Contents

IMPORTANT

WITHDRAWN

A01B-PWFU-R08C-ISIQ-CVWX

REGISTRATION CODE
REGISTRATION CODE

HERE IS YOUR REGISTRATION CODE TO ACCESS MCGRAW-HILL PREMIUM CONTENT AND MCGRAW-HILL ONLINE RESOURCES

For key premium online resources you need THIS CODE to gain access. Once the code is entered, you will be able to use the web resources for the length of your course.

Access is provided only if you have purchased a new book.

If the registration code is missing from this book, the registration screen on our website, and within your WebCT or Blackboard course will tell you how to obtain your new code. Your registration code can be used only once to establish access. It is not transferable.

To gain access to these online resources

1. **USE** your web browser to go to: **www.mhhe.com/bivins5**

2. **CLICK** on "First Time User"

3. **ENTER** the Registration Code printed on the tear-off bookmark on the right

4. After you have entered your registration code, click on "Register"

5. **FOLLOW** the instructions to setup your personal UserID and Password

6. **WRITE** your UserID and Password down for future reference. Keep it in a safe place.

If your course is using WebCT or Blackboard, you'll be able to use this code to access the McGraw-Hill content within your instructor's online course.

To gain access to the McGraw-Hill content in your instructor's WebCT or Blackboard course simply log into the course with the user ID and Password provided by your instructor. Enter the registration code exactly as it appears to the right when prompted by the system. You will only need to use this code the first time you click on McGraw-Hill content.

These instructions are specifically for student access. Instructors are not required to register via the above instructions.

The McGraw-Hill Companies

Mc Graw Hill **Higher Education**

Thank you, and welcome to your McGraw-Hill Online Resources.

0-07-298088-5 t/a
Bivins
Public Relations Writing, 5e

The McGraw-Hill Companies

Mc Graw Hill Higher Education

ng

at

Boston   Burr Ridge, IL   Dubuque, IA   Madison, WI   New York   San Francisco   St. Louis
Bangkok   Bogotá   Caracas   Kuala Lumpur   Lisbon   London   Madrid   Mexico City
Milan   Montreal   New Delhi   Santiago   Seoul   Singapore   Sydney   Taipei   Toronto

Higher Education

To my friend John Mitchell, in memory of Jacy

Public Relations Writing
The Essentials of Style and Format

Published by McGraw-Hill, an imprint of The McGraw-Hill Companies, Inc., 1221 Avenue of the Americas, New York, NY 10020. Copyright © 2005 by The McGraw-Hill Companies, Inc. All rights reserved. No part of this publication may be reproduced or distributed in any form or by any means, or stored in a database or retrieval system, without the prior written consent of The McGraw-Hill Companies, Inc., including, but not limited to, in any network or other electronic storage or transmission, or broadcast for distance learning.

This book is printed on acid-free paper.

   3 4 5 6 7 8 9 0 FGR/FGR   0 9 8 7 6 5

ISBN 0-07-288256-5

Publisher: *Phillip Butcher*
Sponsoring editor: *Phillip Butcher*
Developmental editor: *Laura Lynch*
Marketing manager: *Leslie Oberhuber*
Production editor: *Jennifer Chambliss*
Production supervisor: *Richard DeVitto*
Editorial Assistant: *Marcie Tullio*
Art director: *Jeanne M. Schreiber*
Art editors: *Cristin Yancey and Katherine McNab*
Designer manager: *Kim Menning*
Interior designer: *Caroline McGowan*
Cover designer: *Chris Bivins*
Photo research coordinator: *Natalia Peschiera*
Compositor: *Cenveo Indianapolis*
Typeface: *9.75 x 12 Meridien Roman*
Printer and binder: *Quebecor-Fairfield*

Library of Congress Cataloging-in-Publication Data

Bivins, Thomas H. (Thomas Harvey), 1947–
Public relations writing: the essentials of style and format/Tom Bivins.—5th ed.
    p.cm.
Includes index.
ISBN 0-07-288256-5 (softcover)
1. Public relations—United States. 2. Public relations—United States—Authorship. I. Title.
  HM1221.B538 2004
  659.2—dc22
                                                     2004048114

www.mhhe.com

CHAPTER 6   Crisis Communication 85

CHAPTER 7   News Releases and Backgrounders 102

CHAPTER 14   Design, Printing, and Desktop Publishing 278

Preface

This is a handbook for those who, by intention or by accident, find themselves in the position of writing for public relations. In my years of experience I have had as many questions concerning public relations writing from those not in public relations as from those in the field. Countless inquiries have come from those who, suddenly having been "appointed" publicity chair for their committee, find they don't know the first thing about publicity; or the office manager who has been assigned, ad hoc, the job of putting out a newsletter; or the small-company president who wants to create her own brochures on the new desktop publishing software she just acquired but doesn't have the faintest idea how to proceed. That's why you'll find this book begins with the basics and pretty much sticks with them.

The book is designed to be of aid to both the beginner and the advanced public relations writer. In it, you will find most of the forms of public relations writing, including news releases, backgrounders, broadcast scripts, magazine and newsletter articles, brochures, and print advertising copy.

This latest edition has been updated to include, among other topics, an increased emphasis on writing for and using the new technologies. In addition to Chapter 15, on computer writing and the Internet, Chapter 2 contains an entirely new section on conducting research via the Internet. And for much of the new information, additional Web sites have been listed as online resources.

Other changes and additions to this edition include a whole new chapter (6) on crisis communication. Although crisis communication per se is more in the purview of the strategic planner than the public relations writer, many writers have noted its importance to the practice of public relations. Certainly, no writer should be without basic knowledge of crisis communication. Chapter 8, on annual reports, has been updated to include specifics about not-for-profit annual reports and an entirely new section on writing for corporate responsibility reports. The corporate responsibility report is one of the hottest tools in the corporate strategic plan these days, so much so, that an international organization has grown up around the procedures involved in this new form of social responsibility reporting.

Finally, Chapter 16 is an entirely new chapter on writing for diverse audiences. This information is especially applicable for those working for international organizations or for companies with an international Internet presence.

And, for the first time, there is also a new, comprehensive Web site to support the book at www.mhhe.com/bivins5. On the Web site are two complete reference chapters on style and grammar for downloading. A comprehensive workbook with exercises for each chapter can be found there as well. There is also a brand new supplement—an Instructor's Resource CD—available upon request.

Many of the recommendations contained in this handbook are based on my years of experience as a writer, both in public relations and in general business practice. It is my belief that any public relations writer worthy of the name should become familiar with all forms of writing. After all, good writing is good writing, no matter what the form. The truly good writer is able to work in any medium, like the good artist.

This book is an attempt to put most of the reference material that you, as a public relations writer, would need to successfully complete the work that is so vital a part of your chosen profession—writing.

Acknowledgments

A number of people have helped make this new edition possible. John Mitchell, a longtime friend and faithful user of this book was especially helpful with his many examples of fine work. Seth Walker, former student and now veteran of a number of years in corporate public relations at Intel, provided me with numerous examples of that organization's fine work. My brother, Chris, also provided me with a number of examples from his vast design repertoire for a varied clientele and designed the cover for this new edition. I am also indebted to the educators who reviewed the last edition of this book and made incredibly constructive suggestions for this latest edition: Michael E. Bishop, Baylor University; Bonnye Stuart, Winthrop University; Maggie Jones Patterson, Duquesne University; and Ginni Jurkowski, SUNY Brockport. Every new item that appears here is based on their recommendations. Finally, I am grateful to Phil Butcher, Laura Lynch, and my many new friends at McGraw-Hill for their suggestions and foresight. This new edition is truly a result of their hard work as well as my own. My thanks go to them all. They share in whatever usefulness this book provides to you, the reader.

About the Author

Thomas H. Bivins is a professor and the John L. Hulteng Chair in Media Ethics in the School of Journalism and Communication at the University of Oregon, where he teaches public relations and mass media ethics. He received his Ph.D. in 1982 in telecommunication from the University of Oregon and taught for three years at the University of Delaware before returning to the University of Oregon. Bivins received a B.A. in English and an M.F.A. in creative writing from the University of Alaska, Anchorage, and has over 30 years of professional media experience, including work in radio, television, advertising, public relations, graphic design, and editorial cartooning.

CHAPTER 1

Writing for Public Relations

In this chapter you will learn:

- Why good writing is important to a public relations professional.
- The difference between uncontrolled and controlled information.

- The most often-used tools of public relations writing and how they differ.
- The process of public relations writing.

All public relations practitioners write at some time. Public relations is, after all, communication, and the basic form of communication is still the written word.

Regardless of the prevalence of television, radio, cable, satellite television, and increasingly the Internet, the written word is still powerful. Even the events we witness on television and hear on the radio were written down originally in the form of scripts. News anchors on television are not recounting the day's events from memory; they are reading from a teleprompter. Nearly every entertainment program is precisely scripted—from your favorite sitcom to the *MTV Video Music Awards.* And although it may not seem so, most of what you see on the Internet has been carefully thought out and prewritten prior to its placement on the Web.

It is no wonder today's employers value employees who can communicate through the written word. Employers want people who can write and communicate ideas—who can pull complex or fragmented ideas together into coherent messages. This requires not only technical skill but also intelligence. It also requires a love of writing. Be forewarned: The subjects of public relations writing can seem to many to be crashingly dull; however, for writers who love their craft, the duller the subject, the greater the challenge. Even the most mundane subject can shine with the right amount of polish.

So, the place of writers in public relations is assured. From the president or vice president of public relations to the support staff, writing will be a daily part of life. From enormously complex projects involving dozens of people and whole teams of writers to the one-person office cranking out daily news releases, editing weekly newsletters, or updating Web pages, writing will continue to be the number one concern of public relations. Through it, your publics will come to know you and, for better or worse, develop a permanent image of who you are. It is in your best interest and that of the people for whom you work to ensure that this image is the one you want to portray.

What is needed before you begin to write, however, is knowledge. Being able to spell and string words together effectively does not make a good writer. First and foremost, a good writer must be able to think. To be a good writer you must be aware of the world around you and understand how your writing is going to affect that world.

It is absolutely essential that you think before you write; otherwise, your writing will be only empty words, disconnected from reality, or, worse, unintentionally misleading or false.

WHAT IS PUBLIC RELATIONS WRITING?

All public relations writing attempts to establish positive relations between an organization and its various publics, usually through image-building techniques. Most writing in the realm of public relations falls into two rather broad categories: uncontrolled information and controlled information.

Uncontrolled Information

Information that, once it leaves your hands, is at the mercy of the media, is **uncontrolled information.** In other words, the outlet in which you want the information placed has total editorial control over the content, style, placement, and timing. Such items as news releases are totally uncontrolled. For example, you may write what you think is the most effective, well-thought-out news release ever presented to your local paper, but you never see it in print. Or maybe they do use it, but they leave out all of your skillfully crafted sentences about your employer. In these cases, the newspaper editors have exercised their prerogative to control your information. Once you put it in their hands, they get to decide what to do with it.

Then why, you're probably asking yourself about now, even use uncontrolled information? For at least two reasons. First, it's generally cheaper because you don't have to pay for production or placement costs. Second, your message gains credibility if you can pass it through the media on its way to your target publics. I've sometimes referred to this technique as information laundering (humorously, of course). The fact is that our messages are often viewed by our target publics as having a vested interest—which of course they do. However, when those same target publics see the same message served up by the media, it seems to gain credibility in their eyes. Obviously, this is also true for passing the information through any credible second party such as magazines, opinion leaders, or role models. Thus, the loss in control is usually more than balanced by the overall gain in credibility.

Controlled Information

Information over which you have total control as to editorial content, style, placement, and timing is **controlled information.** Examples of controlled information are institutional (image) and advocacy advertising, house publications, brochures, and broadcast material (if it is paid placement). Public service announcements (PSAs) are controlled as far as message content is concerned but uncontrolled as to placement and timing. To get the most out of any message, you should send out both controlled and uncontrolled information. That way, you can reach the broadest possible target audience, some of whom will react more favorably to one type or the other of your approaches.

THE TOOLS OF THE PUBLIC RELATIONS WRITER

As with any trade, public relations writing uses certain tools through which messages are communicated. The most common are listed here.

- *News releases.* The most widely used of all public relations formats. News releases—both print and broadcast— are used most often to disseminate information for publicity purposes and are sent to every possible medium, from newspapers to radio stations.

- *Backgrounders.* Basic information pieces providing background as an aid to reporters, editors, executives, employees, and spokespersons. This information is used by other writers and reporters to "flesh out" their stories.

- *Public service announcements.* The broadcast outlet most available to not-for-profit public relations. Although the PSA's parameters are limited, additional leeway can be gained by paying for placement, which puts it in the category of advertising.

- *Advertising.* The controlled use of media ensuring that your message reaches your audience in exactly the form you intend and at the time you want. Advertising can be print or broadcast.

- *Articles and editorials.* Usually for newsletters, house publications, trade publications, or consumer publications. In the case of nonhouse publications, public relations articles are submitted in the same way as any other journalistic material. Editorials can be either paid for, as are Mobil's editorials and *Fables,* or submitted uncontrolled and vie for placement with comments from other parties.

- *Collateral publications.* Usually autonomous publications, such as brochures, pamphlets, flyers, and other direct marketing pieces, which should be able to stand on their own merits but which can be used as supporting information for other components in a package. They might, for instance, be part of a press packet.

- *Annual reports.* One of the most-produced organizational publications. Annual reports not only provide information on the organization's financial situation, but also act as a vehicle for enhancing corporate image among its various internal publics.

- *Speeches and presentations.* The interpersonal method of imparting a position or an image. Good speeches can inform or persuade, and good presentations can win support where other, written, methods may fail.

- *The Internet.* Increasingly one of the most important communications tools available in public relations. Writing for the Web is challenging and exciting and can garner results often more quickly than any other format.

Although these are not the only means for message dissemination at the disposal of the public relations writer, they are the methods used most often. Knowing which tool to use requires a combination of experience, research, and intuition. The following chapters do not purport to teach you these qualities. Rather, they attempt to provide you with a framework, or template, from which you will be able to perform basic tasks as a public relations writer. The rest is a matter of experience, and no book can give you that.

THE PROCESS OF PUBLIC RELATIONS WRITING

All forms of writing for public relations have one thing in common: They should be written well. Beyond that, they are different in many ways. These differences are related primarily to purpose, strategy, medium, and style and format. As you will see, these elements are extremely interrelated, and you really can't think about any single element without conceptualizing the others. For example, purpose and strategy are intimately related, and choice of medium is inextricably bound to style and format.

As to purpose, a public relations piece generally is produced for one of two reasons: to inform or to persuade. Strategy depends almost completely on the purpose of a given piece. For instance, a writer might choose a persuasive strategy such as argument to accomplish her purpose, which is to persuade a target audience to vote for a particular mayoral candidate.

The medium you choose to deliver your message will also dictate its style and format. For example, corporate magazines and newsletters use standard magazine writing style (which is to say, a standard magazine style of journalism). Newsletter writing, by contrast, is leaner and shorter and frequently uses a straight news reporting style. Folders (commonly referred to as brochures) are, by nature, short and to the point. Copy for posters and flyers is shorter still, whereas pamphlets and booklets vary in style and length according to purpose. Writing for the Internet may incorporate any or all of these styles in slightly to greatly abbreviated formats.

Beginning here and continuing throughout the book, we will be dealing with these elements of public relations writing: purpose, strategy, medium, and style and format. Before we begin, however, we need to address the issue of planning. That is the subject of the next chapter.

KEY TERMS

uncontrolled information
controlled information

CHAPTER

2

Planning and Research

In this chapter you will learn:

- The four steps in the planning stage of writing.
- What an issue statement is and why and how it is developed.
- The basics of Internet research.
- Why it is important to know your target audience before you develop a PR piece.

- The two types of formal research and their advantages and disadvantages.
- How to conduct a focus group.
- The three types of objectives used in public relations writing.

Almost all writing goes through, or should go through, several stages—the first, and some say the most important, of which is planning. Planning incorporates practically everything you need to know, about both your subject and your audience, to produce a successful written piece, that is to say, a piece that accomplishes what you need it to do. The planning process includes developing an issue statement (the purpose), selecting the proper strategies for accomplishing that purpose, choosing the most effective media to deliver the message, and adhering to the correct style and format as dictated by the media choices. Inherent in all of these steps is research—research into whom to communicate with and how to best communicate with them, and research into how well you communicated. We'll talk about the planning stage of writing in this chapter and the next. This discussion will include all of the elements just mentioned, with the exception of style and format. That is the focus of the remainder of the book.

DEVELOPING AN ISSUE STATEMENT

All communication in public relations has some purpose. It may be to encourage people to vote, or to join your organization, or not to litter, or it may be simply to raise their level of knowledge about your issue. Thus, the first step in any plan whose purpose is to reach a specified audience with a specified purpose in mind is to define the issue or problem being addressed by the communication.[1] Working without a precise definition of the issue is analogous to writing a college term paper without a thesis statement—you have no clear direction to show where you are going and, thus, no way to determine whether you have gotten anywhere when you're finished.

The first step in defining the issue is to develop an issue statement. An **issue statement** is a precise definition of the situation including answers to the following questions:

1. What is the problem or opportunity to be addressed?
2. Who are the affected parties? At this point, it is necessary only to list the concerned parties. A precise definition of publics is the next step in the planning process.
3. What is the timing of this issue? Is it an issue of immediate concern (one needing to be addressed right now), impending concern (one that will have to be addressed very soon), or potential concern (one that you are tracking as needing to be addressed in the near future)?
4. What are your (or your organization's) strengths and weaknesses regarding this issue?

In answering these questions, take care to be as precise as you can. Succinctness is important to clarity, and clarity is of primary importance in the planning

---

[1]The terms *issue* and *problem* are relatively interchangeable depending on how you view the situation. Issue is a more generic term and covers both problems and opportunities; however, many people in public relations persist in viewing most responses in terms of problems. For our purposes, we will use the term *issue* as being more inclusive.

process. It is often wise to answer these questions in outline form and then, working from the outline, to develop an issue statement. Consider the following example. It is necessarily simplistic for demonstration purposes. Most issue analysis at this stage is far more complex; however, the approach is the same and the need for precision and succinctness is no less important.

1. *Issue.* Your company has recently developed a new line of educational software targeted to school-aged children from first grade through high school. Development was time consuming and expensive, and was based on previous research showing a marked trend in education toward computers in the classroom. Marketing and advertising of the new software will be taken care of by your company's marketing department and its outside advertising agency. From a public relations perspective, however, you see an opportunity to capitalize on the growth in educational computing by raising the awareness of key publics as to the importance of this trend and by tying your company's name to that growth.

2. *Affected publics.* Your publics have already been determined in part by the markets who will be using your new line of software. They are educators, administrators, parents, and students.

3. *Timing.* Because this is an opportunity and not a problem, timing is essential. Most opportunities require that you act quickly in order to capitalize on them. Your software is already developed, as is a marketing program. You need to move in advance of, or, at the very least, simultaneously with, the marketing effort.

4. *Strengths and weaknesses.* Your strengths include the availability of existing marketing research that has already determined your target publics, advance knowledge of how the new software will enhance the educational process so that you can focus on those elements, and a wide-open opportunity to set the scene for your product through some public relations advance work.

   Weaknesses might include competition, potential perception of vested interest in any philanthropic effort you might suggest, and the necessity to move almost immediately because of the availability of the product.

An issue statement based on this information might look like the following:

The recent development of our new line of educational software and the coincidence of current trends in educational computing present an opportunity for our company to align itself as a leader in modern education. To do so, we will need to raise the level of attention of key publics concerning the importance of computers in the classroom in such a way that we become closely associated with the trend. We are in a unique position to alert educators, administrators, and parents to the multiple uses of classroom computers and the availability of educational software as an answer to many current classroom problems. A well-placed publicity effort outside of and separate from our marketing plan could help pave the way for eventual increased sales of our software. This publicity effort should not seem to be connected to our product; however, we should not appear to hide our interests in increased sales either. A joint effort with an educational nonprofit organization might be the best approach to take.

This issue statement covers all of the questions posed earlier. The only qualitative difference between the original answers provided to the questions and this statement is the narrative format of the statement. Stating the issue in this form helps others to conceptualize what you already understand and sets the groundwork for further analysis of the issue. Exhibit 2.1 describes how to use a direction sheet to plan your written piece.

Exhibit 2.1

Preparing a Direction Sheet

The first step any public relations practitioner takes before beginning to write is research. Every practitioner needs to understand thoroughly the audience, message, and medium for each communication. Intuition will not suffice. It is important, therefore, to lay the groundwork for any written piece by beginning with a *direction sheet*. A direction sheet is a series of questions you should answer when you begin an assignment. No public relations writer should begin an assignment without one.

A basic direction sheet might include the following information:

- **Subject of the piece.** Is it going to be a new product publicity piece, an announcement of employee promotions, or news about a special event such as a fundraiser or a grand opening?

- **Format.** What form will the information take? Is it to be a news release, a magazine article, a television public service announcement (PSA), or a brochure?

- **Objective.** What do we hope to accomplish by producing this piece? Do we want to educate the general public concerning our hiring policies? Do we want to make engineers aware that we have developed a new product for their use? Do we want to promote the Olympics by associating ourselves with the event?

- **Intended audience.** Exactly who is the target public? Is it homemakers, businesspeople, children, staff members? The audience with whom you decide to communicate will determine the form of the message and probably the medium.

- **Angle.** The angle hooks the audience and establishes the context of the message. It is all-important and one of the toughest components to establish. The angle must be new and interesting. In a print ad, it could be a bold headline. In a television PSA, it might be a peaceful, scenic shot juxtaposed with abrasive audio. In a radio PSA, it might be a humorous context.

- **Key ideas.** These are the salient points you wish to make through your communication. Establishing key ideas is important because they serve as an outline for writing a successful message.

- **Length.** Length depends to a great extent on format. The length should be agreed upon in advance by the party requesting the piece and the writer.

(continued)

(continued)

News releases, for instance, can be from one to five pages long. Article length is usually determined by the publication for which it is intended. Brochure length varies according to layout.

- **Deadline.** This element is usually the most inflexible. Unfortunately, in public relations writing, as in most writing, the finished product is usually needed "yesterday."

When you receive an assignment, try to get as much information as you can in one "client" meeting. This means, be prepared ahead of time with a complete list of questions. Once you have left your client, it is usually difficult to get back in touch.

RESEARCHING THE TOPIC

As is the case in all forms of writing, you must know your topic before you can write about it. Research techniques for this purpose can run the gamut from formal research, such as surveys and questionnaires, to simply checking the library or online services. Increasingly, for instance, information on thousand of subjects can be found free of charge on the Internet.

Regardless of whether it is online or in a file cabinet, organizational research material is generally readily available to most public relations writers. You can check with various departments within your organization for information on your topic and obtain previously published material from in-house and other sources. After you have been at this type of work for a while, you will undoubtedly have a well-stocked "swipe file" in which you have collected everything you or anyone else has ever written about your subject area. In essence, you become a standard journalist gathering background information for a story. You should never start writing until you have sufficient background on your subject.

For many articles, human interest is important. This is where interviews come in. Firsthand information is always best when you can get it. Interview those intimately involved with your topic, and use their information when you write. Interviewing is a special skill, and it takes a lot of practice. The people you interview will determine how informative or interesting your interview will be. Although you can't always control whom you interview, you can prepare so that you can make the most out of your meeting. Exhibit 2.2 gives some tips for a successful interview.

Exhibit 2.2

Tips for a Successful Interview

- **Do your homework.** Collect background information on the people you're going to interview as well as on the topics you're planning to discuss. Don't be embarrassed by your own ignorance of the topics; however, the better you know the topics, the more time you can save by asking for specific details rather than for in-depth explanations.

- **Prepare your interviewees in advance of the interviews.** Contact them well in advance, set a time for the interview that is convenient for them, and make sure they know exactly what you are going to cover and why. That way, they can also prepare for the interview by gathering pertinent information as well as their thoughts. Ask if you can "talk with them" rather than "interview them." A talk puts people at ease; an interview can make them tense and formal.

- **Write down a list of questions that you want answered, working from the general to the specific.** But be prepared to let the interview range according to the interviewees' responses. Often, an answer will open new areas of inquiry or suggest an angle you hadn't thought of before. Be ready to explore these new avenues as they come up. Ken Metzler, journalist, educator, and author of *Creative Interviewing: The Writer's Guide to Gathering Information by Asking Questions* (Allyn & Bacon, 1996), claims that the best interviewers not only should expect surprises but also should ask for surprises in their willingness to explore rather than follow a strict set of questions.

- **If you are going to use a tape recorder, make sure that your interviewee is comfortable with being taped and that you have fresh batteries or that an electrical outlet is available.** And, even though you are taping, always take notes. This physical activity usually puts the interviewee at ease by showing that you are listening, and it serves as a good backup if your recorder stops functioning or your tape runs out.

- **Keep the space between you and your subject free of any object that may be a source of distraction.** Your recorder should not occupy the space between you and your subject. Move it a little to the side, but make sure the microphone isn't obstructed. You should also keep your notepad in your lap, if possible, or simply hold it.

- **Break the ice.** Open your interview with small talk. Try a comfortable topic, such as the weather, or, if you know something about your interviewee, a familiar, nonthreatening topic. For example, if you know your interviewee is an avid golfer, ask if he or she has had a chance to play much lately. Almost any topic will do. Most of the time, something will suggest itself naturally.

- **As your interview progresses, don't be afraid to range freely but be sure to return occasionally to your preset questions.** Although the information you gather exploring other avenues may add greatly to your collection of relevant facts, remember to cover all the ground necessary for your article.

- **If you are ever unsure of a quote or think you might have misunderstood it, ask your subject to repeat it.** Even if you are taping the interview, accuracy on paper and in your own mind is worth the slight pause.

(continued)

(continued)

- **Finally, be prepared to have to remember some key conversation after your interview is officially over.** Most of us are aware of the phenomenon that Ken Metzler calls the afterglow effect, when dinner guests, for example, stand at the door with their coats on ready to go and talk for another 30 minutes. The same thing usually happens in an interview. You've turned your recorder off and put your pad away, and on your way out the door, you have another 10 minutes of conversation. In this relaxed atmosphere, important comments are often made. Remember them. As soon as you leave, take out your notepad and write down the comments or turn on your recorder and repeat the information into it. However, always make sure that your interviewee is aware that you are going to use this information as well. Don't violate any assumed off-the-record confidences.

Remember, get as much as you can the first time out. Most interviews range from 30 minutes to two hours. A follow-up interview, providing you can get one, will never be as fruitful or relaxed as the first one.

USING THE INTERNET FOR RESEARCH

Increasingly, research is being conducted using the Internet. And why not? It is accessible from nearly every computer, and it is much faster than other forms of research. A note of caution, however: Not everything you will need can be found on the Internet. Don't neglect other research sources in favor of exclusive Internet research.

The Internet provides access to a wealth of information on countless topics contributed by people throughout the world. On the Internet, a user has access to a wide variety of services: electronic mail, file transfer, vast information resources, interest group membership, interactive collaboration, multimedia displays, and more. However, the Internet is not a library in which all available items are identified and can be retrieved through a single catalog. In fact, no one knows how many individual files reside on the Internet. The number certainly runs into the many millions and is growing at a rapid pace.

The Internet is a self-publishing medium. This means that anyone with a small amount of technical skill and access to a host computer can publish on the Internet. Remember this when you locate sites in the course of your research. Internet sites change over time according to the commitment and inclination of the creator. Some sites demonstrate an expert's knowledge, whereas others are amateur efforts. Some may be updated daily, whereas others may be outdated. As with any information resource, you need to evaluate what you find on the Internet.

Also be aware that the addresses of Internet sites change frequently. Web sites can disappear altogether. Do not expect stability on the Internet.

One of the most efficient ways of conducting research on the Internet is to use the World Wide Web. The Web offers access to a great deal of what is available on the Internet.

Finding Information on the Internet[2]

Information on the Internet can be accessed in a number of basic ways:

- Go directly to a site if you have the address
- Browse
- Conduct a search using a Web search engine
- Explore a subject directory
- Join an e-mail discussion group or Usenet newsgroup
- Explore the information stored in live databases on the Web, known as the deep Web

Each of these options is described below.

Go Directly to a Site If You Have the Address

A protocol is a set of formal rules describing how to transmit data, especially across a network. The Internet Protocol family includes IP and all higher-level network protocols built on top of it, such as TCP, UDP, HTTP, and FTP. Modern operating systems include services, or daemons, that implement support for specific protocols. Some protocols, like TCP/IP, have also been implemented in silicon hardware for optimized performance. Not every browser can access every protocol. The most commonly accessible protocol is HTTP.

If you know the Internet address of a site you wish to visit, you can use a Web browser to access that site. All you need to do is type the URL (uniform resource locator) in the appropriate location window. The URL specifies the Internet address of the electronic document. Every file available on the Internet has a unique URL. Web browsers use the URL to retrieve the file from the host computer and the directory in which it resides. This file is then displayed on the user's computer monitor.

This is the format of a URL: **protocol://host/path/filename**
For example:

http://www.house.gov/agriculture/schedule.htm—a hypertext file on the Web
ftp://ftp.uu.net/graphics/picasso—a file at an FTP (file transfer protocol) site
telnet://opac.albany.edu—a Telnet connection

Any of these addresses can be typed into the Location window of a Web browser.

Browse

Browsing home pages on the Web is a haphazard but interesting way of finding desired material on the Internet. Because the creator of a home page programs each link, you never know where these links might lead. High-quality starting

---

[2]I am extremely indebted to Laura Cohen, network services librarian, for allowing me to use the information on the University Libraries Web site for the State University of New York at Albany, http://library.albany.edu/internet/research.html.

pages will contain high-quality links. Remember, browsing takes time and is not usually conducive to quick searches.

Conduct a Search Using a Web Search Engine

An Internet search engine allows the user to enter keywords relating to a topic and retrieve information about Internet sites containing those keywords (see Exhibit 2.3). Search engines are available for many of the Internet protocols. For example, Archie searches for files stored at anonymous FTP sites.

Exhibit 2.3

How to Formulate Web Search Engine Queries

There are three steps to a computer database search:

1. **Identify your concept.** When conducting any database search, you need to break down your topic into its component concepts. For example, if you want to find information on the budget negotiations between President Bush and the Democrats, these are your concepts: **Bush, Democrats, budget.**

2. **List keywords for each concept.** Once you have identified your concepts, you need to list keywords that describe each concept. Some concepts may have only one keyword, whereas others may have many. For example:

   Bush

   Democrats

   House speaker

   Budget

   Budget negotiations

   Budget battle

   Budget impasse

   Budget deal

   Depending on the focus of your search, you might use other keywords.

3. **Specify the logical relationships among your keywords.** Once you know the keywords you want to search, you need to establish the logical relationships among them. The formal name for this is Boolean logic. Boolean logic allows you to specify the relationships among search terms by using any of three logical operators: **AND, OR, NOT.**

Search statement	Result of search
World War I AND World War II	Files containing both terms
World War I OR World War II	Files containing at least one of these terms
World War I NOT World War II	Files containing the term World War I but not the term World War II

Some search engines offer Boolean searching without mentioning the logical operators by name. For example, you might be asked to list your search terms and choose that *all* of these terms be searched. This denotes AND logic. Specifying *any* of these terms denotes OR logic. Most search engines use a type of implied Boolean logic, in which symbols or spaces are used to denote logical relationships. For example, **+bears +hibernation** denotes AND logic.

Certain search engines allow you to use a proximity operator. This is a type of AND logic that specifies the distance between words in a source file. For example, AltaVista and Lycos let you use the NEAR operator. Consider this search: **Bush NEAR budget.** In AltaVista, the two terms must be within 10 words of each other in the source file. Lycos allows user-specified distances. This option can help you gain relevance in your search results.

Most Web search engines cannot handle a single search statement that includes all the terms listed in Step 2 above. You may need to repeat your search a few times using terms in different combinations until you get satisfactory results. For example, you may start with **Bush, Democrats, budget negotiations** and connect these terms with AND logic. Take a look at your results. If you are not finding what you want, repeat the search with alternative keywords for the budget concept. Your initial results may give you ideas about which new terms to try.

Search engines located on the Web have become quite popular as the Web itself has become the Internet's environment of choice. Web search engines have the advantage of offering access to a vast range of information resources located on the Internet. Many search engines compile a database spanning multiple Internet protocols, including HTTP, FTP, and Telnet. They may also search multimedia or other file types on the deep Web, often accessible as separate searches (see page 20). Web search engines tend to be developed by private companies, though most of them are available free of charge. A Web search engine service consists of three components:

- *Spider.* Program that traverses the Web from link to link, identifying and reading pages.
- *Index.* Database containing a copy of each Web page gathered by the spider.
- *Search engine mechanism.* Software that enables users to query the index and that usually returns results in term relevancy ranked order.

Keep in mind that spiders are indiscriminate. Some of the resources they collect may be outdated, inaccurate, or incomplete. Others, of course, may come from responsible sources and provide you with valuable information. Be sure to evaluate all your search results carefully.

With most search engines, you fill out a form with your search terms and then ask that the search proceed. The engine searches its index and generates a page with links to resources containing some or all of your terms. These resources are usually presented in term relevancy ranked order. For example, a document will appear higher in your list of results if your search term appears many times, near the beginning of the document, close together in the document, in the document title, or the like. These may be thought of as *first-generation search engines.*

A new development in search engine technology is the ordering of search results by concept, keyword, site, links, or popularity. Engines that support these features may be thought of as *second-generation search engines.* These engines offer improvements in the ranking of results partly because they insert the human element in determining what is relevant. For example, Google ranks results according to the number of highly ranked Web pages that link to other pages. A Web page becomes highly ranked if still other highly ranked pages link to them. This scheme represents an intriguing melding of technology and human judgment.

All search engines have rules for formulating queries (see Exhibit 2.4). It is imperative that you read the help files at the site before proceeding. Online tutorials can also help you learn the rules.

Exhibit 2.4

Tips on Conducting Internet Searches

1. Read the directions at each search site. The technique for formulating a search depends on the search engine you are using. The options available among the different search engines vary widely.

2. If you have a multiterm search, determine which type of Boolean logic you should use. For example, a search about the relationship between latitude and temperature would be formulated as **+latitude +temperature** on many Web search engines for AND logic to apply.

3. Include synonyms or alternate spellings in your search statements, and connect these terms with OR logic.

4. Check your spelling.

5. Take advantage of capitalization if the search engine is case sensitive.

6. If your results are not satisfactory, repeat the search using alternative terms.

7. Try different sources within search engines to diversify your results. Sources can include Usenet newsgroups, Internet FAQs (frequently asked questions), reviewed pages, and more.

8. Experiment with different search engines. No two search engines work from the same index.

9. Try search engines that allow you to search multiple search engines simultaneously. Be aware that you will lose access to advanced query options because not all engines offer them.

10. If you have too many results, or results that are not relevant:
  - Field search.
  - Add concept words. Some search engines allow you to search again within your existing results. Try this option at Hotbot or Lycos.
  - Use vocabulary that is specific to your topic; avoid words with large concepts unless you intend to field search.
  - Link appropriate terms with the Boolean AND (+) so that each term is required to appear in the record.
  - Use term proximity operators if they are available to locate documents in which your terms are close together. Lycos offers a number of term proximity options.
  - If one of your search terms is a phrase, be sure to enclose it within quotation marks (e.g., "global warming").

11. If you have too few results:
  - Drop off the least important concept(s) to broaden your subject.
  - Use more general vocabulary.
  - Add alternative terms or spellings for individual concepts and connect with the Boolean OR.

Try the option available on some engines to find documents related to one or more of your relevant hits. Google, MetaMission, and ProFusion are among the engines that offer this type of feature.

Recommended Starting Points:

- **Google**

  http://www.google.com

  A second-generation search engine that ranks pages by the number of links from pages ranked high by the service. These highly ranked pages are also determined by the number of links to them. The idea here is that a high-quality page will be found and linked to from another high-quality page. Many users find that Google does an excellent job of finding Web documents relevant to their topics.

- **Teoma**

  http://www.teoma.com

  Organizes results into three sections: Web pages listed in link ranked order, experts' links that represent gateway sites, and concept clusters based on topic keywords. The clusters are dynamically generated and allow you to limit the results derived from a search. "Dynamically generated" means the results are generated at the time of the query, not prepackaged in any way, as in a database. The link ranking is a bit different from Google's. Teoma ranks links from pages in the same subject "community" as the topic being searched. They call this subject-specific popularity.

- **Ixquick**

  http://www.ixquick.com

  A good place to try if your topic is obscure or if you want to retrieve results from a variety of search engines with a single search statement. This service searches multiple search tools simultaneously and returns your results in a single list that removes the duplicate files. This type of search processing is called metasearching. Even better, Ixquick returns only the top 10 relevancy-ranked results from the source search services. This means that you can take advantage of the collective relevancy judgment of many tools at once. Other recommended metasearch engines are Ithaki and ProFusion.

Explore a Subject Directory

An increasing number of universities, libraries, companies, organizations, and even volunteers are creating subject directories to catalog portions of the Internet. These directories are organized by subject and consist of links to Internet resources relating to these subjects. The major subject directories available on the Web tend to have overlapping but different databases. Most directories provide a search capability that allows you to query the database on your topic of interest.

Directories are useful for general topics, for topics that need exploring, and for browsing. There are two basic types of directories. *Academic and professional directories* are often created and maintained by subject experts to support the needs of researchers. INFOMINE, from the University of California, is a good example of an academic subject directory. By contrast, directories contained on *commercial portals* cater to the general public and compete for traffic. Yahoo! is the most famous example of a commercial portal. Be sure you use the directory most appropriate for your needs.

Subject directories differ significantly in selectivity. For example, the Yahoo! site does not carefully evaluate user-submitted content when adding Web pages to its database. *It is therefore not a reliable research source and should not be used for this purpose.* In contrast, INFOMINE selects only those sources considered useful to the academic and research community. Consider the policies of any directory that you visit. One challenge to doing so is the fact that not all directory services are willing to disclose either their policies or the names and qualifications of site reviewers. A number of subject directories consist of links accompanied by annotations that describe or evaluate site content. A well-written annotation from a known reviewer is more useful than an annotation written by the site creator, as is usually the case with Yahoo!

Certain directories are the result of many years of intellectual effort. For this reason, it is important to consult subject directories when doing research on the Web. A list of such directories can be found at http://library.albany.edu/internet/subject.html.

Recommended starting points:

- **The Librarians' Index to the Internet (LII)**

  http://lii.org

  Supported by a federal grant, a large number of indexers select and annotate Web resources across a broad range of topics for LII. With its extensive but careful selection, objective and useful annotations, and hierarchical organization, LII might well be thought of as "the thinking person's Yahoo!"

- **The WWW Virtual Library**

  http://vlib.org

  One of the oldest and most respected subject directories on the Web. This directory consists of individual subject collections, many of which are maintained at universities throughout the world.

- **INFOMINE**

  http://infomine.ucr.edu

  A large directory of Web sites of scholarly interest compiled by the University of California. The directory may be browsed or searched by subject, keyword, or title. Each site listed is accompanied by a description.

Join an E-mail Discussion Group or Usenet Newsgroup

Join any of the thousands of e-mail discussion groups or Usenet newsgroups. Usenet is a worldwide distributed discussion system. It consists of a set of newsgroups with names that are classified hierarchically by subject. Articles or messages are posted to these newsgroups by people on computers with the appropriate software—these articles are then broadcast to other interconnected computer systems via a wide variety of networks. Some newsgroups are moderated, that is, the articles are first sent to a moderator for approval before appearing in the newsgroup. These groups cover a wealth of topics. You can ask questions of the experts and read the answers to questions that others ask. Belonging to these groups is somewhat like receiving a daily newspaper on topics that interest you. These groups provide a good way of keeping up with what is being discussed on the Internet about your subject area. In addition, they can help you find out how to locate information—both online and offline—that you want.

E-mail discussion groups can be associated with academic institutions. Many topics are scholarly in nature, and it is not unusual for experts in the field to be among the participants. In contrast, Usenet newsgroups cover a far wider variety of topics and participants have a range of expertise. Be careful to evaluate the knowledge and opinions offered in any discussion forum. Note also that a small number of e-mail groups are cross-posted as Usenet newsgroups. For example, the early music e-mail group EARLYM-L also exists as the newsgroup rec.music.early.

E-mail discussion groups are managed by software programs. There are three in common use: LISTSERV, Majordomo, and ListProc. The commands for using these programs are similar.

A list of Usenet newsgroups can be accessed from within a newsreader program. Web browser suites such as Netscape Communicator include a newsreader. This offers the convenience of Usenet access in a graphical environment as a part of the Web experience.

A good Web-based directory to assist in locating e-mail discussion groups and Usenet newsgroups is Topica, located at http://www.topica.com/.

Explore the Deep Web

The concept of the deep or invisible Web refers to content that is stored in databases accessible on the Web but not available via search engines. In other words, this content is invisible to search engines. This is because spiders cannot or will not enter databases and extract content from them as they can from static Web pages. In the past, these databases were fewer in number and were referred to as specialty databases, subject-specific databases, and so on.

The only way to access information on the invisible Web is to search the databases themselves. Topical coverage runs the gamut from scholarly resources to commercial entities. Very current, dynamically changing information is likely to be stored in databases, including news, job listings, available airline flights, and the like. As the number of Web-accessible databases grows, they will need to be used to conduct successful information searches on the Web.

Other content not gathered by spiders includes nontext files such as multimedia files, graphics files, and documents in nonstandard formats such as Portable Document Format (PDF).

Many search engine sites and commercial portals feature searchable databases as part of their package of services. This phenomenon falls under the heading of converging content. For example, you can visit AltaVista and look up news, maps, jobs, auctions, items for purchase, and so on, all things outside the purview of a spider-gathered index. As another example, Google integrates searches of PDF and Microsoft Office files into its general search service.

Recommended starting points:

- **Profusion**

  http://www.profusion.com/

  Directory of over 10,000 databases, which enables you to search for the database you need, from IntelliSeek.

- **Invisible-web.net**

  http://www.invisible-web.net/

  Directory of high-quality databases on the Web; especially useful to researchers.

- **Search.Com**
  http://www.search.com/
  Directory of approximately 200 topic-based databases, from CNET.

Evaluating Internet Resources

The Web is quickly becoming one of the most-used information sources in the United States and perhaps even the world. However, the safeguards that more traditional information sources have developed over the years to ensure accuracy of information don't exist on the Internet for the most part. Following, then, are some guidelines for evaluating resources on the Internet.

Purpose

Consider the audience
- Consider the intended audience of the page, based on its content, tone, and style.
- Does this mesh with your needs?

Consider the source
- Web search engines often amass vast results, from memos to scholarly documents.
- Many of the resulting items will be peripheral or useless for your research.

Source

- The author or producer is identifiable.
- The author or producer has expertise on the subject as indicated on a credentials page. You may need to trace back through the URL to view a page in a higher directory with background information.
- The sponsor or location of the site is appropriate to the material as shown in the URL.
  Examples:
  - .edu for educational or research material
  - .gov for government resources
  - .com for commercial products or commercially sponsored sites
- If someone's name appears in the URL, the site may be a personal home page with no official sanction.
- A *mail-to* link is offered for submission of questions or comments.

Content

Accuracy
- Don't take the information presented at face value.
- Web sites are rarely refereed or reviewed, as are scholarly journals and books.

- Look for
  - Point of view
  - Evidence of bias
- The information source should be clearly stated, whether original or borrowed from elsewhere.

Comprehensiveness

- Depth of information: Determine if content covers a specific time period or aspect of the topic, or if it strives to be comprehensive.
- Use additional print and electronic sources to complement the information provided.

Currency

- The site has been updated recently, as reflected in the date on the page.
- Material contained on the page is current.

Links

- Links are relevant and appropriate.
- Don't assume that the linked sites are the best available. Investigate additional sites on the topic.

Style and Functionality

- The site is laid out clearly and logically with well-organized subsections.
- The writing style is appropriate for the intended audience.
- The site is easy to navigate, including
  - Clearly labeled *Back, Home, Go To Top* icons or links.
  - Internal indexing links on lengthy pages.
- All links to remote sites work.
- Search capability is offered if the site is extensive.

ANALYZING THE TARGET AUDIENCE

Imagine holding a complex conversation with someone you don't know at all. If you are trying to persuade that person of your point of view, you will have a better chance if you know his or her predispositions in advance. The same holds true for written communication. To write for an audience, you have to know that audience intimately.

A **target audience** is typically defined as the end users of your information—the people you most want to be affected by your writing. What you need to know about your target audience depends to a great extent on your objectives. As discussed previously, public relations writing is typically used either to perform or to persuade. The type of information you gather on your target audience depends a lot on the use to which your particular piece will be put. If you are writing a persuasive publication, for example, you need to know not only who your prospective readers are but also how much they know about your topic, how interested they are, and whether they feel they can or want to do anything about it. With this information in hand you can inform them, address their concerns, and, it is hoped, move them to action. By contrast, think of all those publications you've seen at government agencies or received through the mail as a result of having requested information. Writers of these types of pieces need to know only that you desire their information.

Knowing the audience for whom you're writing is probably the most important factor in planning your message. The success of your writing will be determined, to a great extent, on how well you've aimed your message. The best way to write is to write for an imagined reader, an individual to whom you are speaking directly. To understand this individual, you need to know him or her personally. To do this, you will have to develop a profile of this typical reader, citing both demographic characteristics (age, sex, income, etc.) and psychographic information (behavior patterns, likes and dislikes, attitudes, etc.).

Another important factor to consider at this point is how your target audience feels about your subject. In most persuasive endeavors, there are three types of audiences: those already on your side, those opposed to your point of view, and those who are undecided. As most experienced persuaders know, convincing the hard-core opposition is not a reasonable objective. Persuading those already on your side is like preaching to the choir: Unless you want to stir them to some action, it is a waste of time. Thus, most persuasion is aimed at the undecided. Remember, however, that even the undecided have opinions. Those opinions may not be fully crystallized, which leaves this group particularly open to persuasion.

Conducting Target Audience Research

Methods for collecting information on your target audiences range from informal methods such as simply asking the person who gave you the assignment who the audience is, through secondary research gathered from such sources as the library, the Internet, or your own organization, to fairly expensive formal research. Many writers are put off by the notion of having to gather hard-core information about their readers. Unfortunately, many a message has missed its audience completely, because it was not built around this information.

Although an in-depth discussion of formal research techniques is beyond the scope of this book, you need to understand the importance of such techniques and a bit about how they work. At the very least, you should know enough to ask the right questions of the people you hire to do the survey for you, and enough to translate their findings into plain English. Briefly, then, here are some of the things to look for.

There are essentially two types of formal research: primary research and secondary research. **Primary research** is data collected for the first time and specifically for the project at hand. This type of research is generally more expensive than secondary research because you will have to do everything from scratch, including developing the questions, printing up the survey, collecting the data, and analyzing it. Whether you hire a research firm or do it yourself, it will be costly and take more time. The upside is that it is completely relevant to your current issue (ideally, at least).

Secondary research includes data previously collected, often by third parties, for other purposes and adapted to the current needs. Such data can include demographic information already gathered by another department in your organization, or information gained from research done by other parties entirely outside your company. Secondary research is generally less expensive to obtain and quicker to get hold of compared with primary research. However, it does have to be adapted to your uses and will not always answer all your questions. Conducting a combination of primary and secondary research is usually the best approach.

Regardless of the type of research you use, it must fit your needs. The best way to ensure that it does is to set an objective for your research and then compare the results of your efforts with your original objective. This is most important if you decide to do primary research.

Secondary Research

A visit to the library or the Internet can yield volumes of secondary data. For example, government documents such as the *American Statistics Index (ASI)* can be invaluable sources. *ASI* is a compendium of statistical material including the U.S. Census and hundreds of periodicals that can be obtained directly from the sponsoring agencies, from the library itself, or on the Internet. *ASI* also publishes an alphabetical index arranged by subject, name, category, and title.

Other sources of market information include the Simmons Market Research Bureau's annual *Study of Media and Markets.* This publication includes information on audiences for over a hundred magazines, with readership delineated by demographic, psychographic, and behavioral characteristics. When using such secondary research, you will find much information that is not directly applicable to your target audience. You have to know not only where to look but also how to decipher what you read and apply it to your needs.

Primary Research

Once you've decided to use primary research, you'll need to decide how to collect it. The two most common methods of primary research are focus groups and surveys.

Focus groups. Focus groups have become a fairly commonplace practice for those in advertising, marketing, and public relations. The technique requires that you assemble a small group (usually not more than 10 people or so) from your target audience, present them with questions or ideas, and ask for their reactions. Your approach can be relatively formal (a written questionnaire to be filled out following the presentation) or informal (open-ended questions asked in an open discussion among the participants).

The key to a successful focus group is to design your questions in advance and cover all the areas you need to analyze. Be sure to explore whether your message's language is appropriate to your audience. Some of the questions to be considered are as follows: Is the message difficult to follow or does it have too much jargon or too many technical terms? Does your audience understand the message? Does the message speak to them, or do they feel it is meant for someone else? Is the medium appropriate? Would your readers take time to read the message if it came to them in the mail? As an insert in their paychecks? In the corporate magazine? Answers to these questions should give you a fair idea of how your larger audience will react to your message.

The best way to set up a focus group is to hire a moderator who is experienced in asking these questions and interpreting the responses properly. Don't assume that, because you are the writer and the closest to the project, you can interpret audience feedback clearly. Indeed, in most cases you are not the one best suited to act as the focus group's moderator. Moderators are generally trained in marketing or sociology and are used to eliciting responses from people without biasing the answers. This is not a skill that is beyond most public relations people, but it does take a bit of training. Exhibit 2.5 describes in detail how to conduct a focus group.

Exhibit 2.5

How to Conduct a Focus Group

1. **Specify what you are trying to find out before you conduct the focus group.** Don't go into a focus group without a clear idea of your objective. Instead, develop a list of objectives for your focus group study. List exactly what you hope to discover from this meeting. Are you trying to find out whether your target audience will read stories about other employees? Do they react differently to different colors? To which color or combination of colors do they react most favorably? You are trying to get your group to react to various stimuli you present to them.

2. **Decide on a moderator.** It is best to hire someone who has done this before. Focus group moderators are experienced people with special skills in leading others into answering questions and reacting to stimuli without revealing what they are looking for. Moderators moderate—that is, they lead the discussion, call on different respondents, and keep the discussion going without allowing a free-for-all to occur. If cost is a factor (and good moderators can cost a bit), you might consider conducting the focus group yourself. However, if you have never conducted a focus group or seen one conducted, you should attend a session or two before you attempt it yourself.

3. **Schedule according to your participants' needs, not yours.** If members of your target audience are busiest during certain hours of the day or days of the week, don't hold your focus group during those times. Make the meeting convenient for them. This courtesy will help put them in a cooperative frame

(continued)

(continued)

of mind. Know your audience and their special needs when you schedule. For example, if day care is an issue, perhaps you can arrange for it. If lunch is the only time you can hold your meeting, provide lunch.

4. **Select your participants properly.** Develop a valid method for picking members of your target audience. In most cases, you need only a representative cross-section of your audience. For example, if 60 percent of your readers are women aged 25 to 35, make sure that 60 percent of your focus group members are women in that age group. Holding a focus group with nonrepresentative participants is self-defeating. If you are in doubt about whom to select, develop a screening questionnaire that will tell you whether the respondents are really part of your target audience.

5. **Provide for payment.** Nearly all focus groups are paid. Most people won't participate for the fun of it (although some like having their opinions counted). Base what you pay on whom you are interviewing. Professionals, such as physicians and attorneys, should receive around $100, whereas others may be happy with $20–$50 for the session. Make sure your participants know they will be paid. The screening questionnaire is a good place to mention it.

6. **Like the airlines, always overbook.** If you need 10 people, book 15 or 20. Invariably some will not show up. If everyone does, just take them as they arrive, and turn away the rest once you've reached the number you need. But pay everyone, including those you don't use.

7. **Meet with your moderator and set up guidelines for the study.** It is best to use your objectives as a starting point and to develop a set of procedures from them for the focus group interview. Lay out these procedures step by step so that if you conduct more than one focus group, you will be able to follow exactly the same procedures in each session.

8. **Sit in on the focus group as an observer if possible** and if your moderator doesn't think it will be obtrusive. Always allow yourself to be introduced and don't interrupt or talk during the session.

9. **Provide refreshments, even if it's just coffee or juice.** Most people expect some amenities in addition to the payment they receive. It also helps to put them in a better frame of mind.

10. **The day of the focus group, make sure everything you will need for the meeting is ready and on hand.** You'll be surprised how often you show up to find that someone else is using your reserved room. Or you count on someone else to bring the overhead projector, and he or she forgets. Or you find you need to have pencils on hand, or paper, or wastebaskets, or any number of small items that can make or break a focus group meeting. As with everything else, it is best to make up a list of everything you will need to do or bring prior to the meeting. Then, arrive an hour early and check off your items on the list.

11. **Hold the focus group.** Whether you are the moderator or someone else is, the following guidelines apply equally:

    - **It is a good idea to audiotape or videotape a focus group.** Many nuances of expression and voice aren't captured by simply taking notes or relying on written responses. If you use audiotape, make sure you have enough tape for the entire session. Also make sure that it is good-quality tape and that your recorder will pick up everyone in the room. Don't rely on that tiny recorder you use to tape reminders to yourself. If you videotape, you'll need to hire a camera operator. Just positioning a stationary camera and turning it on won't do because you'll never be able to cover everyone in the room at once. And, if you do decide to tape, let your participants know in advance and remind them again when they are seated and ready to start. Don't rely completely on the tape, however. Use it as a backup and always take complete notes. If the tape fails, for whatever reason, notes may be all you have. Also, note taking makes the participants feel that you are doing your part as well.

    - **Always put your group at ease by telling them something about yourself, why you are conducting this study, and the fact that it is entirely informal and open.** Have the participants introduce themselves. Make sure they understand that you expect each one of them to play a part and that everyone's opinion counts equally. Stress that there are no right or wrong answers.

    - **A warm-up question that is easy to handle—something fun, yet thought-provoking—is a good way to get started.** For example, if part of your study is to gauge reactions to the new look of your newsletter, you might begin by asking each participant to tell you his or her favorite color.

    - **Remember, a moderator moderates.** Don't lose control of the group discussion. To ensure that everyone gets an opportunity to speak, try going around the table allowing each member of the group to answer each question, and don't ask a new question until everyone has answered the question on the floor. By contrast, don't be afraid to veer from the point if an interesting side issue is raised. Just make sure everyone has a chance to respond to each issue in turn. If you find that one or two people tend to dominate the answers, focus on the quiet ones for a while, draw them out, and encourage their participation. Remind the group that everyone's opinion counts.

12. **There is no set length for a focus group study.** Having said that, an hour to an hour and a half should be enough time to get what you need without tiring your participants. If you do go 90 minutes or longer, take a break midway through.

(continued)

(continued)

13. **When the meeting is over, thank the participants personally for their help and make sure they are paid before they leave.**

14. **Immediately after the focus group study is over, sit down with your notes and begin answering the questions you couched as objectives when you began this whole process.** This is only the beginning, however. Don't draw hasty conclusions until you've had a chance to look at everything in context (including any tape you might have made of the meeting). Once you have a handle on the big picture, assemble all the evidence in the form of answers to your questions. Note if anything is incomplete. Perhaps you should have asked something else about reader interest in a particular area. Maybe you didn't probe deeply enough as to color preferences. Make note of these shortcomings so that if you conduct another focus group study, you can include expanded questions.

15. **Draft a final report, even if it's to yourself, covering everything you found out through the focus group study.** Send copies to appropriate parties and file a couple copies for future information. (Or for future editors of your newsletter. They'll thank you for it.)

Surveys. An equally important primary research option is the survey. The three most common methods of survey data collection are the face-to-face interview, the telephone interview, and the mailed questionnaire. Each has advantages and disadvantages.

The *face-to-face interview* allows you to interpret body language, facial expressions, and other nonverbal clues that help flesh out the responses you're getting verbally. A good interviewer will know how to gauge these nonverbal clues and evaluate them within the context of the verbal answers. The disadvantages of face-to-face interviewing include potential inconsistency in the abilities of interviewers and the general lack of willingness of most people to agree to any but the most perfunctory personal interview.

The *telephone interview,* by far the most common type of interview, also has its advantages and disadvantages. It must be brief (usually five minutes or so) or people won't agree to it. You can interview far more people this way, but you don't get much depth. Random dialing is most often used for telephone interviews; however, not everyone has a phone and thus the sample is not truly random. Lastly, not everyone likes to be interviewed over the phone. If the information you need can be gathered in only a few questions, though, the telephone may be your best bet.

The *mailed questionnaire* is usually the most effective way of gathering in-depth information from a great many people at the same time. Although it may lack the ability to clarify ambiguous questions the way face-to-face interviews can, it does provide for more questions and longer responses than telephone interviewing. And it has a built-in consistency the other methods don't. Answers aren't biased by interviewer miscues (facial expressions, body language), and each question is asked in a uniform way.

Generally, two types of data are collected by survey. **Descriptive data** is basically information that "paints a picture" of the public being studied by its distinctive demographic characteristics—descriptors such as age, income, sex, education, nationality, and so on. This is information you need for your reader profile.

Inferential data is information that allows you to generalize about a larger group or population. This means that the people you choose for your survey must be entirely representative of the larger population you want to reach. This allows you to sample a small segment of your target public and infer from their reactions the reactions of the larger audience. However, inferential research can work only if the sample is chosen completely at random from your larger population. This means that everyone in your target public has an equal chance of being chosen. How do you ensure an equal chance? Easy. Computers have made this type of selection process much easier than it was in the past. All you need is a list of your target population (usually gathered by voter lists, motor vehicles records, and such). Numbers are assigned each person, and a computer selects, at random, those to be surveyed. You should be aware of some variations in the selection process, however. These processes, or sampling methods, are listed in Exhibit 2.6.

Exhibit 2.6

Sampling Methods

Several different types of sampling methods are used in survey sampling. Each fits a specific need of those asking the questions.

- **Simple random sampling** is the easiest. It involves simply selecting the number you need from a master list, at random. This will usually be sufficient if you have a relatively homogeneous group with few or no differentiating characteristics.

- **Systematic sampling** adds a bit more process to the process by assigning (again by computer) an interval number. This means that the computer will select, at random, a starting number and then another number that will decide who is chosen next. For example, the computer chooses person number 2,067 as the first person to be mailed a survey. It then picks an interval number, say 43. This number is added to 2,067, giving us 2,100—the next person to be sent a survey—and so on. The same interval number is used each time.

- **Cluster sampling** is useful if you need to interview only the head of each household, for instance, or 20 out of 56 houses in a subdivision, or people in 4 of the 10 counties of a state. Clusters are chosen using the same methods as above, only the population list is shorter because you're using larger initial units than individuals.

(continued)

(continued)

- **Stratified random sampling** implies that you will randomly select your sample based on further defining characteristics. For example, if your population is divided by income level (say, 20 percent over $50,000, 30 percent $20,000–$50,000, and 50 percent under $20,000) you'd need to select the same percentages in your sample.

- **Quota sampling,** by contrast, uses a set number from each mutually exclusive grouping within your population. This way, every voice is given attention. So, for example, within your population you may have a group (say, rape victims) who comprise a very small percentage of the overall target public. Using a stratified sample, you might not get the input you need from this group. Why? Because in the sample you may end up with only one or two people who fall into that category even though their opinions may be very important to you. If you draw an equal number of people from each of the subgroups whose opinions you need, you will have a better idea of the variance of opinion. Or you may not get a valid reading of opinions within that group if you limit yourself to a truly representative sampling size relevant to the population. In fact, many researchers will simply oversample a smaller subgroup to get a valid response from within that group and then weight the response in the overall final analysis.

The final question on any survey is one you must ask yourself: What does it all mean? If you've asked the right questions, and if you've selected your samples according to your needs and totally at random, then you should be able to analyze the answers in a way that is meaningful to you and your employer. This implies that you've carefully planned out the survey in advance, including the questions to be asked and the method of gathering the data. It also assumes that you or whomever you hire to do the asking knows what they're doing.

Typical problems in survey design include the following: Not enough people were sampled, the sample wasn't truly representative of your overall population, important questions were left out or questions were open to too much interpretation (see Exhibit 2.7 for types of survey questions), and your findings aren't related to your objective. Think about the possible shortcomings of any survey prior to spending your valuable time and money on something that might not prove to be worth it.

Exhibit 2.7

Types of Survey Questions

I. An open-ended question:

Who would you like to see elected president?

2. A closed-ended question, with unordered answer categories:

Who would you like to see elected president?

a. Larry   c. Curly   e. Donald Duck

b. Mo   d. Mickey Mouse

3. A closed-ended question with ordered answer categories:

For each of these candidates, please indicate how much you would like that individual to be elected president.

	Strongly favor his election	Somewhat favor his election	Somewhat oppose his election	Strongly oppose his election
a. Larry	1	2	3	4
b. Mo	1	2	3	4
c. Curly	1	2	3	4
d. Mickey	1	2	3	4
e. Donald	1	2	3	4

4. A partially closed-ended question:

Who would you like to see elected president?

a. Larry   c. Curly   e. Donald

b. Mo   d. Mickey   f. Other (specify)

5. Ladder scale question:

On a scale from 0 to 10, where 0 means you rate the job the president is doing as extremely poor and 10 means you rate the job the president is doing as extremely good, how would you rate the job President Fillmore is doing now?

Extremely poor   **Extremely good**

0   1   2   3   4   5   6   7   8   9   10

6. Likert scale question:

How likely do you think you will be to vote for President Fillmore in the upcoming election?

1. Very likely

2. Somewhat likely

3. Neither likely nor unlikely

4. Somewhat unlikely

5. Very likely

7. Semantic differential question:

Question   How would you characterize Millard Fillmore as president?

Good - Bad

Weak - Strong

(continued)

(continued)

Decisive	Indecisive
Immoral	Moral
Intelligent	Stupid

Anticipating Audience Expectations

Once you know who your audience is and how they feel about your subject, one final question must be answered if you expect to be successful: Why are they going to be paying attention to what you've written? If you don't know why your audience is reading your message in the first place, you certainly can't know what they expect to get from it. Ask yourself these questions:

- *What does my audience already know about my topic?* Never assume they know anything about your subject, but don't talk down to them either. How do you reach a compromise? Find out what they do know. Remember, people like to learn something from communication. It is best, however, to limit the amount of new information so as not to overwhelm your readers.

- *What is my audience's attitude toward me or my organization?* Remember the three basic audiences for any persuasive piece. You'll need to determine whether your audience is on your side, against you, or unconvinced. To the extent possible, try to determine your audience's image of you or your organization. Determining audience attitude is often an expensive proposition because it usually requires formal research. If time or money constraints permit you to make only an educated guess based on a small focus group or even on intuition, that's better than nothing at all. It is much easier to convince others when you know that you already have credibility with them.

- *Is my publication to be used in a larger context?* In other words, is your publication part of a press kit, for instance, or a direct-mail package, or one of many handouts at a trade show? This knowledge will determine your readers' level of attention and their receptiveness. Always consider the surroundings in which your piece will be used if you want it to have the maximum impact.

SETTING OBJECTIVES

Although the overall goal of a public relations campaign will generally be broad (such as, "To improve employee moral"), **objectives** set the concrete steps you will need to take to reach your goal. For public relations writing, these objectives must relate to the purpose of your message and should be realistic and measurable. For public relations writing, there are three types of objectives: informational, attitudinal, and behavioral.

Informational objectives are used most often to present balanced information on a topic of interest to your target audience. For instance, if you are simply attempting to let your employees know that your organization has developed a new health care package, your objective might read something like this:

> To inform all employees of the newest options available in their health care benefits package by the beginning of the October open enrollment period.

Notice that the objective begins with an infinitive phrase ("to inform"). Objectives should always be written this way. Notice, too, that the number of employees is addressed ("all"), and a specific time period for the completion of the objective also is included. In a complete communications plan, this objective would be followed by the proposed tactic for its realization and a method by which its success could be measured. For example:

> To inform all employees of the newest options available in their health care benefits package by the beginning of the October open enrollment period by placing informational folders in each employee's paycheck over the next two months. Personnel will keep a record of all employees requesting information on the new health care plan during the open enrollment period.

If your objective is *attitudinal* or *behavioral* rather than informational, your message is probably going to be persuasive. There are three ways you can attempt to influence attitude and behavior:

- You can create an attitude or behavior where none exists. This is the easiest method because your target audience usually has no predisposition.

- You can reinforce an existing attitude or behavior. This is also relatively easy to do because your target audience already believes or behaves in the way you desire.

- You can attempt to change an attitude. This is the most difficult to accomplish and, realistically, shouldn't be attempted unless you are willing to expend a lot of time and energy on, at best, a dubious outcome.

An example of an attitudinal objective is as follows:

> To create a favorable attitude among employees concerning the changeover from a monthly pay disbursement to a twice-monthly pay disbursement.

Methods for measuring this type of objective range from informal employee feedback to formal surveys of attitudes some time after the changeover has gone into effect.

An example of a behavioral objective is as follows:

> To increase the number of employees in attendance at the annual company picnic by 25 percent by mailing out weekly reminders to the homes of employees four weeks prior to the picnic.

Obviously, measuring the effectiveness of this objective is easier, but if you don't see an increase in attendance, you will have to do some serious research into the reasons why. However, these reasons might not involve your message or its presentation at all. You might simply have picked the Sunday of the big state fair to hold your picnic. Don't automatically conclude that your message is the problem without exploring all variables affecting its desired results.

KEY TERMS

issue statement	secondary research	objectives
target audience	descriptive data	
primary research	inferential data	

EXERCISES

1. You are developing an article for a new type of golf club for a trade publication. Profile your target audience by developing a rough, off-the-top-of-your-head description of the typical reader. Next, check several directories to determine media usage (*Simmon's*, for example), create a demographic profile, and extrapolate some basic psychographic information about your target audience.

2. Now, based on its stated ability to reach the target audience profiled in #1, pick an appropriate publication, cite its circulation and publication policy, and state why this is the most appropriate publication for your message.

3. Write down your goal for learning to write for public relations. In general terms, what do you hope to accomplish or where do you hope to be after you learn how to write for public relations? Now, based on your goal, list several objectives that you will need to accomplish in order to reach your goal.

CHAPTER
3

Message Strategy

In this chapter you will learn:

- What a message strategy is and why it is important to develop one before you develop a public relations piece.

- The purpose of informative and persuasive public relations pieces.

- What message strategies work best for conveying information and for persuading, and how each of these strategies works.

- How to choose the appropriate medium (or media) for conveying the message.

Message strategy has to do with developing a message, or messages, that will reach and have the desired effect on your target audience. Your message strategies should logically follow your objectives and contribute either directly or indirectly to them. You will need to develop individual message strategies for each of your target publics, based on what you have learned about them through your research. Remember, the strategy or strategies you use will be determined largely by your audience's makeup, predispositions, and perceived needs.

Most public relations writing is either informative or persuasive by intent, and a number of strategies can be used to accomplish both of these outcomes. Information, for example, may be imparted in a straightforward, expository manner, indicating by style that the message is unbiased. Information may also be imparted using entertainment, as anyone who has ever watched "Sesame Street" knows. In fact, if you are trying to reach an ambivalent audience with information, getting their attention through entertainment may help ensure your success. Persuaders may use entertainment as well, or reason, or emotion to convey their message.

Although persuasion may seem to be separate from "pure" information, it most certainly is not. Most public relations people know, for example, that whether or to what extent a target public changes its mind is due to three variables: (a) whether they are even aware of the issue you are talking about, (b) whether they believe it is important to them personally, and (c) whether they believe they can do anything about it. The extent to which each of these variables is in play with any given target public will dictate the strategy you use in your writing. For example, if the target public is largely unaware of the issue you are dealing with, you will need to inform them first before anything else can be attempted. If they are aware of the issue but don't see its relevance to their personal agendas, then you will have to do some persuading. If they are aware of both the issue and its importance to them but they feel constrained (for whatever reason) from acting, then your job becomes a combination of information and persuasion.

What you have found out about your publics from your prior research will then dictate what strategies to take in your information and persuasion approaches. For example, although entertainment may work well with children, something approaching logic (argument) might have a better effect on businesspeople. Both strategies could be said to be persuasive, their styles simply dictated by the target public.

An informative piece should be balanced and complete. Its purpose is to let readers in on something they may not know or about which they may have an incomplete picture. The intent may be to publicize a new product or service, to set the record straight on a vital issue affecting your organization, or simply to let your readers know what's happening in your organization. Whatever the intent, the informational publication has to stick to just that—information. If your point of view is so strong as to evoke opposition, you probably should be writing a piece to persuade.

Persuasive pieces usually are heavy on the positive attributes of your service, product, or point of view. They need to be written in terms the audience can relate to, and they frequently benefit from the use of words with emotional impact.

Informative pieces can get away with far fewer emotionally packed words and are frequently longer. After all, their aim is to inform what is assumed to be an audience that is already convinced of, or at least interested in, the subject.

INFORMATION STRATEGIES

Writing informative messages is one of the most straightforward tasks in public relations writing. Informative messages should be balanced and unbiased in presentation. Naturally, you can put your own spin on anything you write, but in the information piece you should keep to the facts. Most audiences will see through a persuasive piece thinly disguised as information. Indeed, this is one of the major objections journalists voice concerning news releases. They often say that much of what they receive is really advertising (persuasion) in disguise.

Information can be presented in a number of ways, from dissemination of pure information (called exposition) to entertainment.

Exposition

Two of the most-used forms of **exposition** are narration and description.

Narration (Story Telling)

Telling stories is a natural human inclination. Fortunately for us, it also seems to be a natural need. The popular appeal of documentaries is evidence of our love of story telling, and the enormous success of such cable television innovations as the Discovery Channel speaks to the widespread appeal of this form of information dissemination. Keep in mind that narration as well as the other approaches described here also can be used as persuasive strategies.

Description

This is a method of sharing with our audiences those aspects of our surroundings that have had an impact on us. When used together with narration, we get a very expressive form of narration: fiction. The two most common forms of description are technical description and suggestive description.

- *Technical description* is relatively free from impression. We see it most often in technical journals and manuals. Its purpose is generally instructional.
- *Suggestive description* is more impressionistic and can also be used for persuasion. This is the form taken most often in feature or nonfiction writing.

Entertainment

Entertainment ("sugar-coated" information) is the second major information strategy. Although entertainment is often thought of as not imparting information, like all forms of communication it informs to some extent. Referring to entertainment strategies as sugar coated may seem a bit harsh, but remember that

---

Exhibit 3.1

A Prewriting Checklist for Information Pieces

When writing an information piece, ask yourself the following questions:

- Why would my target audience want to know about this topic?
- What would they want to know about it?
- Is the topic tied to a particular strategy? If so, what strategy? If it is part of an overall persuasive campaign, why am I using an informative approach?
- How much material should be considered "further information" to which interested readers can be referred elsewhere?
- Am I expecting any results from this approach? Make your objectives clear enough to be measurable so that you can later evaluate the results of information dissemination effectively.

Remember, the most valid objective of information is to raise your target audience's level of knowledge or understanding. The reason behind public relations writing may ultimately be to persuade, but in information pieces, bias should be kept to a minimum.

---

the purpose of encapsulating information within entertainment is to make it easier to swallow. We are much more easily informed if we are entertained simultaneously. Again, think of how hugely popular and effective "Sesame Street" has been, or how successful the show "Biography" has been for the cable network A&E. I address entertainment strategies further when I discuss persuasion, below. For a short prewriting checklist for information pieces, see Exhibit 3.1.

THE PROCESS OF PERSUASION

To write persuasively you must understand the process of persuasion, what it is and how it either works or doesn't work. **Persuasion**—moving someone to believe or act a certain way—is difficult in most cases. That's why so many public relations campaigns strive for understanding, not persuasion. The problem, as it turns out, is that human beings have an interesting and frustrating ability to not listen to what is being said to them. This is particularly annoying for public relations people, who are constantly trying to communicate with publics who are simply not paying attention. Once we understand why they aren't listening, we have a much better chance of getting them to pay attention. Ready for a little theory?

Dissonance theory, formulated in the 1950s, says that people tend to seek only messages that are consonant with their attitudes; they do not seek out dissonant messages. In other words, people don't go looking for messages they don't agree with already (who needs more conflict in their lives, right?). This theory also says that about the only way you are going to get anybody to listen to something they don't agree with is to juxtapose their attitude with a dissonant attitude—an attitude that is logically inconsistent with the first. What this means (theoretically) is that if you confront people with a concept that radically shakes up their belief structure, you might get them to pay attention. For example, this is the technique used by some antiabortion activists when they force us to look at graphic images of aborted fetuses. Although the experience may be truly uncomfortable, it reminds even the most ardent abortion rights supporters among us of the costs of the procedure. The attempt is to shock unbelievers into questioning their loyalties.

Later research revealed that people use a fairly sophisticated psychological defense mechanism to filter out unwanted information. This mechanism consists of four so-called rings of defense:

1. *Selective exposure.* People tend to seek out only the information that agrees with their existing attitudes or beliefs. This accounts for our not subscribing to *The New Republic* if we are staunchly liberal Democrats.

2. *Selective attention.* People tune out communication that goes against their attitudes or beliefs, or they pay attention only to parts that reinforce their positions, forgetting the dissonant parts. This is why two people with differing points of view can come to different conclusions about the same message. Each of them is tuning out the parts with which they disagree.

3. *Selective perception.* People seek to interpret information so that it agrees with their attitudes and beliefs. This accounts for a lot of misinterpretation of messages. Some people don't block out dissonant information; they simply reinterpret it so that it matches their preconceptions. For example, whereas one person may view rising interest rates as an obstacle to his or her personal economic situation, another may view the same rise as an asset. The first person may be trying to buy a new home; the second may be a financial investor. Both are interpreting the same issue based on their differing viewpoints.

4. *Selective retention.* People tend to let psychological factors influence their recall of information. In other words, we forget the unpleasant or block out the unwanted. This also means that people tend to be more receptive to messages presented in pleasant environments—a lesson anyone who has ever put on a news conference understands.

What does all this mean? For those of us in the business of persuasion, it means we have a tough job ahead of us. However, the outlook isn't all that bleak. Since the time of the ancient Greeks (and probably before), we have known that people can be persuaded. Once you know how resistant they can be, half the job is done. The rest is knowing how to break down those defenses (or, at least, how to get around them).

PERSUASIVE STRATEGIES

Writing a message that persuades is not easy. First, you have to have a crystal-clear understanding of what you want your readers to do in response to your persuasive effort. This means you have to be able to convey your message in the clearest possible terms and must also be responsive to opposing points of view.

The persuasive message is normally audience centered; that is, persuasive strategy is based on who your audience is and how they feel about your topic. The approach you use probably will be based on audience analysis. For example, your knowledge of your target audience should indicate how receptive they are to either an emotional or a rational appeal. Historically, audiences react best to a combination of both. There are times, however, when a purely emotional or purely rational appeal will be most effective.

In general, audience-centered persuasion will be more successful if you adhere to the following simple principles:

- *Identification.* People will relate to an idea, opinion, or point of view only if they can see some direct effect on their own hopes, fears, desires, or aspirations. This is why local news is more interesting to most people and why global issues remain so distant from most of our daily lives.

- *Suggestion of action.* People will endorse ideas only if they are accompanied by a proposed action from the sponsor of the idea or if the recipients themselves propose it, especially if it is a convenient action. For example, every time you see a tear-off coupon dispenser at a grocery store, the product manufacturer is following this principle.

- *Familiarity and trust.* People are unwilling to accept ideas from sources they don't trust. We will trust even celebrities if they are familiar to us and have good reputations. We certainly trust them to recommend commercial products (such as athletic shoes); however, it is much harder to find spokespeople for image-related issues. That's why we often see occupations rather than specific people used in these pitches. An eco-scientist is a far better spokesperson for a company wanting to go "green" than is any celebrity.

- *Clarity.* The meaning of an idea has to be clear, whether it is an event, a situation, or a message. One of the most important jobs of public relations is to explain complex issues in simple terms. In today's "sound-bite" environment, this has become increasingly difficult. No one is more aware of this difficulty than political campaign advisors. When was the last time you saw a political ad that said anything substantive in 30 seconds? Even so, research shows that some of the best of these ads actually do work.

Remember, a hostile audience usually won't be convinced, a sympathetic audience doesn't need to be convinced, and an undecided audience is as likely to be convinced by your opposition as by you. Different strategies will be used for each of these audiences. For instance, if you are writing for a friendly audience, an emotional appeal may work well. For an undecided audience, a rational appeal supported by solid evidence may work best. If your audience is neutral or disinterested, you'll have to stress attention-getting devices. If they are uninformed, you'll have to inform them. And if they are simply undecided, you'll have to convince them.

As already mentioned, certain strategies are more appropriate to persuasion than to information dissemination. For example, emotional appeals are most often associated with persuasion, not information. That's why, for instance, straight news stories are generally free of such appeals. They are supposed to be as objective (informative) as possible. The most common strategies for persuasion are compliance strategies and argument strategies.

Compliance Strategies

Compliance strategies are persuasive strategies designed to gain agreement through techniques of persuasion based not on reasoned argument (although they may appear to be) but on some other method of enticement. For example offering a reward for the return of stolen merchandise doesn't exactly appeal to altruism, yet it's considered an acceptable method for regaining what is yours. So, although some compliance strategies may appear at first blush to be unethical, a quick review of the following three compliance strategies will reassure you that they need not be.

Sanction Strategies

Sanction strategies use rewards and punishments controlled either by the audience themselves or as a result of the situation. For example, if I'm trying to persuade you that supporting the state lottery is a good thing because the proceeds go to fund education, I can offer you the potential reward of big winnings. Of course, you control whether you are eligible. If you buy a ticket, you are; if you don't, you're not. However, I made you aware and offered you the choice.

Appeal Strategies

Appeal strategies call upon the audience to help or come to the aid of the communicator or some third party represented by the communicator. For instance, I might urge you to "save the whales." I am counting on your sense of altruism to act, mostly because it is so difficult to tie the fate of whales to any personal interest beyond altruism. Of course, this strategy works only on publics prone to act sympathetically.

Command Strategies

Command strategies come in three forms:

- *They may use direct requests with no rationale or motivation for the requests.* The famous "I want you" poster for the U.S. Army is still a great example of this strategy. A more current example is "Got milk?"—the campaign of the American Dairy Council.

- *They may provide explanation accompanied with reasons for complying.* The Army "Be all you can be" campaign is a good example of this one. One of the newer versions of that message plays heavily on the college tuition benefit, for example.

- *They may provide hints in which circumstances are suggested from which the audience draws the desired conclusions and acts in the desired way.* This technique implies that your audience shares certain connotative meanings. For example, the famous (or infamous) Virginia Slims ads suggest that smoking promotes thinness. Another example is the now-famous Godfatherly appeal, "I made him an offer he couldn't refuse." The implicit suggestion is understood between communicator and audience. Nothing explicit need be said.

Argument Strategies

Democratic debate is at the heart of our system of government. It is no surprise then that **argument strategies** are among the oldest types of persuasion at your disposal. Argument strategies, which are persuasive strategies designed to oppose another point of view and to persuade, come in two types: reasoned argument and emotional appeal. Both types attempt to persuade by arguing one point of view against another.

Reasoned Argument

Reasoned argument (also known as logical argument) uses the techniques of rhetoric as handed down from the ancient Greeks. For persuasive messages it is important to understand the psychological state of your audience and build your message around it. This audience-centered approach includes three basic techniques of reasoned argument: the motivated sequence, the imagined question-and-answer (Q & A) session, and messages aimed at attitude change.

Motivated sequence. A common tactic used by persuaders is the motivated sequence, which involves the following five steps:

1. *Attention.* You must first get the attention of your audience. This means that you have to open with a bang.
2. *Need.* Establish why the topic is of importance to the audience. Set up the problem statement—a brief description of the issue you are dealing with.
3. *Satisfaction.* Present the solution. It has to be a legitimate solution to the problem.
4. *Support.* Support fully your solution and point out the pitfalls of any alternatives. Otherwise, your audience may not be able to comprehend completely the advantages of your solution over others.
5. *Action.* Call for action. Ask your audience to respond to your message, and make it as easy as possible to take action.

Imagined Q & A. In the imagined Q & A, the message is structured into a series of questions that the audience might have, followed by your answer to each. Ask yourself the questions your audience might be asking you, such as:

- *Why even talk about this subject?* Tell your audience the importance of your topic to them. Tie your topic to their concerns.

- *For example?* Don't just leave them with your point of view. Give them examples. Support your proposal.

- *So what?* Let them know what all of this means to them, and tell them what you want them to do.

Messages aimed at attitude change. If you really are going to try to change attitude, you had best be aware of the most common techniques: messages aimed at attitude change. Following are some guidelines for constructing persuasive messages designed for attitude or opinion change. The strategy used here is argument.

- *If your audience opposes your position,* present arguments on both sides of the issue. Remember, they already know you have a vested interest in giving your side of the story. By presenting both sides, you portray an image of fairness and willingness to compare arguments. The process appears to be more democratic that way. In most cases, it is advisable to address counterarguments only after you have presented your own side. Here's how it works:

  - *State the opposing view fairly.* Make your audience believe that you are fair minded enough to recognize that there is another side and that you're intelligent enough to understand it.

  - *State your position on the opposing view.* Now that you've shown you understand the other side, state why you don't think it's right—or better yet, not totally right. This indicates that you find at least some merit in what others have to say—even the opposition.

  - *Support your position.* Give the details of your side of the argument. Use logic, not emotion. Show that you are above such tricks; however, don't avoid emotion altogether. Try to strike a balance while leaning toward logic and emotional control.

  - *Compare the two positions and show why yours is the most viable.* If you've done your work well up to this point, then your audience will already see the clear differences between the two sides. Strengthen their understanding by reiterating the differences and finishing with a strong statement in support of your arguments.

- *If an audience already agrees with your position, present arguments consistent with their favorable viewpoint.* This will tend to reinforce their opinions. Not much can be gained by presenting opposing arguments to this audience because they already agree with you. In fact, it might work against you.

- *If your audience is well educated, include both sides of the argument.* Intelligent people will judge your argument by how well you are able to refute counterarguments.

- *If you do use messages containing both sides of the argument, don't leave out relevant opposition arguments.* Audiences that notice the omission (especially well-educated ones) will probably suspect that you can't refute these arguments.

- *If your audience is likely to be exposed later to persuasive messages countering your position, present both sides of the argument to build audience resistance to the later messages.* This is known as the inoculation effect, which basically states that once you have heard me present both my side and the opposing side of an argument, and heard me soundly refute the other side, you are far less likely to listen to the other side at a later time. You have, after all, already heard their side—from me.

Emotional Appeal

Because emotion is common to all human beings, it should come as no surprise that the use of **emotional appeal** as a persuasive strategy is widespread. Most advertising uses emotional appeal to sell products. Parity products, especially, benefit from this technique. A parity product is one that is virtually indistinguishable from other similar products. Bath soaps, soft drinks, and perfumes are examples of parity products. Think about the type of ads you have seen that deal with these products: They are almost always based on an image created by emotional appeal. And not to let public relations off the hook, think of all those politicians who seem to be pretty much alike. How are they differentiated in our minds?

Emotional appeal can be fostered in several ways, the most important of which are the use of symbols, the use of emotive language, and the use of entertainment strategies. I discuss the use of symbols and emotive language in the section on ethics in Chapter 4. Here, I concentrate on entertainment as a way of creating emotional appeal.

Like the techniques of argument, the techniques of entertainment have been handed down to us from the ancient Greeks. The masks of comedy and tragedy are part of our cultural symbolism in the West. Entertainment, by nature, appeals to the senses. As a culture we often refer to a person's sense of humor or someone's sense of the dramatic. As anyone who has kept track of the evolution in beer commercials knows, humor has become the primary focus of many beer manufacturers' ad campaigns. Think of the recent Budweiser campaign using frogs (and then lizards) to imprint name recognition, or the "Bud Bowl," now a staple of Super Bowl mythology. Like many other products, beer is a parity item, and parity products are best differentiated by image, which is often the result of entertainment strategies.

It's easy to spot the uses of drama and humor in advertising, but public relations campaigns frequently use the same approaches in order to persuade. Humor, for example, is especially useful if what you have to "sell" either is opposed by your audience or appears to be distant from their experience. Politicians needing image revamps often turn to humor. Then–Vice President Al Gore could be seen a few years ago cracking jokes about his own stiffness on "Late Night with David Letterman." This was not an accident but rather a carefully planned public relations move to soften his image.

Emotional appeal, like compliance strategies, may seem to be unethical; however, using emotion to draw attention is not inherently so. It may be manipulative (in the sense that its sole intent is to hook the audience), but it is unethical only if it hides the true objective of the message: to persuade.

CHOOSING THE APPROPRIATE MEDIUM OR MEDIA

The final step in the planning process is choosing the appropriate medium or media for your message. Any assumptions you make at this juncture could be disastrous. Selecting the right medium or media is a decision that should be based on sound knowledge of a number of factors. Public relations educators Doug Newsom, Judy VanSlyke Turk, and Dean Kruckeberg, in their book, *This Is PR: The Realities of Public Relations* (Wadsworth, 2003), have suggested a series of important considerations to be used in choosing the right medium for your message:

1. What audience are you trying to reach, and what do you know about its media usage patterns and the credibility ratings for each medium? Many target audiences simply do not watch television or listen to the radio. Others don't read newspapers regularly or subscribe to magazines. You need to know, first, whether your intended audience will even see your message if it is presented in a medium they don't regularly use. Research tells us, for example, that businesspeople read newspapers more than do some other groups, and that they rely on newspapers for basic news and information. Other groups may rely on television almost exclusively for their news and information. For each of these groups, the credibility of the medium in question is vital. For example, businesspeople cite newspapers as a more credible source for news and information than television; however, for many people, television is far more credible.

2. When do you need to reach this audience in order for your message to be effective? If time is of the essence, you'd best not leave your message for the next issue of the corporate magazine.

3. How much do you need to spend to reach your intended audience, and how much can you afford? It may be that the only way to achieve the result you're looking for is to go to some extra expense such as a folder with more glitz or a full-color newsletter. Although every job has budget constraints, it's best to know from the start exactly what it will take to accomplish your objectives.

After you have answered these tough questions, you will need to ask four others:

1. Which medium (of those you've listed in response to your first three questions) reaches the broadest segment of your target audience at the lowest cost? The answer to this question will give you a bottom-line choice of sorts because cost is the controlling factor in answering it. Maybe you can reach all of an employee audience with an expensive corporate magazine but two-thirds of it with a less expensive newsletter.

2. Which medium has the highest credibility, and what does it cost? Here, the correct answer will give you the additional factor of credibility that is key if your audience is discriminating at all. There are always those for whom the least credible of sources is still credible (otherwise, gossip tabloids would go out of business). But, for the honest communicator, credibility is important to the success of any future messages.

3. Which medium will deliver your message within the time constraints necessary for it to be effective? Again, a critical letter distributed via the company intranet may be a lot more timely than a well-written article in next month's corporate magazine.

4. Should a single medium be used or a combination of complementary media (media mix)? Remember, each element in an overall communications program may require a specialized medium in order for that portion of the message to be most effective.

The more you know about your audience, the better you will be at selecting just the right medium for your message. However, you must also understand that media criteria often dictate message and message format. For instance, brochures demand brevity, as do flyers and posters; corporate magazines allow for fuller development of messages; newsletters offer more space than folders but less than magazines; pamphlets offer space for message expansion and place fewer demands on style; annual reports require strict adherence to Securities and Exchange Commission guidelines; and Web pages allow for detailed information on numerous topics. You must also consider cost and lead time for writing, editing, layout, typesetting, paste-up, printing, and distribution.

In short, selecting the most appropriate medium for your message is a complex endeavor. Be forewarned that no assumptions should be made about the acceptability of any particular medium. Until you have considered, at the least, the questions posed earlier, you will probably only be guessing on your choice of an ideal medium.

LEARNING TO ADAPT

One of the hallmarks of a good writer is the ability to adapt to the needs of the audience, the message, and the medium. Public relations writing, unlike many other forms of writing, requires this flexibility. In the following chapters, you will find a variety of writing styles used in different formats. The key to writing for public relations is to learn these formats and adapt your style to each as needed. The road to becoming a good public relations writer has many side tracks, and it is quite easy to let yourself become specialized. But the trick to becoming the best kind of writer is not to let that happen. The greater the variety of writing styles you can learn to use well, the better your chances of becoming an excellent writer.

KEY TERMS

message strategy	dissonance theory	command strategies
exposition	compliance strategies	argument strategies
entertainment	sanction strategies	reasoned argument
persuasion	appeal strategies	emotional appeal

EXERCISES

I. Find a persuasive public service advertisement in a magazine. (Many of the major consumer magazines carry them.) Assess what persuasive strategy it is using: compliance, appeal, command, argument. Rewrite the copy using each of the approaches not used originally.

2. Write down three reasons why you believe this ad was placed in this particular magazine. Based on your reasoning, list three other magazines in which you would place this ad.

3. If you were to use this advertisement in media other than magazines, what would those media be, and why would you pick them?

4. Look through your local newspaper for examples of persuasive writing, excluding advertising. Bring in copies of what you find along with an analysis of what persuasive techniques are being used.

CHAPTER

4

Ethics and Public Relations Writing

In this chapter you will learn:

- Some of the ethical considerations of public relations writing, including unethical persuasive techniques and unethical language use.

- The guidelines for how to ghostwrite ethically.

- The legal aspects of public relations writing, including defamation, invasion of privacy, and copyright and trademark considerations.

Public relations is fraught with ethical dilemmas. No one working in the field would deny this; however, for the writer these dilemmas take a slightly different form than the types of problems faced by others in the field. For instance, many of the ethical quandaries facing public relations people have to do with decisions on large issues—whether to handle a particular political candidate or ethically suspect client; how to deal with the media on a day-to-day basis without lying; what to keep confidential and what to disclose; and whether to do what the client says, no matter what.

It's not that such decisions are beyond the scope of the public relations writer. It's that a writer spends much more time dealing with the technical aspects of his or her job than with the bigger picture. This tight focus, however, comes with its own set of ethical considerations, among which are such quandaries as how to persuade without violating the basic tenets of ethics and good taste, and how to write words that will later be claimed by someone else as his or her own.

ETHICAL CONSIDERATIONS OF PERSUASION

Some people consider persuasion unethical by nature. They believe in a very strict version of the "marketplace of ideas" theory that if you provide enough, unbiased information for people, they will be able to make up their own minds about any issue. Of course, we all know that isn't true. Although our political system is based on this theory, to some extent it is also based on the notion of reasoned argument—that is, persuasion. People who believe fervently enough in a particular point of view aren't going to rely on any marketplace to decide their case. They're going to get out there and argue, persuasively, for their side. Since the time of Aristotle, we've had access to a number of persuasive techniques—some already mentioned. We also are aware of how easily many of these techniques can be turned to unethical purposes. In fact, the most frequent complaint against any form of communication is that it is trying to persuade unethically. This complaint may seem to be leveled most often at advertising, but public relations hasn't gotten off the hook entirely. Discussed here are a number of techniques that, in varying degrees, can be used unethically. All of these techniques have been used in propaganda campaigns, but you will recognize many of them as still being used in both public relations and advertising.

Logic Fallacies

By far the most unethical of the techniques are those codified by the Roman orators over a thousand years ago. These are commonly referred to as **logic fallacies** because they are both illogical and deceptive by nature. Let's look first at these:

- *Cause and effect (post hoc ergo propter hoc).* Don't be put off by the Latin. We see this one in operation all the time. It means that because one thing follows another in time, the second was caused by the first. This tactic is most often used to infer that one thing is the result of the other. Politicians are particularly adept at using this argument. For example, an incumbent may suggest that the national drop in crime rate is the result of his policies when, in fact, it is the continuation of a drop that began before his administration. Or a television ad for the plastic industry may imply that we are a healthier society because meat is no longer sold in open-air markets, exposed to the elements. Although this may be partially true, the overall longevity of any society is the result of multiple factors, not just one.

- *Personal attack (ad hominum).* This means "against the man" and is a technique used to discredit the source of the message regardless of the message itself. Again, we see this one time and again in politics, where policies are left unconsidered while personality assassination runs rampant. Any time you see an argument turn from issues to personality, this unethical strategy is being used.

- *Bandwagon (ad populum).* This is an appeal to popularity. In other words, if everyone else is doing it, why aren't you? McDonald's has been using this strategy for years in its "xxx billion sold" byline. Because human beings are, by nature, group oriented, they already tend to want to go with what's popular. However, as Henry David Thoreau pointed out, the group isn't always right.

- *Inference by association.* This is an argument based entirely on false logic, most often thought of as "guilt by association" or, in some cases, credit by association. The argument usually takes the following form:

Chemical weapons are evil.
X company makes chemical weapons.
X company is evil.

Of course, the argument is logically inconsistent. Although chemical weapons may in themselves be evil, this does not automatically make the entire company evil. The same sort of argument can be made by associating a product or idea with another, already accepted idea. For example, "From the people who brought you. . . ." This statement assumes that because one product is successful or satisfying, all products from the same company will be. And, of course, this argument is used in all those celebrity endorsements: "Wheaties, the breakfast of champions!"

Other Tactics

Several other tactics closely related to inference by association are not necessarily unethical by nature but can be used unethically. Some of the most common tactics are as follows:

- *Plain folks.* This tactic appeals to our need to deal with people who are like us. Plain folks proposes that the speaker is just like the listener and so "wouldn't lie to you." Again, politicians are adept at this approach, but so are corporate executives who sell their own products.

- *Testimonials.* This tactic is directly related to inference by association; however, this technique actually implies that the celebrity spokesperson uses the product or supports the cause. And, of course, this may or may not be true.

- *Transfer.* This technique involves the deliberate use of positive symbols in order to transfer meaning to another message, not necessarily related. The use of religious or patriotic symbols such as a "heavenly choir" or an American flag during a commercial not directly related to such symbols is an example of transfer. Most recently, the ubiquitous use of Beethoven's ninth symphony ("Ode to Joy") in everything from the Olympic Games to cable channel promos is a blatant attempt to bring a sense of high, nearly religious, meaning to the message being imparted.

Unethical Language Use

A final area of ethical consideration, as it relates to persuasion, has to do with the actual use of language. Often called **language fallacies,** these techniques are nearly always used intentionally. The most common are as follows:

- *Equivocation.* Words can, and often are, ambiguous. Many words have more than one meaning. Equivocation refers to using one or both meanings of a word and then deliberately confusing the two in the audience's mind. For example, the word *free* is tossed about quite a bit by advertisers, but does it really mean without cost? When you purchase that big bottle of shampoo that claims you are getting "12 more ounces free!" are you really getting it free? When a press release states that a senior executive has "resigned," does it mean she has quit or that she was fired? In fact, the word *resign* has become something of a euphemism in business and government for being asked to leave.

- *Amphiboly.* This approach uses ambiguous sentence structure or grammar to mislead. For example, "new and improved" products imply that a logical comparison is to be made. However, what are the newness and state of improvement being compared to? How about "X cereal: part of a nutritious breakfast"? What part? Is it nutritious without the other parts? What are the other parts? And if something only "helps" you obtain whiter teeth, what else plays a part?

- *Emotive language.* This technique uses emotionally charged words to shift response from the argument itself to the images invoked by these words. This is a bit like transfer except that it uses words instead of images. Think of the ads that use words such as *freedom, miracle, powerful,* or *younger looking.* Or the news release that refers to a product as revolutionary or a person as dynamic. When we use these words, we've strayed from fact to opinion.

Ultimately, whether or not what you have written is ethical will depend on your ability to be as objective as possible about your own motives. If you wish to deceive, you will. A technically good writer has access to all the tools needed to write unethically. The decision is yours. Remember, persuasion is ethical; manipulation is not.

Ethics and Ghostwriting

Ghostwriting refers to writing something for someone else that will be represented as that person's own point of view. Public relations writers ghostwrite speeches, letters to the editor, annual report letters from the president, and even quotes (see Chapter 7). Ghostwriting is ubiquitous, to say the least. Rhetoricians point out that no president since Abraham Lincoln has written his own speeches in their entirety. Recall that Lincoln wrote the Gettysburg Address on a train ride between Washington and Gettysburg—and, by most accounts, did a fairly nice job.

The days have long since vanished when the busy corporate executive or politician had the time (or the skill) to write his or her own speeches. In fact, we can no longer take it as a given that most of what passes for their words—either in print or spoken forms—are really *their* words. When Reagan press secretary Larry Speakes indicated in his book that he had made up quotes (even "borrowed" quotes from others and attributed them to Reagan), many seemingly incredulous journalists cried foul. Surely they, as most of us, realized that the president simply doesn't have the luxury to write his own speeches anymore. Even John Kennedy, famous for his speeches, didn't write his own. Speakes himself dismissed the accusations as "taking a bit of liberty with my P.R. man's license" in order to "spruce up the President's image."[1]

However—and this is a big "however"—something still bothers all of us about a writer we don't even know putting words into the mouth of someone we do know, or thought we knew. So, the question is, if ghostwriting is to be taken as having been produced by, or at least prompted by, the person under whose name it will appear, is it unethical? Well, yes and no. Some of the best guidelines I know of have been set down by Richard Johanessen in his book *Ethics in Human Communication*, in which he analyzes the ethics of ghostwriting by posing a series of important questions:

- *What is the communicator's intent, and what is the audience's degree of awareness?* In other words, does the communicator pretend to be the author of the words he speaks or over which his signature appears? And how aware is the audience that ghostwriting is commonplace under certain circumstances? If we assume, as most do, that presidential speeches are ghostwritten, then the only unethical act would be for the president to claim to author his own speeches.

- *Does the communicator use ghostwriters to make himself or herself appear to possess personal qualities that he or she does not have?* In other words, does the writer impart such qualities as eloquence, wit, coherence, and incisive ideas to a communicator who might not possess these qualities otherwise? The degree to which the writing distorts a communicator's character has a great deal to do with ethicality.

---

[1] Larry Speakes, with Robert Pack. 1989. *Speaking Out: The Reagan Presidency from Inside the White House*, pp. 169–170. New York: Harcourt.

- *What are the surrounding circumstances of the communicator's job that make ghost-writing a necessity?* The pressures of a job often dictate that a ghostwriter be used. Busy executives, like busy politicians, may not have the time to write all the messages they must deliver on a daily basis. However, we don't expect the average office manager or university professor to hire a ghostwriter. Part of the answer to this question lies in the pressures of the job itself, and the other part has to do with the need and frequency of communication.

- *To what extent does the communicator actively participate in the writing of his or her own messages?* Obviously, the more input a communicator has in his or her own writing, the more ethical will be the resultant image. We really don't expect the president to write his own speeches, but we do expect that the sentiments expressed in them will be his own.

- *Does the communicator accept responsibility for the message he or she presents?* Most communicators simply assume that whatever they say or whatever they sign their names to is theirs, whether written by someone else or not. This is obviously the most ethical position to take.

Remember, if you ghostwrite, you are as responsible for the ethicality of your work as the person for whom it is written. Be sure that you have asked yourself these questions before you give authorship of your work over to someone else.

THE LEGAL ASPECTS OF PUBLIC RELATIONS WRITING

All those who deal in public communication are bound by certain laws. For the most part, these laws protect others. We are all familiar with the First Amendment rights allowed the press in this country. To a certain degree, some of those rights transfer to public relations. For example, corporations now enjoy a limited First Amendment protection under what is known as commercial speech. **Commercial speech,** as defined by the Supreme Court, allows a corporation to state publicly its position on controversial issues. The Court's interpretation of this concept also allows for political activity through lobbying and political action committees.

But, as with most rights, there are concomitant obligations—chief among them is the obligation not to harm others through your communication. The most important don'ts for public relations writers concern slander or libel (defamation), invasion of privacy, and infringement of copyrights or trademarks.

Defamation

Defamation is the area of infringement with which writers are most familiar. Although it is variously defined (each case seems to bring a new definition), defamation can be said to be any communication that holds a person up to contempt, hatred, ridicule, or scorn. One problem in defending against accusations of defamation is that different rules exist for different people. It is generally easier for private individuals to prove defamation than it is for those in the public eye. Celebrities and politicians, for example, open themselves to a certain amount of publicity and, therefore, criticism. Whereas a private individual suing for libel must prove only negligence, a public figure must prove malice. For defamation to be actionable, five elements must be present:

1. There must be communication of a statement that harms a person's reputation in some way, even if it only lowers that person's esteem in another's eyes.

2. The communication must have been published or communicated to a third party. The difference here is that between slander and libel. Slander is oral defamation and might arise, for example, in a public speech. Libel is written defamation, though it also includes broadcast communication.

3. The person defamed must have been identified in the communication, either by name or by direct inference. This is the toughest to prove if the person's name hasn't been used directly.

4. The person defamed must be able to prove that the communication caused damage to his or her reputation.

5. Negligence must also be shown. In other words, the source of the communication must be proved to have been negligent during research or writing. Negligence can be the fault of poor information gathering. Public figures must prove malice—that is, the communication was made with knowing falsehood or reckless disregard for the truth.

There are defenses against defamation. The most obvious is that the communication is the truth, regardless of whether the information harmed someone's reputation.

The second defense is privilege. Privilege applies to statements made during public, official, or judicial proceedings. For example, if something normally libelous is reported accurately on the basis of a public meeting, the reporter cannot be held responsible. Privilege is a tricky concept, however, and care must be taken that privileged information be given only to those who have a right to it. Public meetings are public information. Only concerned individuals have a right to privileged information released at private meetings.

The third most common defense is fair comment. This concept applies primarily to the right to criticize, as in theater or book critiques, and must be restricted to the public interest aspects of that which is under discussion. However, it also can be construed to apply to such communications as comparative advertising.

Privacy

Most of us are familiar with the phrase *invasion of* **privacy.** For public relations writers, infringing on privacy is a serious concern. It can happen very easily. For example, your position as editor of the house magazine doesn't automatically give you the right to use any employee picture you might have on file, or to divulge personal information about an employee without his or her prior written permission. Invasion of privacy falls roughly into the following categories.

- *Appropriation* is the commercial use of a person's name or picture without permission. For instance, you can't say that one of your employees supports the company's position on nuclear energy if that employee hasn't given you permission to do so, even if the employee supports that position and has said so to you.

- Private facts about individuals are also protected. Information about a person's lifestyle, family situation, personal health, and the like is considered to be strictly private and may not be disclosed without permission.

- *Intrusion* involves literally spying on another. Obtaining information by bugging, filming, or recording in any way another's private affairs is cause for a lawsuit.

Copyright

Most of us understand that we can't quote freely from a book without giving credit, photocopy entire publications to avoid buying copies, or reprint a cartoon strip in our corporate magazine without permission. Most forms of published communication are protected by **copyright** laws.

The reasons for copyright protection are fairly clear. Those who create original work, such as novels, songs, articles, and advertisements, lose the very means to their livelihood each time their novel, song, or article, or advertisement is used without payment.

All writers need to be aware that copyrighted information is not theirs to use free of charge, without permission. Always check for copyright ownership on anything you plan to use in any way (see Exhibit 4.1). You may want to rewrite information, or paraphrase it, and think that as long as you don't use the original wording you are exempt from copyright violation. Not so. Prescribed guidelines exist for use of copyrighted information without permission. You may use a portion of copyrighted information if the following conditions are met:

- It is not taken out of context.
- Credit is given to the source.
- Your usage doesn't affect the market for the material.
- You are using the information for scholastic or research purposes.
- The material used doesn't exceed a certain percentage of the total work.

Just remember, never use another's work without permission.

Trademarks

Trademarks are typically given for the protection of product names or, in certain instances, images, phrases, or slogans (see Exhibit 4.1). For example, several years ago, Anheuser-Busch sued a florist for calling a flower shop This Bud's For You. The reason, of course, is that the slogan was commonly recognized as referring to Budweiser beer. The Disney studios have jealously guarded their trademarked cartoon characters since the early 1930s, and their trademark appears on thousands of items. Charles Schultz's *Peanuts* characters are also

---

Exhibit 4.1

Symbols for Protected Material

© **Copyright.** Used to protect copy of any length. Can be "noticed"—or marked—either without actual federal registration (which limits protection under the law) or with registration (which expands the degree of legal protection). "Noticing" is simply stating that something is copyrighted, for example, "copyright Thomas H. Bivins, 2004." This can be done with or without an accompanying copyright symbol.

® **Registered trademark.** Used to protect any word, name, symbol, or device used by a manufacturer or merchant to identify and distinguish his or her goods from those of others. This mark indicates that the user has registered the item with the federal government, allowing maximum legal protection.

™ **Trademark.** Similarly used, but as a common law notice. In other words, material marked this way is not necessarily registered with the government and thus has limited and not full legal protection.

---

used for hundreds of purposes, all with permission. Even advertisements that mention other product names are careful to footnote trademark information.

One of the main reasons for trademark protection is to prevent someone not associated with the trademarked product, image, or slogan from using it for monetary gain without a portion of that gain (or at least recognition) going to the originator. Another important concern is that the trademarked product, image, or slogan be used correctly and under the direction of the originator. Certain trademarked names, such as Xerox, Kleenex, and Band-Aid, have for years been in danger of passing into common usage as synonyms for the generic product lines of which they are part. The companies that manufacture these brand names are zealous in their efforts to ensure that others don't refer, for example, to photocopying as Xeroxing, or to facial tissue as Kleenex. In fact, one of the legal tests for determining whether a brand name has become a synonym for a generic product line is whether it is now included in dictionaries as a synonym for that product.

As harmless as it may seem, using the term *Xeroxing* in a written piece to refer to photocopying, or the simple use of a cartoon character on a poster announcing a holiday party, may be a trademark violation. The easiest thing to do is to check with the originator before using any trademarked element. Often, the only requirement will be either to use the true generic word (in the case of a brand name) or to mention that the image, slogan, or name is a trademarked element and give the source's name.

KEY TERMS

logic fallacy	commercial speech	copyright
language fallacy	defamation	trademark
ghostwriting	privacy	

EXERCISE

Look for a print advertisement in a magazine or newspaper that you think uses unethical or questionable persuasive techniques. Indicate which techniques are used in the ad, and answer the following questions:

- What do you find unethical about the ad and the approach taken?
- Why do you think this approach was used?
- What would you do differently to sell this product or service in order to make the persuasive appeal ethical?

CHAPTER

5

Media Relations and Placement

In this chapter you will learn:

- How journalists judge news value.
- The difference between hard news and soft news.
- How to work with the media, including getting to know journalists and their jobs.

- How to successfully get your public relations message placed in the media.

Public relations practitioners are professionals. So are journalists. Professionals, in the ideal sense, work together for the public welfare. Why, then, do public relations people see members of the media as adversaries, going out of their way to dig up the dirt? And why do reporters—whether print or broadcast—often see public relations people as "flaks," paid to run interference for their clients?

Actually, there is a little truth in both points of view and both sides have a number of legitimate complaints. Public relations people often are charged with covering up or stonewalling, whereas reporters often do seek only the negative in an issue. Obviously, this is far from a perfect relationship between professionals.

Part of the problem stems from a lack of real understanding in both camps of how the other operates. There is little you can do to make journalists find out more about public relations, but you can do much to improve your own knowledge of how the media operate, what media people want from you, and what they are capable and not capable of providing.

WHAT IS NEWS?

The most common stumbling block to a good working relationship between public relations and media professionals is a mutually agreed-upon definition of the concept of news. Research has shown that most journalists judge news value based on at least some of the following characteristics:

- **Consequence.** Does the information have any importance to the prospective reading, listening, or viewing public? Is it something that the audience would pay to know? Remember, news value is frequently judged by what the audience is willing to pay for.

- **Interest.** Is the information unusual or entertaining? Does it have any human interest? People like to transcend the everyday world. Excitement— even vicarious excitement—often makes good news.

- **Timeliness.** Is the material current? If it isn't, is it a whole new angle on an old story? Remember, the word *news* means "new." This is one rule frequently broken by public relations practitioners. Nothing is more boring than yesterday's news.

- **Proximity.** For most public relations people seeking to connect with the media, a local angle is often the only way to do it. If it hits close to home, it stands a better chance of being reported.

- **Prominence.** Events and people of prominence frequently make the news. The problem, of course, is that your company president may not be as prominent to the media as he or she is to you.

If your story contains at least some of the above elements, it stands a chance of being viewed as news by media professionals.

Journalists often make a distinction between hard news and soft news. Although there are no fixed definitions of hard and soft news, some pretty self-evident differences exist between the two. **Hard news** is information that has immediate impact on the people receiving it. By journalists' definition, it is very often news people need rather than news they want. **Soft news** is just the opposite: It is news people want rather than news they necessarily need. A story about a local teachers' strike is hard news. One about a new swimming program at the YMCA is soft news. A story about a corporate takeover is hard news. One about the hiring of a new celebrity spokesperson is not.

The problem is that many public relations people believe that journalists view everything they send them as soft news. Of course, this isn't so, and many public relations writers have discovered that both hard and soft news often will be used by media outlets looking to fill time or space. In addition, much of what passes for soft news often is viewed as public interest information by the various media.

The other thing to understand about hard and soft news is that hard news frequently is perishable whereas soft news is not. In other words, a story on an important stockholders' meeting in which a buyout is announced is not only perishable but also timely. By contrast, a new development in a product line or a promotion within your organization probably is not perishable—it will still be news a week from now.

WORKING WITH THE MEDIA

The media are a powerful force, and they can do a lot for you—or a lot against you. The determining factor may well be how much you know about media professionals and appreciate their jobs, and how well you get to know them as people.

Get to Know Journalists' Jobs

Learn all you can about the media outlets and the individuals with whom you will be dealing on a regular basis. Journalists have a tough life. I know—so do you. Having some journalism experience goes a long way toward understanding the frustrations of the job. Many public relations practitioners have had prior journalistic experience or education. Most journalists, however, haven't experienced public relations work firsthand. Thus, it is often up to you to make the relationship work.

Talk to journalists. Ask them for their guidelines on gathering news. Get to know how they write and what they choose to write about. Most news outlets will gladly provide you with guidelines for submitting everything from feature stories to publicity. Follow them. Know their deadlines and keep to them as if they were your own—in a way, they are. At the same time, try to let media people know what you do. Show them your style. Ask them for hints on how to make it more acceptable to their needs. Everybody likes to be asked his or her professional opinion.

Get to Know Journalists as People

To begin working with media people, you have to meet them first. If you're new to your job, the first step is to get out and introduce yourself. Now, no self-respecting reporter is going to be in his or her office when you drop in. They're busy people, and they're probably out covering stories. If they have an 11:00 P.M. deadline, they may not be back in the office to write their stories until after 6:00 P.M. And with the advent of laptop computers and online transmission capabilities, many reporters now file directly from the field. So how do you meet them?

Call first. Tell them who you are and how what you're doing relates to their work. Keep it brief, just a quick "Hello, I'm new in town. You'll be hearing from me soon, anything I should know?" If you can't get them by phone, try e-mail (although many reporters give out their e-mail addresses only to their closest contacts to keep the traffic volume down). If you get a chance to meet in person, do so. Again, be brief, keep it professional, and don't get away without asking them what you can do to make *their* jobs easier.

Remember, this is a two-way relationship. Journalists need your information as much as you need their medium for your messages. Be available at all times and make sure they know how to get in touch with you at a moment's notice. Always give them your home phone number. News happens after five o'clock, too. If you cooperate, they'll cooperate.

Establishing a rapport with the media is your first concern; however, a word needs to be said here about courting the press. Most journalists who deal in hard news don't react well to being courted. That is, they aren't likely to change anything they think or write because you invited them out to lunch. Although we've all heard stories about unethical journalists, I prefer to assume that every reporter has professional scruples. You should too. They may well go out to lunch with you, especially if you have a story that may interest them, but they are very likely to pick up their own checks. The sole exception might be the trade press. Trade journalists are used to receiving samples of products they are writing about. Everything from small parts to expensive equipment is loaned out to the various trade publications for these purposes. For most media, though, the golden rule of media relations is, *Let them know you by your work, not by your checkbook.*

Guidelines for Dealing with the Media

So now you're ready to meet the media in a working situation. What do you do? Although there are no guidelines that can cover every possible situation, following are a few that will help you to keep your encounters professional and as pleasant as possible:

- *Always be honest.* It takes a lot of hard work to build credibility, and nothing builds credibility like honesty. It takes only one mistake to ruin months of credibility building. If you are honest with the media, they will be fair to you. But remember, fair to them means balanced and objective. They will tell all sides of a story, even the negative. You should be willing to do the same.

- *Establish ground rules early on in your relationship.* Among the most important of these rules is that everything is on the record. If you don't want to see it or hear it the next day in the newspaper or on television, you'd best not say it to a journalist today. Although I usually advise public relations practitioners (and others) to always stay on the record, there are some accepted circumstances under which journalists are *supposed* (and that's a big *supposed*) to honor your off-the-record comments.

- *Not-for-attribution.* This is the home of the "sources close to the White House" quote. Honest public relations practitioners generally stay away from this one. It smacks of leaks and fear of attribution. This is one of the key ways the media often are manipulated into running with information on which they would normally require confirmation. Let's face it, without attribution, how does anyone know the opinion is even valid?

- *Background.* In my estimation, this is the only useful justification for going off the record. Going off the record to fill in background, without which a reporter might misconstrue your statements or misunderstand your position, is a legitimate procedure. Keep in mind, however, that it is open to the same potential abuse as any other off-the-record comment.

- *Always answer a reporter's phone calls.* Never avoid returning a call, either because you're afraid of what the reporter will ask (in which case, you're in the wrong business), or because you haven't done your homework. If the reporter doesn't get it from you, the ideal source, he or she will have to get it from less reliable sources, and you don't want that to happen.

- *Give media people what they want, not what you want.* Ideally, they can be the same thing. The key, of course, is to make your information newsworthy, following the criteria listed earlier.

- *Along the same lines, don't bombard journalists with a daily barrage of press releases.* Nothing that happens that often is newsworthy. The reporters and editors who receive your releases know this and are very likely to stop reading your information.

- *Don't assume reporters are out to get you.* If you've established a good working relationship with them, they are probably going to seek out your help, not try to assassinate you.

- *Don't try to intimidate reporters.* They'll resent it. Don't let your boss talk you into this one. You are the liaison, the media relations person. It's your job to get along, and nobody wants a friend who tries to intimidate him or her into doing something.

- *Don't plead your case or follow up on stories.* The nature of publicity is to let the media handle it once you have released it. If you want more control than that, take out an ad.

Guidelines for Interviews

Although being interviewed by reporters or setting up interviews for reporters with your clients aren't exactly public relations writing, they do help you visualize further the proper relationship between reporter and public relations person. With that in mind, following are some guidelines for interview situations. Some are similar to the guidelines already covered; others are specific to the interview situation:

- *Everything is on the record.* As with everything else in which a reporter is involved, keep any comments strictly on the record. If you don't want your words printed on the front page of tomorrow's paper, don't say them out loud to a reporter.

- *Provide background.* Give interviewers all the background they need to bring them up to speed on the topic at hand before you begin the official interview. They may not have read your media backgrounder or done any homework on your client prior to the interview (although they have if they're good reporters). As with everything else you say, keep the background information free of anything you don't want printed or run on the air.

- *Know the topic.* If you don't know the topic, why are your being interviewed? The same applies to any spokesperson you may have chosen for the interview. Always choose the person who knows the most about the issue being discussed, not just the company president or yourself. Nothing is more embarrassing than to have to constantly beg ignorance.

- *Anticipate touchy questions.* If something hot is happening with your client, the interviewer is there to ask about it. Assume this always to be true. If the interviewer doesn't ask the tough question, just consider yourself lucky; however, be prepared to answer it in your way and with your spin if he or she does.

- *Always answer questions that are already a matter of public record.* For example, if you have just filed a quarterly return with the Securities and Exchange Commission and it contains information about your organization's economic status that is less than flattering, guess what? It's public information by law, and you might as well be prepared to address it if it comes up.

- *Be completely honest.* Truth is the major responsibility of all communicators. If you ever lie to a journalist, he or she will never trust you again. Remember, credibility is difficult to obtain, but it takes only one lie to lose it forever. The following three guidelines are related to this one.

- *Answer questions directly.* Don't rush, guess, dodge, or stonewall when answering questions. Reporters become frustrated quickly when you try to avoid answering a question. Ultimately, it's best just to get to the point if you want to maintain your credibility.

- *If you don't know the answer, say so.* Offer to get back to the interviewer with the answer as soon as you can. You can also offer to put him or her in touch with someone who does know the answer, but then you lose control of the spin factor.

- *Keep it cordial, no matter what happens.* Never lose your cool. This puts you at a disadvantage because you automatically become defensive in such situations. If this happens, you lose control of the interview and you hurt your own image as a public relations professional.

- *Look professional.* This may seem self-evident, but you're a professional. If you look like one, you will enhance your credibility, and this will enhance the importance of your message.
- *Offer help later if needed, and give it.* If you've promised to follow up, do it. Make yourself available for any follow-up questions that the interviewer may have and assure him or her that it is no trouble. However, don't call the interviewer just to check on the progress of the story.

Guidelines for Correcting Errors

Finally, what do you do if you discover an error in the subsequent story a reporter produces? If the error is minor, ignore it—no sense badgering a reporter or editor over minor details. If the error is important, however (regardless of whether the error was caused by you or by the reporter), it needs to be corrected. Here are some guidelines for doing so:

- *Always be as diplomatic as possible.*
- *Contact the reporter immediately.* If it's your fault, say so and ask if it's too late to get the error corrected before publication. Don't take a great deal of time pointing out the error. Just mention it and ask if it can be fixed.
- *Remain calm and courteous.* If you seem agitated, the reporter will get suspicious. If it's the reporter's fault, he or she may even get angry.
- *If the story has already been run, ask for a correction.*
- *If the reporter is unwilling or unable to redress the error, don't automatically go over his or her head*—unless correcting the error is worth more than your relationship with the reporter.
- *If all else fails, write a letter to the editor correcting the error.* Keep it short and to the point. And, above all, keep it rational. Don't pout, and don't point fingers.
- *Finally, ask the reporter if there is anything you can do in the future to prevent this sort of thing from happening again.*

MEDIA PLACEMENT

Knowing journalists will enhance your chances of placing valuable information with them. But you can't rely on personal contact for everything. Placing public relations materials with the media requires up-to-date information on all of the possible outlets for your materials, as well as the ability to physically get your message to the media.

Deciding Where to Place Your Message

Naturally, the number and type of media outlets will depend on your business. If you are in the automotive industry, trade journals will be a vital link between you and your publics. If you work for an organization that is strictly local, then your media contacts will be limited to the local media. Local interest news will be important, too, within the communities in which your plants or offices are located. If you work for a regional or even a national operation, then your contacts will expand accordingly. Whatever media you deal with, it is important to keep updated directories and lists that meet your particular needs with the least amount of wasted information.

Media Directories

A good directory is an indispensable tool for the media relations specialist. **Media directories** come in all sizes and address almost every industry. Publishers of directories offer formats ranging from global checkers that include a variety of sources in every medium, to specialized directories dealing with a single medium.

A number of excellent directories for media placement are available. Here are some of the major ones:

- *Bacon's PR and Media Information Systems,* a series including *Bacon's Publicity Checker* (two volumes covering editorial contacts in the United States and Canada, magazines organized by industry, daily and weekly newspapers, and all multiple publisher groups); *Bacon's Media Alerts* (a directory of editorial profiles covering editorial features and special issues, often planned months in advance, for both magazines and newspapers); *Bacon's Radio/TV Directory* (a listing of every television and radio station in the United States, listed geographically); and *Bacon's International Publicity Checker* (editorial contact information on magazines and newspapers in 15 Western European countries). Bacon is also available online at http://www.bacons.com. Like many of the other services listed below, Bacon online offers sales of their directories, links to online sites for media outlets, and a host of other Internet services.

- *Burrelle's Media Directory,* organized similarly to *Bacon's* and published on a similar schedule. Both *Bacon's* and *Burrelle's* also provide clipping services separate from their directories. Burrelle's is also available online, at http://www.burrelles.com.

- A series published by Larrison Communications that includes *Medical and Science News Media; Travel, Leisure and Entertainment News Media;* and *Business and Financial News Media.*

- *Editor & Publisher,* a series of several media guides including the well-used *Editor & Publisher International Yearbook* (a collection of newspapers divided into dailies and weeklies and covering everything from local and national publications to house organs and college papers). *Editor & Publisher* hosts a comprehensive online service with links to hundreds of media outlets worldwide from its Web site at http://www.editorandpublisher.com.

- *Standard Rate and Data Service (SRDS),* used primarily by advertisers, this multivolume set is one of the most exhaustive resources available. If you are looking for every magazine published in the United States, in every category imaginable, this is your directory. *SRDS* also provides information on electronic media and newspapers. *SRDS* can be found online at http://www.srds.com, which provides an extensive electronic service as well as links to many other useful sites.

Most of the online sites listed here don't substitute for printed directories. In fact, most of them offer these directories for sale as part of their online services. For the time being, printed directories (in some cases available on CD-ROM) are still the industry standard; and because the prices of these directories can range into the hundreds of dollars, you will need to be fairly selective. When choosing a directory, keep the following key points in mind:

- The directory should be current. If it is not updated at least once a year, its uses are limited.

- The directory should cover the geographic area in which you operate and in which you want your organization's message to go out. You may not need a national directory if your operation is strictly local or statewide. Many states publish directories of all kinds of information, such as almanacs, that include media addresses.

- If your primary target is trade publications, then you need to choose a directory that lists them. *Standard Rate and Data Service* (http://www.srds.com) for instance, publishes a constant stream of listings, including business and industry directories.

- If you are a heavy user of broadcast media, your directory should include broadcast listings.

- The directory should list names of editors, news directors, and so on, and their addresses. Make sure this information is current. Nothing is more embarrassing to you and more infuriating to them than to receive a press release addressed to the previous editor.

- Make sure circulation is listed for print publications and listening or viewing audience for broadcast outlets. You don't want to waste an excellent story on a tiny-circulation trade publication when you might have reached a much larger audience.

The most important point to remember about media selection is never to place anything in a publication you haven't read personally. What may sound like an excellent publication in a directory may turn out to be second rate for your purposes. After some time in your particular field, you will become familiar with its leading publications. Until then, read them all. Remember, your image is tied to their image.

Media Lists

Directories are essential, but they are not the only tools you will need to keep up to date with media relations. **Media lists** are just as vital to your job. They are a more personal tool than directories because they contain details about local contacts and all the information you need to conduct business in your community. Media lists may include regional and even nationwide contacts depending on the scope of your operation. A media list, once compiled, should be updated by hand at least once a month. This job can usually be handled efficiently by clerical staff once the list is compiled. It takes only a 30-second phone call to each of the media outlets on your list to verify names and addresses. In the long run, the routine of updating will pay off. Using a computer is a great way to compile and maintain a media list. Computer software designed specifically for media lists is available from a number of distributors.

In compiling a media list, you will need to include most of the following items:

1. Name of the publication, radio or television station, particular show (for talk shows), and so on.

2. Names of editors, reporters, news directors, etc.

3. Addresses, including mailing and street addresses if they are different. You may need to hand deliver a press release on occasion, and this can be difficult if all you have is a post office box number.

4. Telephone and fax numbers for the media outlets as well as for each of the people on your list. Many media outlets can now accept computer-generated press releases through normal telephone lines or satellite-transmitted video or audio actualities (prerecorded video or audio). Include such details in your media list.

5. Any important editorial information such as style guidelines, deadlines, times of editions (morning and evening), dates of publication for magazines, times of broadcasts, use of actualities, photo requirements, and use of fax or electronic transmission (and applicable phone numbers).

Getting Your Message to the Media

Once you have decided where to place your information, you have to get it there. Again, you have a number of choices, depending on what you are sending and to whom.

- *You can mail it.* This takes more time, but if your information is not perishable, this may work just fine. Thousands of news releases and information pieces are still mailed every day.

- *You can hand deliver it.* Reserve this one for important or timely information. Hand delivery used to be the norm; now it's a lot of trouble. However, it can pay off in that it still receives a bit more attention than other forms of delivery.

- *You can fax it.* Nearly everyone has a fax machine these days. The biggest problem with this delivery method is quality. If all you're sending is text, then it's fine. But if pictures are an important consideration, this may not be your first choice.

- *You can transmit it electronically via computer.* This can be accomplished in several ways. You can use standard e-mail, e-mail attachments, Web site message dumps, or direct dumps to the medium itself. Many media have direct lines for such purposes. One of the benefits of using a computer is that images can also be transmitted, often with excellent results.

In lieu of delivering the message yourself, you may choose to use a placement agency. **Placement agencies** are outfits that will take your information, such as a press release, and send it out to a great many media outlets using their regularly updated media lists and computerized mailing services. Many of these firms mail out hundreds of releases for you—at a tidy cost.

Placement agencies will provide you with many more mailings than you might have gotten from your personal mailing list, but much of what is mailed out is not correctly targeted and ends up as waste coverage. As any business editor will tell you, the majority of press releases received are not relevant to the publication, and many originated from placement agencies in other states. You are often better off targeting the media with which you are most familiar and that you know are at least interested in your information.

The sole exception might be the computerized agencies such as *PR Newswire* (http://www.prnewswire.com). Organizations such as this send out your release electronically, over a newswire—just like the Associated Press. Media outlets can subscribe (free of charge) to the service and will receive your release—along with hundreds of others—sorted by subject and other descriptors. They can scan by subject, look at the lead only, or pull up the whole release. This method substantially reduces the amount of paper they have to plow through and at least guarantees subjects of interest to them. Your advantage is that you can target locally, regionally, or nationally. Of course, the price of placing the release increases with its coverage.

Fitting Your Information to Your Outlet

You need to know as much as possible about the media outlet to which you are sending your information. Never submit information blindly to publications you've never read or to stations you've never watched or listened to. Picking a trade publication out of *SRDS* just because it has a large circulation doesn't ensure that it is the type of publication in which you want to see your story.

The key, of course, is to read the publication, watch the television station, or listen to the radio station first. By doing so, you also will learn about the outlet's style and will be able to tailor your release accordingly.

If you are writing for a trade journal, don't automatically assume that the one you have chosen is similar in style to others in the industry. Remember that publications often are differentiated by their styles when they deal with similar subject matter.

Understanding Radio and Television Placement

Before placing information on the radio, you will need to understand the concept of **format.** Whereas placement of your message on television requires familiarity with the various program offerings of the stations you are dealing with, placement on radio is usually determined by the format of the station—usually designed around the type of music it plays or information it provides. For example, some stations play only top-40 hits. These stations usually cater to a teenage audience. Other stations play only classic rock or jazz, or provide news. Their listeners vary according to their format. A radio format, or programming format, or programming genre, refers to the overall content broadcasting over a radio station. Some stations broadcast multiple genres on a set schedule. Over the years, formats have evolved and new ones have been introduced. In today's age of radio, many radio formats are designed to reach a specifically defined segment or niche of the listening population based on such demographic criteria as age, ethnicity, background, and the like.[1]

Determining what radio station you place your message on depends on what your target audience listens to, and that is determined through audience research. Any radio sales manager will be able (and quite willing) to provide you with detailed analyses of the station's listening audience. All you have to do is match your target audience profile with the station's listener profile. If, for instance, your target audience regularly listens to jazz, then you would be best served to place your message on a station using a jazz format. Exhibit 5.1 lists the most common radio formats and their respective target audiences.

Exhibit 5.1

Standard Radio Format Types and Definitions

Many formats are defined below with descriptions of each. Within each type are subtype and niche formats that usually target their format to an even more defined target audience. The following formats are geared toward the United States, Canada, and Latin America. Please note that formats can fall into different categories than the way they are organized here.

News, Talk, and Sports Formats

News/Talk. Stations with news/talk programming feature a heavy concentration of news—local, regional, and global news, as well as sports, weather, and traffic. Along with the news, stations will feature talk programming, including the presentations of views and listener participation call-in segments and shows. Many news/talk stations also carry live local sports coverage in the evenings and on weekends. A variety of this format is the *full service* format. Popular many years ago, this format included a mix of news, talk, and music presented in a conservative fashion. In larger U.S. markets and markets located near the U.S./Mexican border, it is also common to have one or more news/talk station in Spanish. Almost all news/talk stations can be found on the AM dial.

News/Information. Similar to the news/talk formats, but this format has little listener participation and call-ins. Stations with this format are usually linked through satellite and originate from a regional or national level rather than

(continued)

[1]This definition and the format list in Exhibit 5.1 are courtesy of Thomas C. Hokenson, TV RadioWorld, http://www.tvradioworld.com/directory/Radio_Formats/.

(continued)

consisting of local programming. An example of this format includes BBC's overseas broadcasting.

Sports. This format features programming related to the sporting world. Most stations with a sports format include sports news, sports talk shows, and of course live coverage of local and national sporting events. A large majority of sports-format stations are found on the AM dial.

Talk. Stations with this format concentrate on a variety of talk programming. (News still can be heard at least at the top of the hour during the morning and evening drives.) Many of these stations will carry popular syndicated talk show hosts, such as Mancow, Rush Limbaugh, and Howard Stern throughout the day, as well as segments of local call-in periods. Varieties of this format include a *hot talk* format and a *gay/lesbian issues* talk format. Most talk stations are found on the AM dial, but they are also on the FM dial in larger markets.

News/Talk-Business. Also known as news-talk-financial, this format is the most popular offspring of the news/talk format. Stations with this format concentrate their news, information, and talk segments on the business world. Stations with this format are usually in larger markets and are on the AM dial.

Farm/Agriculture. This format is another offspring on the news/talk format. Stations with this format concentrate their information on the agricultural world. During weekday business hours, you can receive updates on financial livestock and crop prices. During off-business hours and weekends, most stations will have some type of music format, usually country, adult contemporary, or oldies music. Stations with this format would be found in smaller markets and rural areas and are usually on the AM dial.

Political. This format is most popular in Europe, especially France, and in other nations with less restrictive media guidelines. The aim of these stations is to provide listeners with news and information, promote the beliefs of the organization that owns the station, and stir up intellectual conversation over the airwaves for the betterment of listeners.

Country Music Formats

Country. As one of the more popular formats, some type of country format is found on more stations than is any other type of format. Country music origins date back to the 1920s but have progressed over the decades to include such styles as western swing, bluegrass, honky-tonk, urban cowboy, and today's new country.

Hit Country. As a variety of the country format, hit country stations concentrate their play lists on current country hits of today and the past few months. Other names for this format include new country, hot country, or young country.

Classic Country. As another variety of the country format, classic country stations concentrate their play lists on classic country hits, also referred to as gold country or oldies country. These play lists include country songs from the 1970s to the early 1990s.

Ranchera. This format of country is best known in Texas, the southwestern United States, and throughout Mexico. In a very loose definition, *ranchera* is more or less a flavor of country music in the Spanish language, but if you ask a Spanish-speaking person, they might tell you this is the best form of country music.

Contemporary Hit Music Radio

CHR. Dubbed mainstream pop music radio, CHR (contemporary hit radio) stations play a variety of popular music of today and the past few years (or decades). There is little emphasis on new and cutting-edge music. Today, a good majority of CHR-format stations, especially in larger markets, slant their music play lists toward another music format (rock or urban). These formats are defined below.

CHR-Pop. This format also is referred to as CHR-top 40. In comparison to CHR-rhythmic, CHR-pop has the same basic elements, slanted more toward rock and alternative songs. Play lists consist of new, cutting-edge music, current hits, and popular hits of the past 6 to 12 months. The target audience is young adults and adults, aged 15 to 30 years.

CHR-Rhythmic. Although a good number of songs will be played on both CHR-pop and CHR-rhythmic stations, the difference between the formats is that CHR-rhythmic leans toward more hip-hop, rap, and dance songs, rather than rock and alternative. Play lists consist of new, cutting-edge music, current hits, and popular hits of the past 6 to 12 months. The target audience is also people aged 15 to 30 years.

CHR-Dance. This is another flavor of popular music with a slant toward dance hits and dance remixes of popular songs. Play lists consist of new, cutting-edge music, current hits, and popular hits of the past couple of years. The target audience is also people aged 15 to 30 years.

CHR-80s. This format is one of the newest and is quickly gaining in popularity across the United States. One can also argue and win that this format belongs with the oldies formats. The music played on stations with this format is just as it sounds, pop music popular during the 1980s and sometimes the early 1990s. The target audience is adults aged 25 to 35 years.

CHR-Español. Also known as Latin pop, this niche format will be found in markets with large Hispanic populations and in cities near the U.S.-Mexican border. Music found on stations with this format will include top pop songs from the Spanish-language charts. Throughout Mexico and South America, the format is simply known as CHR-pop, but such stations normally play a mix of English- and Spanish-language artists.

Tejano. As a local flavor of pop music, *tejano* is bound and geographically defined in Texas, the southwestern United States, and northern Mexico. *Tejano* music is hit music by artists originating in and around the state of Texas.

(continued)

(continued)
Adult Contemporary Music Formats

Adult Contemporary. Simply referred to as AC, adult contemporary music is aimed at people aged 30 years or older. These stations offer lively contemporary music of the past decade or two without cutting-edge music, rock, or rap music. Artists popular on these stations include Madonna, Lionel Ritchie, Mariah Carey, Elton John, and Amy Grant, just to name a few.

Hot AC. Stations with this format have a slightly younger target audience than the AC format. More upbeat music and more cutting-edge music are prevalent. Hot AC is a hybrid between pop and AC music, with an almost exclusive concentration on current hits and music of the past 12 months.

Modern AC. Stations with this format have a slightly younger target audience than the AC format. More upbeat music and more cutting-edge music are prevalent. Modern AC is a hybrid between hot AC and modern rock music, with an almost exclusive concentration on current hits and music of the past 12 months.

Soft AC. Also known as easy listening or beautiful music, this format is targeted to people aged 35 years or older. In comparison to the AC format, soft AC music can span from the past four decades and consists of a large majority of love ballads from popular artists and less upbeat-type music.

AC-Oldies. This format is a blend of AC music and country music. The format is aimed at people aged 30 years or older and is usually found in smaller markets or rural populated areas. Music offered on these stations ranges from the 1960s to the 1990s.

AC-Romantica. This format is the Spanish-language version of the AC format defined above. A large majority of music is performed by Spanish-language artists, and the presenters speak in Spanish. The target audience is adults aged 30 years or older in the Spanish-speaking community.

Other AC Formats. Other hybrids of the AC format exist. Such hybrids include *rock AC, rhythmic AC,* and a variety of Spanish-language AC hybrids.

Rock and Alternative Music Formats

Modern Rock. Also known as new rock or alternative rock, this format is mainstream alternative rock music. There is a high concentration of cutting-edge and current hits and music from the past 6 to 12 months.

Active Rock. Stations with this format concentrate their music on popular rock songs of today and a variety of popular rock and classic rock songs of the past two decades.

Adult Alternative. Also known as AAA, this format offers a hybrid of modern rock and progressive, alternative, and classic rock music aimed at an older target audience than both modern rock and active rock.

Alternative. A format that grew up in the 1980s on college radio stations, alternative music can still be found on noncommercial and college- or student-run radio stations. Music is usually cutting-edge and less mainstream and includes local artists. It may include some punk, dance, industrial, or heavy metal music.

Classic Rock. This is one of the more popular music formats throughout the United States. Most markets contain one classic rock station, but it is common to have two stations with this format. Classic rock stations' play lists include popular rock hits of the 1970s, 1980s, 1990s, and possibly a few hits from today. A variety of this format is *album-oriented rock,* or AOR. The difference between these two formats is that classic rock stations play released singles, whereas AOR stations will play music from popular artists, including cuts not released as singles, known as album-cuts.

Americana. This format features a mixture of adult alternative, blues, and progressive country music.

Heavy Metal. This format has a much harsher, louder sound (listen at your own risk) than rock itself. Such music could be found on college- or student-run stations and several Internet-only stations.

Urban Music Formats

Urban Contemporary. Usually listed simply as urban and may also be known as R&B (rhythm and blues), the urban contemporary musical genre reflects a large number of black music recording artists who play rap, hip-hop, house, and soul as well as new artists. Urban formats are generally aimed at younger audiences.

Urban AC. Urban AC stations are aimed at an older audience. Play lists at these stations include more soul and ballads and less rap and hip-hop music.

Rhythmic Oldies. Nicknamed jammin' oldies, this format is relatively new in the radio format world. Play lists at stations with this format include urban oldies, Motown hits, and a number of upbeat disco and dance retro hits of the late 1970s, 1980s, and early 1990s.

Urban Oldies. This genre features black music recording artists such as Motown from the 1950s, 1960s, and 1970s.

Jazz and Classical Music Formats

Smooth Jazz. Also titled new AC/smooth jazz, and sometimes nicknamed new age jazz, this genre is more of a format than a music style. Today, most major markets contain one station with this format. The style of music played on smooth jazz stations includes recent and current adult contemporary hits as well as new and recent upbeat jazz recordings. Often, programming segments include ambient or world beat music.

Jazz. Traditional jazz music can usually be found on public radio stations and college-run radio stations. Jazz music found on these stations play a variety of

(continued)

(continued)

jazz music recorded throughout the past few decades. *Latin jazz* stations can be found throughout Latin America, with a heavy emphasis on Latin jazz recordings.

Classical. Classical music is known as serious music to those why enjoy it. Classical music can usually be found on public radio stations and college-run radio stations, but most major markets feature one full-time commercial classical music station.

Oldies and Nostalgia Music Formats

Oldies. The type of music one can expect to hear on stations with this format include hit songs from the 1950s, the 1960s and sometimes the 1970s, including such artists as Elvis Presley, the Rolling Stones, and Motown artists. A large majority of oldies-format stations focus on 1950s and 1960s music, but with the popularity of the oldies format over the past decade, many stations now specialize in a certain decade or music type. Two of the more popular formats are Classic Hits and Standards.

Classic Hits. Generally playing 1970s and 1980s pop and rock music, these stations tend to be a hybrid of oldies and classic rock.

Standards. Also known as nostalgia or adult standards, this format plays contemporary, soft music popular between the 1930s and 1960s but may include big band and swing music. Artists include Tony Bennett, Nat King Cole, Natalie Cole, and Barbara Streisand. A majority of adult standards stations are found on the AM dial.

Big Band. Also termed swing (depending on the decade), this format is similar to standards, except the music spans from the 1920s through the 1940s and is more upbeat. A large majority of this music is programmed within noncommercial stations, college-run stations, or Internet radio stations.

Oldies-Español. Popular in markets with large Hispanic communities, this format concentrates on popular Spanish-language oldies hits of the 1950s, 1960s, and 1970s.

MOR. Standing for middle of the road, this format was popular in decades past but has become all but extinct in today's radio world. This format combines news, information, and music. Music would include popular songs of the time (most of which are played on oldies and adult standards stations today).

Other Oldies Formats. In addition to the formats listed above, several other oldies formats are defined and explained throughout these listings. These different types include rhythmic oldies (see under Urban Music Formats), urban oldies (see under Urban Formats), CHR-80s (see under Contemporary Hit Music Radio), and classic rock (see under Rock and Alternative Music Formats).

Spanish and Latin Music Formats

General Information. Spanish-language formats can be found in nearly every major U.S. city. The larger the Hispanic population, the more Spanish-language stations you can listen to in a market. Most formats are similar to existing formats, such as news/talk and several other formats listed here: *tejano,* CHR-*español* (see under CHR Formats), AC-*romantica* (see under AC Formats), and oldies-*español* (see under Oldies and Nostalgia Music Formats).

Regional Mexican. This musical format includes Spanish-language artists of Mexico, Latin America, and even the local areas of broadcast, with a mix of *romantica, mariachi,* and tropical music. It is mainly targeted to Mexican and Spanish-speaking residents living within the United States.

Other Music Formats. Of the most popular, *tropical, salsa,* and *merengue* top the list. Other styles, which differ in beat, style, and even geographical origin, include *cumbia, sabrosita, mambo, andean, bossa nova, samba, tango, mariachi, bachata,* and many others. Throughout Latin America and in larger U.S. markets, a station or two will play combinations of the above musical styles.

World Music Formats

General Information. *World music* is a very general term used to describe popular musical formats outside the United States. Stations that claim their format as world music are simply playing a mix of a number of the formats described here.

Reggae, Soca, Calypso. Popular music native to the Caribbean islands. All three formats have distinctive sounds. In general soca is a much faster beat than reggae tends to be. Stations with a *Caribbean* music format play a mix of the three along with some pop and urban hits.

Hawaiian. Popular native music of the Hawaiian islands. Sometimes known as island music, this term refers to music of any of the Pacific islands.

Traditional Music Formats. Of course, every nation or geographical region has a musical type of its own, most commonly referred to as traditional music. Examples include traditional Dutch folk (in Holland), traditional Greek music of the Greek isles, and traditional Turkish music native to Turkey, just to name a few.

Religious Formats

Religious. Religious-format stations vary in tone, presentation, and denomination, but the basics are preaching and instructional programming and may include some music.

Contemporary Christian. This contemporary and pop music format is based on Christian music and artists.

Christian Rock. This rock and alternative music format is based on Christian music and artists.

(continued)

(continued)

Black Gospel. Upbeat religious music typically heard in predominately black churches. Stations typically include preaching and instructional programming.

Southern Gospel. Country- and soft rock–based religious music. Stations typically include some preaching and instructional programming.

Other Religious Formats. *Islamic* and *Buddhist* religious broadcasters are more common in Asia, Europe, and Africa. The basic goals are to preach spirituality, use positive words, and promote the goals of the organization, but stations do vary in format and presentation. Most will include elements of news, talk, music, and educational programming.

Public, Government, and Community Radio Formats

Public. Public radio became possible in the United States in 1967 through the creation and partial funding by the federal government of National Public Radio (NPR). Public radio also depends on funding through local contributions from listeners. Today, several other public radio organizations exist, many at a local level or in partnership with NPR. Programming varies on public radio but usually contains news and information as well as a musical format, such as classical or jazz music. Public radio is commonly affiliated with a college or university.

Community. Community radio is similar to public radio except that community radio is partially funded through local government and listener contributions and depends on volunteers to help run the station. Community radio is popular throughout the world, and for many smaller, rural towns (20,000 people or less), such stations serve as the only radio broadcaster. Community stations are commonly broadcast in a native language.

Tourist. Tourist radio stations provide local tourist information and information relevant for travel in the region. These stations are commonly multilingual and contain prerecorded material broadcast over and over, changing periodically. These stations are often low-powered AM or FM stations.

Local Government. In the United States, many local city governments broadcast very-low-powered AM or FM stations that provide local information, such as on town events, or airport information. Information is usually prerecorded.

State Owned. In many countries, the federal government operates a radio network, usually with some type of news, information, and music format. Sometimes there may be several channels that specialize in a format. Some may also be local provincial or metropolitan-run stations. In some instances, the state-operated radio station is the only legal broadcaster in the nation.

TIS. The acronym stands for traffic information systems. These stations provide real-time traffic updates in metropolitan areas. These stations are usually low-powered AM or FM stations broadcasting from several transmitters throughout metropolitan areas.

Time. Time stations are mostly found on shortwave and are almost always owned and operated by national government agencies. These stations mainly broadcast such information as time-of-day, usually by regular voice announcements or digital time code, and standard time intervals, usually by transmitting brief audio tones or ticks at regular intervals, such as once per second. Time of day is usually given in coordinated universal time. All time-related aspects of these stations, from the time-of-day information to the actual frequencies on which they transmit, are obtained from atomic clocks.

College and School Radio Formats

College. These stations are owned by a university, college, or community college and are usually operated by a student organization through volunteer time. Most all college stations operate in the college band, 88FM to 92FM, in the United States. Such stations often are available only via cable radio. The programming includes a variety of local news and school information but also includes some type of music format such as free-form, progressive, alternative, classical, or jazz.

Student. This format is similar to college radio, but these stations are owned by a local high school or grade school and are usually maintained by a student organization within that school. These stations also include school information and a music format of some type.

Other Radio Formats

Children. Variety programming aimed at a target audience aged 5 to 15 years. Programming includes music, games, stories, and educational programming. The most popular broadcaster in this format is Radio Disney. *Youth programming* is similar, but the target audience is aged 10 to 15 years.

Ethnic. This format refers to any station broadcasting in a foreign language (as opposed to the common language). These stations provide news, information, and music to a specific ethnic group. This type of station is common in the United States, Canada, and Europe. These stations often are brokered, but if a large enough base ethnic population exists, a full-time commercial AM or FM station will be present. In the United States and Canada, the most popular ethnic stations include *Chinese, French, Korean, Japanese, Polish, Portuguese (Brazilian), Russian,* and *Vietnamese.* Some stations broadcast in several languages (too many to list). These are noted as *multilanguage* stations.

Examine the formats and styles of all publications or broadcast shows you would like to accept your information, and then prepare your material in a style as close to theirs as you can. For example, if you are prerecording public service announcements for use on various stations, you might want to put a different music track on each spot, depending on the format of the station with which it will be placed. Nothing is quite so jarring to listeners of a classical music station as to have their entertainment interrupted with a message surrounded by a rock

Exhibit 5.2

Standard Television Dayparts

Early morning	M–F 7:00 A.M.–9:00 A.M.
Daytime	M–F 9:00 A.M.–4:30 P.M.
Early fringe	M–F 4:30 P.M.–7:30 P.M.
Prime access	M–F 7:30 P.M.–8:00 P.M.
Prime time	M–Sa 8:00 P.M.–11:00 P.M.
	Su 7:00 P.M.–11:00 P.M.
Late news	M–Su 11:00 P.M.–11:30 P.M.
Late night	M–Su 11:30 P.M.–1:00 A.M.
Saturday morning	Sa 8:00 A.M.–1:00 P.M.
Weekend afternoon	Sa–Su 1:00 P.M.–7:00 P.M.

music background. Although a rock music station might carry a spot with a classical music background, the opposite is probably not true.

Television is much easier to figure out. It is the medium that reaches the broadest segment of the population. Rather than depending on formatting to attract a single audience, television depends on different programs and times of day to attract different audiences. Program types include drama and adventure, news, talk, daytime serials, and sports, among others. Each program type draws a particular target audience. Time of day is also a factor in determining when to air a television commercial. Standard television time blocks (known as dayparts) are listed in Exhibit 5.2.

Just as in radio, a television sales manager will be able to give you detailed statistics on viewing audiences by program and time of day. You will need to consider the following questions before you place your message with either a radio or television station:

- If radio, what format does the station use? If television, what programs are appropriate to my message?
- Will the station take taped actualities (for interviews or reactions)? If so, what kind of tape? Reel-to-reel? Cassette? If it is video for television, will the station want one-inch tape, or three-quarter or half-inch cassette? Can they use slides? How about slide-tape?
- What length spot will the station use? 10-, 20-, 30-, or 60-second spots?
- Who will write the copy? Will I write and submit it, or will I simply give the station the information? Will the station use scripts I have written for its announcers to read?
- Will the station provide production services, or will I have to have my message prerecorded?
- How much lead time does the station need? For production? For placement?

All of these considerations—and probably a few more—will have to be taken into account before you can work successfully with the broadcast media. All of this information should be included in your media list.

Broadcast Cover Letter

Before you send any information to a radio or television station in the form of a **spot** (a written script or prerecorded message designed specifically for broadcast), make sure it is accompanied by a cover letter explaining the content and a mail-back card of some kind through which the station can let you know when and if your spot was aired. Exhibit 5.3 is a generic example of such information.

Exhibit 5.3

Cover Letter and Mail-Back Card

> The American Tuberculosis Foundation
> 1212 Folger Street
> New York, New York 00912
>
>
> Dear Program Director:
>
> Smoking and lung disease are issues that affect all of us in some way. The recent concern over second-hand smoke has resulted in considerable debate. In an effort to help "clear the air," the American Tuberculosis Foundation hopes you will run the enclosed radio/TV spots for the education of your listening/viewing audience.
>
> Since our campaign started in January, over 300 radio/TV stations around the country have responded by airing the "Your Good Health" spots. We hope that you will join them in serving your listening/viewing audience.
>
> For your convenience, we have provided you with a mail-back card. By filling out this important evaluation, you will help us to better serve our common interests in the future.
>
> Thank you,

(continued)

(continued)

MAIL-BACK CARD:
"YOUR GOOD HEALTH"

I have aired or intend to air the following spots:
(circle appropriate length).

10 sec.　　20 sec.　　30 sec.　　60 sec.

Radio　　　　　　Television

The spots aired the following times and dates:

Day	Times

PRESS KITS

One of the most common methods of distributing information to the media is via the **press kit.** Press kits are produced and used for a variety of public relations purposes. They are handed out at product promotion presentations and press conferences; they are used as promotional packages by regional or local distributors or agencies; and they are part of the never-ending stream of information provided by organizations to get their messages out. When a press kit (also known as a press packet), is used properly, it can aid message dissemination by adding the right amount of unduplicated information to the media mix.

Not all industries still use the traditional, printed press kit. For example, in much of the high-tech industry, the press kit may be "going the way of the dodo bird."[2] Tech or business reporters tend to like technology and don't mind linking to Web sites for more information or to download photos. Sometimes, an online press kit rather than a print version will be developed.

Intel, for example, delivers two major resources for tech and business reporters during major news and product launches (in addition to a press release over

---

[2] E-mail correspondence with Seth Walker, Intel Public Relations. Much of this discussion on the changing uses of press kits is from that correspondence.

the Business Wire news portal, typical interviews, automated phone responses, etc.) First, they always update their online pressroom at http://www.intel.com/pressroom. Journalists used to working with Intel know to go there first. Second, for big launches, Intel creates a "virtual press kit," which can also be viewed and downloaded at their online pressroom. In addition, Intel has at times held an on-line press conference during which press call into a phone bridge while following along with an online presentation from their desks.

Note, however, that traditional press kits are very much alive with mainstream media like *Ms.* and *Marie Claire* magazines. Many of the editors simply want to pull art from the kits and hand it to their art directors. They also don't like to search around on the Internet and jump from link to link. Press kits are also popular in many countries overseas where Internet access is limited or art budgets are severely constrained. In addition, countries such as Japan have well-known and well-established public relations practices that require public relations professionals to place printed material in certain places for reporters. This, of course, doesn't stop the media from going online for traditional press kit material, but it certainly limits the practice.

A press kit usually is composed of a number of information pieces designed specifically for use by the media (see Exhibit 5.4). Enclosed within a folder with a cover indicating who is providing the kit and its purpose, a press kit usually includes something like the following:

- A table of contents
- A news release
- A backgrounder or a fact sheet
- One or two other information pieces such as:
  - Already-printed brochures
  - Company magazines or newsletters
  - An annual report
  - A feature story or sidebar, if appropriate to the subject matter
  - A biography (or biographies) and accompanying photos

Anything fewer than these items is generally a waste of folder space. If you have only a few items to disseminate and wish to avoid the cost of producing folders, use plain, manuscript-sized envelopes. These are cheaper than folders, you might already have them in stock with your address printed on them, and they are ready for mailing.

The contents of a press kit can vary greatly, depending on the intent of the kit. For example, a press kit for a corporate product introduction briefing might include these items:

- News release on the new product
- Color photo and cutline (caption)
- News release on the product content (the material used to manufacture the product)
- Black-and-white photo and cutline of other products made from the manufactured material

Exhibit 5.4

Press Kit

Label on cover designates which medium and reporter receives this particular kit

Agenda, Welcoming Letter, List of Participants, Brochures

News Release & Backgrounder

Photograph

Business Card

Press Kit Folder (Inside pockets hold information)

- News release describing another application of the material
- Black-and-white and color photos of that application
- Backgrounder on the material.
- In-house magazine article tear sheet on the material
- Color brochure on the material and its uses
- News release on new materials being developed
- Hard copy of the product presentation speeches

Press kits can serve many purposes and should include enough information to meet the needs of their audiences. The key to assembling a useful kit is to keep in mind the needs of those receiving the information.

If you are providing a press kit to the media for a press conference, it should include some, but not necessarily all, of the following items:

- A cover letter explaining the kit and a table of contents listing each item in the kit, with each item listed as appearing on the right or left side of the folder.
- A basic fact sheet outlining the participants at the press conference, the relevant dates, and any facts or figures that might be unclear.
- A backgrounder explaining the relevance of the current topic in a historical context.
- News releases of about one and one-half pages for both print and broadcast media. Give both releases to each reporter.
- Any feature stories or sidebar-type information that might be of interest to reporters. Be sure it is relevant.
- Any photos or other visual materials that might add to the stories. Include cutlines.
- Biographies on any individuals playing an important part in the event the press conference covers. Include photos as well, if available.
- Any already-produced information pieces that might be of interest to the media, such as brochures, in-house publications, and the like.

Once you have assembled a press kit, make sure that all of the media get a copy, even those reporters who do not attend the event your press kit is designed to cover. Press kits are most effective when used with a good, up-to-date media list. By labeling your press kits with the names of the various media outlets prior to your event, you will know immediately after the event who showed up and who didn't. You can then mail the remaining kits to the prodigal media.

COOPERATION IS THE KEY

Whether or not your message is delivered to your target audience depends a great deal on the cooperation of the mass media. It is in your best interest to foster a professional relationship with media representatives whom you deal with regularly. If they respect your professionalism in meeting their (and, by inference, their audiences') needs, you will be rewarded with cooperation—and that is a major step in the right direction.

KEY TERMS

consequence	hard news	format
interest	soft news	spot
timeliness	media directory	press kit
proximity	media list	
prominence	placement agency	

EXERCISES

1. Assume you work for a local not-for-profit agency that works with homeless youth. Put together a media list composed of those outlets most likely to publish information on your organization. Explain why you have chosen these media and not others.

2. Call local media outlets and ask for copies of their publicity guidelines. Write up a comparison of how they differ and are alike, and what you make of the differences.

3. Tour a local newspaper, a local radio or television news operation, or any other appropriate location where news is a primary part of the operation. Write a brief report explaining what you learned and how you think it would affect your ability to do your job as a publicist.

4. Visit a local not-for-profit agency and see what kind of printed information they have available. Do you think it is enough? Do you think it is effective? If possible, meet with the agency's public relations person and see if you can obtain copies of any materials produced specifically for media use.

5. Look through your local paper for any articles you suspect were the result of publicity placement. Explain why you think so.

6. Put together an informational press kit on an organization of your choice. This could be the place where you work or are an intern. It could be your school or department, the student union, or an organization where you volunteer. Find as many informational pieces as you can for inclusion in the kit. Write up a basic explanation of the purpose of the kit and a table of contents. Pick out an appropriate folder design and color, and assemble the final product. Be prepared to explain why you chose the pieces you included and why you left others out.

CHAPTER

6

Crisis Communication

In this chapter you will learn:

- What a crisis is and how to prepare for one in advance.
- How to manage a crisis once it occurs.
- How to respond to the media during crises.

Crises are the hobgoblins of public relations. Traditionally, public relations practitioners were hired to do two things: deal with the media and handle crises. Over the years, of course, the job has become much more complex. However, being able to handle a crisis is still considered one of the most important aspects of a job in public relations. In most cases, proactive communication practices should limit crises. Constant monitoring of the environment in which your organization operates should help alleviate what we normally refer to as unforeseen events. However, there will always be crises, and every organization can benefit from a crisis communication plan. With a good crisis communication plan, it is entirely possible to manage a crisis effectively and to minimize damage to reputations, operational effectiveness, and sales. According to the Ontario, Canada, Ministry of Agriculture and Food, "Effective crisis management begins with planning and advance-preparation. A major benefit of crisis planning is that being prepared for trouble can often lead to crisis prevention. And what better way to deal with a crisis than by averting one?"[1] What follows in this chapter are suggestions on how to handle crisis situations. Although not strictly in the domain of public relations writing, crisis communication is nonetheless an integral tool in a writer's toolbox. It is ultimately better to have a "best-laid plan" than no plan at all.

WHAT IS A CRISIS?

The crisis communication plan for CHS Cooperatives/Land-O-Lakes states that

> A crisis is any kind of out-of-the ordinary event with the potential to damage the reputation of our business. Crises can develop quickly and unexpectedly or can be situations that build over a long period of time. They can be directly tied to an operation, like a spill, or the cause may be external, like weather. In all instances, a crisis is a situation that creates a need for a clear, concise and immediate communications response.[2]

Sandra Clawson-Freeo, of Northern Illinois University, defines a crisis as

> any situation that threatens the integrity or reputation of your company, usually brought on by adverse or negative media attention. These situations can be any kind of legal dispute, theft, accident, fire, flood or manmade disaster that could be attributed to your company. It can also be a situation where in the eyes of the media or general public your company did not react to one of the above situations in the appropriate manner.[3]

In other industries, crises may take specific forms. For example, in the crisis plan for the Ministry of Agriculture and Food for Ontario, Canada, the chief concern is with food safety.

---

[1] Ministry of Agriculture and Food, Ontario, Canada, http://www.gov.on.ca/OMAFRA/english/research/risk/crcpm.htm.
[2] CHS Cooperatives/Land-O-Lakes, http://www.mbrservices.com/commtools/crisis.cfm.
[3] Sandra K. Clawson-Freeo, Northern Illinois University, http://www3.niu.edu/newsplace/crisis.html.

A safety, health, or environmental crisis is an unplanned event that triggers a real or perceived, or possible threat to safety, health, or environment, or to the organization's reputation or credibility. A crisis has the potential to significantly impact the company's operations or to pose a significant environmental, economic, reputational, or legal liability.[4]

CRISIS PREPARATION

Planning for how to deal with a crisis before it happens prevents inappropriate actions that could be taken later when emotions and stress levels are high. An organization can take a number of steps in advance of a crisis to help ensure that it will be manageable when it does occur. Identifying vulnerabilities is a good first step. It shows you where your weak points are in respect to certain types of crises that might occur within your industry. For example, fires are a common threat to any organization; however, nuclear waste disposal would not be a threat for a school district, nor would tornados pose a threat to an oil company's property in Alaska (although earthquakes probably would). The idea is to list the realistic threats to your organization. Following are some worksheets that can help you identify and assess your vulnerabilities.[5] You should develop a set of your own worksheets particular to your industry or organization's needs. For example, if you deal with a local hospital, your list might include large-scale medical emergencies (outbreaks of disease, for example) as well as response to power outages and various natural disasters (see Exhibit 6.1).

Exhibit 6.1

Worksheets for Assessing Vulnerabilities

Complexity (List the top five most complex events)

Example: Explosion or fire at a chemical plant

1. _____

2. _____

3. _____

4. _____

5. _____

(continued)

---

[4] Covello V. 1995. Risk Communication Paper, Opening The Black Box Risk Conference, Mcmaster University. Cited by the Ministry of Agriculture and Food, Ontario, Canada.
[5] CHS Cooperatives/Land-O-Lakes, http://www.mbrservices.com/commtools/crisis.cfm.

(continued)

Probability (List the top five most likely events)

Example: Closing of operations due to storm damage

1. _____
2. _____
3. _____
4. _____
5. _____

Staff capability (List the top five events according to your staff's ability to physically respond to crisis)

Example: Fire in warehouse

1. _____
2. _____
3. _____
4. _____
5. _____

Media interest (List top five events most likely to attract media coverage)

Example: Toxic releases, explosions, or spills

1. _____
2. _____
3. _____
4. _____
5. _____

Elected official interest (List the top five events most likely to get politicians' attention)

Example:

1. _____
2. _____
3. _____
4. _____
5. _____

Also remember that, as a public relations professional, your job is to communicate every day, not just in a time of crisis. One of the best ways to ensure that you will weather a crisis is to build community trust in advance. Establish a reputation within your community for honest communication. Develop solid relation-

Exhibit 6.2

Key Messages

What are our business goals?

1. _____

2. _____

3. _____

What image do we want to have with our customers and community?

_____

_____

_____

List three key messages that blend business goals with image goals.

1. _____

2. _____

3. _____

How can we convey this?

1. _____

2. _____

3. _____

ships with all your stakeholders. Remember that during a time of crisis, people's first reaction will be based on what they already know about you. If they are forming an opinion for the first time during the crisis, you haven't done your job. The reputation you have going into a crisis is the best defense against damage to your organization's reputation coming out of it. Ask yourself what your desired image is and develop messages consistent with that image (see Exhibit 6.2). The best offense is always a good defense. Being prepared means accomplishing the following:[6]

- Know your vulnerabilities; address them to the extent possible.
- Keep an eye on the competition; if they have a problem, you may, too.
- Monitor the media for issues that may be surfacing.
- Be part of your community.
- Provide media training for on-site management.

[6] CHS Cooperatives/Land-O-Lakes, http://www.mbrservices.com/commtools/crisis.cfm.

- Develop a key contact list for crises.
- Build relationships in your community and industry.
- Maintain background information on your operation.
- Reinforce key messages whenever possible.

Pulling Together a Crisis Team

You will need to pull together a **crisis team,** generally composed of managers in key areas including those areas most likely to be hit by a crisis. Look over the materials you have collected on potential crises. Analyze them. Hold a planning session and, at the conclusion, designate one or more members of the team to develop the crisis preparation and response plan.

Whether or not this initial crisis team becomes your official crisis management team, a copy of the team roster should be attached to the crisis plan and should include cellular phone numbers and beeper numbers. Crises have a way of happening when you least expect them, and you need to get in touch with the team members wherever they are. The list should designate each team member's responsibility in the event of a crisis.

The people selected for the crisis management team should generally have the same qualities that make good managers in any situation. The team should include people who are:[7]

- Perceptive
- Intuitive
- Knowledgeable in one or more functional area
- Able to accept additional responsibility
- Clear thinkers
- Decisive
- Calm under stress
- Capable problem solvers

Choosing a Spokesperson

One individual should be designated as the primary spokesperson to represent the organization, make official statements, and answer media questions throughout the crisis. Selecting the right crisis communication spokesperson is essential. How your organization handles all aspects of the communication necessary during a crisis will make or break your organization in the eyes of the public. Also, having one spokesperson for all media communication is best to ensure the consistency of messages and response communication. A back-up to the designated

[7] Ministry of Agriculture and Food, Ontario, Canada, http://www.gov.on.ca/OMAFRA/english/research/risk/crcpm.htm.

spokesperson should be identified to fill the position in the event that the primary spokesperson is unavailable.

Your primary spokesperson should be someone who is articulate and able to maintain composure under stress. Also, he or she should be someone who has solid credibility within the community. Whenever possible, the designated on-site spokesperson should undergo media interview training in advance of any crisis.

In addition to the primary spokesperson and the back-up spokesperson, individuals who will serve as technical experts or advisors should be designated. These resources might include a financial expert, an engineer, a leader in the community, or anyone your organization deems necessary during a specific kind of crisis.

Criteria for the spokesperson, back-up spokesperson, and crisis communication expert are:[8]

- Comfortable in front of a television camera and with reporters
- Preferably, skilled in handling media and skilled in directing responses to another topic
- Skilled in identifying key points
- Able to speak without using jargon
- Respectful of the role of the reporter
- Knowledgeable about the organization and the crisis at hand
- Able to establish credibility with the media
- Able to project confidence to the audience
- Suitable in regard to diction, appearance, and charisma
- Sincere, straightforward, and believable
- Accessible to the media and to internal communication personnel who will facilitate media interviews
- Able to remain calm in stressful situations

In addition to the designated and back-up spokespeople, other parties involved in the crisis—police, fire department, health officials, and the like—will each have a spokesperson. It is important to obtain the identity of each additional spokesperson as early as possible so that all statements and contacts with the media can be coordinated among the individuals and their organizations and interests whenever possible.

CRISIS MANAGEMENT

Here are the basic steps you should take when an incident occurs:

1. Notify key individuals (crisis team, etc.)

---

[8] Sandra K. Clawson-Freeo, Northern Illinois University, http://www3.niu.edu/newsplace/crisis.html.

2. Notify on-site spokesperson if appropriate (this person should already have been selected).

3. Inform on-site security if necessary.

4. Get the facts straight.

5. Designate message and media center.

6. Develop key messages.

7. Develop response statements.

8. Develop response and designate spokespersons for other audiences if needed.

9. Monitor local news media to determine how the story is being reported.

10. Update information and response regularly.

Vehicles for notifying key audiences include the following:

- Internal mechanisms for reaching consumers, employees, sales force, and the like
- Customer hotline
- Mailing lists and fax numbers for local, state, and federal government offices
- Mailing lists and fax numbers for customers, suppliers, distributors, unions, interest groups, trade organizations, and so on
- A section of the organization's Web site devoted to such information
- The media, both general and trade specific

The crisis communication preparation worksheet in Exhibit 6.3 can help you determine in advance your specific audiences, spokespeople, key messages, and communication tools. The worksheet is useful during an event for gathering factual information, developing messages specific to the incident, and preparing a response.[9]

Designating a Message and Media Center

Select a place to be used as a **message and media center.** It should be some distance from offices of the crisis communication team, spokesperson, and emergency operations center to ensure that media don't end up in the middle of the action and can't accidentally bump into people they shouldn't be talking to. If there is a visual (a fire or rescue operation), don't make the media center in such a remote site that they can't see what is going on because they may not show up, and if they do you will lose their confidence and you may appear to be hiding something. Locations for interviews and press briefings should be decided by the crisis communication team.

Keep a **contact log** to record all telephone calls from the media or other parties inquiring about the crisis. This will help to ensure that the many callbacks

---

[9] CHS Cooperatives/Land-O-Lakes, http://www.mbrservices.com/commtools/crisis.cfm.

Exhibit 6.3

Crisis Communication Preparation Worksheet

Key contacts: _____

_____

Who will serve as on-site spokesperson? _____

Where could media briefings be held? _____

Who are our audiences?

   I. _____

   2. _____

   3. _____

   4. _____

   5. _____

What are our key messages?

   I. _____

   2. _____

   3. _____

How will we get the word out?

_____

_____

_____

---

required are not overlooked. It will also assist in the post-crisis analysis. The contact log should contain the following information:

- Date
- Name of caller
- Questions(s) asked
- Telephone number
- Person responsible for response
- Additional follow-up needs

It is essential that you establish a media policy immediately (in fact, it should already be in your plan). Generally speaking, only the designated on-site or company spokespeople should have contact with the news media during times of crisis. Employees should be instructed on a regular basis to refer all media inquiries to the operation's management or the on-site spokesperson during a crisis situation. If it is later determined that a specific employee should be made available for a media interview, that individual must receive advance preparation from an on-site spokesperson or other designated person.[10]

Developing a Message

Key to effective message development is the recognition that individuals are unique and that each is going to respond to a message using his or her own filters of knowledge and experience. Risk messages need to be personalized enough to provide a framework for individual action, recognizing the practical constraints of tailoring a message to each member of a target audience. The message should also be repeated, using a variety of media.[11] In general, risk messages should:[12]

- Relate the message to the audiences' perspectives, emphasizing information relevant to any practical actions that individuals can take
- Be couched in clear and plain language
- Respect the audience and its concerns and seek strictly to inform the recipient
- Clearly state the existence of uncertainty
- Avoid risk comparisons that trivialize the concern
- Ensure completeness, including the nature of the risk, the nature of the benefits that might be affected if the risk were reduced, the available alternatives, uncertainty in knowledge about risks and benefits, and management issues

Vincent Covello, director of the Center for Risk Communication in New York City, has offered the following guidelines for talking about risk:[13]

- Be balanced and honest.
- Focus on a specific issue.
- Pay attention to what the audience already knows.
- Tailor statements to the specific needs of the audience.
- Place the risk in an appropriate context.
- Include (at least) the specific information needed to resolve the decisions that members of the audience face.
- Use a hierarchical organization so that people who want only answers can find them quickly and people who want details can also find them.

---

[10] CHS Cooperatives/Land-O-Lakes, http://www.mbrservices.com/commtools/crisis.cfm.
[11] Needleman, C. 1987. "Ritualism in communicating risk information." *Science/Technology and Human Values* 12: 20–25.
[12] Ministry of Agriculture and Food, Ontario, Canada, http://www.gov.on.ca/OMAFRA/english/research/risk/crcpm.htm.
[13] Covello, V. T., Fischhoff, B., Kasperson, R. E., and Morgan, M. G. 1993. "Comments on 'the mental model' meets 'the planning process'." *Risk Analysis* 13: 493.

- Be respectful in tone, and recognize that people have legitimate feelings as well as thoughts.
- Be honest about the limits to scientific knowledge.
- Consider and address the broader social dynamics in which risks are embedded.
- Subject statements to careful empirical evaluation and iterative refinement.

When developing messages, you need to acknowledge that the risk exists and address what has happened and what is being done. Remember that how messages are conveyed during a crisis is of paramount importance and that being seen as a credible and trustworthy source of information is extremely critical. To increase the chances of maintaining, or possibly enhancing, the organization's level of credibility and trust in the eyes of its audience, consider the following guidelines for information release:[14]

- Early release sets the pace for resolution of the problem.
- If you wait, the story may leak anyway.
- You have better control of accuracy if you are first to present the information.
- More time is available for meaningful public input if information is released promptly.
- People are entitled to information that affects their lives.
- Information release may prevent similar situations elsewhere.

Responding to the Media

Communicating effectively with the media in a crisis is critically important. It's also important to remember, however, that the news media are not an audience. Groups such as employees, customers, and the general public are audiences; television, radio, and newspapers are tools by which your message will be carried. The media hunger for information and sources is insatiable in the first stages of a crisis. Given this reality, it is important to work with journalists to help them provide a responsible and accurate reporting of the event. With focus and planning, you can successfully use the news media to get your messages to your key audiences.

The media work in cycles, usually dictated by their deadlines. During a crisis, you will need to become even more acutely aware of those deadlines, and their effects on media behavior, and act accordingly. The National Education Association has developed an extensive set of guidelines designed specifically for school shootings but broadly applicable to other crises. The rest of this section describes some of their guidelines for dealing with the media.[15]

---

[14] Hance, B. J., Chess, C. and Sandman, P. M. 1988. *Improving Dialogue with Communities: A Risk Communication Manual for Government.* Environmental Communication Research Program, Rutgers University, New Brunswick, NJ. 83 pp.

[15] The National Education Association "Crisis Communication Guide & Toolkit," http://www.nea.org/crisis/b2home.html.

1. Establish a Perimeter

Immediately following a crisis, reporters, photographers, satellite trucks, and engineers operating various media equipment may attempt to move in on the site. A perimeter line should be immediately established across which only staff, rescue crews, and law enforcement may pass. Official badges or vests should be issued to these personnel for identification. A location should be identified for media to set up working operations.

The location should allow the media to access pictures of the affected area and information from spokespersons at a distance where they will not interfere with emergency crews. Remember that in many crisis situations, law enforcement may assert control over the site. Therefore, as part of crisis response plans, agreements should be forged between the organization and law enforcement about where perimeter lines are drawn and media camps allowed, and how collaboration may occur in making such decisions.

2. Provide Statements, Press Releases, and Fact Sheets

Within the first hours following a crisis, a press statement should be released providing only confirmed facts. Remember, if you don't communicate immediately, you lose your greatest opportunity to control events. Your first news release should include, at a minimum, the who, what, when, and where of the situation. According to Sandra Clawson-Freeo, "If you do nothing more than show concern for the public and for your employees in your first press interaction, you are already on the right track."[16]

Statistics and information sheets should be widely distributed to the media in a number of formats—including faxes, Web updates, and e-mail alerts. National and out-of-town media outlets unfamiliar with the area will need this information to fill in details about the organization in their stories. Fact sheets and organizational profiles will help answer frequently asked questions.

These fact sheets should be prepared ahead of time and ready to distribute prior to the crisis. Many organizations already have such information posted on their Web sites. Take care to protect the privacy rights of employees and others. Many organizations have a strict policy regarding the release of employee information. Make sure you are aware of your organization's policy and any applicable state and federal laws.

3. Schedule Regular Press Briefings

Depending on the circumstances, the organization should schedule regular briefings with the press to disseminate information and answer questions. Media advisories alerting the press to the time and location of such briefings should be distributed well in advance. If possible, briefings should be scheduled at times that consider reporter deadlines. Mornings and early afternoons are preferable.

---

[16]Sandra K. Clawson-Freeo, Northern Illinois University, http://www3.niu.edu/newsplace/crisis.html.

The format should include opening remarks by the spokesperson outlining new information and action being taken and resources the public can draw upon for help. The remarks should also convey concern for the community and any victims, and confidence and pride in the action and ability of staff and other crisis responders. After brief remarks, questions can be taken. The question-and-answer period should be kept very short. The spokesperson should close the briefing by announcing the time and location of the next press briefing, if possible. Communication staff should stay at the briefing to be available upon the spokesperson's departure to record any questions or requests for information that can be fulfilled at a later time.

4. Use the Internet

The Internet is the perfect vehicle for reaching many people with critical information quickly. When answering media queries, direct reporters to the organization's Web site for continuously updated information. It is important that the Web site follow through on that promise, or it will not be regarded as a fast, reliable source of information. Driving as much traffic to the Internet as possible will help reporters receive information more quickly and will free up communication staff for other activities, such as gathering information to disseminate on the Web.

5. Field Media Inquiries

Responding to media inquiries effectively requires a deliberate system and policy that fulfills requests quickly, consistently, and with the best information. Following are some strategies for achieving these goals:

- *Create a priority system for coding and organizing requests, using a two-sided query sheet.* One side of the query sheet is designated for requests for information or answers to specific questions; the other side is designated for requests for interviews and includes information such as the type of medium (radio, television, print), the deadline for the interview, the context for the interview and story (what is the story about and who else will be consulted), and how long the interview will likely last.

- *Create a script for those answering the phones to follow in processing the requests.* Instruct those answering the phones to stick to the script and remember that they are not authorized to be quoted. If asked for their names, the volunteer staff assigned to fielding queries should respond, "I am an employ helping the organization fulfill media requests and am not an official spokesperson. All statements attributed to the company must come from an official spokesperson. If you will give me your name and telephone number, I will see that it gets to an official spokesperson. Thanks for your cooperation. As I'm sure you can imagine, we are fielding many calls."

- *Maintain a master list of questions that need to be answered and assign volunteers to seek those answers.* The document should be constantly updated and expanded and can serve as a frequently-asked-questions reference for volunteers. Only answers that have received official approval should be added to the list.

6. Assert Control and Set Parameters

Do not be afraid to set and assert parameters for media coverage. For instance, media do not have the right to roam unsupervised on private property or the right to interfere with normal comings and goings or your organization's work schedule. If necessary, coordinate with law enforcement and public safety officials.

Parameters on media coverage on private property (buildings and grounds) protect employees and staff. Such parameters should be a consideration in the organization's crisis response plan. The designated parameters can be enforced by denying violators access to regular press briefings.

Reporters will likely want to interview employees and other staff about the incident. Communication staff can help facilitate this effort by identifying employees who are comfortable granting interviews and have constructive messages to deliver.

7. Provide Guidance for Those Agreeing to Be Interviewed

Employees and staff do not have an obligation to do media interviews. Of course, reporters have a right to seek interviews, and employees have a right to tell their story to the media. However, employees and others should agree to interviews only after considering and carefully thinking about the following:

- *What is your story, and what do you hope to accomplish by telling it?* Some employees may feel that if they grant an interview with one reporter, that it will somehow reduce the quantity of requests from other reporters. The opposite is true. Once you appear in a news story, other reporters will see your name and seek you out for an interview for their media outlet. They may also express a sense of entitlement to an interview and demand to know why one media outlet was accommodated over another.

- *Are you comfortable with the parameters for the interview?* Have you discussed with the reporter the context for the story and his or her expectations for your input? Ask in advance for specific questions that will be asked and find out who else will be interviewed for the story. If you are uncomfortable with any aspect of the story, you are within your rights to set conditions and parameters.

- *Are your family and colleagues supportive of the interview?* What are the likely implications of your appearing in a story?

- *Where will the interview take place?* If the interview takes place in an open area or in a place where other reporters have access, there is a strong possibility that other reporters will stake out the area and seek you out for an interview for their media outlet.

- *Does the reporter have a reputation for fairness and sensitivity?* Past behavior is a strong predictor of future behavior.

- *Have you discussed the interview with communication staff?* They are media relations professionals and can help you prepare for the interview and provide insight into what to expect and avoid.

If employees do choose to do an interview, make sure they have done some homework and know how to deal with reporters. Following are some suggestions from the National Education Association:

- Ask the reporter about others being interviewed for the story, so that you can see how your comments might be framed.
- Write down the messages you would like to communicate and make sure that you repeat them often. Use bridging phrases to provide opportunities to articulate your main points (e.g., It's important to remember that . . . , The bottom line here is . . . , This issue hinges on . . .).
- Make sure that your comments focus on your main points. Do not count on off-the-record comments being kept confidential. Think carefully how your words may be used in and out of context. Don't leave room for confusion or for your words to be taken out of context.

8. Work to Produce Constructive Media Coverage

Communication staff should work with the media in an effort to avoid sensationalism and to put as positive a spin on the situation as is possible.

Exhibit 6.4 offers additional suggestions on working with the media.

Exhibit 6.4

Tips for Dealing with the Media

In working with the media, the most important thing you can do is to remain in control of the situation. Most members of the media are just trying to do their jobs. Your task is to assist them, while preserving and enhancing your operation's reputation. You can accomplish this by doing the following:

- *Cultivate positive relationships.* Good media relations doesn't begin when a crisis begins. Be proactive in providing information and story ideas throughout the year.
- *Practice full disclosure and honest, open communication.* You will gain credibility later at the crisis scene.
- *Maintain controlled access.* Members of the media, particularly television and still photographers, will want visual images. You must determine where they can go, when they can go, and how many can go. (It is possible to allow access to only one still and one television camera and request that they provide a "pool feed" to others.) Work with on-site safety and response officials to maintain a consistent and safe approach.

(continued)

(continued)

- *Establish times and places for responding.* There is no law that requires anyone to immediately begin responding to a reporter's questions. It is appropriate to ask for time to gather updated information. It is also appropriate to set a specific place and time for conducting interviews. This will enable you to focus on your key messages, review factual information, and position your operation in the best light.

- *If you don't know, say so.* It is human nature to want to answer questions, but it is risky to share information you're not certain about. During times of crisis, factual information may be difficult to acquire. Never speculate, especially with the media. If you don't know, say so. Speculation or inaccurate information reported in the media can be difficult to correct. It can damage your credibility and even lead to legal repercussions. It is always better to offer to follow up with the reporter when information is available.

- *Don't speak off the record.* The best rule to follow in dealing with the media is to assume that everything, even casual conversation, is on the record.

- *Emphasize positive action being taken.* Many people refer to this as spin. There is nothing wrong with accentuating the positive; however, don't gloss over the negative. People will think you're hiding something or assume you are guilty of something.

- *Do not refuse to speak to the media.* Refusing to speak to the media is not a productive response. It will not prevent coverage but will deny you the opportunity to inform and communicate with the public.

- *Never give personal information about a staff member or employee.* Personal information should be released only at the discretion of the individual in question or his or her immediate family.

- *Do not answer hypothetical or speculative questions.* This will only fuel rumors, and that is the last thing you want.

- *Share information with all those affected by a statement before releasing it to the press.* This is especially true for public information officers in school districts, law enforcement, and the like.

- *Show concern and compassion.* Although facts are important, whenever possible strive to show empathy and concern for any individuals—employees or others—who may have been involved in an incident.

RECOVERY AND REBUILDING AFTER THE CRISIS

The final stage of crisis management is assessing the damage and rebuilding the organization's reputation after the crisis. The progression from the actual crisis to the recovery phase can happen only after a predefined action—which signifies that the crisis is officially over—has been executed.

Going through a crisis is never a pleasant experience, but it can produce some beneficial results. Throughout a crisis situation you can communicate your concern about product safety and demonstrate your accessibility and openness. Turning the crisis into a positive experience requires a number of steps both during the crisis and ongoing after the situation has subsided. This is the time to assess the effectiveness of your organization's crisis communication plan and make any necessary updates or changes.

KEY TERMS

crisis team
message and media center
contact log

EXERCISES

1. Locate a crisis plan for an organization. It can be any type of organization: corporation, social service agency, school. Bring the plan to class. If you found it on the Internet, print it out and bring it in. Be prepared to discuss how closely it adheres to some of the guidelines covered in this chapter. At points at which it doesn't seem to match, discuss the reasons why you believe it doesn't. Do you think this is a good plan? Why or why not?

2. Draft a crisis communication for yourself. Imagine a possible, realistic emergency you might be involved in (a fire, earthquake, tornado, riot) during which people would need to know from you how you are and what is happening. As part of your plan, consider the following questions:

   - Who should be contacted? Why?

   - Who would be on your crisis team? Why?

   - Who would be your spokesperson (if you couldn't be) with the media, with officials wanting to talk with you, and with other interested parties?

   - What other crisis issues would you need to take care of? Because this is a personal plan, it might include such things as purchasing a cell phone, leaving friends with contact numbers, and so on. Use your imagination.

CHAPTER

7

News Releases and Backgrounders

In this chapter you will learn:

- What a news release is and why it is important to public relations professionals.
- How to write various forms of news releases, including publicity releases, product news releases, and news releases for broadcast.

- What a backgrounder is and how to write one.
- What a fact sheet is and how to write one.

The news release has been called the workhorse of public relations. Every day, thousands of news releases are sent out all over the country to newspapers, magazines, and radio and television stations. Some newspaper editors receive as many as a thousand a month. Of these, only a minuscule number are ever used, and most of these are severely edited. Why, then, do public relations professionals and the people who employ them continue to use news releases? Because they remain effective. They are still used by newspapers and trade journals to pass along information about events and occurrences that reporters might not otherwise have the time or the inclination to cover.

The key to effective news releases is not so much in the writing, although we certainly concentrate on that, but in the placement. As we saw in Chapter 5, knowing when something is newsworthy and when it is not, and knowing your contacts in the media and their schedules and guidelines, are the most important elements of news release writing.

As a writer of news releases, you will become a reporter. It is essential that you understand journalistic style in order to present your releases in the proper format. Remember that reporters and editors are used to seeing one style of writing on a daily basis. That style fits their papers, and they are unlikely to print anything that doesn't conform. Remember, too, that although the reporter is responsible only to his or her editor, you are responsible to both the editor and the people you work for. This means that you must accommodate both the style of the newspaper and the needs of your employer. It is not an easy fence to walk, but as a public relations practitioner you have to try to keep your balance.

WHAT IS A NEWS RELEASE?

A **news release** is information that you wish released to the press, usually the print media. Although all news releases have format in common, there are different emphases:

- Basic **publicity releases** cover any information occurring within an organization that might have some news value to local, regional, or even national media.
- **Product releases** deal with specific products or product lines. These are usually targeted to trade publications within individual industries. They can deal with the product itself, consumer use of the product, or a particular business or marketing angle.
- **Financial releases** are used primarily in shareholder relations; however, they are also of interest to financial media. Many local, regional, and national general media have financial highlights sections.

One of the most important points to remember is that all news releases should contain at least three elements: publicity, angle, and story. These elements may overlap or be quite distinct from one another, but they are all there. The **publicity** value of a news release is sometimes hidden while the story is the perceived reason for writing the release, at least from the media's point of view. The **angle,** by contrast, may be simply the hook that attracts media attention. Often it is the same as the story but not as often the same as the publicity value. The reason, of course, is that most media aren't interested in your organization receiving publicity; they are interested in a story their audience wants to know about.

WRITING A NEWS RELEASE

The style of the news release is that of the straight news story: It begins with a lead, expands on the lead, and proceeds to present information in decreasing order of importance. This style, known as the **inverted pyramid style,** allows an editor to perform his or her job—that is, to edit—from the bottom up. A good news release also utilizes accurate quotes.

The Lead

The **lead,** or opening sentence of the news release, is all-important. As every journalist knows, the lead is the hook that entices the reader into your story. For the public relations practitioner, too, the lead is a hook to entice the editor into running your release. Don't ever get the notion that any news release you send out will automatically be printed or that it will even be printed the way you wrote it. The fact is, even if you have written the most appealing news release ever seen at the *Daily Planet,* most editors feel an obligation to edit. Indeed, you will be lucky to have the information in your release placed at all. This should not deter you, however, from writing a good release. You have to sell the editor first before your release will ever be seen by anyone else, and that's where a well-written lead comes in.

Editors often take less than 30 seconds to peruse a news release. Their decision to print the message depends a lot on how you present yourself in the headline (title) and the lead. Most editors use several measures to determine whether your release will be used. Who you are, in terms of your past record of providing only legitimate news, is the first important consideration. Once past that, your headline or title should tell them whether your release is important to them (more on this later). Finally, your lead should summarize the relevancy of your story.

The **summary lead** is by far the most common type of news release lead. A good summary lead will answer the key questions: who, what, when, where, why, and how. The **delayed lead** is used to add drama to a news story; however, this type of lead is usually reserved for feature stories and is not appropriate for straight news. Thus, we concentrate here on summary leads.

Before you write the lead, you must first decide on a theme. Try to determine what is unique about the event covered by your release. Although news releases should generally be considered as straight news stories and must be informative, they don't have to be boring. To illustrate, look at the summary lead from a release distributed by the Electronic Products Producers Association:

"The present condition of the software market is such that companies involved in software development should be able to capitalize on current economic trends. This means that new product development should allow the earliest investors a significant niche in the market." This statement was made by Mr. James L. Sutton, President of Associated Products Corporation, during a speech at the Fall convention of the Electronic Products Producers Association held in Syracuse, New York.

Now consider this revised version of the same lead:

A leading electronics industry executive declared today (October 21) that the computer software market is wide open to new investors.

"The present condition of the software market is such that companies involved in software development should be able to capitalize on current trends," said James L. Sutton, president of Associated Products Corporation. "This means that new product development should allow the earliest investors a significant niche in the market."

Sutton's prediction of a dynamic market was made in a speech given at the Fall convention of the Electronic Products Producers Association in Syracuse, New York.

Notice how the second lead has broken up the quote and used the proper journalistic form for *attribution* ("said James L. Sutton"). The opening paragraph has been rewritten to include most of the pertinent information:

Who?	A leading electronics industry executive.
What?	Declared a wide-open computer software market.
When?	Today (October 21). Notice the inclusion of the actual date in parentheses. This is to let the editor know that the "today" you are speaking of is October 21. If the paper receives the release on October 20 but doesn't publish the information until October 22, they will need to correct the copy to read "yesterday."
Where?	Left until the final paragraph. (It isn't always necessary to squeeze all of the information into the first paragraph.)
Why?	Included in the explanatory paragraph following the lead. Of all the information, "why" is the most likely to be left out of the lead because it usually takes the most explanation and invites the interested reader to look further.
How?	In a speech. Also left for the final paragraph.

Remember that you are responsible for the ordering of points in your lead and in your news release. The more interesting you can make the information by order of presentation, the better it will read. Notice also how much shorter the sentences seem in the revised version. In fact, there is only one more sentence than in the original, but because the quote is broken up and the attribution is placed in the middle, the sentences seem much shorter. Although it is wise to present most of the key information early in the release, only the most important elements need appear in the lead. The rest can follow in logical order.

A publicist's lead is likely to differ from one written by a newspaper reporter. The following examples, written for a local newspaper, illustrate the difference:

Publicist's Lead
Francis Langly, former Director of Research and Development at Rogers Experimental Plastics Company, will be awarded the prestigious Goodyear Medal on

June 6 in Indianapolis at a banquet held in his honor. Awarded by the American Chemical Society, the Goodyear Medal is the premier award for work in the field of specialty elastomers.

Reporter's Lead
Francis Langly, 24 Cedar Crest Drive, will receive the Goodyear Medal at the annual meeting of the American Chemical Society. The conference is being held in Indianapolis on June 6.

Although neither of these examples is particularly original—public relations releases rarely are—the differences in content and style exist for a reason. Consider these questions:

- Why is the address left out in the publicist's lead?
- Why is Langly's title included in the publicist's lead?
- What is the difference between the phrases "will receive" and "will be awarded"?
- What is the significance for the publicist in pointing out that the Goodyear medal is the premier award in the field?

Answers to these questions illustrate the differences between hard news and publicity, and between the publicist's and the journalist's objectives.

Quotations and Attributions

Quotations add interest to your news release. It is always good to obtain usable quotations and then to place them at appropriate spots throughout the release. It is never a good idea to begin a news release with a quote. Because news releases are considered straight news stories, a quote fails to come to the point soon enough. As was illustrated above, quotes need not be written as complete sentences followed by the attribution; they can be broken up by the attribution. You don't need to follow every quotation by an attribution, especially if it is understood that the same person quoted earlier is still being quoted. A good rule is to repeat an attribution if more than one paragraph has elapsed since it was last given. Of course, if you change the source of the quotation, you will need to designate the change by a new **attribution.** Don't be afraid to work with the form of attribution, and don't use the same form each time. Consider the following:

Johnson, a long-time trucker, doesn't like the strike. "This layoff has really affected my family," he said. The strike has been in effect for three months. "We're down to eating beans out of a can," he said. Johnson has three small children and a $500 a month house payment. "I don't know what I'm going to do about my bills," he said.

Although the form of attribution ("he said") is correct, its repetition is monotonous. There are a number of ways of attributing a quotation that can add variety to releases. For example, you can paraphrase points of the quote, combine quotes, or simply use one attribution between two quotes. Look at this revised version:

Johnson, a long-time trucker, doesn't like the three-month-long strike. "This layoff has really affected my family," he says. "We're down to eating beans out of a can."

Johnson, who has three small children and a $500 a month house payment, says he doesn't know what he's going to do about his bills.

Notice that the tense of the attribution has also been changed to the present. News releases need to sound as timely as possible, which includes using the present tense in attributions if possible. If you are dealing with a story that is obviously past, then the attribution must reflect this.

Most news-writing classes and most journalists adhere to the rule of using only the last name in an attribution. News releases, by contrast, must follow the conventions set by the originating organization. In most cases, even if you do insist on attributing a quotation to "Mr. Jones" or "President Smith," the news editor will delete the honorific. You will have done your job by using the conventions of your employer. In the long run, that is all you are expected to do.

The accuracy of quotations is obviously important, but even though reporters must be absolutely accurate, public relations writers can have some leeway. An illustration will help explain. Suppose you work for Rogers Experimental Plastics Company (REPC). You are writing a release on a new product line and are quoting the company president. You have interviewed the president, and he knows you are writing the release. He is also aware of what he said; however, because he will probably be reviewing the release before it is sent out, he will correct anything he doesn't like. As a writer and an employee, you have the creative ability and leeway to "invent" a quotation as long as he approves it. No employer will fault you for putting well-written words in his or her mouth. Suppose in your interview the president had said,

I don't think anything like this new plastic has ever been seen—at least not around this area of the world. It may be the greatest thing since sliced bread and who knows how much money we'll make from it.

You may write in your release,

Paul Johnson, President of REPC, is excited about the new product. "We've come up with a totally new concept in plastic," he says. "I expect that the market for 'Plagets' in the West will be tremendous."

All you've done is tidy up the quotation and make it more interesting. Remember that you may only doctor quotations that will be checked for accuracy and approved by the party to whom they are attributed. It is a good rule to make sure that anyone you interview receives a copy of the finished release before it is distributed. There is nothing like a libel suit to sober up a writer! Another legitimate way of presenting unclear or clumsy quotations is to paraphrase or use indirect attribution. This is fine for news stories written by reporters, but news releases can benefit a great deal from well-written quotations.

Finally, if you want to help prevent serious editing, or even elimination, of your quotations (and your sources' names) you must learn to protect your quote. In other words, learn to use information that is vital to the understanding of the story as quotes rather than the fluff quotes often provided by those giving you the assignment. For example, consider the following:

> "This is an exciting day for all of us," says Delphi CEO Robert Altus. (Any self-respecting editor would edit out this nearly meaningless quote. It's painfully clear that it was included in order to get the CEO's name in the release.)

Instead, you could write this:

> "The merger of Delphi and TransAmerican airlines will more than double the workforce available to both companies currently," says Delphi CEO Robert Altus. (Although it may still be clear that this quote provides for mention of the CEO's name, it has a greater chance of staying because it provides important information.)

Used in this way, quotes can be placed strategically, based on the level of importance of the information. Fluff quotes, of course, belong at the end of the release—if used at all.

Local Interest

Local media outlets like local stories. For most public relations writers, news releases can almost always be oriented to a local audience. The real problem is finding just the right local angle—the one that will entice the newspaper into running the story. Some basic guidelines will help you in your placement:

- If you are releasing a story with national as well as local interest, try to construct your release so that any local information is interspersed throughout the release. This way, it will be difficult to cut out the national information, which might not be of interest to a local editor, without harming the local angle.

- Avoid commercial plugs. Editors recognize advertising instantly and will simply round-file (trash) your release. Keep your local angle newsworthy.

- If you are sending only to local media and you reference a local city in your release, omit the name of the state.

- Above all, don't strain to find a local angle where there is none.

Suppose that you are assigned to write a release that has national importance and you want to target it for a local paper, the *Seattle Times*. You know from your interview with William J. Hoffman, chief systems engineer of Associated Products Corporation of Syracuse, New York, that he went to high school and college in Seattle. Based only on this little bit of knowledge, the piece can be localized. In addition, you could try to place a version of the release in the *Lincoln High Review* and another version in the University of Washington *Husky* (the alumni paper). Your leads might look like this:

> *For the* Seattle Times
>
> William J. Hoffman, Seattle native and Chief Systems Engineer for Associated Products Corporation (APC) of Syracuse, New York, has been credited with developing a revolutionary educational software line.

For the Lincoln High Review
William J. Hoffman, a Lincoln High School graduate and former president of the
LHS Electronics Club, has been credited with developing a revolutionary educa-
tional software line.

For the University of Washington Husky
William J. Hoffman, a University of Washington graduate with honors in Engineering, has been credited with developing a revolutionary educational software line.

You might think that the Lincoln High School angle is too much of a strain. If
you do, don't use it. Every angle, however, is worth at least some consideration.
You'll be surprised how your placements can multiply if you ask the right questions in your interviews and construct the right angles from the answers.

Remember, though, that the focus of your release isn't always the local angle;
that is only the hook. Don't slight your real story in favor of the local angle, no
matter how interesting it is. In the samples above, for instance, Hoffman is the
angle, but the software is the story. The trick is to lead with the angle, move to
the story, and keep the two so intertwined that any editor will have difficulty sep-
arating them.

NEWS RELEASE FORMAT

Although public relations practitioners often incorporate the conventions of their
organization into their news releases, a standard news release format exists. Exhibit 7.1 provides a sample news release, with all format elements in place.

- News releases typically are written on plain, white bond paper with no deco-
  rative border.

- Margins are one to one-and-a-half inches on all sides.

- The address of the sender is placed in the upper left-hand corner of the first
  page. This identifying block should include the complete address, name of
  the contact person (usually the person who wrote the release), and telephone numbers. It is especially important to include a night telephone number as well as a daytime number. Remember, newspapers don't shut down at
  night, and if an editor wants to use your release but needs further or clarify-
  ing information and can't reach you, the release may get dumped.

- The release date appears on the right margin, slightly lower than the bottom
  of the address block. This portion provides the editor with exact information
  concerning the appropriate timing for the release. More about release
  dates later.

- The body of the release begins about one-third of the way down the page,
  allowing some white space for comments or notes from the editor. If there
  is to be a title—and titles are entirely optional—it should come between
  the address block and the body of the release, flush left. Typically, the title
  does not extend beyond the address block by more than a few characters,
  which usually means that it will be stacked (broken into two lines on top

Exhibit 7.1

News Release Format

Company or Client Name
and Address Here
Contact: (Your Name)
Day Phone:

Night Phone:

Release Date and Time

THE TITLE GOES HERE, ALL UPPER

CASE AND UNDERLINED LIKE THIS

The Point of Origin Dateline Goes Here -- The body of the release should begin one-third of the way down the page to leave enough room for the editor or copy person to write remarks. The release proper should be all double spaced for ease of readability and editing.

Be sure to use normal indents and consistent spacing between paragraphs. It is not necessary to triple space between paragraphs. All information should be presented in descending order of importance, ending with the least important items in case last-minute editing results in the bottom of your release being lopped off.

Remember to leave at least one-inch margins all around, but resist the urge to leave huge right-hand margins in order to stretch your information.

When you arrive at the bottom of the first page, leave at least a one-inch margin and indicate either the end of your release (-30-) or that more information follows (-more-). If more information follows, try not to break paragraphs or sentences in the middle. Never break a word and complete it on the next page.

.-30-

of each other). The title should be in all caps, single-spaced, with the last line underlined.

- The body of the news release is double-spaced. Never single-space a news release. Paragraphs usually are indented with normal spacing between paragraphs. Some companies prefer no indention and triple-spacing between paragraphs, but the standard is indented.

- If the release runs more than a page, the word *more* is placed in brackets or within dashes at the bottom of the page.

- Following pages are identified by a slug line (abbreviated title) followed by several dashes and the page number at the top of the page, usually either flush left or flush right.

- The end of the release is designated in one of several ways. Use the word *end* or the number *30* either in quotation marks or within dashes, or the symbol #####.

Timing and Dating Releases

When do you want your release to be published or broadcast? If you have just written a release about an important meeting that will be held tomorrow (January 23) but you don't want the information that will be presented at that meeting to reach the public prior to the meeting, you will have to say so on your release. Although it is wise not to send out releases too far in advance of an event, it is also wise to be as timely as possible—which means getting your release to the media outlet beforehand.

Release dates and times can be designated in a number of ways. Regardless of which method you choose, the time and date belongs just slightly below the address block, flush right. The most common designations are as follows:

- *Release with no specific time frame.* This type of release is by far the most widely used and is usually designated by *For Immediate Release.* Other phrases include *For Release on Receipt* or *For Release at Will.* It is unnecessary to add a date to this type of release statement.

- *Release with specific date.* An example of this type of release designation would be *For Release January 23 or Thereafter,* or if you need to be even more specific, *For Release January 23, 10:00 P.M. or Thereafter.* Other options are *Hold for Release, Friday, January 23, 10 A.M.,* or *For Release after 10:00 A.M., Friday, January 23.* This type of release statement could be used, for instance, if you want all the media to carry it at one time, or if the event is occurring at a future date but you want to release the information early.

Datelines

Datelines are used to indicate the point of origin of your news release if, for some reason, that is important. Datelines are important to foreign correspondents to enable readers to appreciate that a story originated at the location where it happened. For public relations practitioners, a dateline may serve the same purpose. It alerts the editor that your release concerns an event either reported from or happening at a certain geographical location. Datelines should be placed immediately preceding the opening of your release proper, on the same line:

> Springfield, OH—Rogers Experimental Plastics Company (REPC) has announced the development of a versatile new plastic widget that has the potential for use in a number of industries from automotives to electronics.

If the city is well known, there is no need to include the name of the state (e.g., New York, Los Angeles). If the name of the city may be popular in a number of states, you would want to designate the state (as in the example above, to differentiate Springfield, Ohio, from Springfield, Oregon, or Springfield, Kentucky, or any number of Springfields). However, if the release is intended for a statewide press only, you can get by with just the name of the city. Also, if any confusion might arise from use of the city name only, include the state (e.g., Moscow, Idaho, or Moscow, Russia).

Exclusives and Specials

If your release is an **exclusive** (intended for only one paper), make sure the editor knows it. Remember that an exclusive can be sent to only one publication. A **special,** by contrast, is a release written in a certain style, intended for a specific publication, but being released elsewhere as well (see Exhibit 7.2). Both designations should be noted immediately below the release information as follows:

> For Immediate Release Exclusive to the *Daily Planet*
> For Release February 24 or Thereafter Special to the *Daily Planet*

PRODUCT NEWS RELEASES

Product publicity often has little or nothing to do with advertising. In its strictest sense, advertising refers only to the purchasing of time or space in which to run a message. Product publicity is not paid for; it is a far more subtle art. You must be able to construct informative passages concerning a given product without actually pitching the product. This is not an easy task. The minute an editor detects a sales pitch, the release gets thrown out.

Most product publicity goes through several stages: product introduction (usually via news releases to trade media), articles in which the product is reviewed after testing (written by the trade publications themselves), and user articles (submitted by the public relations writer focusing on actual users of the new product). This section covers only product introduction releases.

Product releases serve a multitude of purposes, from providing pure information about a single product to publicizing other companies and other products. It is quite common to mention contributing manufacturers in a product release. For example, if you develop a basic plastic that is then used by a leading headphone manufacturer in its product design, it is usually acceptable to mention that company's use

Exhibit 7.2

Exclusives and Specials

Deer Point Development, Inc.
Box 1387
Deer Point, Michigan 72493
Contact: Warren Bailey
Day Phone: (714) 555-6635
Night Phone: (714) 555-1765

For Immediate Release
Special to the Deer Point Sentinel

NEW PLANT TO OPEN IN DEER POINT

A new plant designed to manufacture high tech components for automobiles is scheduled to
be opened in late July according to Eleanor Maston, president of Deer Point Development, Inc.
(DPD). The two-building facility will encompass over 55,000 square feet and be housed on a five-
acre plot near the Doe River. Maston's company was instrumental in the planning, acquisition of
land, and contracting of firms for the construction of the new plant. The plant will be owned and
operated by Auto-Tech, Inc. of Albatross, Maine—a long-time member of the automotive peripher-
als industry.

Maston predicts that over 800 new jobs will be created by the plant's construction. "Auto-Tech
has assured us that they intend to hire the majority of their plant workers from the local community,"
she says. "They plan to bring in only a bare-bones management crew from the outside to begin with,
and train local people from the ground up."

According to Maston, DPD first learned of the scheme last December when Auto-Tech president
Wilson Klatchki contacted her. The New England-based company was seeking to expand into the
high-tech industry and needed a plant close to the major automobile manufacturers in Detroit. Deer
Point seemed like the perfect solution.

"Auto-Tech felt that our proximity to Detroit was ideal," Maston says. "They wanted to be close
without having to build in the city itself."

The site was chosen for its availability and scenic location, according to Maston. "Because high
tech is basically a 'clean' industry, being located near Doe River poses no environmental problems,"
she says.

Construction of the plant began in February and is expected to continue through the summer.

-30-

Exhibit 7.3

Product News Release

Tall Drink of Water, Inc.
435 Lasado Circle
Watertown, NY 10056
Contact: Myrna Hofman
Phone: (121) 555-1222   For Immediate Release

NEW FOUNTAIN DISPENSES

COLD, HOT, AND ICE WATER

Watertown, NY—-A new water fountain that dispenses cold water, hot water, and ice has been marketed by Tall Drink of Water, Inc. (TDW) of Watertown, NY. The new fountain, which already is appearing in offices across the country, operates on an entirely new system for compartmentalizing water supplies.

According to TDW president and co-founder, Willis Reed, the new fountain represents four years of hard work. "We spent a lot of time on this new fountain," he says. "It's a whole new concept in water fountains. We did some initial research on office water consumers and found that they wanted not only cold water, but also hot and iced water as well."

The new fountain uses a system of valves that pass the water from the building plumbing system through the fountain in a series of stages. The incoming water is captured first in a central reservoir. From this central pool, the liquid is siphoned off to the cold water tank. This tank feeds the main drinking spout for normal water needs. Ice is produced in a refrigerated tank located next to the cold water reservoir and dispensed through a separate opening in the side of the fountain. On the opposite side of the fountain is the hot water dispenser, which feeds off a heater tank located above the main reservoir.

"It's the addition of the ice maker that makes our fountain unique," says Reed. "We use a Handy-Ice III manufactured by FREON, Inc. in Asbury Park, NJ," he says. "The Handy Ice III produces ice at a rate that far exceeds anything else on the market today. A number of other manufacturers already make dual purpose fountains, but ours covers the entire range of drinking needs."

Reed indicates that the new fountain will probably be marketed in areas with noticeable seasonal
-more-

shifts. "We expect that areas that have pronounced seasonal temperature fluctuations will have the greatest need for our fountain," he says. "But almost any office where people have different tastes in beverages is a potential market." Reed explains that in any given office environment, 75 percent of the staff will be satisfied with just plain water; however, the other 25 percent will use a fountain for making hot drinks such as tea and soup in the winter and iced drinks in the hot months. He also expects that the very availability of such a fountain will increase its usage.

# # # # #

of your product. There is always the chance that the headphone manufacturer will reciprocate. In fact, many such joint arrangements are formalized when products are publicized. Consider the release in Exhibit 7.3 about a new water cooler.

Can you tell whom the publicity is for? From the address block you learn that the company that manufactures the fountain is sending out the release; however, a second company is also mentioned. The manufacturer of the ice maker is given some free publicity. In many cases, this is a good thing to do. Of course, you don't want to give your competition a helping hand, but it never hurts to help your friends. Often, it's difficult to determine the real publicity point in a product release. If the release in Exhibit 7.3 had been written and distributed by an agency or by FREON, Inc., then the bottom-line publicity would be for the ice maker, through publicity for the fountain. This approach is not uncommon in product publicity and is not usually considered unethical.

Product news releases are arranged slightly differently from other releases. Although they certainly follow the normal inverted pyramid style of decreasing order of importance, they are quite obvious in their inductive approach to the product definition. In other words, product releases usually proceed from a general statement concerning the product (often an announcement that the product is on the market) to specific information about the product's attributes, characteristics, and applications. The end of the release is usually reserved for company background—full name, relationship to parent or subsidiary companies, and branch locations or the location at which the specific product is made. The release in Exhibit 7.4 reflects this pattern of organization. Note that

Exhibit 7.4

Product News Release

Intel Corporation
2200 Mission College Blvd.
P.O. Box 58119
Santa Clara, CA 95052-8119

Intel Corporation
2200 Mission College Blvd.
P.O. Box 58119
Santa Clara, CA 95052-8119

CONTACT: Shannon Johnson
                      (408) 765-7770
                      shannon.johnson@intel.com

News Release

INTEL LAUNCHES INTEL™ CENTRINO ™ MOBILE TECHNOLOGY

New Capabilities Unwire Mobile PCs to Change Where and How
People Compute and Communicate

SANTA CLARA, Calif., March 12, 2003 – Intel Corporation today introduced Intel® Centrino™ mobile technology, integrating wireless capability into a new generation of mobile PCs that will bring business users and consumers greater freedom to connect in new places and in new ways.

Representing Intel's best technology for mobile PCs, Intel Centrino mobile technology includes a new mobile processor, related chipsets and 802.11 wireless network functions that have been optimized, tested and validated to work together. In addition to wireless communications, Intel Centrino mobile technology includes features designed to enable extended battery life, thinner and lighter notebook designs, and outstanding mobile performance.

"Unwiring the PC will change the way people use computers, allowing them to communicate, be productive or be entertained wherever and whenever they want," said Craig Barrett, Intel's chief executive officer. "Our focus on integrating all the elements of mobility allows Intel Centrino mobile technology to deliver an outstanding wireless computing experience and marks the first time we've put a combination of technologies under a single brand. This breakthrough innovation, together with industry-wide investment and WiFi hotspot deployments, brings new computing and communications capabilities to businesses and consumers, adding value to mobile PCs."

Intel Centrino mobile technology-based notebook PCs are available immediately from leading computer makers worldwide. System pricing will start as low as $1,399, comparable to today's mainstream notebooks. Computer shoppers can identify these notebooks by a Centrino brand logo featuring a striking magenta color and the Intel Inside™ mark.

--more--

Intel/Page 2

Accelerating "Hotspot" Deployment Worldwide

Hotspots—locations where users can connect using 802.11 wireless technology—are on the rise, enabling users to be more mobile than ever. According to industry analyst firm IDC, there will be more than 118,000 hotspots worldwide by 2005.**

Using truly mobile notebook computers can change the way people live. With notebooks based on Intel Centrino mobile technology, a business traveler can check office email or read the hometown newspaper online while waiting for a flight at the airport, and still have battery life left to watch a DVD movie on the plane ride home. A real estate agent can check the latest listings wirelessly while dining with prospective home-buyers. A financial planner can check the market and activate client orders while at a seminar without compromising on the performance necessary to run the most demanding office applications. Students can register for next semester's classes or seek a part-time job from the college library, all on a sleek, light-weight system that won't drag them down.

As part of the introduction of Intel Centrino mobile technology, Intel has been working with leading wireless network service providers, hotels, airports, retail and restaurant chains worldwide to accelerate deployment and increase awareness of wireless public hotspots. In addition to marketing and promotional activities, Intel developed the Wireless Verification Program which includes engineering and testing of Intel Centrino mobile technology with various access point devices, software combinations, hotspot locations and wireless service providers to verify they are compatible, further enhancing the end user's wireless experience. Intel's efforts worldwide have already resulted in thousands of verified hotspots. The company expects to verify more than 10,000 by the end of the year.

Intel has also created a standardized worldwide Wireless Identifier Program that includes signs to help users identify where they can connect wirelessly. The program informs users that a particular service provider's network has been verified with Intel Centrino mobile technology.

In addition, the company last year created a $150 million fund to invest in companies that are helping to expand and accelerate the infrastructure and capabilities required to make wireless computing ubiquitous.

Intel, the world's largest chipmaker, is also a leading manufacturer of computer, networking and communications products. Additional information about Intel is available at www.intel.com/pressroom.

--more--

(continued)

(continued)

Intel/Page 3

Intel, Intel Centrino, Pentium, SpeedStep technology are trademarks or registered trademarks of Intel Corporation or its subsidiaries in the United States and other countries. Other names and brands may be claimed as the property of others.
*For more information on Intel's mobile performance, visit: www.intel.com/performance
**IDC, 2003.
****Note: Important Information: Wireless connectivity and some features may require you to purchase additional software, services or external hardware. Availability of public wireless LAN access points limited. System performance measured by MobileMark* 2002. System performance, battery life, wireless performance and functionality will vary depending on your specific hardware and software configurations. See http://www.intel.com/products/centrino/more_info for more information.

--30 –

Intel, like many other product manufacturers, frequently uses footnotes to explain difficult concepts, provide additional information sources, and confirm trademarked names.

A number of industries don't use the inverted pyramid style for news releases. These industries typically use a more feature-oriented style, usually owing to the media outlets to which they typically send the releases, and also because of the nature of the industries themselves. For example, the clothing and fashion industry has developed a features-oriented media. So have the food and beverage industry and the entertainment industry. News releases produced for these and some other industries will usually be constructed more like features.

Some interesting hybrids are born of a combination of industries. For example, the release in Exhibit 7.5 is from computer industry giant Intel, but it is targeted to a different type of audience than they usually focus on. It could be seen as a combination of both product and feature release. Exhibit 7.6 is the first page of an Intel release that is even more feature oriented in its lead.

Exhibit 7.5

Feature-oriented Release

Intel Corporation
2200 Mission College Blvd.
P.O. Box 58119
Santa Clara, CA 95052-8119

News Release

CONTACT: Seth Walker
            (503) 264-2190
            seth.walker@intel.com

INTEL GOES INSIDE HOLLYWOOD FOR A NEW GENERATION OF FILMMAKING

Visual Effects Leader Industrial Light & Magic
Using Intel Technology at the Core of its Desktop Workstations

SANTA CLARA, Calif., July 22, 2002 – Hollywood has found an unlikely ally in its efforts to lower costs in the increasingly complex world of digital filmmaking: Intel Corporation.

Industrial Light & Magic* (ILM), a division of Lucas Digital Ltd. LLC, today revealed its latest Intel technology deployment of 600 Pentium® 4 processor-based animation workstations. ILM is one of many studios adopting Intel technology to assist with the future of filmmaking.

"The visual effects industry has traditionally been a land of proprietary systems and software," said Cliff Plumer, ILM's chief technology officer. "At ILM, we're increasingly using Intel-based systems to expand our range of software choices for animation and compositing. In fact, having Intel at the core of our desktop systems provides greater quality and productivity because the technology can handle more iterations with greater frequency. We can now run any operating system we want."

ILM began using Intel-based systems on "Star Wars: Episode II -- Attack of the Clones," and then with "Men in Black II" and "Minority Report." They are currently employed in the development of "Star Wars: Episode III," "Harry Potter and the Chamber of Secrets," "The Hulk" and "Terminator 3: The Rise of the Machines."

-- more --

(continued)

(continued)

Intel/Page 2

Use of Intel technology is on a rapid rise in Hollywood because of the convergence of four key factors. First, the performance of Intel-based systems over the past two years has consistently surpassed that of proprietary systems, while system costs have come down. This has led to significant savings for studios. Next, major studios are increasingly outsourcing the rendering of digital effects to "render farms" that use large banks of small servers, and in that model Intel's high-volume, high-performance, low-cost, any-software approach makes sense. In addition, studios are now using a variety of operating systems, and Intel technology provides them the most flexibility. Finally, the results of Intel's multi-year effort to make movie software more Intel-friendly has borne fruit. Applications from such companies as Adobe*, Alias/Wavefront*, Digital Domain*, Discreet*, Macromedia* and Softimage* have reached critical mass.

Large studios are now using or have recently used Intel technology to help create some of Hollywood's leading movies. DreamWorks*, which used Intel-based systems in the Academy Award*-winning "Shrek" and recent hit "Spirit: Stallion of the Cimarron," continues to expand its Intel-based work, and is now testing Itanium® 2-based systems. Weta Digital Ltd.* recently announced it is using hundreds of Intel® Xeon™ processor-based servers for its work on the "Lord of the Rings" trilogy. The first movie of the trilogy, "The Lord of the Rings: The Fellowship of the Rings," won four Academy Awards, including Best Visual Effects. Walt Disney Pictures* recently disclosed plans to use Intel-based Hewlett-Packard* workstations and data-serving computers for work in its animation division. Digital Revelations, a Hollywood studio owned by actor Morgan Freeman, is utilizing mostly Intel Architecture in its development of "Rendezvous with Rama," scheduled for release in 2003. Sony Pictures Imageworks recently used more than 600 Intel processors in creating visual effects and animation for the recent "Spider-Man" blockbuster and "Stuart Little 2," in addition to evaluating Intel® Itanium®-based systems.

"Imageworks chose Intel-based systems for its newest server farm due to the open, scalable nature of the technology and its superior price-performance," said George Joblove, vice president of technology, Sony Pictures Imageworks.

Intel, the world's largest chip maker, is also a leading manufacturer of computer, networking and communications products. Additional information about Intel is available at www.intel.com/pressroom.

-- 30 --

Intel, Intel Xeon, Pentium and Itanium are trademarks or registered trademarks of Intel Corporation or its subsidiaries in the United States and other countries
* Other names and brands may be claimed as the property of others.

Exhibit 7.6

Feature-oriented Release Lead

Intel Corporation
2200 Mission College Blvd.
P.O. Box 58119
Santa Clara, CA 95052-8119

Feature Release

CONTACT: Stephen Bonsignore
GCI Group
(212) 537-8094
HYPERLINK: sbonsignore@gcigroup.com

Claudine Mangano
Intel Corporation
(408) 765-0146
claudine.a.mangano@intel.com

HOME MOVIES GET THE STAR TREATMENT
Powerful PCs Help Families Create, Enhance and Preserve Home Movie Memories

NEW YORK, Dec. 2001 – Consumers may not realize that their VHS and 8mm home movies can degrade to the point of being unusable within 15 years.[1] Ralph Bond knows this only too well.

When Bond watched a 16-year-old VHS videotape of his children's first steps, he was shocked – not by how much they had grown, but at how close he had come to forever losing a precious video memory.

Damaged by the passing of time, the tape's crispness was gone, a dark band was creeping from the edge of each frame to the center of the action, and a pink hue tinted the true colors of the entire tape. Bond, consumer education manager at Intel Corporation, learned from personal experience – and just in time.

Home Movie, Meet the PC

The key to preserving precious home movies is to make them digital, and a powerful personal computer is an invaluable tool to ensure that every special moment is captured in time – not destroyed by it.

"Powerful home PCs coupled with a digital camcorder, new software applications and CD or DVD recorders give consumers a gateway to creative freedom and fun with their home movies," Bond said. "Whether it is creating new home movies or preserving memories filmed many years ago, digital video is a hot application for PC users and all the necessary tools are widely available."

-- more --

WRITING NEWS RELEASES FOR BROADCAST

Radio is meant to be heard, and television is made to be seen and heard. That means you have to write for the ear or for the ear and eye. Simplification is the key to broadcast writing. Because it is harder to absorb the spoken word than the written word, concepts need to be pared down to the bare bones. Sentences must be shorter, speech more colloquial, and complex issues distilled to their essence. One of the major advantages of using broadcast media is repeatability: Listeners may hear or see a message many times in the course of a single day or a single week. Even so, you must learn to write as though your audience will hear or see your message only one time.

Consider the differences between the following leads written for two different releases: one meant for print, the other for radio.

Print

INDIANAPOLIS, June 6—Francis Langly, former Director of Research and Development for Associated Products Corporation (APC), today received the American Chemical Society's (ACS) Goodyear Medal—ACS's most prestigious award—for his work in the field of specialty elastomers.

Radio

At an awards luncheon in Indianapolis today, a Wilmington native received the highest honor of the American Chemical Society. The prestigious Goodyear Medal—awarded for work in the field of specialty elastomers—went to Francis Langly, former Director of Research and Development for Associated Products Corporation.

Although both releases are approximately the same length, noticeable differences exist that raise some interesting questions:

- Why doesn't the broadcast release start with a dateline?
- Why not use the abbreviations ACS and APC in the broadcast release?
- What is the reason for beginning the broadcast release with the location rather than the name, as in the print release?

Datelines are not needed in broadcast releases because they won't be read. The point of origin usually becomes clear through the narrative. Abbreviations are too confusing when heard on the air. It is always advisable to use the entire name, unless the abbreviation has become commonplace usage. Finally, beginning with location in broadcast helps set the scene. This approach is peculiar to broadcasting and is a carryover from drama, in which a scene is set prior to any dialogue.

Use the medium to your advantage. If you are using radio, set the scene first, then populate it with real people and easy-to-understand facts. Remember, a news release for radio or television is just that—news. It is intended for the same purpose as a print news release—to be used as news. The closer to acceptable news style it is, the better your chances of getting it broadcast. Prepare your releases for broadcast media using the same format you would use for a print release. Exhibit 7.7 illustrates a broadcast release.

Exhibit 7.7

Broadcast Release

Society for Needy Children

4240 Welxton Avenue

Newhope, MN 78940

Contact: Lucille Bevard

Day Phone: 555-8743

Night Phone: 555-9745

For Immediate Release

A little girl stood for the first time today to receive a new teddy bear and a check for $75,000 from the Society for Needy Children. Eight-year-old Mary Patterson accepted the check on behalf of the children at the St. Mary Martha's Children's Hospital. The money represents the culmination of a year-long fund-raising drive by the Society.

The money is earmarked for a new ward to be devoted exclusively to the treatment of crippling diseases in children. One of the first beneficiaries will undoubtedly be little Mary, who has been disabled by congenital arthritis since birth. Along with her new teddy bear, Mary and the other children at the hospital will be using a new physical therapy center donated through a matching grant from the Friends of St. Mary Martha's.

Hospital Administrator Lois Shelcroft says that the check and the new therapy center are just the first step, and that the Society for Needy Children has promised to continue their fundraising efforts on the hospital's behalf in the coming year. Society spokesperson Jane Alexander says that the next fund-raising drive, scheduled to begin in September, will provide funding for a new lab.

# # # # #

After reading the release in Exhibit 7.7, consider these questions:

- Why is paraphrase used instead of direct quotation in this release?
- Does the lead establish a sense of place prior to coming to the point?
- Can you locate all the elements of a lead within the release?
- Are they where they should be in order of importance?
- If you were a news announcer, what additional information would you want to have before you ran this story?

Remember, no matter what the type of news release, it is still information you will lose control over once it is sent out to the media. They are your primary audience. You must learn to write for them first. To the extent that you do this, your releases will have a greater chance of reaching any other audience.

BACKGROUNDERS

Backgrounders are in-depth information pieces. As the name implies, they provide background information for anyone wishing it—reporters, ad copywriters, speechwriters, and editors. Backgrounders are almost always prepared by the public relations staff. A good backgrounder is comprehensive yet concise. It should never be used to espouse company policy or philosophy—that is reserved for controlled media, such as ads and editorials.

Backgrounders frequently accompany news releases in press kits. They usually supply enough information to fill in any gaps left by the release. Often, they are just insurance against getting called in the middle of the night by a reporter who is editing your news release and in need of some background. Other times, they are important sales pieces, setting up a historical need for a new product.

To make a backgrounder comprehensive, the public relations writer must research as many sources as possible, including old articles, brochures, reports, news releases, and materials published outside the organization. Backgrounders can also benefit from personal interviews. As with news releases, backgrounders are more readable if they contain firsthand information.

A backgrounder should begin with a statement of the issue being addressed. Because it is not a news story or news release, it need not be presented as a lead nor need it follow the inverted pyramid style. Most backgrounders, however, do follow a basic pattern:

1. Open with a concise statement of the issue or subject on which the accompanying news release is based. Try to make it as interesting as possible. This opening statement should lead logically into the next section.
2. Follow the opening with a historical overview of the issue. You should trace its evolution—how it came to be—and the major events leading up to it. It is

permissible here to use outside information. For instance, if you were writing a backgrounder on a new surgical technique, you would want to trace briefly the history of the technique's development and tie this in with information on techniques that had been used in the past. It is advisable to name your sources in the body of the text when appropriate. Readers of backgrounders want to know where you got your information.

3. **Work your way to the present.** This is the meat of your backgrounder. You want to explain the issue you opened with and its significance. Be factual. Remember, a backgrounder is an information piece, not an advertisement or the place to sell your company's philosophy.

4. Present the implications of the issue being discussed and point the direction for future applications. Even though a backgrounder is a public relations piece, it needs to be carefully couched in fact-based information.

5. **Use subheads where appropriate.** Subheads negate the need for elaborate transitions and allow you to order your information logically. Subheads need to be carefully chosen and should contribute to understanding.

6. Most backgrounders are four or five pages in length. Let your information dictate your length; however, don't become long winded or pad your document. Editors will recognize fluff immediately. The object of a backgrounder is to provide information and answer anticipated questions, nothing more.

The backgrounder in Exhibit 7.8 was used as an accompanying piece to a news release touting the advantages of a fire-resistant latex foam for use in upholstered furniture and mattresses. After you have read it, consider the following questions:

- How does it follow the recommendations for writing a backgrounder?
- How does it differ?
- Does it trace the history of the issue adequately?
- Does it bring the reader up to the present and cover the current status of the issue?

Can you tell from reading this backgrounder that it was meant to sell a product? Probably not, unless you knew in advance that it was part of a product-related press kit. The object of a backgrounder is to provide background, not to sell anything. In this particular backgrounder, information is provided concerning fire safety and the need for purchasers of upholstered furniture to be aware of the dangers of fire.

The next step is to present readers with a suggested action. This can, and often does, come in the accompanying product news release. Thus, the trick to writing backgrounders is to make them relate to your subject without actually pushing your product, philosophy, or service.

Exhibit 7.8

Backgrounder

CONTENTS, NOT STRUCTURE, POSE THE MOST FIRE HAZARDS

Losses to fires are costing billions of dollars and claiming thousands of lives each year in the United States. The National Fire Protection Association handbook states: "Fire resistive construction is an important life-safety measure. However, severe fires may occur in the contents of fire resistive buildings, and highly combustible decorations and interior finish materials may more than offset the value of noncombustible structurals." In fact, of all the contents common to residential, commercial, and institutional occupancies, the most often underestimated is the hazard from burning upholstered chairs and mattresses.

Although the many desirable features of a fire resistive building cannot be overlooked, there is no such thing as a "fireproof" building. Regardless of the construction type, there are always combustibles within the building. Generally, contents fires present a greater life safety hazard to building occupants than the eventual ignition of the structure. In fact, the cause and early stages of fires are related to the building contents and interior finish materials and not the structure.

No matter what the construction type, the contents fire must be controlled in order to achieve life safety. A parallel may be drawn between a contents fire in a fire resistive building and a fire in a furnace. The contents are the fuel and the building is the furnace.

Statistics Show Furniture Fires on the Rise

The Consumer Products Safety Commission recently stated that last year there were about 62,000 bedding fires which caused 930 fatalities. Another 35,000 fires in upholstered furniture took 1,400 lives, prompting the Commission to declare that these materials are the "biggest killer of all the products under the jurisdiction of the agency."

The National Bureau of Standards had earlier reported that mattresses, bedding, and upholstered furniture were involved in 45 percent of the fatal fires they reviewed where the materials first ignited could be identified. They concluded that "any inroads that can be made into the furniture problem promises greater fire-death reduction than any other type of strategy."

Building Design Not the Answer

As for building design, recent well-publicized fires have resulted in new provisions to building fire codes; however, over 90 percent of the buildings that will be in use in the year 2000 have already been built. Reliance on these new fire codes for personal safety may, in fact, be unwarranted.

Although building design and fire protection devices are important, they do not guarantee the

-more-

safety of the occupants. Many fires develop too rapidly for fire systems, such as sprinklers, to control. Fires can spread past a sprinkler head to another area before the sprinkler head operates. Another fire might smolder for hours, producing deadly smoke and gases but not enough heat to cause operation for the sprinkler system. In addition, property loss is most closely related to fire-resistant building materials which would have to be incorporated into future structures. Building contents most strongly affect human safety.

Fire Reduction Not Yet a Reality

A decade ago, the National Commission on Fire Prevention and Control reported that fire was a major national problem, ranking between crime and product safety in annual cost. They were appalled to find "that the richest nation in the world leads all the major industrialized countries in per capita deaths and property loss from fire." The efforts of this commission focused attention on fires and resulted in the establishment of a goal to reduce the nation's fire losses by 50 percent in the next decade. That goal has not be realized.

Recent fire loss data from the National Fire Prevention Association suggests that we have performed poorly in our efforts to reduce the nation's fire losses. Multiple death fires, killing three or more people, have increased 70 percent in the past decade. In fact, fatalities in this group rose 37 percent between 1972 and 1980, and fires in this category are increasing at an average rate of 7.5 percent a year.

The estimated property loss from just building fires in the United States last year was about $6 billion, an increase of almost 7 percent from the year before. Further analysis of the estimate for fire loss data this year shows that:

— Educational facilities lost $184 million, an increase of 82.2 percent over last year's figures.

— Institutional facilities lost $38 million, up 52 percent.

— Areas of public assembly lost $356 million, up 9.2 percent.

— And residential occupancies, such as hotels, motels, and apartments, lost $3.3 billion, up 7.1 percent from last year.

Judging from this data, it is apparent that the goal of reducing fire losses by 50 percent has not been met. In fact, fire losses are steadily increasing in most cases. Why? In answering this question,

(continued)

(continued)

---

some important points must be taken into consideration:

— Contents may more than offset the value of noncombustible building materials, and

— The flammability properties of the contents are critical to life safety.

Although most new buildings are constructed in accordance with a national building code such as the National Fire Protection Agency (NFPA) 101 Life Safety Code or a similar code, no national code regulates upholstered seating or mattresses. And although a Federal mattress flammability standard exists, its effectiveness has been questioned by both the Consumer Products Safety Commission and the National Bureau of Standards. As a result, a concrete fortress could be built according to code and filled with furniture that burns like gasoline. Larger buildings can contain tons of such furniture.

The Burden of Safety Is on the Buyer

In the absence of codes specifically meant for furniture, the burden of safety falls on the person selecting furniture for a residence, commercial structure, or installation. Greater care must be taken to select the most fire-resistant furniture available for a particular need. In judging these needs, the hazards to which the furniture might be exposed should be considered, such as the likelihood of cigarette burns, open flames, proximity of fuel or other combustibles, and population density. For example, in areas with a high level of vandalism, materials with a good open flame resistance might be needed, while furniture prone to accidental ignition may only need to be cigarette resistant.

The ultimate test of any furniture is, of course, how it will perform in an actual fire. It is obvious that fire-resistant structures are not enough to ensure life safety. If the nation's fire losses are to be reduced, then the potential hazards of furnishings must be considered.

-end-

FACT SHEETS

Fact sheets contain just that—facts—and nothing more. If you have a lot of figures, for example, or a few charts that help explain your topic more easily, or simply a few itemized points you want to make, then a fact sheet is the form to use. A fact sheet is usually only one page, sometimes printed on both sides. It should elaborate on already presented information, such as a news release, and not merely repeat what has already been said.

For example, if you have written a news release about the relocation of a facility to a new site, the news release undoubtedly discloses the newsworthiness of the event with particulars on when the move is to take place, for what reasons,

Exhibit 7.9

Fact Sheet

University of Northern Washington

Museum of Natural History Fact Sheet

The University of Northern Washington Museum of Natural History will move into a new building on the east side of campus by March of 1996. The museum is being relocated as part of the university's $45 million project to expand and modernize its science facilities.

Future Location:
On the northwest end of a university-owned parking lot on East 23rd Avenue, between Renton and Box Streets. The parking lot is being redesigned so that no parking spaces will be lost as a result of the new building.

Construction timeline:
Five months, beginning in late summer.

Cost:
$635,000

Fund-raising goal:
$150,000 to complete and equip the building.

Balance left to be raised by mid-August:
$72,500

Pledges to date: $77,000

- $32,500 from former UNW football coach Arlyss Thompson to build the storage area for the geology collection.
- $22,500 on a one-to-two challenge match pledged by Thompson for construction costs.
- $22,500 from Seattle philanthropist Frazier Crane, to match half of the Thompson challenge, on the condition that the rest of the money be raised from other sources.

Other funding sources:
$485,000 allocated by the university from the $8.1 million Department of Energy grant for the first phase of the capital construction program to build modern science facilities on campus.

Square feet:
11,000 with a 9,100 square-foot courtyard. Total square footage of existing building is 10,689.

Special features:
Air-conditioned and climate-controlled to protect the highly fragile collections.

Advantages:
Improved public access and increased public parking.

#

2900 Provender Drive • Alderdale, Washington 99304 • (206) 345-8749

and the like. A fact sheet, however, can elaborate in interesting ways. For example, you might want to itemize costs, or break out major donations made toward the move, or elaborate on size of facility with square foot comparisons.

Take a look at Exhibits 7.9 and 7.10. These fact sheets are slightly different, but each contributes to forming a more complete story. The first fills in the numbers on a museum move, and the second supports a product press kit for a line of vitamins.

Exhibit 7.10

Fact Sheet

VITAMIX **VITALSTATS**

Vitamix International
P.O. Box 9234
Westphalen, Ohio 76456

Vitamix Vital Statistics

- About 2/3 of U.S. households reported making dietary changes in the past survey year for reasons of health or nutrition. Of these, 43% cited weight control as the primary reason for the changes.

- 53% of the adult population surveyed have tried to control weight during the past year by "staying away from fattening foods and/or eating less"—up from 48% the year before.

- 18% of the adult population surveyed this year reported the use of "low-fat" food/beverage options as part of weight control strategy.

Population Overweight/Obese

- According to the data collected in the most recent Health and Weight Loss Survey (HWLS), 32% of the men and 36% of the women aged 20-27 were 10 percent or more above their desirable weight.

- 14% of the men and 24% of the women were 20 percent or more above their desirable weight in the same HWLS survey.

- 7 million Americans are classified as extremely obese.

- 30% of all males and 49% of all females surveyed by the National Center for Vital Statistics said they considered themselves overweight.

- More than half of those surveyed in a recent Aerobic 4 National Fitness Survey said "it would be beneficial to lose weight."

Weight Control Diets

- At any given time, at least 20% of the population are on some kind of weight-loss diet.

- 33% of those surveyed in the Aerobic 4 National Fitness Survey said they are dieting either to lose or maintain weight.

- 56% of women aged 25-34 said they were dieting in a recent Nielsen Survey.

# # # # #

KEY TERMS

news release	inverted pyramid style	exclusive
publicity release	lead	special
product release	summary lead	backgrounder
financial release	delayed lead	fact sheet
publicity	attribution	
angle	dateline	

EXERCISES

1. Tape a television talk show. As you view the tape, take notes of the answers of the person being interviewed. Write up your "quotes." Watch the tape again, comparing the actual answers to your cited quotes. Note the differences.

2. Pick a news story from your local paper. Rewrite the lead of the story stressing as many different facets of the story as possible. Turn in both the original story and your leads. Work up each lead and following paragraph ideas using the News Release Outline Form in Exhibit 7.11.

3. Pick a product that interests you. Write a product news release targeted to a trade publication in that industry outlining the virtues of your product in a nonadvertising approach. Use a media directory such as *Standard Rate and Data Service* or go to the library or local newsstand and pick out a target publication. Be prepared to explain why your release shouldn't be considered advertising.

4. Assume you are writing a news release on yourself highlighting a recent accomplishment. It can be on literally anything. Where would you place the release? Think of where you've been and what you've done and what potential media sources serve those locations. Make a media list complete with addresses. Devise a separate lead for each outlet.

5. Locate a product-oriented feature story from a mass consumer magazine or trade publication. Go over the story carefully and pull out items that relate only to pure information about the product and develop an outline for a product backgrounder based on this information. What further information would you need to work up a complete backgrounder on the product?

Exhibit 7.11

News Release Outline Form

News Release Outline Form

Objective of Release: _____

_____

Lead:

_____
_____
_____
_____

Paragraph 1 (Main Idea):

_____

Paragraph 2 (Main Idea):

_____

Paragraph 3 (Main Idea):

_____

Paragraph 4 (Main Idea):

_____

Paragraph 5 (Main Idea):

_____

CHAPTER

8

Annual Reports and Social Responsibility Reports

In this chapter you will learn:

- What an annual report is and who its audiences are.
- The contents of a typical annual report.
- How to write for an annual report.
- What a not-for-profit annual report is and how it differs from a corporate annual report.

- The contents of a typical not-for-profit annual report.
- The presentation of both types of annual reports.
- How to judge your annual report.
- What a social responsibility report is and why they are produced.
- Guidelines for producing a social responsibility report.

ANNUAL REPORTS

Annual reports are probably the least read of all house publications. Recent research indicates that about half the stockholders who receive them spend less than 10 minutes looking at them. And 15 percent of all stock analysts don't read them at all. Nonetheless, over 10,000 U.S. corporations are required to produce and issue annual reports. Closer to 50,000 reports may be produced annually because a great many not-for-profits, public agencies, universities, and countless other organizations also produce them, even though they're not required to do so (see Exhibit 8.1).

The history of the annual report dates from the Securities Exchange Act of 1934, which requires publicly traded companies to provide their investors with a yearly financial statement. This law also requires that an annual report be delivered to stockholders no later than 15 days before the annual meeting. Quarterly reports also have to be filed.

Beginning in 1980, the Securities and Exchange Commission (SEC) mandated that additional information be added, including financial data covering the past five years and an expanded discussion and analysis of the company's financial condition. It's not surprising, then, that annual reports increase in size and complexity each year—so much so, in fact, that a few years ago General Motors asked the SEC to allow them and other companies to develop and file an abbreviated, summary annual report.

In 1987, the SEC ruled that companies could publish such a report as long as they included all of the elements required by law as either appendices to the abbreviated report or in another formal document, such as the already required Form 10-K. Critics worry that this new flexibility allows companies to selectively cut bad news from their most visible communication vehicle. They argue that most stockholders will read only the annual report, believing it complete. Although some companies have experimented with the summary annual report, at this writing, most companies still produce the lengthy report already familiar to stockholders.

These days, most large corporations, and many small ones, have their own Web sites on the Internet. Most of these sites include links to their annual reports. However, many of these abbreviated reports include only what the company considers to be important sections (generally the president's letter and some summary tables). It appears that hard-copy annual reports are still the best way to get a complete financial picture of an organization, at least for the time being.

Besides the annual report, companies issue several other financial reports:

- *Quarterly reports.* These reports are similar to annual reports except that the former are issued every three months and are less comprehensive.
- *10-K Reports.* Larger firms issue 10-K reports that are more detailed than annual reports. A 10-K report provides detailed information about divisions and subdivisions of the company. These reports are sent to stockholders only by request.

shareholder's name, and all who hold stock are commonly allowed to vote on is-sues affecting the corporation whose stock they hold. A corporation doesn't have to issue stock. In fact, many small and large companies are privately owned and do not issue stock. Issuing stock allows a corporation to diversify and build its base of capital. Once stock is issued, the company is considered to be publicly traded; that is, anyone wishing to purchase stock may do so.

Typically, a share allows the owner one vote for each share owned and entitles the owner to a share of the assets of the company in the form of dividends or other distributions. The more stock a shareholder owns, the more voting power he or she has and the greater the share of assets (and losses). The corporate an-nual report is the one place most shareholders turn to for information on their company and its stock.

Annual Report Contents

No two annual reports are alike; however, the SEC does require certain elements to be present, including the following:

- Certified financial statements for the previous two years
- An explanation of any difference between these financial statements and statements filed in another form with the SEC
- A summary management analysis of operations for the past five years
- Identification of the company directors' principal occupations
- Stock market and dividend information for the past two years
- Notice of Form 10-K availability
- A brief description of both business and line of business
- Any material differences from established accounting principles reflected in the financial statements
- Supplementary inflation accounting

The form this information takes is what makes annual reports different from each other. To accommodate the SEC guidelines, annual reports have developed certain standard mechanisms for housing the required information:

- A description of the company, including its name, address (headquarters, subsidiaries, and plant sites), its overall business, and a summary of its opera-tions, usually in both narrative and numerical form.
- A letter to stockholders including an account of the past year's achievements, an overview of the industry environment and pertinent markets, and a dis-cussion of future business and investment strategies.
- A financial review as set forth by SEC regulations listed above.
- An explanation and analysis of the financial review that outlines the factors influencing the financial picture over the past year.

- A narrative report covering anything from a discussion of subsidiaries to details on corporate philanthropy. Many companies use the annual report as a forum in which to discuss social issues or beat their own public relations drum, as it is one of the best publicity tools available.

According to the Annual Reports Library in San Francisco, annual reports usually have nine, distinct sections. Most are required.

1. *Chairman of the board letter.* Within the first five pages. Covers changing developments, goals achieved (or missed), actions taken, and industry conditions. One or two pages maximum.

2. *Sales and marketing.* Closest to the front. Usually written by the marketing department. Describes where the company sells and where it makes most of its money. The scope of lines, divisions, and operations should be clear.

3. *Ten-year summary of financial figures.* Front of report is better. Usually provided by the chief financial officer (CFO).

4. *Management discussion and analysis.* Before financial statements. Written by CFO. Discusses significant trends over past two years.

5. *Certified public accountant's (CPA) opinion letter.* Either before or after financial statements. Written by certified public accounting firm.

6. *Financial statements.* Provided by CFO or chief accounting officer.

7. *Subsidiaries, brands, and addresses.* Last few pages. Usually provided by legal department.

8. *List of directors and officers.* Last or second to last page. Usually provided by corporate secretary.

9. *Stock price.* Analysts want this. Best to have near front of report. Usually provided by corporate secretary. Should contain where traded, stock symbol, high/low history, and price and dividend trends over time.

Writing for Annual Reports

There are generally two ways to produce an annual report: You can write it in house, or you can farm it out to an agency. Frankly, agencies—including those that specialize in annual reports—produce the bulk of these publications. However, with the advent of desktop publishing, more organizations are considering in-house writing and production.

No matter who writes it, the bulk of an annual report is taken up with tables, charts, and flashy photographs. In fact, critics charge, annual reports often try too hard (and too blatantly) to sweeten a bitter financial pill with a lot of pretty sugar coating. Many annual reports stand guilty of this charge, but countless others perform a valuable informational service to shareholders and members. In fact, because they are good message vehicles, a great many not-for-profit organizations are now producing annual reports even though they don't have to (see p. 141). The modern annual report has become a major tool in any organization's public relations arsenal.

Writers produce only a small portion of the annual report, but it includes the sections most often read by shareholders: the president's letter and the narrative report.

The President's Letter

Some really awful president's letters can be found in annual reports. The reason cited most often for this quality problem is the SEC guidelines telling them what they have to talk about. Fortunately, these guidelines don't tell writers how to talk about what they have to talk about. There is no reason these letters have to be crashingly dull, wordy, and confusing. What impresses the everyday shareholder is honesty, a straightforward writing style, and no fluff.

The following examples opt for the numbers-up-front approach in the mistaken belief that readers want it that way:

[Company name] expanded its financial base in 2004 and substantially increased the number of property interests in its investment portfolio. A $47 million common stock offering, completed in June, plus a $40 million public offering of mortgage notes and common stock purchase warrants in December 2004 were among the financial resources that permitted [company name] to increase the number of its property interests to 191 by adding 99 real estate investments during the year.

The year 2004 was a successful one for [company name]. Net income was up substantially, over 27 percent greater than 2003's results, to a record $305.6 million, as the economy moved into a strong recovery. On a per-share basis, our earnings were $9.50, an increase of 13 percent, reflecting both the issuance of additional common stock during this past year, as well as the preferred stock issued during 2004.

The next example at least begins with an interesting image of a "corporate renaissance":

We are in the midst of a corporate renaissance, and 2004 was a strong reflection of the growth, diversification, and enthusiasm that typifies [company name].

We had a record performance in 2004 in many areas. For the first time, net income exceeded $1 billion, at $1.2 billion. Sales reached an all-time high of $13.4 billion—up more than $2 billion from the 2003 level. The list of records also included earnings per share at $6.47; and operating income, which at $2.3 billion was up 69 percent from the previous record.

And what about bad news? This letter buries it under a barrage of industry buzzwords such as *maximizing profitability:*

[Company name] continued its strategy of maximizing profitability in basic markets and businesses in 2004. All these areas of the Corporation had a truly excellent year. Unfortunately, the property and casualty reinsurance lines of the Insurance Group, which are not a part of our basic long-term strategy, incurred continuing heavy losses, significantly lowering our overall profitability. Reflecting this impact, [company name]'s consolidated net income of $106.3 million was about flat with 2003, although earnings per share increased marginally to $4.02 from $3.96 reflecting a slightly reduced number of common shares outstanding.

Finally, here's a letter that approaches a mixed year with an interesting, number-free narrative approach:

> External forces produce both opportunities and challenges—and 2004 had its share of both for [company name] and its businesses.
> During the year, some of the external forces facing our four business segments served to expand revenues and growth. Others had a dampening effect, calling for effective counter-measures.
> The mix of forces at work included . . . [bulleted list follows]
> We worked to take advantage of those external forces that offered opportunities, and to overcome the challenges posed by others.

If you can write the letter yourself, and simply route it for the president's approval, you'll get better results than you would if the president drafted it. When you do it yourself, keep in mind a few points. Because most of the rest of the report is numbers, it's best to keep numbers in the letter to a minimum. Keep your letter short, and keep its language friendly and simple. This way, you'll be able to cover the SEC bases without boring your readers.

The Narrative Report

The body of the annual report is your only chance to write anything without numbers—or, at least, with a minimum of numbers. Here is where you get to describe the company, its operations, its people (a favorite focus of many reports), and its future in detail. The only problem is one of space. Remember, you can't leave out anything required by the SEC. And you don't want to leave out anything that makes your company look good.

One of the best ways to decide on content is to have the people in charge of the various divisions or subsidiaries submit brief lists of the year's highlights from their down-in-the-trenches perspective. Make your needs known in plenty of time to get responses from your contacts. And leave the final compiling and writing to one person so that the entire report has a single style.

A quick word about that style. Depending on a company's image, the style of an annual report can vary greatly. Some are formal to the point of being stiff. Others are too informal and leave shareholders with a feeling that the company is being loosely run. The best and most appropriate style is somewhere in the middle.

As with the president's letter, you don't have to begin your narrative report with numbers. In fact, it benefits greatly from a little introduction. There is no reason why annual reports have to be boring reading. The following introductions to the narrative report sections of two different annual reports are fairly good examples of what can be done to lend a modicum of interest to an otherwise often dull subject:

> To come up with a winner in global competition, you have to provide the highest quality . . . the greatest number of choices and the most innovative solutions to a customer's needs, regardless of location.
> In meeting that challenge, [company name] uses a system of "global networking": to choreograph its worldwide response by product, function, and geographic area. Networking teams enable [company name] to draw upon its resources

around the world and to respond quickly no matter where customers may be headquartered.

There are many ways to define shareholder value . . . and many ways that companies strive to create it. But at [company name], the strategy has been three-pronged:

- Utilizing existing resources within the company to diversify into four separate businesses.
- Acting on opportunities to build and strengthen these existing businesses.
- Keeping abreast of trends that hold promise for the future.

Use numbers to augment your narrative—don't let numbers be the entire focus. Although annual reports are intended to spell out a company's financial environment, they communicate more often with average people than with financial analysts. Financial analysts won't rely on an annual report as their sole information source. Many shareholders will, so it has to be written in a style they will understand.

Striking just the right tone, in both writing and design, is the most important ingredient in producing an annual report. In fact, so much depends on design that many annual reports emphasize form at the expense of function.

Design for design's sake is still common. Be careful not to let the report's look overpower the written information. Ideally, form and function should work together to achieve a real sense of the company that readers care enough to own.

These days, it's quite common for annual reports to appear online; however, most are still presented in PDF format, preserving the look of the original print publication. For a comprehensive look at what's available online, take a look at http://www.reportgallery.com.

The Not-for-Profit Annual Report

Increasingly, annual reports are being produced by organizations other than publicly traded corporations. The overriding reason is that stakeholders always benefit from seeing where their money is being spent or how their efforts are being rewarded. A donor to a local charity wants to know where his or her money went. Did it go directly to support the charity's constituents? Was part of it diverted to administrative costs? An accounting of expenses and an assessment of how the organization did during the previous year will go a long way toward ensuring continued involvement.

Like its corporate counterpart, the not-for-profit annual report should be targeted to all your stakeholders. Here is a list of potential stakeholders:[2]

- Volunteers and fundraisers
- Boards of directors, management, or trustees

[2] Much of what follows was gleaned from two excellent Internet sources: the Dundee Voluntary Action of Dundee, Scotland (http://www.d-v-a.org.uk/factsheetwar.htm), and the Annual Reports Library in San Francisco (http://www.zpub.com/sf/arl/arl-non.html).

- Staff
- Service users
- Members
- Clients/Beneficiaries
- Potential staff
- Partners
- Local groups
- Voluntary organizations in same field of work
- Local press
- Local community
- Donors—current and potential
- General public

When structuring your annual report, remember that most of your constituency will read it with an eye to accuracy. Opinion surveys show that this is about the only information about a not-for-profit that many people actually trust. This is your opportunity to let people know exactly what you stand for and how you conduct your business. Consider the following when structuring your annual report (see also Exhibit 8.3):

- Explain what the organization does and what more needs to be done.
- Communicate why the organization does what it does, how and on what it spends its money, and the rationale behind its actions.
- Address the assumptions that the public makes about the organization.
- Demonstrate accountability and transparency.
- Inspire confidence by showing a spirit of openness about how the organization is managed, its policies, and its performance.
- Demonstrate how the organization's achievements represent good value for donors.

Exhibit 8.3

Checklist of What to Include in Not-for-Profit Annual Report

General Information

- All contact details—full mailing address, telephone and fax numbers, e-mail and Web site addresses
- Charity number/Company Limited by Guarantee status and Company Registration number if appropriate
- Year of annual report

- List of members of committee or board and their positions
- The full title of the organization if it is usually known by its initials
- Organizational structure

What the Organization Does and How Well
- An explanation of what the organization does, who it helps, and how it does so—with figures and examples
- The organization's strategy and how it is implemented
- Activities in which the organization has been involved
- An interpretation or measure of effectiveness against some standard or previous achievement (e.g., increase in figures from previous year)
- Developments and achievements of the past year
- Future plans, including risks
- Examples of how what the organization has done fits its aims and objectives

The Involvement of Others
- Partnership activity (e.g., local authority, health board, joint work with other voluntary organizations)
- Use of volunteers; effect of their contribution
- Thanks to personnel—management, staff, volunteers, clients

Donors
- Acknowledgement of support
- Thanks to donors
- Use of donors' logos where required

Finances
- Accurate balance sheet
- Explanation of unusual items on balance sheet
- Explanation of support services costs (e.g., administration)
- Details of fundraising, its effectiveness, and how much it has cost
- What the money is being spent on
- Projection of future financial position

Not-for-Profit Annual Report Contents

Non-corporate annual reports usually consist of four sections:

1. *Chairman of the board letter.* The chairman of the board's letter is much the same as in a corporate report, except that the focus in usually on human capital rather than financial capital. Accomplishments are usually described with broad strokes because the next section will provide the details.

2. *Description section.* In this section, the activities of the organization are described: what it has accomplished over the past year and who has supported it.

3. *List of directors and officers.* Many public agencies and not-for-profits have boards of directors drawn, usually, from the local community. Listing the board members and agency officers gives an idea of the caliber of the individuals associated with the organization. Most agencies try to cull board members from a cross-section of the community. They often are officers in other, for-profit organizations or are simply well-respected community members.

4. *Financial statement.* As with the corporate annual report, the financial statement is one of the most important areas. This statement often includes the following sections:

   - *CPA opinion letter.* The CPA opinion letter tells the reader whether something is out of whack with the organization's finances. Qualifications are carefully inserted here and should be an indication of any problems. If there are no qualifications, the letter will be short and simply state that the organization has followed standard GAAP (generally accepted accounting principles in the United States) rules.

   - *Income statement.* The income statement shows what money came in and where it went. The percentage of revenues going to salaries, management services, and fundraising expenses are important to consider. For example, the National Charities Information Bureau (NCIB) recommends that organizations spend at least 60 percent of annual expenses for program activities.

   - *Balance sheet.* The balance sheet shows where funds have been placed over the years. The NCIB recommends that organizations (a) have net assets available for the following fiscal year of not more than twice the current year's expenses or the next year's budget, whichever is higher, and (b) not have a persistent or increasing deficit in unrestricted net assets.

   - *Footnotes.* Footnotes are important to read because they can alert the reader to lawsuits, litigation, IRS problems, loans to directors or officers, loans for other purposes, and "extraordinary charges."

Presentation

Presentation is extremely important in an annual report. That is why profit-making corporations will spend hundreds of thousands of dollars on a single issue. Although not-for-profits can rarely afford that kind of outlay, there is no reason why a charitable organization's report can't look professional. Most organizations today have access to desktop publishing software that can produce professional-looking documents. The trick is to locate someone within your organization who has an eye for design (or hire someone) to help you with the annual report. It will pay off in the long run.

Judging Your Annual Report

Following are some guidelines that can help you decide whether your annual report has done its job:[3]

- Does the front cover demand readership? Has the report utilized not only an intriguing cover statement but also, on inside pages, textual callouts, boldface lead-ins, action subheads, bulleted paragraphs, and the like? Does the report contain an open, inviting layout; solicit readership on every page; and have an action-filled index? Is the design approach present throughout, including in the back of the report?

- Is the writing sprightly, and does the text eschew jargon? Are complex words avoided?

- Does it contain little more than a letter to shareholders and an operations review? Or does it aim to inform fully, presenting items such as a special editorial section, a glossary of terms, and a mission statement?

- Does it shed light on the competition, market position, and market share? Does it provide a well-organized (and presented) breakdown of operations, results, and prospects? Are the competition and customers named?

- Has management wholeheartedly assumed responsibility, alongside the auditors, for the financials?

- Does the document contain biographical data on the officers and directors—more than simply their age and year of affiliation?

- Does it have a discernible point of view—a theme well-conceived and woven throughout, more than simply stated on the cover?

- Does it communicate a favorable identity of the organization through its look and its articulation of the organization's identity, business, and performance?

- Does the financial disclosure cover more than the five-year data the SEC requires? Are charts and graphs fully explained?

- Is there honesty throughout? Is bad news delivered without subterfuge or delay? Are there any noticeable conflicts between the report's parts?

- Is there clear CEO involvement (whether actual or perceived) in the shareholder letter?

- Does the CEO unequivocally present a revelatory view of the firm and provide substantive insight into where it's headed?

SOCIAL RESPONSIBILITY REPORTS

An interesting publication that has gained a lot of prominence lately in both corporate and not-for-profit circles is called the **social responsibility report.** It is

---

[3] These guidelines are taken in part from an excellent Web source on annual reports produced by Sid Cato. The original list was developed in 1984 and is copyrighted by Cato Communications, Inc., http://www.sidcato.com/criteria.htm.

often presented much in the same way as an annual report. The basis of the social responsibility report is good citizenship—especially in the areas of economic, environmental, and social responsibility. According to sociologist Ann Svendsen, the "wider community of stakeholders . . . are insisting that corporations be socially and environmentally responsible. And this wider community is becoming more assertive about the right to be informed and to influence corporate decisions."[4]

The result has been the **social audit,** part of the result of which may be the social responsibility report. Social audits are sometimes conducted by outside firms to determine areas in which the organization has acted responsibly or could use improvement. In the case of some organizations, such as Ben & Jerry's and the Body Shop, the audit was stakeholder oriented and directed.[5] In cases such as these, and when organizations conduct their own social audits, they are often verified by an external auditor, much in the same way as an annual report.

Purpose of Social Responsibility Reports

A number of reasons—all of them good ones—exist for conducting an annual social audit and producing a social responsibility report. Vasin, Heyn & Company CPAs and Management Consultants list the following:[6]

Perception Reasons
- Business partners, suppliers, and customers favor doing business with reputable organizations.
- A good image attracts potential employees, especially in competitive hiring modes.
- Government and public groups may be more accommodating or open on community impact issues.
- Donors and volunteers are more willing to contribute if the not-for-profit supports the same values they do.

Business Reasons
- Philanthropic programs can open new markets.
- Strong employee support services help reduce absenteeism and turnover and improve employee productivity.
- Community involvement helps a strong corporate culture, which results in innovation, higher quality, and more commitment.

[4] Ann Svendsen, "Social Audits Good for the Bottom Line," published in *The Globe & Mail* Business Ethics column, February 12, 1998. Reprinted online by the Center for Innovation in Management, http://www.cim.sfu.ca/pages/resources_social_audits.htm.
[5] See their social responsibility reports online at http://www.benjerry.com/our_company/about_us/social_mission/social_audits/2001/index.cfm and http://www.thebodyshop.com/web/tbsgl/env_how_we_engage.jsp.
[6] Vasin, Heyn & Company CPAs and Management Consultants, http://www.vhcoaudit.com/responsibilityaudits.htm.

- Future competitiveness and success depends on the health of the communities in which the business operates.

- Well-defined ethics programs can protect against legal exposure, fines, and sanctions.

- Environmental management increases efficiency in materials and energy use, thus lowering costs.

- Monitoring social responsibility can prevent fraud and organizational wrongdoing.

Altruistic Reasons
- "It is the right thing to do."

- "We have an obligation to share our success."

- "We have a responsibility to give something back to the community."

Coverage of Social Responsibility Reports

What the report covers depends on the organization. The most accepted three areas are economic impact, environmental impact, and social impact. The key is to show how your organization contributed in all these areas, while maintaining, it is hoped, its integrity as an ethical organization in all its dealings. Following is a detailed listing of most of the critical areas of social responsibility:[7]

External Environment
- *Social responsibility and new opportunities.* Contributing to solving or reducing social problems.

- *Community relations.* Extent of openness and support to people around the organization and to (local or national) government, stakeholder groups, action groups, churches, educational institutes, health care institutes, and others.

- *Consumer relations.* Extent of openness toward consumers and recognition of rights of consumers: safety, information, free choice, and being listened to.

- *Supplier relations.* Extent of openness toward suppliers and recognition of rights of suppliers: information, participation in design.

- *Natural environment (e.g., pollution packaging) and future generations.* Execution of legal requirements, research into current and future technical and environmental developments, and consideration of environmental issues regarding packaging and (recycling). Respect for biodiversity and needs of future generations.

- *Shareholders' relations.* Extent of openness regarding social effects of the activities of the organization (especially with regard to investment decisions).

---

[7] Peter Kok, et al, "A Corporate Social Responsibility Audit within a Quality Management Framework," *Journal of Business Ethics* 31: 285–297, 2001.

Internal Environment

- *Physical environment.* Safety, health, ergonomic aspects, structure, and culture.
- *Working conditions.* Demands in relation to recruitment, selection, promotion, part-time work, working on Sundays, medical aspects, and retirement.
- *Minorities and diversity.* Extent to which attention is given to minorities, diversity, and multiculturalism.
- *Organizational structure and management style.* Empowerment and involvement.
- *Communication and transparency.* Top-down and bottom-up communication, use of information technology, and review of information flows: relevance, timeliness, detail, and accuracy.
- *Industrial relations.* Extent to which communication takes place about expectations, needs, values, and norms in society.
- *Education and training.* Needs of employees, current and future knowledge and skills, review of training budget, personal development, quality assurance of training process, and evaluation of training results.

Internal and External

- *Ethics awareness.* Attention to ethical issues in relation to work and the business; involvement of employees in developing codes of behavior, values, and ethical codes; stimulation of broad ethical discussion among all parties.

Writing for Social Responsibility Reports

There really isn't much difference between writing for a social responsibility report and an annual report. The only real difference is the lack of SEC, or any other, legal regulations. You can put in pretty much whatever you'd like; however, as a general rule, it should conform to the three areas of economic impact, environmental impact, and social impact. Many, if not most, social responsibility reports follow a format developed as part of the Global Reporting Initiative (GRI).

According to *Corporate Responsibility* magazine, GRI is a long-term, multistakeholder organization and process whose mission is to develop and disseminate globally applicable *sustainability reporting guidelines,* most recently revised and released in mid-2002. The guidelines are designed to assist reporting organizations and their stakeholders in articulating and understanding contributions of the reporting organizations to sustainable development. Business, social and environmental advocates, labor, the financial community, the United Nations, and other stakeholders worldwide collaboratively developed the guidelines.[8]

> By drawing thousands of partners and hundreds of organizations into its multistakeholder process, GRI continues to work toward excellence of CR disclosure, maximizing the value of reporting for both reporting organizations and users alike.[9]

[8] "Bringing Concrete Expression to Corporate Responsibility: The Fundamental Role of Sustainability Reporting,"*Corporate Responsibility* magazine, online version, http://www.responsiblepractice.com/english/standards/gri/.
[9] "Bringing Concrete Expression to Corporate Responsibility: The Fundamental Role of Sustainability Reporting,"*Corporate Responsibility* magazine, online version, http://www.responsiblepractice.com/english/standards/gri/.

The GRI guidelines are designed to do the following:

- Present reporting principles and specific content to guide the preparation of organization-level sustainability reports
- Assist organizations in presenting a balanced and reasonable picture of their economic, environmental, and social performance
- Promote comparability of sustainability reports, while taking into account the practical considerations related to disclosing information across a diverse range of organizations, many with extensive and geographically dispersed operations
- Support benchmarking and assessment of sustainability performance with respect to codes, performance standards, and voluntary initiatives
- Serve as an instrument to facilitate stakeholder engagement

Social Responsibility Report Contents

Social responsibility reports are organized into five sections that GRI considers both logical and necessary:

1. *Vision and strategy.* Description of the reporting organization's strategy with regard to sustainability, including a statement from the CEO (see Exhibit 8.4)
2. *Profile.* Overview of the reporting organization's structure and operations and of the scope of the report
3. *Governance structure and management systems.* Description of organizational structure, policies, and management systems, including stakeholder engagement efforts
4. *GRI content index.* A table supplied by the reporting organization identifying where the information listed in Part C of the guidelines (organizational profile, and scope and content of the report) is located within the organization's report
5. *Performance indicators.* Measures of the impact or effect of the reporting organization divided into integrated, economic, environmental, and social performance indicators

GRI is careful to point out that these sections cover only basic report content. Reporting organizations might also have additional sector-specific or organization-specific information to include in their reports. However, in order to be considered in accordance with GRI guidelines, an organization must conform with further conditions stated in the rest of the document. Organizations are encouraged to use the guidelines flexibly, to meet their specific purposes, however. For example, each of the above sections provides detailed information on how to accomplish them as well as suggestions for tailoring them to particular needs.

A good example of the kind of flexibility allowed those following GRI guidelines is the CEO statement in Exhibit 8.5. It comes from the Intel corporate responsibility report for 2002. Notice that the CEO doesn't gloss over the economic downturn of the preceding year. An organization's philanthropy turns on its economic well-being. Despite the presence of this bad news, the overall tone is upbeat and the organization's commitment to social responsibility is clearly stated.

The statement is clearly in accordance with GRI guidelines. In fact, at the beginning of the report, a boxed disclaimer states that the report was developed using GRI guidelines. The complete guidelines can be downloaded in PDF format from GRI at http://www.globalreporting.org/guidelines/2002.asp. A downloadable version of the complete Intel report can be found at http://www.intel.com/intel/finance/gcr02/index.htm.

Exhibit 8.4

GRI Vision and Strategy Guidelines

This section encompasses a statement of the reporting organization's sustainability vision and strategy, as well as a statement from the CEO.

Statement of the Organization's Vision and Strategy Regarding Its Contribution to Sustainable Development

This statement presents the overall vision of the reporting organization for its future, particularly with regard to managing the challenges associated with economic, environmental, and social performance. This statement should answer, at a minimum, the following questions:

- What are the main issues for the organization related to the major themes of sustainable development?
- How are stakeholders included in identifying these issues?
- For each issue, which stakeholders are most affected by the organization?
- How are these issues reflected in the organization's values and integrated into its business strategies?
- What are the organization's objectives and actions on these issues?

Reporting organizations should use maximum flexibility and creativity in preparing this section. The reporting organization's major direct and indirect economic, environmental, and social issues and impacts (both positive and negative) should inform the discussion. Reporting organizations are encouraged to draw directly from indicators and information presented elsewhere in the report. They should include in their discussion any major opportunities, challenges, or obstacles to moving toward improved economic, environmental, and social performance. International organizations are also encouraged to explicitly discuss how their economic, environmental, and social concerns relate to and are affected by their strategies for emerging markets.

Statement from the CEO (or Equivalent Senior Manager) Describing Key Elements of the Report

A statement from the reporting organization's CEO (or equivalent senior manager if other title is used) sets the tone of the report and establishes credibility with internal and external users. GRI does not specify the content of the CEO statement; however, it believes such statements are most valuable when they explicitly refer to the organization's commitment to sustainability and to key elements of the report. Recommended elements of a CEO statement include the following:

- Highlights of report content and commitment to targets
- Description of the commitment to economic, environmental, and social goals by the organization's leadership
- Statement of successes and failures
- Performance against benchmarks such as the previous year's performance and targets and industry sector norms
- The organization's approach to stakeholder engagement
- Major challenges for the organization and its business sector in integrating responsibilities for financial performance with those for economic, environmental, and social performance, including the implications for future business strategy

The CEO statement may be combined with the statement of vision and strategy.

Exhibit 8.5

CEO Statement: Intel Corporate Responsibility Report

While the world at large may shift its attention from the environment to workplace programs to corporate governance, at Intel, we remain focused on all aspects of corporate citizenship. Doing things right is a deeply embedded value. With this report, we continue the effort we began in 2002 to provide updates on our programs and performance in the area of corporate responsibility.

On the whole, 2002 was a difficult year for the high-tech industry. As much as I'd like to profess unfettered optimism for the year ahead, I'm taking a cautious view of 2003 as well. Intel hasn't been shielded from the high-tech slowdown. Learning from the '90s, companies today have a better understanding of what technology to pursue and how to spend and invest their money. Ultimately, this supports Intel's goal to deliver innovative products in high volume at lower prices than proprietary efforts make possible. In the short term, however, the entire industry feels the effects of this conservative approach to technology and investment.

Economic conditions aside, 2002 was a year of excellent results and challenges alike:

- Intel remained at world-class levels of health and safety performance. At the same time, we are addressing a challenge to reverse an uptick we have seen in the number and severity of employee injuries in the workplace.

(continued)

(continued)

- We met all of our environmental targets, including our first global waste recycling goals, and achieved worldwide certification to ISO 14001 for all of our manufacturing operations.

- Our education team surpassed all of its goals, making a real educational impact in more than 50 countries. We set out to teach 500,000 teachers worldwide how to incorporate technology tools and resources into their curricula. By the end of 2002, we had exceeded that goal by 350,000 teachers. In addition, by the end of 2002, we had opened 62 Intel® Computer Clubhouses in 13 U.S. states and Washington, D.C., and in 10 other countries. My statements in last year's report remain true today and for the future. Corporate responsibility isn't a program to complete; it is a discipline we apply to our jobs. We are proud of what we have accomplished, and we are prepared to do more. We remain focused on accountability and transparency in our environmental, health and safety (EHS) reporting—and on our long-term commitment to being a good neighbor in our communities and a great place to work for our employees.

The skill and dedication of our employees have brought us through two tough years. Their continued commitment to Intel, our mission and our values will make us even more successful in the years ahead. I am proud to work with each and every one of them.

KEY TERMS

annual report	social responsibility	social audit
quarterly report	report	
statistical supplement		

EXERCISES

1. Bring in an annual report for either a profit or not-for-profit organization. Be prepared to analyze its approach including writing style, layout and design, and approachability.

2. Critique the president's letter from the annual report you have chosen. Analyze its strengths and its weaknesses. Rewrite any portions that you think could benefit from your changes.

3. Imagine yourself as an organization seeking investors. Describe yourself in a president's letter for your personal annual report. Consider the following: What was your past year like? How would you state your shortcomings so that they don't sound quite so bad? What do you see as the strengths that would make you a good investment? Why would anyone want to invest in you? Paint as good a picture as possible about your potential for success next year.

CHAPTER

9

Newsletters, Magazines, and Feature Writing

In this chapter you will learn:

- The various types of newsletters and why they are used.
- How to research, write, and design a newsletter.

- The purpose of house magazines and how to create them.
- How to write in the feature style.

NEWSLETTERS

Every day in the United States thousands of **newsletters** are published and distributed to hundreds of thousands of readers. It is estimated that some 50,000 corporate newsletters alone are published each year in this country. Most newsletters are internal publications in the sense that they reach a highly unified public—employees, shareholders, members, volunteers, voting constituencies, and others with a common interest. In fact, if you ask any self-respecting communication professional for the most effective means of reaching a primarily internal audience, the response will most likely be the newsletter.

Types of Newsletters

Newsletters are as varied as the audiences who read them; however, they do break down into several different types:

- *Association newsletters* help a scattered membership with a common interest keep in touch. Profit and not-for-profit associations and almost every trade association in the United States publish newsletters for their members, often at both national and regional levels.

- *Community group newsletters* are often used by civic organizations to keep in touch with members, announce meetings, and stimulate attendance at events. The local YWCA or Boys Club newsletter might announce their schedules, whereas a community church group newsletter distributed throughout surrounding neighborhoods might be a tool for increasing membership.

- *Institutional newsletters,* perhaps the most common type of newsletter, are usually distributed among employees. Used by profit and not-for-profit organizations, they are designed to give employees a feeling of belonging. They frequently include a balanced mix of employee-related information and news about the company.

- *Publicity newsletters* often create their own readers. They can be developed for fan clubs, resorts (some resort hotels mail their own newsletters to previous guests), and politicians. Congressional representatives often use newsletters to keep their constituencies up to date on their activities.

- *Special interest newsletters* developed by special-interest groups tend to grow with their following. *Common Cause,* for instance, began as a newsletter and has grown into a magazine representing the largest lobbying interest group in the United States.

- *Self-interest or "digest" newsletters* are designed to make a profit. The individuals or groups who develop them typically offer advice or present solutions to problems held in common by their target readers. These often come in the form of a sort of digest of topics of interest to a certain profession. In the public relations profession, for instance, you'll find *PR Reporter, PR News, Communicate, O'Dwyer's Newsletter, Communication Briefings,* and many more.

Why a Newsletter?

Why indeed? Most newsletters address an internal public, with the exception of those that target single-interest groups—such as professionals and executives—outside a formal organizational structure. The goal of most newsletters, then, is communication with a largely internal public (see Exhibit 9.1).

Downward and Upward Communication

In the ideal organizational structure, communication flows both vertically (upward and downward) and horizontally. The newsletter is a good example of **downward communication.** It fulfills part of management's obligation to provide its employees formal channels of communication. **Upward communication** provides employees a means of communicating their opinions to management. Ideally, even downward communication channels such as newsletters permit upward communication through letters to the editor, articles written by employees, surveys, and so forth. Newsletters can also provide horizontal communication (i.e., a newsletter that covers a whole industry and is distributed among similar organizations), but this type of newsletter is rarely produced within an organization; rather it originates from outside.

Newsletter or Something Else?

Why a newsletter instead of a magazine, booklets, bulletin boards, or (heaven forbid) more meetings? You can ask yourself several questions when deciding whether a newsletter is the publication that best suits your purpose:

- What is the purpose of the publication? Is it to entertain? Inform? Solicit?

- What is the nature and scope of the information you wish to present? Longer information is probably better suited to a longer publication such as a magazine; shorter, to brochures or folders. If your information is strictly entertaining or human interest in nature, it may also be better received within a magazine format.

- Who, exactly, are you trying to reach? All employees from the top down? A select few (the marketing department, the credit department, the vice president in charge of looking out windows)?

- How often do you need to publish it to realize the objectives you set in answering the previous questions? Newsletters are best suited to situations requiring a short editorial and design lead time.

Newsletters are best for small publication runs and information that needs a quick turnover. They handle information that is considered necessary but disposable (much like a newspaper, which in a sense the newsletter mimics). However, this is generally, but not universally true. Many fine newsletters are designed to be kept. Health and financial newsletters, for instance, are often hole-punched so that the reader can save them in ring binders. For the most part, though, they are considered disposable.

Exhibit 9.1

Newsletter Examples

EWEB NEWS YOU CAN USE

SPRING 2003

Pipeline

EWEB cuts budget to shield customers from lingering effects of energy crisis, BPA electricity rate increases

RATES UPDATE

ike other public utilities in the Northwest, the Eugene Water & Electric Board gets most of its electricity from the Bonneville Power Administration.

This federal agency is responsible for marketing hydroelectric power generated at three dozen dams in the Northwest. The BPA supplies Northwest homes, businesses and schools from Everett to Ashland with almost half the electricity they need.

For decades, EWEB and other public utility customers have enjoyed the benefits of plentiful, ultra-cheap power produced by these hydroelectric dams. EWEB currently buys almost 70 percent of the power it needs from Bonneville (the rest comes mainly from EWEB's own hydroelectric facilities).

But as every electricity consumer in the Northwest knows, power isn't so cheap any more. Bonneville, rocked by a financial crisis brought on by the 2001 energy crisis, increased the price of electricity it sells to utilities by almost 50 percent in October 2001. These local utilities, including EWEB, were forced to pass on those higher costs to consumers.

Generators convert water into electricity at Bonneville Dam, which was built in 1938.

But while the West Coast energy "crisis" has begun to fade from memory, its impact on electricity costs has not. Since late 2001, Bonneville has continued to increase the price of the electricity it sells to Northwest utilities and has announced it may raise rates by another 15 percent or more again this October.

EWEB's elected commissioners, well aware that the poor economy has put financial hardships on many customers, have been wrestling with these ever-increasing Bonneville-related power costs, which will reach almost $10 million by early fall.

Fortunately for customers, EWEB has cut its budget substantially and has found a number of one-time cost savings to avoid raising electric rates so far. These $9 million in cuts and other savings include freezing wages and salaries, reducing the work force by 6 to 10 employees, putting off new vehicle purchases, cutting conservation services and reducing the hours EWEB offices are open to the public.

"EWEB commissioners have worked hard to minimize rate increases by cutting the utility's budget

continued on page four

EWEB

OPPORTUNITIES
to speak to the elected
Board that guides EWEB.

Founded in 1911, the Eugene Water & Electric Board is one of the oldest publicly owned electric utilities in the Northwest. Today, EWEB is Oregon's largest customer-owned utility.

The citizens of Eugene elect a five-member Board of Commissioners, which retains full control of the utility and sets policies that guide its operation.

Commissioners meet on the first and third Tuesdays of every month, beginning at 7:30 p.m., in the North Building at 500 E. Fourth Ave. Time is reserved at each meeting for you to speak to the Board on any utility-related issue.

In This Issue

FEATURES
Rates Update
ENERGY STAR®
Slow the Flow
New Board Member

HIGHLIGHTS
Earth Works
Quick Read
McKenzie Currents

PRSRT STD
U.S. POSTAGE PAID
Eugene OR
Perm No. 59

POSTAL CUSTOMER

Eugene Water & Electric Board
PO Box 10148
Eugene OR 97440-2148

WINTER ISSUE 2000

FRESH AIR

JOURNAL

Windpower and Wildlife

In terms of the environment, no energy resource is entirely benign – even windpower. A key issue for windpower is the potentially negative effect on both resident and migratory bird populations, particularly raptors such as eagles, hawks and other birds of prey.

Since the Foote Creek Rim wind project in Wyoming included the Bonneville Power Administration, the federal National Environmental Policy Act (NEPA) required a formal Environmental Impact Statement (EIS). Part of this extensive on-site assessment included surveys and field studies of resident and migratory bird populations, as well as other wildlife.

Because of the rural nature of the Foote Creek Rim environment, a variety of birds were identified during a number of site surveys. Specifically, the EIS noted the presence of several native species of raptors and other birds that are on — or are candidates for — the Endangered Species Act (ESA) list. The list included bald eagles, peregrine falcons and mountain plovers.

In addition to their listing as a threatened species under the ESA, bald eagles are also afforded protection under the Bald Eagle Protection Act. While some bald eagles were sited during the surveys, no nests were found within the project area.

At the time of the surveys in 1994, peregrine falcons were listed as endangered under the ESA. However, while a small number of these birds were reported in the project area, no nesting sites were identified. In 1999, the U.S. Fish and Wildlife Service removed the peregrine falcon from the list of threatened and endangered species. Even though the peregrine falcon is no longer on the list, the bird's recovery rate will continue to be monitored.

At the same time, the mountain plover was considered a "species of concern," but was not formally listed. Today, however, the mountain plover is proposed for listing as a threatened species, and mature birds and nesting sites were found at the project site.

A Peregrine Falcon (Falco peregrinus)

Wind Turbine Design Focuses on Protective Measures

Once the EIS was completed, the permit focused on a number of "reasonable and prudent measures" that the developer, SeaWest Energy Corporation, could integrate into the design of the project to reduce the impact on these birds. SeaWest also consulted with other federal agencies, including the Bureau of Land Management and the Wyoming Game and Fish Department. As a result, the project designers incorporated a number of protective measures into the design of the facility to keep the impact of the wind machines on bird species to a minimum.

For example, a key measure was to locate the wind turbines away from the edge of the rim, where resident raptors tend to soar on wind currents while hunting. Another design feature was to paint the turbine and blades with an ultraviolet coating to make them more visible to birds.

see **BIRDS** page 2

Fresh Air Journal is a publication of Eugene Water & Electric Board for EWEB customers who support energy resources that are renewable, sustainable and have minimal impact on the environment.

EWEB
Windpower.

Once a newsletter is deemed a successful way to reach constituents, many companies use them for multiple purposes. Here we see two different uses of the newsletter format from the same company. *Pipeline* is the regular quarterly newsletter of the Eugene (Oregon) Water and Electric Board. It is large (11-by-15½-inch) and is printed in full color. Its general focus is news about how to save energy and its associated costs. *Fresh Air Journal* contains information specific to wind generation of power. It is a more standard 8½-by-11-inch in size and is also printed in full color.

Newsletter Content

To determine a newsletter's content, you must first know your audience. Is it totally internal, or a combination of internal and external? Your audience and its interests will dictate, to a large extent, the topic and direction of your articles.

Depending on the type of newsletter you are publishing, the focus will be broad or narrow. For example, when you write for an internal, employee public, you must carefully balance information with entertainment. You must please management by providing information it wants to see in print and you must please the employees by providing information they want to read. Otis Baskin and Craig Aronoff, in their book *Public Relations: The Profession and the Practice* (West, 1983), present a rule of thumb for an appropriate mix in an internal publication (not necessarily a newsletter) aimed primarily at an employee audience:

- 50 percent information about the organization—local, national, and international
- 20 percent employee information—benefits, quality of working life, etc.
- 20 percent relevant noncompany information—competitors, community, etc.
- 10 percent small talk and personals

Given that most newsletters are fairly short, such a complete mix may be impractical; however, a close approximation will probably work. Remember, though, that this mix is appropriate only for publications such as institutional newsletters.

By comparison, most horizontal publications tend to focus on items of interest to a more narrowly defined target public. For example, a newsletter for telecommunications executives may concentrate on news about that industry, omitting human interest items, small talk, or industry gossip. In fact, almost every newsletter targeted to executives contains only short, no-nonsense articles. The reason, of course, is that busy executives simply don't have the time to read the type of article that interests the average employee.

Newsletter Objectives

Newsletters, like any well-managed publication, will achieve best results if objectives are set and all actions follow logically from them. Objectives relate to your publication's editorial statement. Editorial statements shouldn't be pie-in-the-sky rhetoric; they should reflect the honest intent of your publication. If your intent is to present management's story to employees, then say so up front. An editorial statement can be an objective, or it can serve as a touchstone for other objectives.

For example, from the editorial statement in the previous paragraph you could reasonably derive an objective such as "To raise the level of awareness of management policies among all employees by X percent over the next year" or "To provide an open line of upward and downward communication for both management and employees." Whatever your objectives, make sure they are measurable. Then, you can point to your success in reaching them over the period of time you specified. You should also have some means by which to measure the success of your objectives. If your objective is simply "To present management's message to employees," how will you measure its success or failure? Don't you want to find out if just presenting the message was enough? How will you tell if anyone even read your message or, if they did, whether they responded in any way?

Make your objectives realistic and measurable, and once you have set them, follow them. Use them as a yardstick by which to measure every story you run. If a story doesn't help realize one of your objectives, don't run it. If you just can't live without running it, maybe your objectives aren't complete enough.

Newsletter Articles

Most newsletters are journalistic in style. They usually include both straight news and feature stories and range from informal to formal depending on the organization and its audience. Usually, the smaller the organization, the less formal the newsletter. Large corporations, by contrast, often have a very formal newsletter with a slick format combining employee-centered news with company news.

The responsibility for writing the newsletter is almost always handled in house, although some agencies produce newsletters on contract for organizations. In-house personnel tend to be more in tune with company employees and activities. Sometimes the writing is done in house, and the production—including design, layout, and printing—is done by an agency.

If you produce your own newsletter, you are limited only by expense and imagination. A standard newsletter is usually 8½-by-11-inch or 11-by-17-inch folded in half. It averages in length from two to four pages and is frequently folded and mailed. Many are designed with an address area on the back for mailing (see Exhibit 9.2).

Article length varies. Some newsletters contain only one article, whereas others include several. An average four-page newsletter uses about 2,000 words of copy. Depending on the focus of the newsletter, articles can range in length from digest articles of less than 100 words to longer articles of 600 words for newsletters that cover only one or two topics per issue. The trend today is toward shorter articles, especially for the newsletter aimed at the businessperson or corporate executive. Even for the average employee, newsletter articles usually need to be brief. Most newsletters make use of simple graphics or photographs. Although most are typeset or, increasingly, desktop published, many are simply typed.

Because newsletters inform and entertain, articles should be written in an entertaining way. Usually, news about the company or strictly informational pieces utilize the standard news story style, except that there is no need to use the inverted pyramid because newsletter stories are seldom edited for space from the bottom up. Employee interest pieces tend to use the feature story style. Feature-type articles for newsletters should be complete, with a beginning and an ending (see more detailed discussion of feature writing later in this chapter).

Where Do Stories Come From?

There are many ways to come up with acceptable ideas for articles. Sometimes you might receive ideas from employees or management. Sometimes a news release or a short piece done for another publication will spark enough interest to warrant a full-blown newsletter article. Whatever the source of the idea, you must evaluate the topic based on reader interest and reader consequence.

Exhibit 9.2

Newsletter Folds

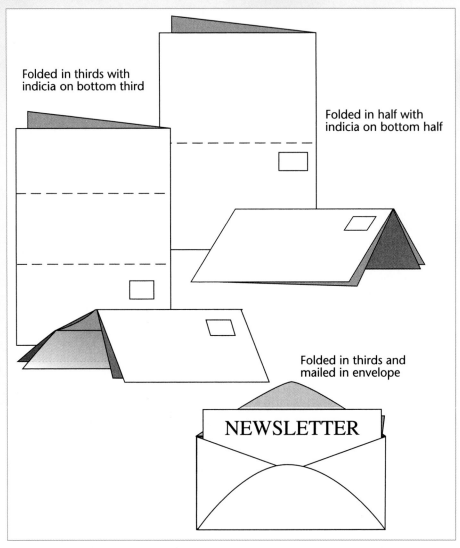

Folded in thirds with indicia on bottom third

Folded in half with indicia on bottom half

Folded in thirds and mailed in envelope

NEWSLETTER

Clockwise from bottom: standard 11-by-17-inch, four-page folded in thirds and mailed in business envelope; standard 11-by-17-inch, single folded in thirds with post office indicia on bottom third (usually folded and stapled); standard 11-by-17-inch folded in half with indicia on bottom half (usually folded and stapled).

If you're familiar with your audience's tastes, you can quickly determine their interest. To evaluate consequence, ask yourself what they will learn from the article. Although light reading is fun for some, an organizational publication isn't usually the place to engage in it.

Every newsletter editor will tell you that getting story ideas isn't all that hard. Finding someone to write the stories is. There are several methods for enlisting writers. If you are putting out an in-house publication, try assigning beats like at a newspaper. If you're lucky enough to have a staff, assign them to different types of stories perhaps by department or division, or by product or service. If you don't have a staff, rely on certain people in each department or division to submit stories to you. Sometimes the simple promise of seeing their name in print is enough inducement.

You can also send employees a simple request form, spelling out exactly what you are looking for. The information you get back will be sketchy, but you can flesh it out with a few phone calls (see Exhibit 9.3). This is an especially good method of gathering employee-related tidbits that don't deserve an entire story but should still be mentioned. One method for organizing your shorter stories is to group them according to topic. For example, group all stories relating to employee sports, or all stories about employee community involvement, or promotions, and so on.

Of course, if your publication is a narrowly focused horizontal publication, you may end up doing most of the research and writing yourself. Many such newsletters are truly one-person operations. Because desktop publishing allows a single person to act as reporter, editor, typesetter, and printer, this type of publication is enjoying a rebirth.

Whatever system you use to gather stories, as editor you will probably be doing most of the writing as well as the editing.

Researching Stories

If you write most of your own stories, you know that every topic must be researched thoroughly. The first step in a normal research process is to do a literature search to determine whether your article has already been written. If it has, but you still want to explore the topic for your specific audience, then try another angle.

Next, gather background information. Try to get specifics. You can't write about something you don't know a lot about personally. It also pays to get first-hand information. Interview people who know something about your topic. Not only will you get up-to-date information, but you may end up with some usable quotes and some new leads. (See Chapter 2 on interviewing tips.)

Don't forget the library. Many a fine article has been written based on a library visit. Library research is among the most valuable, and one of the cheapest, forms of research. In any event, most articles will be fairly complete and accurate if you do a little background research and conduct an interview or two. Because newsletter articles are usually short, this is about all the information you can use.

Exhibit 9.3

Employee Information Sheet

Employee Information Form
For Newsletter Articles

Employee Name: _____

Department: _____

Position: _____

Do you have any information pertaining to promotions, awards, service recognition, etc. that might
be of interest to fellow employees? If so, please give details below.

Do you have any story ideas for the employee newsletter?
Please list your suggestions below.

If you are directly involved in any of the above information, would you be willing to be interviewed?

Would you be willing to write any or all of an article relating to any of the ideas mentioned above?

Please return this form to the Corporate Communications Department, #302.

Design Considerations

No discussion of newsletters would be complete without some mention of design. Most people who engage in newsletter writing and editing today also lay out their own newsletters. With the advent of desktop publishing, that job has become increasingly easy.

We've already seen how most newsletters are simply 11-by-17-inch pages folded in half, giving us four panels, or pages, to work with. However, once we include the design elements that will make our newsletter attractive enough to be picked up by readers, there's not all that much room left for words. Exactly how much room will depend on your design capabilities.

What most designers especially love about newsletters is the wide variety of available formats. Just picking one can be a challenge. A newsletter can take on any number of disguises, ranging from the standard 11-by-17-inch format folded down to a four-page 8½-by-11-inch size, to a lengthy magazine-like format folded and stapled, to a tabloid newspaper, to a tabloid-sized magazine-type format known as a magapaper. Audience needs and cost are the most important deciding factors in picking a format for your newsletter.

No matter what format you ultimately decide on, you will be stuck with it for quite some time. If you are going to have enough information to fill a 12-page magazine format four times a year—good, use a magazine format. If not, try something smaller. If you need to insert your newsletter in a monthly billing envelope, try something even smaller. If size is what attracts your audience, and you usually don't have to mail your newsletter, try a magapaper or a tabloid (even these can be mailed—they just cost a lot more).

Whatever you decide, remember that your design elements must fit your format. Large formats call for larger artwork. Small formats call for shorter articles. White space is an extravagance in a bill stuffer but not in a tabloid. Folding and mailing differ immensely among the various sizes. Suit your format to your needs.

The well-designed newsletter won't shout "look at my look." Instead, it will simply say, "pick me up and read me." More than anything else, the design you choose and the skill you use in implementing that design will be nearly subliminal to the message you impart. As mentioned earlier, the nonverbal message imparted through choices of paper, color, and format is as important as anything you have to say. If you fail to entice your readers through these subtle nuances, you may not have any readers.

To get the most out of a newsletter, you must design it with your target audience always in mind. Are they a conservative, business executive group? Shouldn't your newsletter reflect that conservatism? Are they an artistic, easygoing audience? Shouldn't your newsletter appeal to their sense of freedom of expression? In fact, your newsletter has to appeal to your readers' sense of what is correct for them—both in the information you provide and in the packaging in which you provide that information.

Take a look at Exhibit 9.4 for some of the essential elements of a newsletter front page. Although there isn't time or space to cover newsletter design in detail here, refer to Chapter 14 for more information on design and working with printers.

Exhibit 9.4

Newsletter Front Page

This illustration shows some of the more important design elements of a typical newsletter. (1) The banner or name of your newsletter. Make sure it neither overpowers your front page nor is overpowered by other elements on the page. (2) The headline. Typically, there should be only one major head on the front page. Make it large enough to draw attention but not so large as to overpower your banner. (3) Photos and illustrations. Don't scrimp on size. Draw attention to your stories with large photos and illustrations. Just make sure they are of a quality worthy of the attention. (4) Body copy. Flush left, ragged right if columns are wide (two or three columns); justified if narrow (four or more columns). (5) Table of contents. Don't assume it has to be boxed. Try an open format for a change. (6) Rules and boxes. Use them to delineate your columns or to set apart items.

Exhibit 9.5

Newsletter Style Sheet

As you can see from this simple style sheet, you'll have to make numerous design considerations as editor of your own newsletter. The fun is in the experimenting. Don't give up until you have it the way you want it.

Style Sheet: <u>On Line</u>

Newsletter of the Public Relations Student Society of America, University of Oregon Chapter

<u>Page size</u>—11 by 17 inches, one-page, printed front and back, vertical tabloid layout. Margins 3/4 inch on all sides. Folded in thirds for mailing. Self-mailer on bottom third of back page. 60 pound white, semi-matte finish.

<u>Grid</u>—Five columns for normal text layout. Four or five columns for boxed or feature items. One pica between columns with a hairline rule.

<u>Body text</u>—10-point Times, auto leaded, flush left, first indents 1/4 inch.

<u>Captions</u>—9-point Times italic, flush left, run width of photo, 1/2 pica beneath photo.

<u>Lead article headline</u>—24-point Optima bold, set solid, reversed on 40% screen. Run full width of page (five columns).

<u>Two- and three-column heads</u>—18-point Optima bold, leaded 19, flush left running width of article. Reversed on 40% screen.

<u>Pull quotes</u>—14-point Optima italic, centered, one- to three-column width as needed. Two-point line one pica above and one-point line below as needed to fill space.

<u>Masthead copy</u>—9-point Optima, flush left, one-column width.

<u>Ink color</u>—Black ink run on preprinted blanks with banner in PMS 4515.

Style Sheets

To maintain consistency in your newsletter from issue to issue, you will need to develop a **style sheet.** A style sheet is a listing of all of the type specifications you use in your newsletter. It should be as complete as possible, and every member of your staff should have a copy. Style sheets are especially important if you are sick or on vacation and someone else has to produce an issue or two of your newsletter. It will tell them at a glance what it probably took you hours to determine when you first started. Exhibit 9.5 shows a typical style sheet. As you can see from this simple style sheet, you'll have to make numerous design considerations as editor of your own newsletter. The fun is in the experimenting. Don't give up until you have it the way you want it.

MAGAZINES

When we speak of magazines, most of us think of our favorite consumer publication (e.g., *Time, Newsweek, National Geographic, Atlantic Monthly*); however, for our purposes, we are speaking primarily, but not exclusively, of the house publication. Recent research has shown that house publications are the least looked to form of organizational communication. Guess what's first? Face-to-face communication. That's not surprising, but it doesn't mean that the house magazine is dead (although it has taken on some new forms in the computer age). What it does mean is that the magazine should contribute to open communication rather than be relied upon as the sole source. It also plays another role. Unlike most print media an organization might have access to, the house publication is a totally controlled medium—that is, the organization producing it has sole editorial control. The company can go on record through its house organ, state its position on a controversial issue, or simply tell its story its way. In other words, the house organ is still a good public relations tool.

The typical house organ is meant for an internal public—usually employees, shareholders, and retirees. Sometimes, though, it is offered to the external public. A publication like *Weyerhaeuser Today* stresses a broader emphasis, with articles often dealing with the industry as a whole and subjects of interest to those outside the company. Because the house organ is, at bottom, still a public relations piece, its thrust remains company oriented. Even a seemingly unrelated story will, in some way, eventually relate to the organization.

The house publication is usually in either magazine or newspaper format (or sometimes in the hybrid magapaper format). Both communicate with their various publics efficiently. Unless the company is large enough to produce a slick in-house publication, the house organ will be sent out to an agency for design and printing. Sometimes the agency will even provide writers to work up the stories; however, the best articles still come from writers inside the company who know and work with the people they write about.

Content and Format

Like their smaller cousin, the newsletter, house magazines usually present the following editorial mix:

- 50 percent information about the organization—local, national, and international
- 20 percent employee information—benefits, quality of working life, raises, etc.
- 20 percent relevant noncompany information—competitors, the community, etc.
- 10 percent small talk and personals

How you organize these elements is important. You should lead your reader through your magazine in a logical order that is pleasing and interesting. There is no single organizational format for house magazines. What is important is that you find a place for all relevant information, a place inclusive enough to house similar information from issue to issue.

Before you even start (or if you're overhauling an existing publication), you need to set some objectives. To make sure your reasons for publishing a house magazine are realistic, ask yourself some questions:

- Are my goals and objectives consistent with the goals and objectives of the organization itself? What am I really trying to get out of this? The temptation is very real, especially for creative people, to produce a magazine for simple ego gratification. Don't succumb to it. Have good, solid reasons for publishing.

- Can I attain these objectives through another, more effective method? Can I achieve good downward communication through an existing newsletter or more frequent meetings?

- Can I attain these objectives in a more cost-effective way? House magazines are expensive to produce. As usual, budget restrictions will have the final say.

Once you have answered these questions, and you have satisfied yourself that your prospective audience will benefit from your publication, you can decide on its proper organizational format.

Most house magazines contain very much the same type of editorial information as newsletters. The following items are listed in the approximate order in which they might appear (allowing for overlap in the case of articles):

- *Table of contents.* Usually runs on the front page.
- *Masthead.* Gives publication information (editor, publisher, etc.) and usually runs on the table of contents or second page.
- *Editorial.* Can be in the form of a "President's Column," a signed editorial from management or the publication's editor.
- *Letters.* If the publication is designed for two-way communication, a letters column is a common addition.
- *News notes.* A quick (and brief) look at what's happening around the organization. You can get a lot of these in two or three pages. This is a good place for employee information as well.
- *Articles.* News and feature articles make up the bulk of the magazine and should have a consistent order of their own. For instance, the cover story should always appear in the same approximate location in each issue.
- *Announcements.* Usually boxed but sometimes run as regular columns for job placement, promotions, etc. This is another good place for employee interest pieces.
- *Calendar.* Upcoming events of interest to readers.

Remember, there is no hard and fast rule for formatting your magazine, but stick to whatever method you choose. Your readers look for consistency. If the format changes every two issues, you'll quickly lose your readers.

Types of Articles

House publication articles range from straight news to complete fiction, and include everything in between. Most, though, are either straight news or feature. A vast array of writing styles can justifiably be called magazine writing. Articles or ideas for articles that don't seem to fit one particular magazine format, or even one section of a magazine, may well fit into another. For example, let's say you interview an employee on a job-related topic such as benefits. In the course of your conversation, you discover that he builds model ships for a hobby and, in fact, has won several competitions. You gather enough information for a how-to article on building model ships as well as enough for a feature on the employee. Neither of these ideas may fit into the story you originally set out to do; however, they may fit into another section on employees or one on hobbies. The lesson, of course, is never discard information just because it doesn't fit into your present assignment. Even if the tone or style of the article or information doesn't seem to fit one category, it may well fit another.

Articles for house publications tend to be shorter than those for consumer magazine articles or even trade journals (dealt with below). The average length of most house publications in magazine format is around 12 pages. Article length runs about 1,000 words or less for features (about four typed pages). Considering that magazine column width is about 14 picas for a three-column spread, and that articles are usually accompanied by photographs or artwork and headlines, subheads, and blurbs—a 750-word article may cover several pages.

TRADE JOURNALS

Trade journals are a valuable source of information for those who work within a specific industry. They provide news and stories dealing with the concerns and products of that industry. Trade journals accept product press releases readily and are an excellent target for placement. They usually have a section devoted specifically to new products and will usually place your release, edited, of course, in this section.

For those desiring more attention, trade journals also accept articles written on products, concepts, and services of interest to their specific audiences (i.e., the industries they serve). These are normally submitted in the manner of any freelance magazine article. First, you query the journal by letter explaining that you have an article idea, what it is, and why you think it might fit the journal's format and be of interest to its readership. If you receive a positive response, send the article, carefully following the journal's editorial style. Trade journals, like consumer magazines, often have author's guidelines explaining their style, average length, manuscript requirements, and so on. Follow these guidelines explicitly if you want to get published or get your client the publicity you were hired to provide.

The variety of trade journal articles is immense. They can range from feature-type articles using human interest, through straight news stories on products and services, to light fluff articles on travel and entertainment. To determine what style best fits your idea and their magazine, obtain a copy of the publication and read it thoroughly. Never submit an article to a magazine you haven't read.

Get a copy of one of the numerous media directories that list all of the publications by industry (see Chapter 5). For my money, *Standard Rate and Data Service* provides the most comprehensive look at trade publications of any on the market. Almost every industry has a trade journal, sometimes a number of them. For instance, there are trade journals for golf course groundskeepers, race track owners, thoroughbred breeders, paper manufacturers, supermarket owners, table waiters, bartenders, railroad workers, airline workers, and almost every other trade imaginable. One or more of these will fit your needs.

FEATURE WRITING FOR NEWSLETTERS AND MAGAZINES

We have seen that much of what public relations writers produce is in so-called straight news format, or inverted pyramid style. This is always true of news releases and can be true of anything written that is deemed straight news as opposed to a feature. We now know what straight news is, but what is a feature?

A feature can be construed as almost anything that isn't straight news. In fact, *feature* has several meanings. As used in the term *feature story,* it simply means the main story or cover story in the publication. In its broader sense it means an article that features something as its central point or theme. This something may not necessarily be the message of the story or its publicity angle. It is most often the story itself. For example, you've been asked to do a story on a new product—say, a plastic lining that can be used as a bed for soil or sod to keep it from eroding or slipping. Instead of doing a straight news story on the product itself, you opt to do a feature story on a user of the new product. Maybe you find a golf course that's using the new underliner to rebuild its greens, and the focus of the story becomes the golf course. The publicity angle or the message about the new product becomes almost secondary. Featuring the golf course adds an extra dimension to your product story and sets it in context. In fact, the most useful element of a feature story approach is that it presents a context. Not every straight news story can do that.

Feature Style

Feature style is usually less objective and provides less hard information than straight news style. Features generally take a point of view or discuss issues, people, and places. The style is more relaxed, more descriptive, and often more creative than straight news style. Read over the straight news story in Exhibit 9.6. Next, look at the opening paragraphs of the feature story in Exhibit 9.7. This story is on the same topic as the straight news example, but the approach is quite different.

Exhibit 9.6

Straight News Story

Newsletter

AMHCA story

Page 1 of 1

Counselors' Association "hires" PRSSA

The American Mental Health Counselors Association (AMHCA), a representative association for community counselors, has hired the Public Relations Student Society of America (PRSSA) to develop and implement a series of communication projects. The projects began last spring when a committee of five PRSSA members developed a public relations plan for AMHCA. The comprehensive plan is targeted at present and potential members. The two main objectives of the plan are to strengthen AMHCA as a membership organization and to create awareness of AMHCA among its target audiences.

After receiving approval for the plan from AMHCA board members, PRSSA was asked to develop more specific projects. This fall, a committee of eight PRSSA members worked on two projects. The first was to develop a logo and slogan for AMHCA to be used on all informational materials. The logo, now finished, symbolically represents the safety and shelter of a hearth, utilizing a stylized Hebrew symbol for home and well-being. The second project involved redesigning an existing AMHCA brochure. The committee developed a whole new layout and cover design.

The committee will also continue to develop projects during the winter and spring terms. The main project will be a series of brochures for AMHCA. The brochures will range from information on membership to information on mental health counseling. Other upcoming projects include writing a series of public service announcements to be broadcast nationally for Mental Health Week in March.

"Overall, the project has been a great experience for all of us involved," said committee chairperson, Wendy Wintrode.

Exhibit 9.7

Feature Story

AMHCA story

Page 1 of 1

Clearing Up the Confusion over Mental Health

What's the difference between a therapist, psychologist, psycho-
therapist, psychiatrist, and a counselor? If you don't know, you're
among the millions of people who are confused about the multi-
tiered mental health counseling field.

In an effort to clear up some of the confusion, the American Mental Health Counselors Association (AMHCA) has "hired" a university
student group to produce a public information campaign for them.

The Public Relations Student Society of America (PRSSA) at the
University of Oregon has been retained by the association to develop a program of information that will better define the various
roles contained under the umbrella term "mental health counselor." Jane Weiskoff, regional director of AMHCA says that the
confusion seems to stem from a misconception over what constitutes a "counselor." "In the mental health profession, there is a
perceived hierarchy," she says. "Psychiatrists are seen as being at
the apex of the field with psychologists, therapists, and other counselors falling into place under them. We'd like to clarify and possibly alter that perception."

Part of the plan, which has already been produced and approved,
is to establish and maintain contact with current AMHCA members
through a series of brochures and an updated and redesigned association newsletter. These informational pieces will carry the message that mental health counselors come in a variety of forms with
a variety of educational and training backgrounds, and that each
of these levels is suited to certain types of counseling. The goal is
to establish credibility for certain of the counseling functions not

(continued)

(continued)

---

fully recognized at this time by the general public and the mental health profession. . . .

[For illustration purposes, part of the story has been deleted here.]

If committee chairperson Wendy Wintrode has her way, the term "mental health counseling" will soon have a completely different, and definitely more expanded, definition. "We want everyone to know that professionalism doesn't begin and end with a small clique at the top—it is the guiding force behind the entire field of mental health counseling."

The facts are still here, but the focus in on creative information presentation. The lead is a question (a typical delayed lead strategy). Answering that question becomes part of the story itself. Quotes are used liberally. They not only validate and lend credibility to the subject discussed but also add human interest.

Human interest is a key characteristic of much feature writing. It can be simple inclusion of the human voice in a story, or it can be an entire profile, featuring a single person. Although the term *profile* usually refers to a feature story done on a person or on one aspect or issue relating to a person, individual companies or products may be profiled as well (discussed in more detail later).

The following is from a profile on a corporate legal department and its new head. Notice how the scene is set in the lead before the subject is introduced.

> Sitting behind a cluttered desk, boxes scattered around the office—some still unopened—is the new head of Associated Products Corporation's Law Department, Ed Bennett. Ed is a neat man, both in appearance and in speech. As he speaks about the new Law Department, he grins occasionally as though to say, "Why take the time to interview someone as unimportant as a lawyer?" That grin is deceiving because, to Ed and the other attorneys who work for Associated Products Corporation, law is serious business.

To add human interest is merely to add the human element to a story. Information without this element is only information. With it, information becomes more interesting, more personal, and more attuned to readers' experiences. As a further example, consider the following lead:

> Somewhere north of Fairbanks, long after the highway disappears into the low growth and stubby trees, Seth Browner is stalking an elusive prey—his health. Seth is one of 20 hikers involved in the inaugural "hiking for health" program. Seth hopes the program will give him an opportunity to see the outdoors up close for the first time in his life, and provide him with something he badly needs right now. Six months ago, Seth's doctor told him if he didn't exercise he would die.

And, if you're trying to reach people with your message—I mean really reach them—injecting human interest is often the best way to do it.

Writing the Feature Story

Feature stories, unlike straight news stories, must have a definite beginning (the *lead*), middle (the *body*), and end (the *ending*). Developing these elements takes patience, practice, and organization. Exhibit 9.8 points out the elements of a feature story.

The Lead

Always start at the beginning. A good lead is the hook that entices the reader into reading the complete piece.

Your lead must tell the reader what the story is about. It is not necessary to cram everything into the lead; however, you must include enough information so that the reader doesn't have to search for your topic. For straight news articles, the lead needs to come right to the point with the facts up front. For a feature, the delayed lead may be used. In this type of lead you create ambiance, then place your story within the environment you have created, but it must still come to the point before the end of the second paragraph. Consider the following leads:

A Lead for a Horse-Racing Trade
For some time now, the sound of heavy machinery has been echoing through the rolling green countryside and heavily forested groves of eastern Maryland. But that sound will soon be replaced by the sound of galloping horses as they take to the newly banked turns and straightaway at what is being billed as "the most innovative thoroughbred training and sports medicine facility in North America."

One for the Hospital Industry
The scene is a standard hospital room designed with fire safety in mind: a very low fuel load, floors of asbestos tile, walls of gypsum board on steel studs, and a ceiling of fiberglass panels. The hospital is built in accordance with the National Fire Protection Agency Life Safety Code and has received the Joint Commission on Accreditation of Healthcare Organization's maximum two-year approval.

Late in the evening, a patient accidentally ignites the contents of his trash can, which in turn ignite the bed clothes and, eventually, the mattress. The ensuing fire is a disaster, and despite the correct operation of all fire systems, multiple fatalities occur and the entire hospital wing is a total loss. Why? There are no fire standards on the upholstered furniture in this hospital, and the mattresses meet a federal code designed to retard fires from smoldering cigarettes, not open flames.

A Lead for a New Product Aimed at Highway Engineers
You're traveling along at high speed—the familiar clackety-clack of the rails beneath your feet. But wait a minute. You're not on a train, you're in an automobile, and that familiar sound beneath your feet is the result of deteriorating pavement joints that have been repaired with the usual "hot pour" method.

And an Article for Golf Course Superintendents
Valleyview Country Club had a problem—the 12th hole was sinking again. For almost 40 years, the facilities people at Valleyview had been rebuilding the green. In

fact, it had been rebuilt three times over that period of time, but each time with the same results—in a matter of a few years, the green would begin to sag again. This time, it was almost bowl-shaped and was acting as a funnel for rainwater that was draining from its outer edges into its concave center.

Although you may not have guessed it, all of these leads come from articles announcing new products or new applications for established products. Remember, even the most mundane subject can benefit from a creative treatment. Your readers will read your story only if they like your lead.

Other techniques for beginning your story include leading with a quote and placing it in context, or using metaphor, simile, analogy, anecdote, and other interest-getting devices. Although most of us forgot these literary tools the minute we left freshman composition, we shouldn't assume that good writing can get along without them. Look over the following literary uses of metaphor, simile, and analogy and then compare them with the feature article leads that follow them:

- A metaphor says that one thing is another:

CAULIFLOWER IS NOTHING BUT A CABBAGE WITH A COLLEGE
EDUCATION.
—Mark Twain

TREE YOU ARE,
MOSS YOU ARE,
YOU ARE VIOLETS WITH WIND ABOVE THEM.
—Ezra Pound

- A simile says that one thing is like another:

THOUGH I MUST GO, ENDURE NOT YET
A BREACH, BUT AN EXPANSION,
LIKE GOLD TO AIRY THINNESS BEAT.
—John Donne

IN TIME OF PERIL LIKE THE NEEDLE TO THE LODESTONE,
OBEDIENCE, IRRESPECTIVE OF RANK, GENERALLY FLIES TO HIM
WHO IS BEST FITTED TO COMMAND.
—Herman Melville

- Analogies make hard-to-understand ideas easier to grasp by placing them in reader context or, as in the following example, by making a point of view more understandable through humor:

SOAP AND EDUCATION ARE NOT AS SUDDEN AS A MASSACRE, BUT
THEY ARE MORE DEADLY IN THE LONG RUN.
—Mark Twain

The following leads show even the most mundane subject is of interest to someone and deserves the most interesting treatment possible. Pay particular attention to the number of scene-setting or descriptive words used in these leads:

Leading with a Quote

"Steelhead trout are an elitist fish; they're scarce, big, beautiful and they're good fighters," says Bob Hooton, Fish and Wildlife biologist responsible for steelhead on Vancouver Island. (*Salmonid,* newsletter of the Canadian Dept. of Fisheries and Oceans)

Leading with an Anecdote

If past experience is an indication, the telephones at our Client Services Center in Laurel, Maryland, will rarely stop ringing on December 16. That day the Center begins accepting calls for appointments to review diaries from the fall radio survey. (*Beyond the Ratings,* national newsletter of Arbitron)

April 1 marks the beginning of a new era in banking—and a new dawn of satellite communications. On that day a clerk in Citicorp's Long Island, New York, office will make history by picking up the phone and dialing a Citicorp office in California. (*Telecommunications Week,* national newsletter published by Business Research Publications, Inc.)

Leading with an Analogy

You've heard the adage "two heads are better than one." What about 40? The Division's plants, more than 40 of them, are "putting their heads together" in the form of a division-wide information sharing project recently released. (*Action Connection,* employee newsletter of Weyerhaeuser Packaging Division)

Setting the Scene

It's 5:30 on a Monday afternoon and you've just finished one of those days. Not only did the never-ending pile of work on your desk cease to go away, but you just received two additional A priority assignments. On top of that, the phones wouldn't stop ringing and the air conditioning wouldn't start working, even though the temperature hit 95. (*Spectra,* employee newsletter of the SAIF Corporation)

It's pretty quiet at Merwin Dam in southwest Washington. Two generators are running. The water level is down a little so folks along the reservoir can repair some docks while the weather stays nice.

   For the 21 people working at the dam, it's business as usual. But, there is a subtle change. There's no longer a threat hanging over their heads that Pacific might not own or operate the dam. The court case that could have forced Pacific to give it up was finally resolved at the end of February. (*Pacific Power Bulletin,* employee newsletter of Pacific Power)

Leading with a Metaphor or Simile

   Recession fears faded like presidential candidates this spring. Markets were jolted by the February employment release, which showed an increase in employment of over 500,000. . . . The mood has gone full circle as there is renewed focus on the strength of the economy with its 5.4 percent unemployment rate, and the whiff of higher inflation in the air. (*Northwest Business Barometer,* a quarterly economic review for customers from U.S. Bank)

The Body

Once the lead is conceived and written, the story must elaborate on it. If possible, make points one by one, explaining each as you go. Get the who, what, when, where, and how down in the most interesting way possible—but get to the point early.

The body of the article must support your main point, preferably already made in the lead, and elaborate on it. It should contain all the information your reader needs to understand what you are trying to say. Obviously, it's in your best interest to present your ideas clearly. Working from an outline is the best way to ensure that you have covered all your key points in a logical order.

You should anticipate questions your reader might have, and answer them satisfactorily. Remember to use logical transitional devices when moving from one point to another. Subheads, although helpful to the reader, don't alleviate the need for thoughtful transitions. Back up your statements with facts and support all generalizations with specifics. Although magazine and newsletter feature stories seldom use footnotes, they are not completely inappropriate. Usually, however, citations can be taken care of in the body of the text. If, however, you are quoting someone, be sure to use attribution. Don't just give the person's name. A person's title or job may lend your quote authority if that person is considered knowledgeable or an expert on your subject.

In a feature, cover the news angle in a more people-oriented way. Paint word pictures to help readers hear, smell, and feel the story. If your story has a possible human-interest angle, use it. It helps your readers relate to the message through other human beings. Above all, don't be afraid to experiment with different approaches to the same topic. Try a straight news approach, then a human-interest angle or maybe a dramatic dialogue. Whatever approach you use, try to make your story specific to your audience. Remember, they are major players in your scripts, in reality or vicariously.

Exhibit 9.8

Feature Story Structure

The lead paragraph incorporates many of the basic elements of a newstype lead, including who, what, where, and how. It also delays the discovery of the topic until the second sentence by setting the scene first.

The second paragraph is the bridge from the lead to the body of the story. It begins with a factual statement and ends with another.

APC's Answer Man

You might have noticed, if you've been in the new headquarters building at Associated Products Corporation long, a rather harried figure dashing madly up and down the halls. That man with the worried expression is Dave Martin. Dave, in a sense, is the ombudsman for APC's new building. He's the man who fields all the complaints, large and small, that have to do with everything from desk positioning to major malfunctions.

Dave's official title reads: Manager, Headquarters Facilities and Services. This constitutes a promotion for Dave, who previously was Manager, Technical Services. It also constitutes quite a lot of heartburn.

The job was almost a matter of evolution for Dave, who became associated with the project through working with Bob Allen, project manager for the new building. Dave continually found himself involved with planning of space allocation, since this was a natural carryover from his former job. He cites the speed at which the building was completed as one of the major factors for his almost sudden immersion in the project.

An undertaking of this magnitude usually takes years to complete. The space layout itself, which usually takes six to eight months, took only six to eight weeks. Dave and the planners worked night and day setting up seating arrangements for each department. These arrangements had gone through each department weeks before but had to be thoroughly scrutinized by the architects and planners before implementation.

Dave realizes, of course, that not everyone is going to be completely happy with his or her particular arrangement, but no major changes can be made until after the first of the year. There are several reasons for this. "The move itself will take up to 60 days to complete," says Dave, "during which time furniture will constantly be arriving." According to Dave, each piece has been designated for a particular spot in the new building, and last minute changes would only serve to confuse further what will doubtless be a confusing move as it is.

Telephones have already been assigned to particular individuals and can't be moved, and the special ambient lighting fixtures built into the desks provide light for a specific grouping of furniture. Moving a desk would mean disrupting the lighting scheme for a particular area, which would affect more than just one person. All of these factors lead Dave to stress acceptance of the new floor plan, at least for the time being. According to Dave, psychological adjustment to new surroundings normally takes about 30 days. A great deal of complaints handled prior to that time are likely to be adjustment oriented. Those are the complaints he would like to avoid initially.

Paragraphs 3 through 6 follow a sort of chronological order, based on the construction of the new building, and provide background information.

(continued)

(continued)

Paragraph 7 comes back to the subject (focusing on the human angle) and expands on position and point of view.

> Dave's new position will have him on the fourth floor as part of the Industrial Relations Department, where he will be in charge of the expanded reproduction facilities as well as Office Services, which handles supplies, PBX operation, mail service, and messenger service. Dave is going to be monitoring almost every aspect of the new building. He will handle the janitorial contract, the plant contract (yes, Virginia, there will be greenery inside too), and snow removal. As Dave says, "If the building has a problem during the day, I'll hear about it first." Dave's only concern right now is that he will receive too many complaint calls like, "I don't want to sit next to Joe" or "I can't see the window from here." With all of the major problems involved in a move of this magnitude (by the way, he's also in charge of getting everybody into the building), Dave doesn't need to hear the "personal" problems each employee is bound to have.

The closing paragraph refers to the opening paragraph as a technique for gaining closure.

> So, if you see this man with the harried expression in his eyes rushing around the halls of APC's new headquarters building, have a heart. Remember that Dave, like a modern-day Atlas, bears the weight of six floors on his shoulders. Just say "Hi," give him a smile, and learn to live with your new desk for a while.

The Ending

The most powerful and most remembered parts of your article will be the beginning and the end. Good endings are as difficult to write as good beginnings. However, there are only a few ways to wrap up an article and bring your readers to closure (a sense that they are satisfactorily finished): summarize your main points **(summary ending),** refer back to the beginning in some way **(referral ending),** or call for action **(response ending),** although this last type of ending is rarely used in feature article writing. Consider the following leads with their respective endings:

- Posing a question in the lead/summary ending:

Lead

Name the oldest civilization in North America. If your anthropological information is such that you pinpointed the Aleut peoples of Alaska, you are both well-informed and correct.

Ending

"Intellect and knowledge, technical skills, helpfulness, and concern for the truth are still the hallmarks of Aleut culture," observes the Connecticut anthropologist, Laughlin. Such virtues are valuable assets, ever more useful as the 21st century approaches, and the bedrock on which the best that is Aleut may find permanence and continuity.—Richard C. Davids for *Exxon USA*

- Setting the scene in the lead/referral ending:

Lead

For one emotion-filled moment on July 28, when the Olympic torch is lit atop the Los Angeles Memorial Coliseum, this sprawling California city will be transformed into an arena of challenges and champions. But that magic event, shared with two billion television viewers around the world, will mark more than the beginning of the XXIII Summer Olympic Games.

Ending

For GTE employees worldwide, perhaps some of that special thrill can be shared by just watching the Games on television, and knowing that whenever gymnastics, fencing, water polo, volleyball, yachting, or tennis are televised, those images and sounds will have passed through the hands of 425 fellow employees—GTE's team at the Olympics.—Bill Ferree for *GTE Together*

- An anecdotal lead/summary and referral ending:

Lead

In 1737, Benjamin Franklin wrote in the *Pennsylvania Gazette* of an auroral display so red and vivid that some people thought it was a fire and ran to help put it out.

Ending

Although the effects of auroral activity on the lower levels of the earth's atmosphere are more apparent, the effects on the upper atmosphere are not, and we are only now beginning to understand them. With more understanding, we may eventually view the aurora with a more scientific eye, but until that day comes, it still remains the greatest light show on earth.—Tom Bivins for National Bank of Alaska *Interbranch*

Common Types of Features

Although several standard types of feature articles are appropriate for magazines and newsletters, the most common is the **profile.** The profile is most typically a feature story written specifically about a person, a product or service, or an organization or some part of it. It literally profiles the subject, listing facts, highlighting points of interest, and—most important—tying them to the organization.

Regardless of the subject of your article, you are writing for a specific organization and the article must have some bearing on it—direct or indirect.

The Personality Profile

Personality profiles are popular because people like to read about other people, whether these people are just like them (so that they can easily relate) or very different (so that they can aspire or admire). Of course, a personality profile should do more than just satisfy human curiosity, it should inform the reader of something important about the organization itself by putting it in the context of a biographical sketch. For example, this lead was written for a brief profile on an award-winning engineer:

> When Francis Langly receives the Goodyear Medal this spring, it will represent the symbolic crowning of a lifetime of dedication to the field of chemistry. Awarded by the Rubber Division of the American Chemical Society, the Goodyear Medal is the premier award for work in the field of specialty elastomers—an area that Langly helped pioneer. When Langly makes his medalist's address to the gathering in Indianapolis in May, his comments will be a reflection of almost 50 years of innovation and development, which began in 1938 when he joined Rogers Experimental Plastics Company as a research chemist.

What does this say about the organization? It implies, for one thing, that the company is obviously a good one to have such a well-respected person work for it for so long. A profile like this calls attention to the merits of the organization by calling attention to someone who has something to do with it—or, in some cases, to someone who benefits from its services or products. Consider the following lead:

> Guy Exton is a superb artist. His oils have hung in galleries all over the country. But, for nearly five years, he couldn't paint anything. In order to paint, you typically need fingers and a hand, and Guy lost his right hand in an auto accident in 1993. But now, thanks to a revolutionary new elastomer product developed by Rogers Experimental Plastics Company (REPC), Guy is painting again. He can grip even the smallest of his paint brushes and control the tiniest nuance through the use of a special prosthetic device designed by Medical Help, Inc., of Franklin, New York. The device, which uses REPC's Elastoflex membrane as a flexible covering, provides minute control of digits through an electromechanical power pack embedded in the wrist.

One of the most common types of personality profiles is the Q & A (question-and-answer format). This style typically begins with a brief biographical sketch of the person being interviewed, hints at the reason for the interview, and sets the scene by describing the surroundings in which the interview took place. For the remainder of the piece, speakers are tagged Q or A. Sometimes, the interviewer is designated with the publication's name (for example, *The Corporate Connection* might be shortened to CC). Likewise, the interviewee might be designated by his or her last name.

The descriptive narrative tells the story of the individual being profiled from a third-person point of view. Naturally, quotes from the subject may be included, but sometimes a successful profile is simply a biographical sketch and won't necessarily need quotes. The profile in Exhibit 9.9 is a mixture. Although some brief quotes are included, most of the profile is simple biography.

Exhibit 9.9

Personality Profile

When Francis Langly receives the Goodyear Medal this spring, it will represent the symbolic crowning of a lifetime of dedication to the field of chemistry. Awarded by the Rubber Division of the American Chemical Society, the Goodyear medal is the premier award for work in the field of specialty elastomers—an area that Langly helped pioneer. When Langly makes his medalist's address to the gathering in Indianapolis in May, his comments will be a reflection of almost 50 years of innovation and development, which began in 1938 when he joined Rogers Experimental Plastics Company (REPC) as a research chemist.

Born in Brooklyn, New York, in 1915, Langly received his B.A. in chemistry and his Ph.D. in organic chemistry from Cornell in 1939. His first position at REPC was in the Chemical Department at the Experimental Station near Ravenswood, Vermont. At the outset of World War II, he was working on the synthetic rubber program addressing the problem of an adhesive for nylon tire cord for B-29 bomber tires. These studies eventually culminated in the development of the vinyl pyridine adhesives so widely used today.

Langly's background in organic chemistry led to his transfer to the Organic Chemicals Department at the Johnson Laboratory in Stillwater, Oklahoma, where he discovered the first light-fast yellow dyes for cotton; and during the next 10 years, he led the task force that developed dyes for the new synthetic fibers that were fast becoming a mainstay of American fashion.

From his work in dyes, Langly moved on to work in fluorine chemical research. The small research team he headed is credited

(continued)

(continued)

with the discovery of a family of new elastomers. The team at that time had, what Langly calls, "a very special business in fluorine chemicals," but no solid applications yet for these quickly developing products. Langly and his group knew that they had something distinctly different and new in the field of elastomers. To an inventor, of course, the invention comes first. It didn't seem to trouble him that there was little or no market at that time for these new products. "There was no surprise in development," Langly says. "We understood the properties of the products we were developing and were sure that markets would eventually open up."

Chief among these early fluorelastomers was Axon, a polymer that could resist extremely high temperatures, toxic chemicals, and a broad range of fluids. Other products, however, were gathering attention in industry and defense, and the company was eager to market these already-accepted materials. In fact, the Axon project was sidetracked in the early 1950s, when it was thought that the Langly research team could be better utilized in work on an already existing product. In a way, this turned out to be a profitable diversion. Although the proposed research turned out to be a dead end, a small pressure reactor system that had been designed to build EP rubbers was converted to make fluoropolymer and used as a pilot plant to produce Axon.

According to Langly, "You rarely have a chance to fill a vacuum with something entirely new." And Axon was entirely new. The Air Force had been searching for some time for a product that could withstand very low and very high temperatures and was impervious to oil for use as engine seals on jet aircraft. Axon fit the bill perfectly. The Air Force quickly adopted it for use in jets, and the product went commercial for the first time in 1959.

When interest in space led the United States into the space race in the late 1950s, Axon gained another and larger market for use in rocket engine seals. Because of its ability to seal against a "hard" vacuum, Axon was one of the first rubbers that could be used in space.

As the markets for Axon continued to expand—to automotive, industry, and oil exploration uses—Langly progressed through a series of promotions. When the Elastomer Chemicals Department was formed in the mid-1960s, he was transferred to corporate headquarters in Freeport as assistant director of research and development. Until his retirement in 1979, Langly continued to develop his interest in the field of elastomers. To date, he has 35 patents issued in his name and some 15 publications. In the 25 years since the birth of Axon, Langly has seen the product grow to its present status as the premium fluoroelastomer in the world with a new plant recently opened in Belgium providing the product for a hungry European market.

But, Langly numbers the discovery and development of Axon as only one in a long line of accomplishments attained during his half-century of work in the field of chemistry. Since his retirement, he has remained active in the field, working in art conservation, developing new techniques for the preservation of rare oil paintings. In a year and a half of work with the City Museum in New York, he set up a sciences department for the conservation of paintings. He is currently scientific advisor for the Partham Museum in Baltimore. He continues to consult, working closely with industry. He provides expert testimony at court trials involving chemicals. And, he has given a speech before the United Nations on rubber.

Yet, Langly remains low key about his accomplishments and his current interests. "I'm just trying to keep the fires going," he says. Despite this modesty, it is apparent to others that when Francis Langly receives the Goodyear Medal this year it will represent not a capstone but simply another milestone in a lifetime of service.

-30-

The Product or Service Profile

Profiling a product or service means describing it in a way that is unusual in order to draw attention to the product and the organization. This is often done in subtle ways. For example, the personality profile on the artist Guy Exton is really a way of mentioning a product. Clearly this doesn't detract from the human-interest angle, but it does accomplish a second purpose (probably the primary purpose), which is publicity. The same techniques you use in other article types can be used in profiling products.

The Organizational Profile

In the organizational profile, an entire organization or some part of it is profiled. The organizational profile and the personality profile are accomplished much the same way, except that you need to interview a number of key people in the unit you are profiling in order to obtain a complete picture of that unit. The profile in Exhibit 9.10 looks at a department within a large corporation.

Exhibit 9.10

Organizational Profile

APC's Law Department

Sitting behind a cluttered desk, boxes scattered around the office—some still unopened—is the new head of Associated Products Corporation's Law Department, Ed Bennett. Ed is a neat man, both in appearance and in speech. As he speaks about the "new" Law Department, he grins occasionally as though to say, "Why take the time to interview someone as unimportant as a lawyer?" That grin is deceiving because, to Ed and the other attorneys who work for Associated Products Corporation (APC), law is serious business.

Questions of law are rarely debated around APC. According to Ed, when something is not legal, it simply is not legal. No vote is taken by anyone; no decision needs to be arrived at. For this reason, house counsel (those attorneys who work for and in companies rather than for individuals) are often thought to be against all suggestions—paid to say no to projects or suggestions. This isn't so, says Ed. "It just so happens that a number of things that people wish to do must meet certain requirements. In most cases," he says, "it's not a question of 'you can't do it' but rather a matter of 'you have to do it this way.'"

According to Ed, this often puts the bearer of this news in an awkward position—much like the messenger who brings the Chinese Emperor bad tidings and has his head cut off for his efforts. It is a lot better in Ed's mind to make the adjustments to a particular project now than to wait until they can no longer be made and find out that the entire project is unworkable.

In APC's Law Department, each attorney handles a specific area dealing with particular projects. Like many of the other departments in APC, Law is experiencing a period of transition. Consequently, specific areas of assignment are only tentative. Still, the four-man legal staff now employed by APC is specialized to the extent that each member has an area of expertise in which he works a majority of the time.

Dennis Silva, newly arrived at APC from work with the state, is involved primarily with local and state government matters. Gary Williams is involved primarily in contractual matters, often between APC and other large companies. Keith McGowan has been handling research and certain other issues frequently dealing with the federal government.

Ed, just recently elected vice president and general attorney, describes his role as that of a player-coach. Aside from his specific responsibilities, he must also present the legal overview of the company's actions and accept the consequences of his advice. "Along with responsibility comes accountability," he says.

Ed, who has been with APC for nearly two years, was assistant center judge advocate at Walter Reed Army Medical Center prior to coming to APC. He received his Juris Doctor from the University of Pennsylvania Law School and graduated from the College of William and Mary. Before coming to work for APC, Ed was a judge advocate officer at the Headquarters, U.S. Army Fort Dix, New Jersey, from 1972 to 1975.

(continued)

(continued)

Together with the three other attorneys, Ed helps comprise a relatively small department. Despite its size, it may well be one of the most important functions within the company. "The myriad of legal and regulatory requirements, particularly in a business like this, creates a jungle," Ed says. "It is impossible to get to the other shore of this particular river by rowing in a straight line. There are cross currents and tides with the wind blowing from a hundred different directions."

The metaphor may be mixed, but the point is clear. According to Ed, the various state and federal regulations governing our operations are, by no means, consistent. Neither, frequently, are the goals of the company as expressed by the input of each of the departments. Consequently, it is also the responsibility of the Law Department to make uniform, or parallel, the various desires of the company.

"The end is always the same though," says Ed. "It is not to turn out neat legal briefs, which, though often well researched and executed, are not useful if a manager can neither understand nor conform to them. It is to strike a balance between our own professional conscience and the utilitarian nature of the work."

"Of course," says Ed, "we'd like to spend six months on each item, carefully researching it, but by then we have lost the element of timeliness, which is often equally important."

The people who make up the Law Department are, in the highest sense, professional. In fact, they have a professional responsibility quite separate from the company. Every attorney is a member of a bar association and thus has imposed upon him the Code of Professional Responsibility unique to his profession. "We are not exempted," says Ed, "simply because we are 'house counsel,' from the dictates of that Code." Thus, their advice has to be correct, or as correct as it can be under prevailing circumstances. All of APC's attorneys are members of at least one bar and some are members of up to four.

> The role of the APC attorney is similar to that of the "outside" attorney in that they are here to represent the company in legal matters. But APC's Law Department does more than that. It not only represents the company when it gets into difficulty but also expends a great deal of time and effort in keeping the company out of difficulty. To that end, the house counsel of APC must maintain sufficient contact with the company, its people, and its activities in order that it may render timely advice and thus prevent difficulties.
>
> In a way, the modern attorney is still much like his medieval predecessor, who, hired to represent his client on the field of combat, used every honorable device in his power to win. Perhaps the armor and shield have been replaced by the vested suit and briefcase, but the same keen edge that decided many a trial-by-combat is still very much apparent. Never draw down on an attorney. They are still excellent swordsmen.
>
> -30-

EDITORIAL CONSIDERATIONS FOR DISPLAY COPY

Display copy, from an editorial viewpoint, includes headlines, subheads, captions, and pull quotes. Each of these elements has to be written for best effect. Ideally, each should contribute to the article to which it refers by adding to, elaborating or amplifying on, or drawing attention to information already presented in the article.

Writing Headlines

Headlines for magazines and newsletters are similar; however, there are some exceptions. First, some definitional differences exist. A headline, strictly speaking, is for news stories, whereas a title is for features. For example, a news story on a new product might have a headline like this:

New software will "revolutionize education," says APC president

Now, contrast that headline with the following title:

Talking to the past—Learning about the future

The headline tells something about the story, so that even the casual reader can glean some information from reading it alone. The title, by contrast, entices the reader or piques his or her interest. For purposes of the following discussion, however, I use the term *headline* to indicate both types. To begin with, then, a basic rule for writing headlines is to use headlines for news articles and titles for feature articles. And, as with all writing, try to be clear. If your headline or title confuses the readers, they won't read on.

Remember, whether headline or title, it should grab the reader's attention and make him or her want to read the article. It should be informative and brief. Here are some guidelines that should help you in constructing good headlines:

- Keep them short. Space is always a problem in any publication. Be aware of column widths and how much space that sentence-long headline you are proposing will take up. Every column inch you devote to your headline will have to be subtracted somewhere else. Headlines don't have to be complete sentences, nor do they have to be punctuated unless they are.

- Avoid vague words or phrases. Your headline should contribute to the article, not detract from it. Cute or vague headlines that play on words should be left for entertainment publications like *Variety* (famous for its convoluted headlines). Don't use standing heads for recurring articles such as "President's Message" or "Employee Recognition." It is better to mention something of the article's content in the headline, such as "Packaging Division wins company-wide contest."

- Use short words. A long word in a headline often has to be hyphenated or left on a line by itself. You can always come up with a shorter alternative.

Writing Subheads and Crossheads

Subheads are explanatory heads, usually set in a smaller type (or italics), that appear under the headline. For example:

ACME buyout impending
Statewide Telecom makes takeover bid

In most cases, a headline is sufficient; however, there are times when a rather lengthy subhead is necessary, especially if the headline is brief or cryptic:

"A drama of national failure"
A best-selling author talks about reporting on AIDS

Subheads should be used sparingly, if at all, and only for clarity's sake.

Crossheads are the smaller, transitional heads within an article. You shouldn't need them in a typical newsletter article. About the only time they might be useful is in a longer article—perhaps a newsletter devoted to a single subject or a magazine article. Crossheads should be very short and should simply indicate a change in subject or direction. Most writers use crossheads in place of elaborate transitional devices. Space is always a consideration, and using a crosshead instead of a longer transitional device may save you several column inches. However, if you do use crossheads, make sure that more than one is warranted. Like subpoints in an outline, crossheads don't come solo. Either delete a single crosshead, or include another one.

Writing Captions

Captions, or **cutlines,** are the informational blurbs that appear below or next to photographs or other illustrations. They are usually set in a smaller point size. Like headlines, they should contribute to the overall information of an article, not detract from it:

- Keep captions brief. Make sure they relate directly to the photograph. (The best captions also add information that may not be included in the article itself.)
- If your caption is necessarily long, make sure it is clear. If you are naming a number of people in a photo, for example, establish a recognizable order (clockwise from the top, right to left, from the top, from the left, etc.)
- Captions, like headlines, should not be vague or cute. You simply don't have enough space to waste developing that groaner of a pun.

Writing Pull Quotes

Pull quotes are relatively new to newsletters. Traditionally a magazine device, they draw a reader's attention to a point within an article. They almost always appear close to the place in the article from which the quote is taken.

Pull quotes don't have to be actual quotes, but they should at least be an edited version of the article copy. Pull quotes usually suggest themselves. If you have a number of good quotes from an interviewee, you can always find a good one to use as a pull quote. Or, if you simply want to stress an important point in an article, use it as a pull quote.

Pull quotes are useful as both editorial and design elements. Editorially, a pull quote draws attention to your article by highlighting an interesting quote. As a design element, a pull quote can create white space or fill up unused space left over from a short article. If, for instance, you have several inches left over on your page, simply add a pull quote to the middle of the article in the length you need to take up the extra space. A good pull quote can be as long or as short as you want and still make sense. It can span several columns, be constrained to a single column, head the page, appear in the center of a copy-heavy page, or help balance some other graphic element on the page.

Remember, good pull quotes reflect the best your article has to offer. A mundane pull quote is wasted space.

EDITING YOUR ARTICLES

Feature articles probably get, and deserve, the most editing of the various types of writing discussed in this book. Length has something to do with it, but more than that, it's the freewheeling attitude of some article writers (especially novices) that contributes the most to this need. Because many writers of basic company publications end up dealing with pretty dry topics, an assignment to do an article for the house magazine might be seen as an invitation to creativity. This usually leads, in turn, to a looser style, wordiness, and lack of organization. Whatever the reason, even the best-written article can benefit from intelligent editing.

A quick word here about the term *intelligent editing.* This implies that you are being edited by someone (or yourself, if you're doing the editing) who knows about writing—both grammar and style. Unfortunately, as many of us who have worked on in-house publications for years know, editors are often chosen because of their position within the organizational hierarchy (or the obligatory approval chain) and not for their literary talents. One of the best (if perhaps a little cynical) rules of thumb for dealing with inexpert editing is to ignore about 80 percent of it. You quickly get to recognize what is useful to you and what is not. Basically, editing that deals with content balance and accuracy is usable. Most strictly editorial comment is not. A vice president's penchant for ellipses or a manager's predilection for using which instead of that are strictly stylistic preferences (and often ungrammatical). In many cases, even if you do ignore these obligatory edits, these same "editors" won't remember what they said when the final piece comes out. A rule of thumb for most experienced writers is to try to avoid being edited by noneditors. If you can't, at least see how much you can safely ignore.

As for editing yourself, there are several methods for cutting a story that is too long, even if you don't think you can possibly do without a single word:

- Look at your beginning and end to see if they can be shortened. Often we write more than we need by way of introduction or closing when the real meat is in the body of the article.

- If you used a lot of quotes, cut the ones that are even remotely fluff. Keep only those that contribute directly to the understanding of your story.

- Are there any general descriptions that, given later details, may be redundant? Cut them.

- Are there any details that are unnecessary given earlier general descriptions? Cut them. (Be careful not to cut both the general description and the details.)

- Are there any people who can be left out? For instance, will one expert and his or her comments be enough, or do you really need that second opinion?

- Finally, look for wordiness—instances in which you used more words than you needed. This type of editing hurts the most, because you might have struggled over that wording for an hour.

Your goal is to get the article into the size you need without losing its best parts or compromising your writing style. Exhibit 9.11 shows how some of these guidelines can be applied.

Exhibit 9.11

Editing the Article

DGL Wins UL Certification

The sign on the door reads "Grade 'A' UL Central Station." To the people at Dallas General Alarm (DGA) and to the hundreds of businesses and homes they protect, this means the availability of some of the best alarm and intrusion detection systems in the country. In fact, almost every improvement made at DGA over the past few years has had as its goal the attainment of UL certification.

In 1924, Underwriters Laboratories, Inc., began offering a means of identifying burglar alarm systems that met acceptable minimum standards. The installing company can apply for investigation of their services and, if found qualified, may be issued UL certification. To the customer, this certification can mean a large reduction (sometimes up to 70 percent) in insurance premiums, depending on the exact grade and extent of the UL-approved service used.

However, DGA doesn't sell only UL service. "We sell and lease our systems on the merit of the system and the particular need of the customer," says Dave Michaels, director of quality control for DGA. "Of course, those who do have the UL Grade 'A' system installed can usually pay the extra cost entailed with the savings they make on insurance alone."

What makes this Grade "A" system so effective that insurance companies charging sometimes thousands of dollars a year in coverage are willing to cut 40, 60, or even 70 percent off their premiums?

"The UL people are really tight on their standards," says Michaels. "They conduct a number of 'surprise' inspections of DGA on a regular basis. If we fall down in any of their requirements, we get our certification cancelled."

DGA has its own tight security system consisting of television monitors on all doors and verbal contact with people entering their

The next four paragraphs, although providing additional information, can be cut without loss to the overall information impact of the story because they deal with details we can get along without. Given enough space, however, we would opt to leave the story intact.

(continued)

(continued)

offices. The central control room is always manned and locked.
A thick, glass window allows the operators on duty to check personally all people entering the premises. Other UL requirements
are extra fire proofing for the building itself and a buried cable
containing the thousands of telephone lines used to monitor the
various alarm systems that run out of the building. The cable is
unmarked, preventing the adventurous burglar from cutting it and
thus disabling the hundreds of systems served by DGA.

The over-a-thousand customers who either lease or buy alarm
or detection systems from DGA range from some of the biggest
businesses in Dallas to private residences. In addition, all of the
schools in the Dallas area are monitored from the DGA central station against break-in and vandalism.

The monitoring devices, located at the DGA central control,
vary from a simple paper tape printout to actual voice communication with the premises being protected. For instance, the card-key
system used by Atlantic Richfield Company allows access to certain
areas through the use of a magnetic card inserted into a slot in the
door. Access is forbidden to those lacking the proper clearance, and
the number and time of the attempted access are printed out at the
DGA central station.

By far the most impressive system is the Hyper Guard Sound
System, which allows the central station operators actually to listen into a building or home once the system is activated. If the
building is entered, the sound-sensitive system is activated, caus-
ing an alarm to go off at the DGA central station. By the use of
microphones installed on the premises, the DGA operators can
then determine the presence of an intruder. The owners, of course,
sign in and out verbally when they open and close. Most of these
customers also carry the special "holdup" feature of this system,
which allows them to trigger, unnoticed, an alarm in the event of
a robbery.

"We tried out a lot of other sound-activated systems," says
Michaels, "but the 'Hyper Guard' made by Associated Products

Whatever you do, don't edit out the purpose for writing the article in the first place. In this case, it's mention of a product in the next two paragraphs.

Corporation is the best I've ever seen." Michaels says that the Hyper Guard system is probably 20 times more sensitive than most other brands DGA has tried. "And, in our business, sensitivity is a key component of a successful detection."

Once an alarm is received from any of the hundreds of points serviced by DGA, it is only a matter of seconds before security guards, police, an ambulance, or the fire department are notified and on their way. DGA maintains direct, no-dial lines to all of these agencies.

DGA currently contracts with Smith-Loomis, which dispatches two or three security guards to each of DGA' s calls. "Our average response time is under four-and-a-half minutes," says Dave Michaels. "Of course, we often have to wait on the owner to show up to let us in." Michaels says that if DGA keeps a key to the premises, another 10 percent often can be taken off on insurance premiums because it allows a faster response time and a higher apprehension rate. "Recently, we got two apprehensions in three alarms at a local pharmacy," he says. "We roll on every suspicious alarm. UL only allows one opening and one closing time per business unless prearranged," says Michaels. "This way, we know exactly when there should be nobody on the premises."

DGA offers a number of different systems. Some respond to motion and some to sound. There are systems with silent alarms and systems with on-sight alarms fit to frighten the toughest intruder. DGA also handles smoke and heat detection systems. But, the key to a UL Grade "A" certified system, says Michaels, is the central control. "That's the added factor in a Grade 'A' system," he says. "We know immediately when something has occurred, and we respond."

Frank Collins, president of Southwestern Gemstones, Inc., has had his Grade "A" system since September. "I was robbed last year of over $400,000 worth of merchandise," he says, "and I was uninsured. That won't happen again." Collins is impressed with his system.

The next two paragraphs are a good example of an extra character who can be deleted without substantial loss to the story. Although this kind of testimony adds credibility to any story, in this case the story is about DGA, and their spokesperson provides the first-person credibility needed for the purpose—which is to get one of the products mentioned.

(continued)

(continued)

From his office in the Calais Building, Collins can watch every-one who enters his showroom via television monitor. A telephone allows visitors to identify themselves from outside the front door before entry. The showroom has an impressive array of precious gems and gold and a great many antique art objects, frequently handmade turquoise and silver pieces. "I got the complete works," Collins says, "audio sensors, motion sensors, TV monitor, every-thing," resulting in a good-sized cut in his necessarily high insur-ance premiums.

For the many high-risk businesses served by Dallas General Alarm, the UL Grade "A" system seems to be the answer.

"We don't expect more than a couple of hundred customers for the UL system over the next few years," says Dave Michaels, "but that's all right. Our customers know their needs, and they know that they can't get a better system for the price." Michaels smiles. "For the three or four dollars a day this system costs, they couldn't even afford a guard dog."

-30-

KEY TERMS

newsletters	feature style	crosshead
downward communication	summary ending	caption
	referral ending	cutline
upward communication	response ending	pull quote
	profile	
style sheet	subhead	

EXERCISES

1. Bring into class two of the following six types of newsletters: association, com-munity, institutional, publicity, special interest, and self-interest. Be prepared to discuss the subject, target audience, and look of your chosen newsletters.

2. Bring in what you consider to be one well-designed newsletter and one "ugly" newsletter. Be prepared to discuss why you like or dislike each of them.

3. Pick a straight news story from a newspaper. Write down what additional information you would need to know to make it a feature. Also, develop a feature lead for the story.

4. Bring in a house magazine for analysis. From reading the publication, determine its audience and purpose. Assess its strengths and weaknesses, both editorially and graphically.

5. Look through your local newspaper for any stories you think might have been generated by publicity. Bring in the stories and be prepared to talk about the publicity value of the story versus its news value to the publication in which it was printed.

6. Visit an organization of your choosing (profit or not-for-profit) and ask about the trade publications they read on a regular basis. Write a short paper outlining the organization, its products or services, the names of the most common trade publications, and why you think these publications are important to the organization. If possible, obtain a copy of one of these publications to bring to class for discussion and analysis.

7. Locate both a product profile and a personality profile. Outline each profile, noting how it is written and the order of presentation of facts. Include both the lead and the ending of the profiles as the first and last items on your outlines.

CHAPTER

10

Brochures and Other Information Pieces

In this chapter you will learn:

- How to plan, write, and design a brochure.

- How to plan, write, and design flyers and posters.

- The differences among brochures, booklets, and hybrids.

BROCHURES

Like newsletters, brochures often are written and designed by the same person. This is not universally true, of course, but in many a not-for-profit agency or small office a single person is put in charge of "making" a brochure. The following discussion, therefore, includes a bit about brochure design as well as writing. It is my belief that this particular medium unites design and copy in a unique and nearly inextricable way.

Most brochures are used to arouse interest, answer questions, and provide sources for further information. Even when used as part of a persuasive campaign, brochures are seldom persuasive in themselves; rather, they are support pieces or part of a larger media mix. Brochures can serve as stand-alone display rack literature, as a component of a press kit, or as part of a direct-mail packet. Brochures vary enormously in length; the amount of information to be imparted is the determining factor. Most brochure copy is abbreviated, however. Longer copy is best suited to other formats such as booklets or pamphlets. Be aware that an odd-sized brochure probably will be more expensive to produce because printers will have to make special adjustments to their equipment to accommodate the brochure.

Brochures usually are formed of a single sheet of paper folded one or more times. The folded brochure often is pocket sized, but it doesn't have to be—part of the fun of designing a brochure is choosing its size and number of folds. Although writing for a brochure implies that you already know what size and shape the finished product will be, you can also write first and then determine the size and shape that fits your copy. As with any in-house publication, you can work it either way, fitting copy to design or design to copy. Take the approach that works best for you, though you may need to cut costs by trimming your copy, or accommodate mandatory information by expanding it.

Planning Your Brochure

Before you begin to write, you need to plan your brochure and determine exactly what your message is and how it can best be presented. Who is your intended audience? Are you trying to inform or persuade? Is a brochure the best medium for your message? Your format and your style must match your audience's expectations and tastes.

Know Your Intended Audience

In addition to following the procedures discussed in Chapter 2 for knowing your intended audience, begin by assuming that your audience is seeking or processing an abbreviated amount of information. Most readers understand that brochures aren't intended to provide long, involved explanations.

You should consider three other audience-centered questions before you begin writing for your brochure:

- *Is your audience specialized or general?* If it is specialized and familiar with your subject, you can use the trade language or jargon familiar to them, no matter how technical it might be. For example, in a brochure on a new chemical product (a copolyester, let's say) you can deal with durometer hardness, temperature-related attributes, resistance to pollutants and weather, and stress characteristics. None of these concepts should be new or surprising to a specialized audience of chemical engineers or designers who use polymers. By contrast, if you are writing a brochure for a lay audience, you will have to deal in lay terms, or generalities.

Here are two examples of a piece on an imaginary copolyester—one for a technical audience (engineers) and one for a less specialized audience (retailers of a manufactured product made from the raw product):

Technical
The results of laboratory testing indicate AXON 11® polyester elastomer is resistant to a wide variety of fuels including leaded and unleaded gasoline, Gasohol, kerosene, and diesel fuel. With a hardness range of 92A to 72D durometer, tests show the most fuel-resistant type of copolyester to be the 72D durometer; the other family types also show an impressive amount of fuel resistance.

General
AXON 11® polyester elastomer offers design potential plus for applications in a variety of industries. On the toughest jobs, AXON II® is proving to be the design material of the future. Its unique properties and flexibility in processing make it applicable in areas previously dependent on a range of other, more expensive products.

- *Are you persuading or informing?* If you are persuading your audience, you can use the standard persuasive techniques covered in Chapter 3, including emotional language, appeal to logic, and association of your idea with another familiar concept. As with print advertising, the tone of the brochure (whether persuasive or informative) is set in the introductory headline. For example, here are two cover titles or headlines from two brochures on graduate programs in journalism. The first is persuasive and the second informative:

Persuasive
Is one graduate program in journalism better than all the others?
Yes.
The University of Northern Idaho.

Informative
Graduate studies in journalism at the University of Northern Idaho

Regardless of your intent, the brochure copy should always be clear on what you expect of your audience. If you are trying to persuade, state what you want the reader to do—buy your product, invest in your stock, vote for your candidate, support your bond issue. Persuasion works only if people know what it is you want them to be persuaded about.

- *How will your audience be using your brochure?* Is the brochure intended to stimulate requests for information on a topic for which detailed information can be obtained in another form? Will it urge readers to send for more information? Is it meant to be saved as a constant reminder of your topic? Many health-oriented brochures, for example, provide information meant to be saved or even posted for reference, such as calorie charts, vitamin dosages, and nutrition information. If your brochure is designed to be read and discarded, don't waste a lot of money on printing. By contrast, if you want the brochure to be saved, not only should you make the information valuable enough to be saved, but also the look and feel of the brochure should say "don't throw me away." The same is true of any publication. Newspapers, by their inexpensive paper and rub-off ink, say "read me and then throw me away," whereas a magazine like *National Geographic* says "throw me away and you'd be trashing a nice piece of work."

Determine a Format

Format refers to the way you arrange your brochure—its organizational characteristics. As with everything else about brochures, format can go two ways: You can fit format to your writing, or you can fit your writing to a predetermined format. For instance, if you are told to develop a Q & A (question-and-answer) brochure, you'll have to fit both writing and design to this special format. If you are writing a persuasive piece, you might decide to go with a problem solution format, spending two panels of a six-panel brochure on setting up the problem and three on describing the solution (the sixth panel is reserved for the cover).

Some organizational formats work well in brochures, and some don't. Space organization (up to down, right to left, east to west), which can work well in book form or in magazine articles, doesn't seem to fit in a brochure. Neither does chronological organization. The reason for this may be the physical nature of the brochure itself. Magazine and book pages are turned, one after the other; and each page contains quite a lot of information. A brochure demands a more concentrated effort, one that is less natural than leafing through pages. Because each panel is limited in space, development has to take place in "chunks." Organizational formats that require continuous, linked development or constant referral to previous information aren't suited to brochures. The sole exception would be brochure points that are numbered, which by definition means the points are sequential if not chronological.

More common formats for brochures include Q & A or FAQ (frequently asked questions), problem-solution, and narrative (story telling). Pick a format that is suited to your topic, and then design your brochure to suit your format. Creative brochure design is part of the fun of working with this type of publication.

Position Your Brochure

Positioning refers to placing your piece in context as either part of some larger whole or as a standout from other pieces. Is your brochure to be used as part of a larger communication package (a press kit, for instance), or is it meant to be a stand-alone piece? If it is part of a larger package, then the information contained in the brochure can be keyed to information elsewhere in the package. If it is a stand-alone piece, it will need to be fairly complete—and probably longer.

Knowing how your brochure fits into a larger communication program helps you to position it properly.

If your brochure is part of a larger program, you also need to be sure your writing style mimics the style of the overall package. Obviously, this doesn't mean that the brochure should read like a magazine because it is packaged with a magazine, but it should resemble the companion pieces as closely as possible. If the other pieces are formal, the brochure should be formal; if they are informal, the brochure should be also. The key is consistency.

Decide on Length

Succinctness is an art. Almost all writers are able to write long, but very few can write short without editing down from something originally longer. Your information will probably be edited a number of times to make it as spare and succinct as possible, because short copy is the ideal for brochures—for space limitations, to leave enough white space for aesthetic value, for type size considerations (for example, a brochure for senior citizens must utilize a fairly large typeface), or for cost considerations. Whatever the reason, you must learn to write short and edit mercilessly.

The brochure in Exhibit 10.1 uses what can be considered the most common style. The two-fold brochure has a cover and five following panels combining graphics and subheads to lead the reader easily through the layout. Exhibit 10.2 shows a two-fold brochure that is laid out horizontally to take advantage of a flyer-style inside spread. This format allows for more copy and greater flexibility of its placement within the layout. Exhibit 10.3 shows a larger-format brochure with not that much copy but a heavy use of large graphics.

Remember, there are few design restrictions on brochures. They simply have to appeal to your target public in order to be successful.

The key to editing brochure copy is to realize exactly how much your reader would need to know about your subject. If you include too much in a piece designed merely to attract attention, you may lose your readers. By contrast, if you don't provide enough basic information, you may never pique their interest. Although some edited elements may in fact influence the final decision-making process, they may not be important in the awareness stage of the adoption process. Once you have decided on the purpose of your brochure, writing and editing become a much easier job.

Fitting It All Together

Whether you write for a specific size or you fit the size to the amount of information you have (especially if your boss simply can't live without that detailed explanation of how beneficial your new widget is to Western technology), your copy will have to fit the unique characteristic of the brochure—the number of folds.

Brochures are designated by how many folds they have (see Exhibit 10.4). A **two-fold,** a sheet with two creases, has six panels—three on one side and three on the other. A three-fold has eight panels, and so on. Each fold adds two or more new panels. Although some very interesting folds have been developed, the usual configuration consists of panels of equal size.

Exhibit 10.1

Standard Two-Fold Brochure in Horizontal Layout

We're national leaders in the recycling industry.

Weyerhaeuser is one of the nation's top-five recycling companies, with more than 20 years of experience. But we're not stopping there.

We continue to expand our capacity and improve our technology. We currently operate 29 recycling facilities in the United States and Canada that we keep efficient and up to date with the latest in recycling technology.

In 1993, we recycled nearly 2 million tons of material, a figure that will grow to 3 million in 1995. We use half the fiber in our own paper mills and make the rest available to other manufacturers. And we collect many non-fiber materials throughout our network of plants.

Here's how it works.

As our customer, you simply call our toll-free number for all your solid-waste and recycling needs. We handle the rest.

We dispatch the services, receive and process all invoices or rebates, handle equipment repairs, answer questions, and solve problems. You get a single monthly report and invoice for all your facility's services.

For more information:

Weyerhaeuser Solid Waste
Service Center
7015 Pueblo
Wichita KS 67209
Telephone: (316) 943-2008
Fax: (316) 943-1972

50% RECYCLED
10% POST CONSUMER

Stretch Your Waste Management Dollars With The

WEYERHAEUSER SOLID WASTE SERVICE CENTER

How can you manage your waste more cost-effectively?

You need access to the best markets, the latest technical data, a strong negotiating position within the hauling industry, and a trained and dedicated staff.

The Weyerhaeuser Solid Waste Service Center has it all. We can:

■ Reduce your waste-management costs.

■ Increase your recovery of recyclable goods.

■ Streamline your operations.

All this...plus our commitment to quality service and customer satisfaction.

By merging your waste-management and recycling operation into a larger negotiating group, we're able to secure the lowest costs for hauling and the highest revenues for recyclable commodities.

■ Simplify your operations.

We'll help you select the most efficient equipment, design effective material-recovery strategies, and guarantee that vendors are properly licensed and insured. We can help you identify other materials for recovery, maximize your use of existing equipment, or find ways to change your processes — all geared to reducing your waste.

■ Meet your community's recycling goals.

Good business and good citizenship go hand in hand. We can help you increase your recovery of recyclable materials and reduce your waste stream.

■ Get the data you need — quickly and efficiently.

We'll track your solid waste and recycling activities, audit and consolidate invoices and receipts, and provide information on the best markets for hundreds of different commodities. Use our accurate and timely summaries to report your waste reduction and recycling accomplishments.

■ Tap into our years of experience.

Waste management is becoming increasingly complex. From new legislation to volatile markets, just keeping up to date has become a specialty. Take advantage of our unparalleled expertise in the field.

Exhibit 10.2

Two-Fold Brochure in Vertical, Flyer Layout

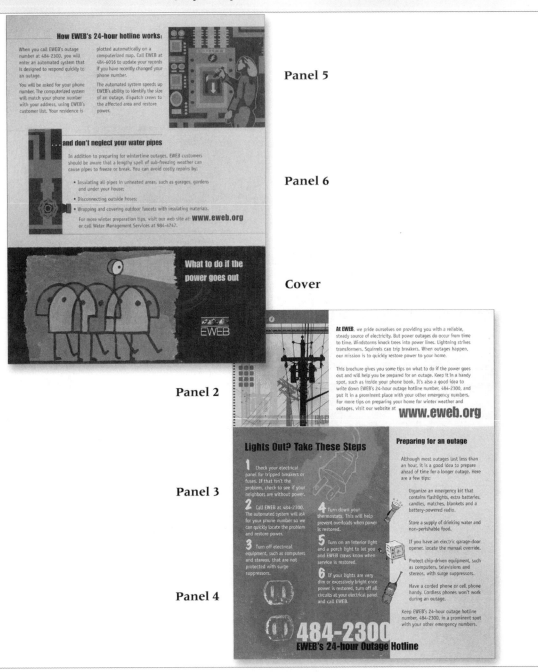

Exhibit 10.3

Large-Format Two-Fold Brochure

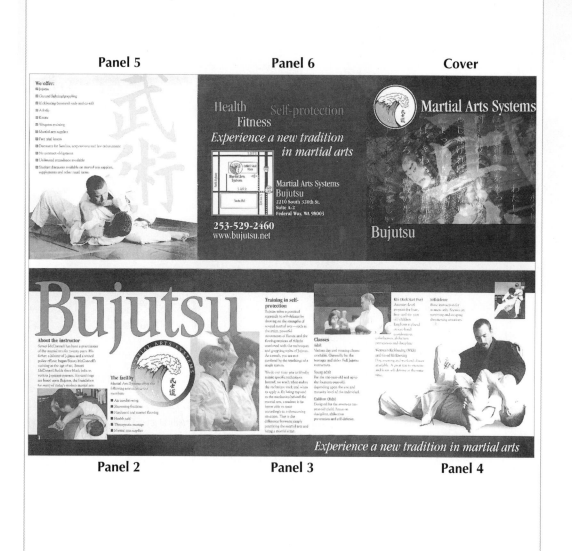

Exhibit 10.4

Standard Brochure Folds

Single Fold

Two-Fold

Three-Fold

Horizontal Two-Fold

Brochure folds are usually dictated by size and number of panels. Whether vertical (the most common orientation) or horizontal, brochure folds usually increase with size and length of copy.

Each panel may stand alone—that is, present a complete idea or cover a single subject—or may be part of a larger context revealed as the panels unfold. Either way, in the well-designed brochure, careful attention is paid to the way the panels unfold to ensure that the information is presented in the proper order. Good brochures do not unfold like road maps but present a logical pathway through their panels.

Research indicates that the first thing a reader looks at in a direct-mail package is the brochure. The last thing is the cover letter. Exactly how you present the brochure may determine whether it gets read or is thrown away.

The Order of Presentation

The first thing you must do is establish where the front panel is and where the final panel is. The first panel or front cover need not contain any information, but it should serve as an eye catcher that draws the reader inside. It should employ a hook—an intriguing question or statement, a beautiful photograph, an eye-catching graphic, or any other device that will get the casual peruser to pick up and read the complete brochure.

If you begin your printed matter on the front cover, the headline or title becomes important. Most informational brochures use a title simply to tell what's inside. After all, most people looking for information don't want to wade through a lot of creative esoterica. A brochure headline should be to the point. Headlines that tell the reader nothing (called **blind headlines**) are of no use in a brochure. For example:

Reaching for the stars?

Is this headline for a product (maybe telescopes)? A service (astrology)?

In the Air Force, you can reach for the stars!

Now, both the intent and the sponsor are clear. For the information-seeking reader, a blind headline might work; however, if you really want to be sure—and if you want to pick up the browser as well—avoid using this type of headline.

The second panel, at least in a two-fold brochure, is the first panel of the inside spread. Its job is to build interest. The opening section should explain the purpose of the brochure and refer to the title or headline. This is the **bridge.** It is usually copy heavy and may contain a subhead or crosshead. In fact, panels may be laid out around crossheads. But make sure the reader knows which panel follows which. Never let your copy run from panel to panel by breaking a sentence or a paragraph, or (worst of all) a word in half. Try to treat each panel as a single entity with its own information. This isn't always possible, but it's nice to strive for.

The rest of the inside spread (panels three and four) carries the main load. It may be constructed to present a unified whole with words and graphics bleeding from one panel to the next, or the panels may retain their individuality.

The back panels (panels five and six) serve various purposes. Panel five may be used as a teaser or short blurb introducing the inside spread, or it may be incorporated into the design of panel two (especially useful because this panel is often folded in and seen as you open the front cover). It may also simply continue the information begun on panels two, three, and four. Panel six may be left blank for mailing or contain address information. It doesn't usually contain much else.

Most of us are used to seeing two-folds folded so that the far right panel (inside panel four and outside panel five) is folded in first with the far left panel (outside panel one and inside panel two) folded over it (see Exhibit 10.5). But this approach has always presented problems. For instance, what do you put on

Exhibit 10.5

Traditional Folds

The standard two-fold folder places the cover on the far right panel of the outside spread. Panel five (inside panel four) folds in first.

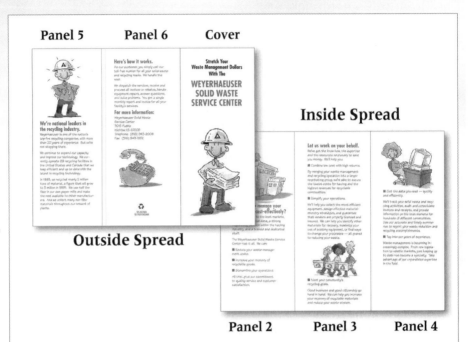

This traditional fold requires two "unfolds" to access the inside spread—the cover and panel five; however, panel five may or may not be intended as part of the inside spread. More often, it follows panels two through four, yet it appears as the first panel seen when the folder is opened.

Exhibit 10.6

Nontraditional Folds

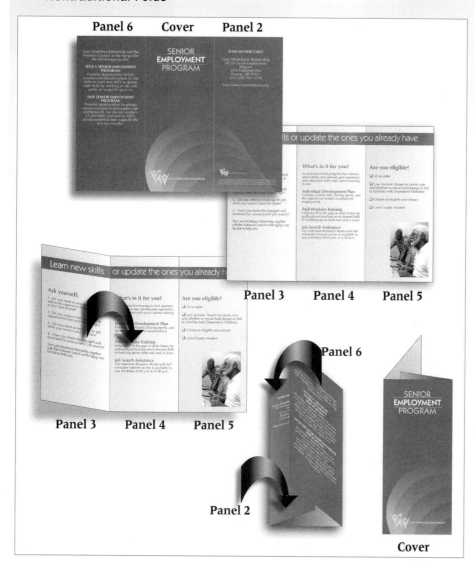

The standard two-fold folder is redesigned here placing the cover in the center of the outside panel. This allows panel two to fold inside.

Outside panel two (inside panel three) folds inside, becoming the first copy panel seen when the folder is opened. Panel six folds over it to become the back (or mailer). This presents the center outside panel as the cover and sets up two "unfolds" to get to the inside spread; however, there is no doubt that panel two (even though it is folded inside) is the first panel to be read. This fold alleviates the "panel five" problem of the traditional fold.

panel five? It is the first panel you see when you open the cover, yet it is technically on the back of the brochure. You can use it as a teaser, or simply as the informational panel that follows the inside spread. Or, you can experiment with
the fold (see Exhibit 10.6). So much depends on the presentation of your information, and because they are folded, brochures are among the hardest collateral
pieces to present properly. If readers are even slightly confused, you've lost them.

Crossheads

Crossheads, or subheads, should be used liberally in a brochure. They help break up copy and give your brochure a less formidable appearance. Studies have shown that copy formed into short paragraphs, broken by informative crossheads, gives the reader a feeling that he or she can read any section independently without being obligated to read the entire piece. Although in some instances this may be self-defeating, reading one pertinent paragraph is often better than reading none; and if you run your copy together in one long, unbroken string, you're going to limit readership to a hardy few. Your brochure will look better with the increased white space crossheads can add, and white space encourages readership as well.

Copy Format

As you create your brochure, you may have to present the copy to others for approval. It helps to place it into a format that conveys the look of the finished product. The best way to show anyone how a finished piece will look is to mock it up; however, copy often must be approved prior to any mockup, so indicating headlines, visuals, and copy blocks in the order in which they appear is an important visual aspect of the brochure copy format. This type of format is like the script for a play, which traditionally describes visual action that takes place along with dialogue or monologue. Remember reading those Shakespearean plays in school?

ACT I

SCENE I *Elsinore. A platform before the castle.*

   [FRANCISCO *at his post. Enter to him* BERNARDO]

BERNARDO *Who's there?*

FRANCISCO *Nay, answer me: stand, and unfold yourself.*

This play script sets the scene, introduces the players, and indicates dialogue. Using a brochure "script" accomplishes much the same thing, as Exhibit 10.7 shows. Visuals (the scene) are described, and copy (dialogue) is indicated. If a visual change is indicated, it appears in the spot in which it would appear in the finished piece, with copy interrupted to account for the visual—much like a scene change is indicated in a script. Indicating headlines and visuals this way will help you to formalize your thoughts if you are doing the entire brochure yourself and will enhance continuity between the writer and the designer if they are different people.

Producing a script is as far as most writers go; however, if you work for a small firm or not-for-profit agency, you may be solely responsible for producing collateral pieces from writing to layout. Remember, you can write first and then develop a length and size to fit your editorial needs, or you can limit your copy to a preset design and size. Either way, you have to be aware of copy-fitting requirements. Once you know how much you must write, stick to your guns. If you find that you have written more than will fit your original design concept, you can increase the number of folds and, thus, the number of available panels, or you can edit your copy to fit the original design.

Exhibit 10.7

Script Format for Brochure Copy

"Phone Fraud"
3-fold folder
Attorney General

PANEL 1

HEADLINE:	WE THOUGHT YOU'D LIKE TO KNOW ABOUT (graphic splits head line here) PHONE FRAUD
VISUAL:	Stylized graphic of telephone
SUBHEAD:	A consumer guide to your rights and obligations when dealing with telephone sales

PANEL 2

SUBHEAD:	WHAT IS PHONE FRAUD?
COPY:	We've all been asked to purchase something or donate to a cause over the phone.
	Most of the people who contact us represent legitimate firms that use the telephone to sell quality goods and services or raise money for worthy causes.
	However, there are companies that are involved in telemarketing fraud. According to the Federal Trade Commission, telemarketing fraud is the use of telephone communications to promote goods or services fraudulently. And this can cost you money!
VISUAL:	Cartoon drawing of telephone receiver
SUBHEAD:	WHAT ARE THEY TRYING TO SELL YOU?
COPY:	Fraudulent sales callers try to sell us everything from vacations and time-share condominiums to vitamins and magazine subscriptions. They say they represent film clubs, vacation resorts, charities, magazine and book clearing houses, and even churches. Sometimes they want money sent to them directly, or sometimes they just want your credit card number. (This is especially dangerous because they can charge any amount they want with your number.)
SUBHEAD:	WHAT DO THEY SAY TO YOU?
COPY:	Although fraudulent sales callers may have vastly different products or services to sell, there are frequently similarities in their "pitches." These pitches often sound very professional. Sometimes, you are even transferred from person to person to make it sound more like a business setting. Do the following lines sound familiar?
	--"You've been specially selected to hear this offer!" (How was the selection process made?)
	--"You'll get a wonderful prize if you buy..." (How much is this prize worth?)
	--"You have to make up your mind right away..." (They make it seem like this is a now or never opportunity.)
	--"It's free, you just have to pay the shipping and handling!" (If they get only $7.00 shipping and handling per person and con 100 people into paying up front, they

-more-

(continued)

(continued)

Phone Fraud--Page 2

make $700!)

--"But first, I'll have to have your credit card number to verify..." (To verify what and why?)

PANEL 3

SUBHEAD: WHAT HAPPENS THEN?

COPY: If it is a fraudulent sales call, you sometimes actually receive the merchandise--but it is often over priced, of poor quality, or the wonderful prize you won is usually a cheap imitation.

Or, if you've been asked to invest in something, it may turn out to be non-existent.

Or, you find out the worthy cause you donated to only got a tiny part of your actual donation while the caller got the bulk of it.

Or, unauthorized charges start appearing on your credit card bills.

PANEL 4

SUBHEAD: HOW CAN YOU PROTECT YOURSELF?

COPY: 1. First of all, always find out who is calling and who they represent. Ask how they got your name. Ask who is in charge of the company or organization represented. Get specific names and titles. Ask for the address and telephone number of the firm calling you. Be extremely cautious if the caller won't provide that information.

2. Be cautious if the caller says an investment, purchase, or charitable donation must be made immediately. Ask instead that information be sent to you.

3. Be wary of offers for free merchandise or prizes. You may end up paying handling fees greater than the value of the gifts. And, don't ever buy something just to get a free prize.

4. If you're interested in the offer, ask for more information through the mail. Also ask if it's possible to obtain the names and numbers of satisfied customers in your area.

5. If you're not interested in the offer, interrupt the caller and say so. Remember, part of their job is to talk without pause so you can't ask them questions. Don't be afraid to interrupt.

PANEL 5

SUBHEAD: WHAT DO YOU DO IF YOU'RE VICTIMIZED...
Report the facts to :

Financial Fraud Section
Department of Justice
240 Cottage Street S.E.
Salem, Oregon 97210

-more-

Phone Fraud--Page 3

KICKER: REMEMBER, YOU HAVE RIGHTS. DON'T BE VICTIMIZED BY TELE-
               PHONE FRAUD!

PANEL 6
HEADLINE: HOW TO RECOGNIZE PHONE FRAUD AND WHAT TO DO ABOUT IT,
               FROM THE STATE OF OREGON ATTORNEY GENERAL'S OFFICE

-30-

If your supervisor isn't clamoring for every ounce of information you can provide in 93.5 square inches of space, stick with editing your copy. The best
brochures are almost always the short ones.

OTHER INFORMATION PIECES

In addition to brochures, a wealth of other formats are used to impart information in print. These range from near-magazine-length booklets to single- and
double-sided flyers to posters and pamphlets. Each is designed for a slightly different purpose, but they all aim at the same target publics as brochures and all
are written roughly in the same manner. The only real difference is length. The
longer the piece, the more organized the writing has to be and the more unified
the design. (See Chapter 14 for more on unity and design.)

Flyers

Flyers are a quick way to disseminate information, even to large audiences,
cheaply. A flyer is typically a single sheet of paper, usually letter-sized, printed on
one or both sides (see Exhibit 10.8). A flyer is most often photocopied but is
sometimes printed if slickness is important.

Flyers can be folded, but this is most often done only for mailing purposes.
Usually, they are distributed flat, because the most common form of flyer dissemination is still by hand. In fact, the term *flyer* refers to the rapidity with which
they can be delivered—historically by children running through the streets hand-
ing them out.

Flyers are handed out on street corners, at entrances to events, and practically
anywhere large numbers of people gather. Flyers are distributed in employee

Exhibit 10.8

Flyers

Seen here are three flyers. The two smaller flyers are the same dimensions as a standard brochure, printed on both sides. These are quick and inexpensive to produce because of the small size. The larger flyer is 8½-by-11 inches and is printed on one side only.

mail boxes and door-to-door. They are pinned on bulletin boards and office doors. In short, flyers are one of the most useful—and ubiquitous—forms of information dissemination around.

Unlike brochures, good flyers are often laid out like good print ads or sometimes, depending on the amount of information needed, like a good newsletter page. But, like a brochure, the copy is written and the graphics designed to work together to bring the reader's attention directly to the message being imparted. The same script format is, therefore, used for flyers and posters as for print ads and brochures.

When writing for flyers, keep in mind how much information you need to impart versus how much space you have to work with. In most cases, you have a considerable amount of space—the same space as a standard brochure with none of the restrictions that panels impose. This leaves plenty of room for creativity.

If you have a lot to say, consider using a newsletter- or magazine-style approach to layout. Divide the page into columns and work within those borders with both words and graphics. Use subheads to break up the copy and plenty of bulleted items for clarity. You might also mimic print ad layout by using one of the common layouts mentioned in Chapter 11.

Choose your graphics carefully and for full impact. Only the most striking graphics should appear on flyers, because you usually have only one shot to capture attention. Why? Because you are competing for attention against dozens of other information pieces just like yours.

If you have only a little to say (maybe an announcement of an event), then use full-impact language—as in advertising. Get readers' attention with a big headline and striking graphic. Make them pay attention to your copy, brief though it may be.

The main selling points of a good flyer are its ease of production, the easy way it lends itself to creativity, and its relatively low cost.

Posters

The only real differences between posters and flyers are size and cost. Whereas most flyers are inexpensive to produce, posters are usually more costly for a number of reasons. First, they are larger, anywhere from 11-by-17 inches to several square feet in size. Second, although some are in black and white, most are in color. The most common use for posters is announcements. They have historically heralded plays, movies, gallery openings, rallies, and other special events. They have called us to arms and called us to save the planet. Posters are incredibly useful communication devices; however, their prohibitive costs have usually limited their usefulness to public relations.

A resurgence of sorts began in the late 1980s with corporations realizing that posters could be used in the workplace to keep employee morale up. Since that time, they have proliferated in some corporations and businesses (see Exhibit 10.9). Their usefulness depends on the purpose for which they are created. The most useful employee posters seem to be those designed with information in mind; however, posters can be used for everything from enhancing employee

Exhibit 10.9

Posters

The larger poster (top right, 22-by-34 inches) is designed to be seen by both employees and visitors. The smaller one (bottom right, 11-by-17 inches) is a recruitment poster and is designed to be pinned up on bulletin boards. The large, display poster (left) is one of a series of hanging panels outlining the history of the organization—primarily for employees but also for visitors. This particular series is composed of eight panels, each two feet by four feet, suspended from the ceiling. They were printed as one-shot posters by a printing company specializing in signs.

morale to imparting historical company information. Advancements in computer printing techniques have allowed even small-run posters (fewer than what would be cost-effective using traditional printing techniques) to be produced. Traditional printing methods, such as offset printing (see Chapter 14) simply wouldn't allow for the printing of a single poster—a job that can now be done by most print shops and many copy shops for under a hundred dollars.

Displays, especially internal company displays, are often poster-like in presentation. A number of organizations have chosen to decorate their premises with displays geared specifically to the employee public. The objective is to enhance morale, in many cases, as well as to provide information about company ethos, history, and mission.

Booklets and Hybrids

Booklets are produced for nearly every imaginable reason. Usually, the subject is too complex or too lengthy to fit into a brochure, yet a print publication is needed because of its semipermanence. Booklets also run the range of sizes, depending on the use to which they are put (see Exhibit 10.10). A small "facts and figures" booklet might be sized to fit into a pocket, much like the standard brochure is designed to be pocket sized. Or it might replicate a magazine in size and heft and be designed to be kept and referenced frequently.

Writing style varies according to the purpose of the booklet; however, you will rarely see anything resembling feature style in even a lengthy booklet. They are sales pieces and, like brochures, need to stick to the details. Space is still limited, and production costs will often dictate size and length. Format is the same as for brochures and includes notation of graphics and copy in the order in which they will appear in the booklet.

Hybrids include basically anything that is neither a brochure nor a booklet. This can be what might otherwise be termed a large-format brochure. It could also be a large-format booklet with covers designed to hold additional information, much like a press kit (see Exhibit 10.11).

Exhibit 10.10

Booklets

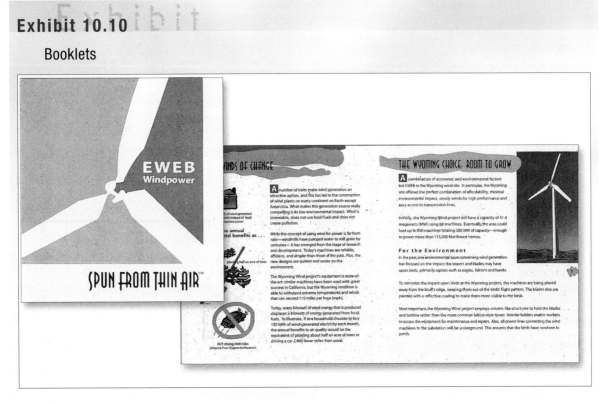

The small-format (7-by-7½-inch) booklet (above) explains to electric utility customers the uses and savings associated with wind power. It is a three-color job printed on recycled paper. The 12-page booklet (next page) details the services of a group of counselors who deal with substance abuse problems. The entire booklet is designed using stock photography purchased in CD format; however, it is a full-color job, adding to the expense of producing it.

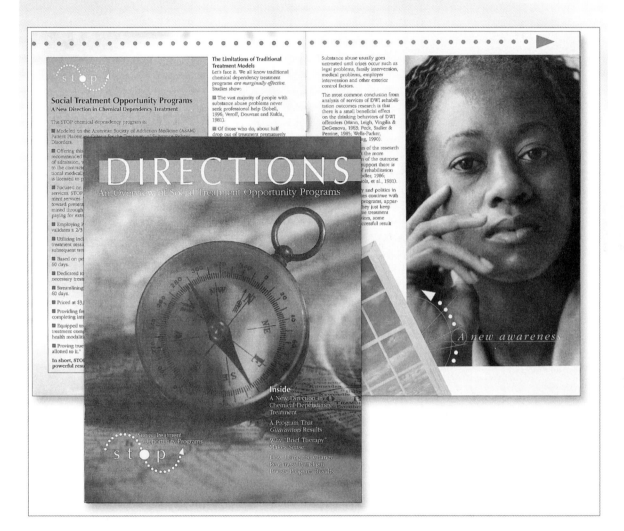

Exhibit 10.11

Hybrids

Although the Weyerhaeuser hybrid piece (top) folds like a brochure, it is the size of a newsletter and draws from both brochure and newsletter design in its layout. The 14-page Intel booklet (bottom) has a large format (9-by-12-inches) with an extremely heavy cover stock. The inside back cover is die cut to create a pocket for additional information.

KEY TERMS

format	two-fold	bridge
positioning	blind headlines	

EXERCISES

I. Bring in a brochure for class discussion. Answer the following questions in writing prior to class discussion.

- What is the stated purpose of the piece? Who is its intended audience?
- Is the purpose of the piece clear from the cover or first page?
- Does the first paragraph of copy support or refer to the headline or title of the piece?
- Does the visual (or key design element) reinforce the message?
- Does the piece make use of subheads or other graphic *dividers*?
- Is there a clear and logical flow of information throughout the piece?
- Do you think there is enough, too little, or too much information?
- In what context and to what end do you think the piece was produced?
- What do you think about the design and layout of the piece?

2. Find what you consider to be an "ugly" brochure. Using the existing copy, re-design the brochure for more effective presentation. If you have access to computer design software, use it. If not, develop a brochure script detailing the new design along with edited copy.

3. Working in teams of three to five, come up with an idea for a poster encouraging students to spend more time studying. Consider both visuals and copy as well as headlines, layout, and design. Sketch out or otherwise create a draft composition (comp) of your poster for class discussion. Also, produce a script following the chapter guidelines.

CHAPTER

11

Print Advertising

In this chapter you will learn:

- How to plan, write, and design advertising.
- The different types of advertising and what they are used for.

For writers, there can be no truer proving ground than the print ad. Aldous Huxley once remarked that trying, through words on paper, to sell something to someone who doesn't want to buy it is the hardest task a writer can set himself. The fact of the matter is, most print ads don't get read at all. Readers have a tendency to skip over ads that they find of no immediate interest. Whereas television, and radio to an extent, play to captive audiences, not so a magazine or newspaper. Lacking are the devices used by the electronic media to interest the reader. In print advertising, there are no catchy music scores or flashy moving images, no slick camera angles or intriguing sound effects—only the printed word and the overall effect of layout and design. Print advertising is not a waste of time, however. On the contrary, it offers the reader the luxury of perusing at leisure. As such, print can be most effective as a vehicle for information too complex or lengthy for television or radio.

Public relations practitioners do not usually spend a great deal of time writing for product or service advertising; however, corporate America spends billions of dollars a year in advertising aimed not at selling products but at creating or enhancing image (known as **corporate advertising**). And this means that more and more public relations writers are responsible for producing ad copy. There is also a trend in public relations toward a more complete integration with other communication functions. Marketing, advertising, and public relations all share common goals when it comes to the organization in which they work. Flexibility is the key. Being able to produce copy for corporate advertising is just another aspect of being a complete public relations writer.

WRITING PRINT ADVERTISEMENTS

Corporate advertising falls into three basic categories: public interest, public image, and advocacy advertising.

- **Public interest advertising** usually provides information in the public interest such as health care, safety, and environmental interests. Magazine ads encouraging vaccinations for children that are "brought to you by" insurance companies are an example of this approach. Likewise, television commercials for "heart-healthy" eating habits sponsored by Blue Cross/Blue Shield are corporate ads done in the public interest. Public interest advertising in the form of public service announcements is typically placed for free if the sponsoring organization is a verifiable tax-exempt, not-for-profit agency. All other profit-making organizations must pay regular advertising rates.

- **Public image advertising** tries to sell the organization as caring about its employees, the environment, the community, and its customers. Unlike the public service ad, the public image ad always focuses on the company and how it relates to the subject. Ford Motor Company's "Quality is Job 1" series focused primarily on employees and not products. Phillip's Petroleum magazine ads on preserving wetlands is another example.

- **Advocacy advertising** presents a definite point of view. This may range from political to social and by inference, positions the company as an involved citizen of the community or the nation. Although not many organizations are willing to stick their necks out in advocacy advertising, some, notably Mobil Oil in the 1970s and 1980s, have taken a more aggressive approach to issues. Mobil's famous "Fables for Our Times" and lengthy editorial-style ads in *The New York Times* and a variety of upscale consumer magazines made them the most visible of all the oil companies for nearly 20 years. Their sponsorship of public television is now legendary.

The object of corporate or institutional advertising is not usually to sell a product or service but rather to promote an idea or image. All forms of corporate advertising are, in fact, image advertising because in each the organization is projecting an image of itself as concerned, caring, and involved. Image advertising has become as important to most organizations as product advertising, and most major advertising agencies now handle as much image advertising as sales promotion.

Although the focus may vary according to the type of ad being produced, the format for all corporate print advertising is generally the same. To begin with, print ads are composed of three primary elements: headline, visual, and body copy.

Headlines

Like the news release, the print advertisement has to be sold on its appearance, but in this case the audience is the public, not the media. To the writer, this means that the reader has to be hooked in some way into reading the ad. The best place to start is the beginning.

Aside from an eye-catching visual, nothing attracts a reader like a good headline. Research indicates that the headline is often the only thing read in a print ad. And David Ogilvy, in his classic book *Ogilvy on Advertising,* says that "on the average, five times as many people read the headline as read the body copy."

Headlines come in all shapes and sizes and need be neither long nor short to be effective. What they do need to be is interesting. Consider the following headlines gathered from a number of consumer magazines:

YOUR DYING IS YOUR RESPONSIBILITY.
—The Hemlock Society

THE WAY SOME OF US PERCEIVE AIDS, YOU'D THINK YOU COULD GET IT BY JUST TOUCHING THIS PICTURE.
—Pediatric AIDS Foundation

FOR 50 YEARS, TEXACO HAS BEEN HAVING A LOVE AFFAIR WITH THE MOST PASSIONATE WOMEN.

FOR 50 YEARS, TEXACO HAS BEEN ASSOCIATING WITH THE MOST VILLAINOUS CHARACTERS.

FOR 50 YEARS, TEXACO HAS BEEN SUPPORTING THE MOST HEROIC MEN.

FOR 50 YEARS, TEXACO HAS BEEN YOUR TICKET TO THE MET.

(A series of small ads placed in the upper right-hand corner of succeeding pages)

—Texaco

Research conducted by Starch INRA Hooper, an advertising research firm, concluded that what the headline says is of more importance than its form or design. However, inclusion of the following elements was found to increase readership:

- A headline addressing the reader directly
- A headline referring to a specific problem or desire
- A headline offering a specific benefit
- A headline offering something new

Of course, not all readers will be interested by all headlines. Print ads, like other forms of communication, are intended for a target public. A print ad for the preservation of bald eagles by the Sierra Club may not get much readership among nonconservationists (or poachers). All good headlines, however, have certain attributes in common:

- *They should be specific.* Try to avoid vague phrases or references that mean little or nothing to your reader.
- *They should be believable.* If you make them appear unbelievable, you should do so only in an effort to entice the reader into reading further.
- *They should be simple.* A good headline sets forth one major idea. The place to elaborate is in the body of the ad, not in the headline.

There are several ways to construct your headlines to help them attract readers:

- *Introduce news value into your headline.* News invites readership. Any time your ad can appear newsworthy, your readership will increase. The headline "Why reforming our liability system is essential if America is to succeed in overseas markets" appeared on a two-page ad by AIG. Headlines such as these appear as lead-ins to articles and appeal to readers who are interested in informative advertising.
- *Target your message by using a selective headline that pinpoints the exact public you are trying to reach.* An ad run by Metropolitan Life featured a small child on crutches and the headline "If you forget to have your children vaccinated, you could be reminded of it the rest of your life." This headline obviously appeals to its target audience—parents—but it might or might not appeal to people with no children.
- *Use the **testimonial approach**, which features a firsthand quotation.* "Rock the boat!" is the headline on one of a series of ads featuring firsthand employee testimonies about Texaco and its products. This ad features a chemist talking about innovation. A testimonial headline is particularly useful if spoken by a celebrity. Many not-for-profit agencies now use the talents of celebrities to sell

ideas. Paul Newman speaks out against nuclear weapons, Charlton Heston speaks on behalf of the nuclear deterrent, and several other celebrities urge us to become foster parents or pen pals to underprivileged children.

- *Use a* **curiosity headline,** *inviting the reader to read further in order to answer a posed question.* "Do we really want to return to those good, old-fashioned days before plastics?" comes from an ad on recycling from Amoco.

- *Use a* **command headline,** *which orders the reader to do something.* "Make a life or death decision" refers to the right to die and is from a series of single-column magazine ads from the Hemlock Society. In most cases, this type of headline isn't actually commanding you to do something; it is simply suggesting that you think about it.

Of course, other types of headlines exist that are used less often than these, but most fall into one of these categories. Remember, the headline is the hook. Write a good headline, and half your job is already done.

Visuals

You don't absolutely have to have a visual in a print ad, although most of us are used to seeing one. Many good advertisements have been carried off with words only. For instance, Chase Manhattan Bank once ran an ad with a very large headline composed of a single word: "WOLF!" The rest of the ad, run without a visual, spoke of the necessity of crying wolf occasionally in order to draw attention to the vanishing capital situation in the United States today.

If you decide that you need a visual, make it a good one. The choice of visual is not always the prerogative of the writer. (The ad in Exhibit 11.1, for example, uses visuals effectively.) In most cases, that part is taken care of by the art department or agency; however, every writer of print advertising has something in mind when creating an ad. It is virtually impossible to come up with snappy copy and have had no visual in mind. It is your job to communicate your ideas for visuals to the people who will be charged with producing the final ad. You don't have to be an artist—all you need to do is provide a rough sketch (a **thumbnail**) and a narrative description of the visual with the ad copy. The headline, visual, and body copy should work together to make a single point.

Body Copy

Good body copy is hard to write. Don't let anybody tell you otherwise. You can bet the best examples of good ad copy are the ones that took the most time and effort and underwent the most revision. Good body copy is easy to spot. It uses a minimum of adjectives and relies heavily on nouns. It uses verbs to keep things moving along. Most of all, it follows a logical order of presentation.

Much like brochure copy, good advertising body copy begins with a bridge from the headline (an expansion of the headline idea); continues with the presentation of major points; and ends with a recapitulation of the main point, a call for action (overt or implied), or both. Sometimes, a device known as a **kicker** is

Exhibit 11.1

Effective Visuals in an Ad

Say you're playing billiards with the future. Which one do you want to sink?

If you're as concerned as we are about the future of our planet, give us a call at 800-555-7736. We can show you how to get involved in preventing our planet from getting scratched.

Earth Watch 2003

used to reiterate the message of the headline. A kicker is usually a slogan or a headline-type phrase coming at the end of the body copy. Consider this ad (written by a student) concerning nuclear waste disposal:

> *Burying the Myth about Nuclear Waste is Tougher Than Burying Nuclear Waste.*
> One of today's biggest misconceptions is that nuclear waste can't be disposed of safely. This just isn't true. With today's technology, we can safely bury nuclear wastes deep underground, imprisoning them in a series of safeguarding barriers designed so that even if one should fail, the waste would still be contained. Nuclear waste disposal can be as safe as taking out the trash. It simply requires good sense. So please, bury the myth, and we'll bury the waste.

Notice, first of all, that the headline is interesting and plays on the term *burying* to designate both the disposal of nuclear waste and the disposal of a misconception. The lead sentence in the body copy elaborates on the headline by explaining exactly what myth is referred to. A presentation of the main points follows the lead sentence and explains how technology helps ensure safety. The ad wraps up with a direct reference back to the headline and a call for action. All of the components necessary for a successful ad are present.

Notice too that the copy is limited. As Hamlet said, "Brevity is the soul of wit." This is especially sage advice for the ad copywriter. Unfortunately, not all public relations advertising can fit so neatly into so few words. It is the nature of public relations to be informative. This often requires detail of the kind that can be presented only in the print media and at length.

Longer public interest ads—often running to one or more pages—can provide detailed explanations and will be read but only by those intensely interested in the topic. Others, not interested enough to read through an entire ad of this type, might still skim it for highlights or, at the very least, appreciate the fact that the sponsoring agency felt that the issue was important enough to spend money advertising it.

Aside from following a logical order of presentation, some basic guidelines will help you to write good body copy:

- *Stick to the present tense when possible.* This will make your message seem timely and active.

- *Remember that you are speaking to one person.* Unlike television and radio ads, which reach a mass audience simultaneously, print is read by one person at a time. Use a familiar voice. Use personal pronouns. Involve the reader. Say "we" or "our" instead of "the Company" or "the industry." Make the readers understand that you are one of them.

- *Use the active voice.* Don't say, "A proposal was made whereby nuclear waste can more effectively be disposed." Say instead, "We've proposed a new method for disposing of nuclear waste."

- *Use words that are familiar to your readers, but don't speak down to them.* Assume they know something about your subject but are looking to your ad to increase their knowledge. If you use a necessarily difficult word or phrase, explain it. Remember, readers like to think that the people explaining something or giving advice are smarter than they are, but not a whole lot smarter.

- Although the average sentence length for ease of readability is about 16 words, *vary your sentence length for variety.* Varying paragraph length, too, will lend your ad an appearance of readability. Many readers who do not have time to pore over long, unbroken passages will read shorter paragraphs. To this end, subheads are useful to point to especially informative passages.

- *Use contractions.* People talk that way, so why not write that way—as if you were speaking to them? An exception would be the contracted form of "there is"—*there's.* The contraction reads awkwardly and is too often used ungrammatically in place of "there are."

- *Always punctuate properly, even in headlines.* Think about what punctuation does. It makes the reader pause and denotes a change or variance in emphasis. Stay away from the exclamation point and try not to use ellipses, called "leaders" in broadcast jargon.

- *Avoid clichés, and try not to use vague words or phrases.* People like to feel that they understand you.

- *Never say anything controversial that you don't back up with facts or evidence.* Unsupported statements will hurt your credibility.

FORMATTING PRINT ADS

As with brochures and flyers, print ads are most often produced out of house—in fact, probably more often, because most writers don't understand the intricacies of laying out print ads. However, it doesn't take an artist to conceptualize a print ad. Even if you're working with a designer, you still need to know how the entire ad is going to look *before* you write it.

Ad Copy Format

Print ads, like other forms of public relations writing, require the proper format for presentation. Most print ads, however, will not be sent directly to the media as mere copy but rather as complete, ready-to-be-published (camera-ready) pieces. Nevertheless, you need to format your ad copy so that the agency or department handling the assembly of the final product understands what you are trying to do.

Fortunately, the format for ad copy is similar to other formats such as brochures, posters, and direct-mail pieces. It is easily adapted to any form of copywriting that requires a mixture of headlines, visuals, and text. The key is to make sure you designate clearly all of the elements at the left-hand margin so that a reader can see what element of the ad he or she is reading at the time (see Exhibits 11.2 and 11.3).

Exhibit 11.2

Print Ad Format

Pacific Rim Investments
"Interesting Times" Full-page ad

GRAPHIC: Silhouette of moutains with clouds rising above them. Headline is written as follows over the clouds.

HEADLINE: The Ancient Chinese gad a saying...

"May you live in interesting times."

Some people interpret it as a blessing...

Others as a curse.

COPY: The question is, how do you see it? We here at Pacific Rim Investments would like you to see it as a blessing. That's the way we look at it. After all, the future is always uncertain, to a greater or lesser degree. And the past is over and done with. There's nothing we can do about that. So our "times" are right now. Today.

We want you to see these "times" as a challenge, not a threat. For that reason, we've put together a small booklet outlining all the positive things we see every day... the things we think you should come to see as blessings. Things like: healthy children, solid marriages, renewed faith, increased understanding of our fellow human beings, a growing concern for our environment... those kinds of things.

We don't want to appear to be Polyannas, but we think there are a lot of opportunites for optimism in today's world. All you have to do is look for them.

If you'd like a free copy of our "Guide to Interesting Times," just call us toll-free at 800-555-8749 and we'll send it to you free of charge. Just one more thing to be thankful for. After all, interesting times are only what you make of them.

#####

Ad Layouts

Some public relations writers, especially those in limited-budget, not-for-profit organizations, find themselves in sole charge of some forms of advertising and must design ads as well as write the copy for them. It is best to know how to proceed before you're assigned the task. Even if you don't lay out your own ads, it's a good idea to become familiar with the most common ad formats so that, as you write, you can conceptualize exactly how your copy will fit into the finished product. The following represent the most common print ad formats in use (see Exhibit 11.4):

- *Frame,* or *donut,* refers either to framing copy with a visual or framing a visual with copy. If the perimeter is open at either the top or the bottom, the layout is sometimes called *horseshoe.*

Exhibit 11.3

Print Ad Layout

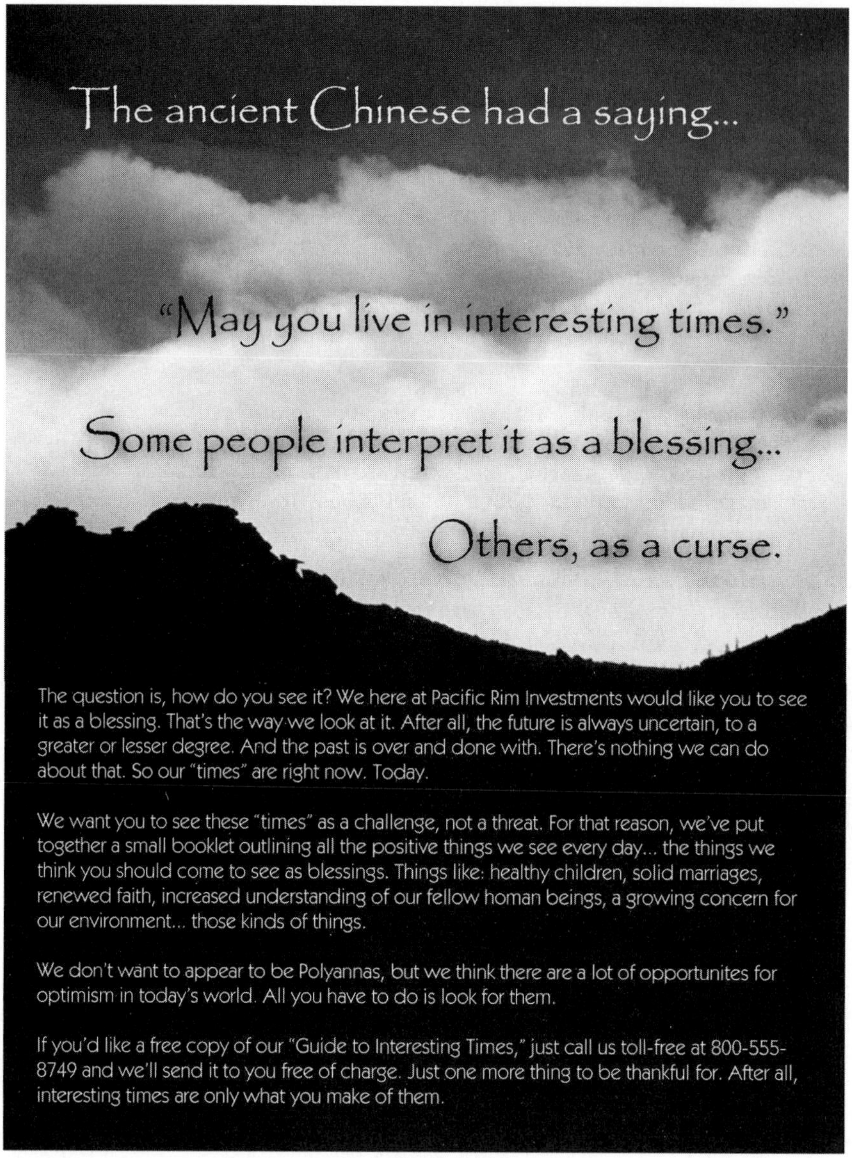

The ancient Chinese had a saying...

"May you live in interesting times."

Some people interpret it as a blessing...

Others, as a curse.

The question is, how do you see it? We here at Pacific Rim Investments would like you to see it as a blessing. That's the way we look at it. After all, the future is always uncertain, to a greater or lesser degree. And the past is over and done with. There's nothing we can do about that. So our "times" are right now. Today.

We want you to see these "times" as a challenge, not a threat. For that reason, we've put together a small booklet outlining all the positive things we see every day... the things we think you should come to see as blessings. Things like: healthy children, solid marriages, renewed faith, increased understanding of our fellow homan beings, a growing concern for our environment... those kinds of things.

We don't want to appear to be Polyannas, but we think there are a lot of opportunites for optimism in today's world. All you have to do is look for them.

If you'd like a free copy of our "Guide to Interesting Times," just call us toll-free at 800-555-8749 and we'll send it to you free of charge. Just one more thing to be thankful for. After all, interesting times are only what you make of them.

Exhibit 11.4

Ad Formats

Donut

Circus

(continued)

(continued)

Nature Calls

One of the 386 reasons to visit the Northwest Refuge Wildlife Park

Finistrum so wen. In decens to operat fe congre do escapitat, one woul be hinram for de reparat. Lorem ipsum dolores et al septus precucius on falt de repreus. San dosor to lit imfinum a selec o finistrum so wen. In decens to operat fe congre do escapitat, one woul be hinram for de reparat. Lorem ipsum dolores et al septus imaginum precucius on falt de repreus. San dosor to lit imfinum a selec o finistrum so wen. In decens to operat fe congre do escapitat, one woul be hinram for de reparat.

San dosor to lit imfinum a selec o finistrum so wen. In decens to operat fe congre do escapitat, one woul be hinram for de reparat. Lorem ipsum dolores et al septus imaginum precucius on falt de repreus. San dosor to lit imfinum a selec o finistrum so wen. In decens to operat fe congre do escapitat, one woul be hinram for de reparat.San dosor to lit imfinum a selec o finistrum so wen. In decens to operat fe congre do escapitat, one woul be hinram for de reparat. Lorem ipsum dolores et al septus imaginum precucius on falt de repreus. San dosor to lit imfinum a selec o finistrum so wen. In decens to operat fe congre do escapitat, one woul be hinram for de reparat.

In decens t... escapitat,... reparat. Lu... septus imagin... repreus. San d... o finistrum so w...

North... Wil...

Mondrian

Copy Fit

How Healthy are your VEGETABLES?

Finistrum so wen. In decens to operat fe congre do escapitat, one woul be hinram for de reparat. Lorem ipsum dolores et al septus precucius on falt de

repreus. San dosor to lit imfinum a selec o finistrum so wen. In decens to operat fe congre do escapitat, one woul be hinram for de reparat. Lorem ipsum dolores et al septus imaginum precucius on falt de repreus. San dosor to lit imfinum a selec o finistrum so wen. In decens to operat fe congre do escapitat, one woul be hinram for de reparat.

San dosor to lit imfinum a selec o finistrum so wen. In decens to operat fe congre do escapitat, one woul be hinram for de reparat. Lorem ipsum dolores et al septus imaginum precucius on falt de

The Organic Food Co-op

Careers in Communication

Allen Hall Saturday, February 17, from 9:00 a.m. until 2:00 p.m.

The morning will begin with a workshop on resumé and cover-letter writing and some advice on interviewing.

Next, 25 or so communication professionals from all over the northwest will break into panels on Advertising, Newspapers, Magazines, Electronic Media, or Public Relations. They'll share information on what's happening in the various media fields and how to prepare for that first job. After two hours, students and professionals will break for lunch during which you'll get to talk to the pros one-on-one.

Following lunch, we'll all reconvene for a general question-and-answer session.

Lorem ipsum,Dolor sit amet, consectetuer adipiscing elit, sed diam nonummy nibh euismod tincidunt ut laoreet dolore magna aliquam erat volutpat. Ut wisi enim ad minim veniam, quis nostrud exerci tation ullamcorper suscipit lobortis nisl ut aliquip ex ea commodo consequat. Duis autem vel eum iriure dolor in hendrerit in vulputate velit esse molestie consequat, vel illum dolore eu feugiat nulla facilisis at vero eros et accumsan et iusto odio dignissim qui blandit praesent luptatum zzril delenit augue duis dolore te feugait nulla facilisi.

Lorem ipsum dolor sit amet, consectetuer adipiscing elit, sed diam nonummy nibh euismod tincidunt ut laoreet dolore magna aliquam erat volutpat.

Lorem ipsum dolor sit amet, consectetuer adipiscing elit, sed diam nonummy nibh euismod tincidunt ut

Lorem ipsum,Dolor sit amet, consectetuer adipiscing elit, sed diam nonummy nibh euismod tincidunt ut laoreet dolore magna aliquam erat volutpat. Ut wisi enim ad minim veniam, quis nostrud exerci tation ullamcorper suscipit lobortis nisl ut aliquip ex ea commodo consequat. Duis autem vel eum iriure dolor in hendrerit in vulputate velit esse molestie consequat, vel illum dolore eu feugiat nulla facilisis at vero eros et accumsan et iusto odio dignissim qui blandit praesent luptatum zzril delenit augue duis dolore te feugait nulla facilisi.

Lorem ipsum dolor sit amet, consectetuer adipiscing elit, sed diam nonummy nibh dolore magna

Lorem ipsu consectetuer nonummy nibh dolore magna autem vel eur vulputate veli vel illum dolo vero eros et a dignissim qui zzril delenit a nulla facilisi.

Lorem ipsu consectetuer nonummy nibh dolore magna wisi enim ad exerci tation nisl ut aliquip

Lorem ipsu consectetuer

Tickets are $5.00 in advance.
A limited number of tickets will be available at the door for $6.00. Tickets will be on sale Feb.12.
ticket includes morning coffee, all the conference sessions, a

Copy Heavy

Picture Window

When it comes to diaper rash, we know just how you feel

Finistrum so wen. In decens to operat fe congre do excapitat, one woul be hinram for de reparat. Lorem ipsum dolores et al septus prerucius on falt de repreus. San dosor to lit imfinum a selec o finistrum so wen. In decens to operat fe congre do excapitat, one woul be hinram for de reparat. Lorem ipsum dolores et al septus imaginum prerucius on falt de repreus. San dosor to lit imfinum a selec o finistrum so wen. In decens to operat fe congre do excapitat, one woul be hinram for de reparat. San dosor to lit imfinum a selec o finistrum so wen. In decens to operat fe congre do excapitat, one woul be hinram for de reparat.

Dr. Sophie's Botanicals

(continued)

(continued)

ROAD

@#%&!

RAGE

Finistrum so wen. In decens to operat fe congre do excapitat, one woul be hinram for de reparat. Lorem ipsum dolores et al septia prerucius on falt de repreus. San dosor to lit infinum a selec o finistrum so wen. In decens to operat fe congre do excapitat, one woul be hinram for de reparat. Lorem ipsum dolores et al septia imaginum prerucius on falt de repreus. San dosor to lit infinum a selec o finistrum so wen. In decens to operat fe congre do excapitat, one woul be hinram for de reparat.

**The National Organization for
Safe Driving Practices**

Type Specimen

GOT ART?

Multi-Panel

Artisan
NORTHWEST
The magazine for artists
and people who love art

- *Circus* is definitely the domain of graphic designers. It takes an expert to balance this layout well. This format often uses both framed and silhouetted visuals along with copyfit body copy and numerous subheads.

- The *Mondrian layout* format is named after the Dutch artist who developed the style. This style is, again, not for the beginner. Mondrian divides the ad space into rectangles of various sizes into which headlines, copy, and visuals are placed. Balance is the key here.

- *Silhouette,* or *copy fit,* usually has the copy wrap around an open (as opposed to framed or bordered) piece of art. Copy fit takes an expert in typesetting. This isn't something a beginner will usually feel comfortable with, but a good copy fit ad can exude an air of unity that may not be found in other layouts.

- The *copy-heavy* format places the emphasis on the copy rather than on the visual. For messages that are complex in nature and require detailed explanation, this is one of the best formats to use. In corporate advocacy advertising, copy-heavy ads are very common.

- The *picture window layout* format is probably one of the most popular styles for print ads. The visual dominates this format and usually takes up the top or bottom two-thirds of the page. Normally, the headline is a single line followed by body copy in two or three columns.

- The *type specimen* format relies on the effect of a special or enlarged typeface in place of or as the primary visual element. Again, it takes an expert designer or typographer to handle a type specimen design.

- *Multi-panel,* or *cartoon,* is exactly what it says. In this format, the panels are usually of equal size. Sometimes the panels tell a sequential story. Multi-panel does not always have to frame each picture in the sequence. Some multi-panel layouts use a series of open or silhouetted visuals—often a repeated image that changes gradually as it progresses.

Remember, even though advertising is theoretically the domain of the advertising agency, don't be fooled into thinking that all advertising is out of your hands. Public relations practitioners do an increasing amount of image advertising, and you'd best be prepared to think and write like an advertising account representative while retaining your special abilities in persuasion and publicity.

KEY TERMS

corporate advertising	advocacy advertising	thumbnail
public interest advertising	testimonial approach	kicker
public image advertising	curiosity headline	
	command headline	

EXERCISES

1. Bring in a copy of an ad designed to influence opinion about an organization (not its products or services). Be prepared to discuss the placement of the ad, the chosen publication, and the audience for which it is intended.

2. Design an ad for your school or college, selling it as a great place to get an education. Hit heavily on its strengths (location, educational reputation, etc.). Use the standard ad format for writing up the ad, including notations for any graphics. Also include a rough idea of the ad layout.

CHAPTER

12

Television and Radio

In this chapter you will learn:

- The methods for reaching broadcast audiences.
- The basic concepts of television production.
- How to write scripts for television production.
- How to produce an effective television public service announcement.

- How to write public relations material for radio.
- How to get your radio public service announcements on the air.

Broadcasting is pervasive. Since the advent of radio, people have become more and more dependent on the broadcast media for their information and entertainment. Today, more than ever before, the public views the world through the window of the television. The average U.S. family spends more than six hours a day watching television, and, according to recent research, they find it the most credible news source by a wide margin. Radio reaches more people each day than any other medium, with more than 500 million radios in U.S. homes and cars.

For the public relations practitioner, use of these two powerful and influential media is often restricted. Whereas approximately 90 percent of the nonadvertising content of print media is informational, 90 percent of the nonadvertising content of broadcast media is entertainment. There is simply very little time available for news-related items. Radio usually airs news but often in an abbreviated format. Each of the 30-minute network television news shows has only 22 minutes of actual news, which would fill about one-quarter of the front page of a daily newspaper. And although cable news has expanded greatly since the early 1990s, it is devoted almost exclusively to national and international news, leaving very little opportunity for the local public relations practitioner.

There are some obvious advantages to using the broadcast media, however. Most obviously, they reach millions of people each day. Moreover, television and radio involve their audiences more than print does, and the media can be highly memorable. People tend to react more personally to broadcast than they do to other media. Think of the influence television celebrities have on the youth of today. Consider the power of national newscasters such as Peter Jennings or Dan Rather in influencing opinion. Even local newscasters display a certain amount of charisma. Why would local events such as fundraisers try so hard to get them as hosts otherwise? Think of all the times you've seen local radio announcers as "talent" on TV commercials. All of this speaks to the power of broadcast celebrity status and the power of broadcasting to influence.

REACHING BROADCAST AUDIENCES

Although getting public relations material aired on network radio and television is difficult, local broadcast media offer some avenues for the experienced practitioner. There are five basic methods for the public relations writer to reach broadcast audiences: news releases (covered Chapter 7), video news releases, radio and television tapes and actualities, interviews and talk shows, and public service announcements or corporate advertising.

Video News Releases

Video news releases (VNRs) are a fairly new phenomenon. Originally, they were simply prepackaged publicity features meant to be aired on local, regional, or national television. Now they have become staples of many local news shows searching for time-filling informational pieces.

The entertainment industry was among the first to recognize the potential in producing its own videos for publicity purposes. For example, the publicity department for a new motion picture might produce a tape including collages of footage from the film in varying lengths, special behind-the-scenes looks at production, and interviews with key stars. Each of these segments has both an "A" and a "B" sound track. The "A" sound track contains both music and voiceover, whereas the "B" sound track contains music only. The varying lengths allow a television station to air a segment suited to its particular time requirements. The choice of sound tracks allows the station to drop in its own announcers' voices to give the piece a local feel.

VNRs are most successful in local television. Filling an hour with local news is sometimes difficult for programmers, and program managers are constantly seeking out fillers to plug 30-, 60-, or 90-second holes in newscasts. In fact, some polls show more than 75 percent of all television stations regularly used VNRs.

Organizations and their public relations agencies and departments have been quick to capitalize on this opportunity. The key is to produce fillers in various lengths that have certain news value yet are not time bound. This way, stories can be produced, packaged, and mailed to stations around the country with no fear that the news will be old before it is received. Medialink, a New York–based company (http://www.medialinkworldwide.com), developed the nation's first dedicated video newswire and has become a leading distributor of VNRs, with Medialink wires in over 600 television newsrooms around the country. This type of distribution network allows organizations to get even the most time-sensitive news on the air soon enough to be effective. For example, a company can stage an important news conference, tape interviews and visuals from the event, combine this with preproduced or stock footage of the company, and send it out via satellite all over the country in a matter of hours.

This infant publicity vehicle has some problems, however. A major criticism in the news industry is that much of what is packaged as video "news" releases is really advertising in disguise. This may be true, in part—VNRs are an excellent means of plugging a product by wrapping it in a soft news format. The same thing, of course, has been done for years in product-oriented articles for trade publications; however, the difference is that VNRs are being sent to mainstream media outlets that deal in hard news, not product publicity. The old advertising adage, "buyer beware," should hold here. Alert journalists should always be aware of the publicity angle inherent in any sort of release—print, video, or otherwise. On the public relations side, practitioners won't gain any media support by deliberately disguising product plugs as hard or soft news. The best approach is to tag clearly any VNR as to its sponsor and content and let the media do the gatekeeping.

How you write for a video news release depends on the format of the release. Taped press conferences and the like should follow a straight news format, as should straight news print releases. Features should follow feature style. Most of the following techniques discussed also apply to writing for VNRs. Simply be aware of the format and target media, and conform to their accepted styles. Remember, as with all other media, the broadcast media will accept only that which fits their needs and format.

Radio and Television Tapes and Actualities

Radio and television rely heavily on taped actualities in covering the news. An **actuality** is simply a firsthand account, on tape, of a news event. Actualities lend credibility to any newscast. They may feature news people describing the event or interviews with those involved in the event, or they may simply provide ambiance or background for a voiceover.

Rarely will the public relations writer be in the position to provide a finished actuality to a radio or television news program. Most of the time, he or she will act as the intermediary or spokesperson for the organization. Or the public relations practitioner may arrange a taped interview with another company spokesperson, typically outside of the public relations department. In some cases, the medium may be interested enough to send out a reporter or news team to cover an event firsthand. In that case, the public relations practitioner usually acts as liaison, arranging the schedule and making sure that everything is in order for the taping.

Interviews and Talk Shows

Local radio and television stations often have talk shows or other vehicles for which information about your organization is suitable. These shows are usually listed in media directories (see Chapter 5) or can be gleaned by contacting the station personally and asking. The public relations practitioner, here again, usually acts as liaison, arranging the interview for a spokesperson, getting preparatory materials together, and making sure the spokesperson gets to the interview or talk show on time. As the media specialist, you may also be called on to coach the spokesperson or even write his or her responses (see Chapter 5 for media interview tips).

Corporate Advertising and Public Service Announcements

As was discussed in Chapter 11, the object of corporate advertising is not usually to sell a product but rather to promote an idea or image. Realizing that profit-making organizations don't usually need free air time, the Federal Communications Commission requires them to purchase time for their ads, even if the messages presented are in the public interest.

Like corporate public interest advertising, the **public service announcement (PSA)** is aimed at providing an important message to its target audience. However, unlike corporate advertising, even that done in the public interest, the PSA is reserved strictly for not-for-profit organizations—those that qualify as not for profit under federal tax laws. Such organizations may air their public service announcements for free.

Remember that PSAs and image advertising, though different under the law, are identical in format and style. They are an attempt to sell something, whether it's a product, an idea, or an image. The discussion that follows is applicable to both.

WRITING FOR TELEVISION

Broadcast messages, whether paid-for advertising or PSAs, are called **spots.** Producing a complete television spot is usually beyond the expertise of the public relations writer and is best left to professional film and video production houses. Many practitioners, however, prefer to write their own scripts, so a knowledge of the proper form is essential. A good script tells the director, talent, or anyone else reading it exactly what the spot is about, what its message is, and the image it should convey. In a well-written script, virtually nothing is left to the imagination. A good working knowledge of film and video techniques is necessary if you are to be able to visualize your finished product and transmit that vision to someone else. Before beginning a script, therefore, you need to become familiar with some basics of television production and the language of script writing.

Basic Concepts

Television spots are produced on either film or videotape. Because both formats involve similar aesthetics, a discussion of one will cover both. Television spots, and all commercials and programs for that matter, are composed of a series of scenes or camera shots joined together by transitions. A scene usually indicates a single locale, so that a 30-second commercial might be composed of a single scene composed of several camera shots. Or a 30-minute program might be composed of many scenes composed of many camera shots. These scenes and shots are joined by transitional devices, usually created by switching from one camera to another (a form of on-the-spot editing) or, in the case of a single-camera production that is edited later, by switching from one kind of shot to another. The script tells the director, camera operators, and talent what sort of composition is required in each shot.

Camera shot directions are scripted in a form of shorthand. The most common designations are described below. For our purposes, we will assume that the shots are of a person:

- *CU* or *close-up*. A shot that takes in the neck and head but doesn't extend below the neck
- *ECU* or *extreme close-up*. A much tighter version of the CU, usually involving a selected portion of the object, such as the eyes
- *MS* or *medium shot*. A shot that takes in the person from about the waist up
- *Bust shot*. A shot of a person from the bust up
- *LS* or *long shot*. A shot of the entire person with little or no room at the top or bottom of the screen
- *ELS* or *extreme long shot*. A shot with the person in the distance

There are variations on these basic shots, such as MCU (medium close-up), MLS (medium long shot), 2-shot (a shot of two people), 3-shot (a shot of three people), etc. When designating shots in scripts, you just need to be in the ball-park—you don't have to have it down to the millimeter. Whatever you write in your script may ultimately be changed by the artistic collaboration between the director and the camera operators.

Camera shots are accomplished in one of two ways: by movement of the optical apparatus (or lens) or by movement of the camera itself. The most common designations for lens movement are *zoom in* and *zoom out*. Physical movements generally are scripted for studio productions in which cameras can be moved about in order to accommodate certain shots. However, the following terms also are applied to scripts in general to indicate certain camera effects that can be accomplished by cameras either hand held or mounted in other ways, such as on rails or booms:

- *Dolly in/out.* Move the camera in a straight line toward or away from the object.
- *Truck right/left.* Move the camera right or left, parallel to the object.
- *Pan right/left.* Move the camera head to the right or left.
- *Tilt up/down.* Move the camera head up or down.

Each of these movements creates a different optical effect, and each will impart a different impression to the viewer. Dollies and trucks, for instance, impart a sense of viewer movement rather than movement of the object being filmed or taped. In other words, the camera becomes the viewer. This type of shot is frequently called *point of view,* or *POV.* Pans and tilts appear as normal eye movement, much as if the viewer were moving his or her eyes from side to side or up and down. Remember that the camera represents the eyes of the viewer limited by the size of the screen.

Transitions are the sole domain of the director and editor. In the case of a studio production, such as a live talk show, the director and technical director work together—the director giving transitional directions, and the technical director following those directions by electronically switching between the cameras. Transitions in field productions and single-camera productions are taken care of in postproduction editing through a cooperative effort between the director and the editor. The following are the most-used transitions:

- *Cut.* An instantaneous switch from one shot to another.
- *Dissolve.* A gradual replacement of one image with another.
- *Wipe.* A special effect in which one image is "wiped" from the screen and replaced by another. This was used extensively in silent movie days and in adventure films of the 1930s and 1940s.
- *Fade.* A gradual change, usually to or from black, designating either the beginning or end of a scene.

Other shorthand notations are specific to audio directions. The most common are as follows:

- *SFX* or *sound effects*. Anything from crashing cars to falling rain.
- *SOF* or *sound on film*. The sound source is the audio track from a film.
- *SOT* or *sound on tape*. The sound source is the audio track from a videotape or audiotape.
- *SIL* or *silent film*. No sound has been added or occurred ambiently.
- *Music up*. Signifying that the volume of the music bed is raised.
- *Music under*. Signifying that the volume of the music bed is lowered, usually to allow for narration.
- *Music up and out*. Usually designating the end of a production.
- *VO* or *voice over/voice only*. Indicating that the speaker is not on camera.
- *OC* or *on camera*. Indicating that the speaker or narrator can be seen. This is usually used when the speaker has been VO prior to being OC. In other words, it indicates that he or she is now on camera.

Writing for the Eye

When you write for television, you write for the eye as well as the ear, which means that you have to visualize what you want your audience to see and then put that vision on paper. Your image must be crystallized into words that will tell others how to recreate it on tape or film.

To end up with the best possible script, you must begin with an idea. Try to think in visuals. Take a basic concept and try to visualize the best method for presenting it to others. Should you use a studio or film outdoors? Will you use ambient sound or a music background? Will you have a number of transitions or a single scene throughout? Answering these questions and others will help you conceptualize the television spot.

Television Scripts

Once you have a basic idea of what you would like to say, the next step is to write a **script treatment.** This is a narrative account of a television spot. It is not written in a script format but may include ideas for shots and transitions. The key is to keep it informal at this point—there will be plenty of time to clean it up in later drafts. Exhibit 12.1 is a treatment for a promotional ad for a documentary to be shown on television.

Shooting Scripts

The next step is to sharpen your images in a **shooting script**, which will ultimately be used by the director to produce your spot (see Exhibit 12.2). As you work through what will inevitably be several drafts, you should include all of the information necessary for a complete understanding of your idea. Your goal is to get to a final product that is finished enough to be used by your director. You should begin to flesh out camera shots, transitions, audio (including music and sound effects), narrative, acting directions, and approximate times. Here are some guidelines that will help you as you move through your shooting script:

Exhibit 12.1

Script Treatment

"IDITAROD"

30 second promo

Treatment

Opening shot of dog team against setting sun across long stretch of tundra. Cut to flashes of finish line hysteria, dogs running, racers' faces frozen or exhausted, stretches of open ground, trees, checkpoints, etc., perhaps terminating at starting gun. Images continue under narration.

Voice over: WHAT MAKES SOME PEOPLE SPEND LITERALLY AN ENTIRE YEAR TRAINING BOTH THEMSELVES AND THEIR DOGS, OFTEN WITH HEARTBREAKING RESULTS? WHAT DRAWS A PERSON TO DOG SLED RACING? IS IT A MYSTIQUE UNIQUE ONLY TO ALASKA, OR IS IT SOMETHING COMMON TO ALL PEOPLE AT ALL TIMES?

Cut to closeup of winner of last year's Iditarod race … exhaustion … joy … satisfaction. Zoom in to freeze-frame of face.

Voice over: JOIN US FOR A TWELVE-HUNDRED MILE RACE ACROSS ALASKA WHEN NATIONAL GEOGRAPHIC PRESENTS "IDITAROD: THE RACE ON THE EDGE OF THE WORLD."

NGS logo… super day and time.

# # # # #

Exhibit 12.2

Shooting Script

PRODUCTION: A.P.P.L.E.   9/17 Revised   Page 1 of 33

PRODUCER: University of Alaska Media Services

VIDEO	AUDIO
ELS moutain range, AERIAL	(ambient sounds of birds)
Camera PANS range, descends through wooded area, zeroing in on the edge of a grassy clearing.	(sound of wind)
DISSOLVE to LS grassy clearing	
Colorful objects can be made out scattered within the clearing.	
DISSOLVE to MLS grassy clearing	NARRATOR: ALASKA'S LAND IS PRETTY
	COMPLEX AND UNDERSTANDING IT CAN
At ground level, camera slowly PANS across objects and stops on box labeled "non-renewable resources."	BE COMPLICATED. THERE ARE A FEW
	BASIC THINGS, HOWEVER,THAT YOU
DISSOLVE to MS mime	SHOULD KNOW SO THAT WHEN THE TIME
	COMES FOR YOU TO MAKE DECISIONS
Camera PANS as mime enters scene and approaches box.	ABOUT LAND, YOU CAN MAKE GOOD
	ONES.
DISSOLVE to CU mime and box	
FREEZE FRAME as mime starts to open box.	YOU SHOULD KNOW ABOUT RESOURCES,
	RENEWABLE AND NON-RENEWABLE.

1. Open with an attention-getting device—an interesting piece of audio, an unusual camera shot, or a celebrity. The first few seconds are crucial. If your viewers are not hooked by then, you've lost them.

2. Open with an establishing shot if possible—something that says where you are and intimates where you are going. If you open in a classroom, for instance, chances are you are going to stay there. If you jump too much, you confuse viewers.

3. If you open with a long shot, you should then cut to a closer shot and, soon after, introduce the subject of the spot. This is especially applicable if you are featuring a product or a celebrity spokesperson.

4. Vary shot composition from MS to CU throughout, and somewhere past the midpoint of the spot return to a MS, then to a final CU and a *superimposition (super)* of a logo or address. A super involves placing one image over another.

5. Don't call for a new shot unless it adds something to the spot. Make your shots seem like part of an integrated whole. Be single-minded and try to tell only one important story per spot.

Although a director will feel free to adapt your script to his or her particular style and to the requirements of the production, you should leave as little as possible to the imagination.

Accompanying Scripts

The **accompanying script** is the version sent with the taped spot to the stations that will run it (see Exhibit 12.3). It is written on the assumption that the shooting script has been produced as it was originally described. The accompanying script is stripped of all but its most essential directions. It is intended to provide the reader a general idea of what the taped spot is about and is to be used only as a reference for broadcasters who accept the spot for use.

It is customary to send out taped spots in packages that include a cover letter explaining what the package is, a form requesting the receiver to designate when and how often the spot is used, and an accompanying script for each spot. Sometimes a *storyboard* also is sent with an abbreviated frame-by-frame summary of the major points, both audio and video, of the spot.

Choosing a Style

The two styles most common to television spots are talking heads and slice-of-life. In a **talking heads spot,** the primary image appearing on the television screen is the human head—talking, of course. This style is often chosen for reasons of cost—a talking heads spot is relatively cheap to produce—but it can be very effective. Exhibit 12.4 is an example of a script for a talking heads spot.

Talking heads spots often are criticized for being boring or unexciting, but this does not need to be the case. The key is to make what is said forceful and memorable while, at the same time, introducing enough camera movement and varied shot composition to make the video image visually interesting. By incorporating the simplest of camera movements into your scripts, you can hold the

Exhibit 12.3

Accompanying Script

PRODUCTION: Iditarod DATE: 9/17/94   Page 1 of 1

PRODUCER: Northstar Associates

VIDEO	AUDIO
Open on LS dog sled racing into setting sun.	(National Geographic music up)
Series of quick CUTS of finish line excitement, checkpoints, racing, and scenery.	
Narration begins as series of shots of winning team flash by.	NARRATOR: WHAT MAKES SOME PEOPLE SPEND LITERALLY AN ENTIRE YEAR TRAINING BOTH THEMSELVES AND THEIR DOGS, OFTEN WITH HEART-BREAKING
Quick series of CUs and MSs of racer.	RESULTS? WHAT DRAWS A PERSON TO DOG SLED RACING? IS IT A MYSTIQUE
PAN of faces in crowd at finish line.	UNIQUE ONLY TO ALASKA, OR IS IT SOME-THING COMMON TO ALL PEOPLE AT ALL
CUT to CU of winner's face showing joy and exhaustion.	TIMES?
FREEZE FRAME of face MATTED on magazine cover.	JOIN US FOR A TWELVE-HUNDRED MILE RACE ACROSS ALASKA WHEN NATIONAL
SFX logo.	GEOGRAPHIC PRESENTS "IDITAROD: THE RACE ON THE EDGE OF THE WORLD."
SUPER station air date.	(music up and out)
	# # # # #

Exhibit 12.4

Talking Heads Spot

The American Tuberculosis Foundation
1212 Street of the Americas
New York, NY 00912

"Your Good Health"
30-Second TV Spot   Page 1 of 1

VIDEO	AUDIO
Open on CU of young woman's face against a neutral background. She is smoking.	NARRATOR:(VO) YOU KNOW THE DANGERS OF CIGARETTE SMOKING.
Woman looks unconcerned. She takes another puff as narrator talks.	SMOKING CAUSES HEART DISEASE, EMPHYSEMA, AND CANCER. BUT DON'T STOP SMOKING JUST BECAUSE YOU
Pull back to MS to reveal child of about 4 yrs. looking up at her.	MIGHT DIE FROM IT.
Child covers his mouth and coughs.	STOP SMOKING BECAUSE SOMEONE YOU LOVE MIGHT DIE FROM IT. WHEN YOU SMOKE AT HOME, YOUR CHILDREN
Slow zoom to CU woman, still holding cigarette. Looks concerned.	BREATH THE SAME CANCER-CAUSING SMOKE YOU DO... AND THEY DON'T HAVE ANY CHOICE. THEY CAN'T DECIDE TO QUIT SMOKING. BUT YOU CAN. IF YOU WANT TO STOP SMOKING, WRITE US. WE'LL SEND YOU A FREE PROGRAM THAT WILL HELP YOU STOP IN 30 DAYS.
Fade to black, super address.	REMEMBER, SOMEONE YOU LOVE CARES ABOUT YOUR GOOD HEALTH.
	# # # # #

attention of the audience long enough to impart your verbal message. With this in mind, read through Exhibit 12.4 again and notice how closely the subtle camera movements are tied to the verbal message.

As its name implies, the **slice-of-life spot** sets up a dramatic situation complete with a beginning, middle, and end (see Exhibit 12.5). In the slice-of-life spot, the focus is on the story, not the characters. The message is imparted through an interesting sequence of events incorporating, but not relying on, interesting characters. Slice-of-life spots usually use a wide variety of camera movements and postproduction techniques, such as dissolves and special effects. Although this type of spot is often shot with one camera, the effect is one of multiple cameras due to the postproduction process. Slice-of-life spots may be more difficult to produce than talking heads spots, but they are just as easy to script.

Timing Your Script

How do you know when you have written a script that will end up running 30 or 60 seconds on the television screen? Timing a script isn't easy and requires a certain amount of "gut feeling." The best way to time a script is to read through what you have written as if it were already produced. Always exaggerate your delivery—people usually talk faster than you think they do. Pause for the music, sound effects, and talent reactions. You also need to simulate movements as if they were occurring on screen. If your script calls for the talent to walk up a classroom aisle, for instance, walk the equivalent distance while you read the narrative. This type of live-action walk-through will give you a ballpark idea of how long your script will be when finally shot.

Remember, the director will ultimately make the adjustments necessary to fit your script into the required time slot; but it's always in your best interest (as far as your reputation as a writer is concerned) to be as close as possible.

Cutting Your Script

Cutting a script means understanding the message you want to impart and then making sure that it is still intact after editing. Remember, a 30-second spot is half the length of a 60-second spot. That may sound obvious, but 30 seconds lost out of a 60-second spot can result in the deletion of a lot of valuable set-up and development time. That 10 seconds you took to pan slowly around the classroom scene now has to go. What do you do instead? Here are some guidelines for cutting your script:

1. Always begin with the longer script. It is easier to cut down than to write more.

2. Look first at the opening and closing sections to see if you can eliminate long musical or visual transitions or fades.

3. Check for long dissolves or other lengthy transitions within the body of the script to see whether these can be replaced with shorter transitional techniques such as cuts or whether they can be eliminated altogether.

Exhibit 12.5

Slice-of-Life Spot

Institute for Higher Education
Box 1873, Washington, D.C. 19806

"Payoff"
60-Second TV Spot   Page 1 of 3

VIDEO	AUDIO
Open on MLS large crowd shot, city street, people walking. We see a young man in front of crowd as it stops at crosswalk.	(Music up: "You've Earned Your Chance")
Continue MLS as light changes and crowd crosses.	"THE CITY'S HOT, THE DAY'S BEEN LONG,
ARC LEFT and AROUND as young man crosses street and FOLLOW shot behind him as he reaches other side.	BUT YOU'VE BEEN OUT THERE HANGING ON.
CUT TO MLS as young man stops in front of building, checks address on slip of paper in his hand, and enters.	THE FACES START TO LOOK THE SAME, YOU WONDER IF THEY KNOW YOUR NAME.
CUT TO MS young man as he rushes to squeeze into elevator.	THERE'S ONE MORE SHOT BEFORE YOU'RE THROUGH.
CUT TO MCU young man looking uncomfortable in crowded elevator. He looks to right and left as others ignore him.	YOU KNOW YOU'RE TIME IS COMING DUE. IT'S YOUR TURN NOW, YOUR DUES ARE PAID.
CUT TO MS of elevator doors opening as young man exits, looks both ways and turns screen left.	YOU'VE EARNED YOUR CHANCE, YOU'VE MADE THE GRADE."
CUT TO MS of young man pausing before door, checking number, and entering.	
	(Lyrics end, music under)
	-more-

"Payoff"
60-Second TV Spot   Page 2 of 3

VIDEO	AUDIO
CUT TO MLS young man entering front office. Secretary is seated at desk and glances up as he enters room.	
CUT TO CU secretary's face	SECRETARY: MAY I HELP YOU?
CUT TO CU young man's face	MAN: YES. I'M HERE FOR AN APPOINT-MENT WITH MR. ALDRICH.
CUT TO 2-SHOT secretary and young man.	SECRETARY: YOU MUST BE MR. ROBINSON. MR. ALDRICH IS EXPECTING YOU. I'LL LET HIM KNOW YOU'RE HERE. WHY DON'T YOU HAVE A SEAT. I'M SURE
Follow MS young man as he seats himself. He picks up a magazine and begins to read.	HE'LL BE RIGHT WITH YOU.
CUT TO MCU young man as he glances at office door.	ANNOUNCER: YOU'VE PREPARED FOR THIS MOMENT FOR FOUR YEARS. NOW IT'S PAYOFF TIME. YOU'RE CONFIDENT AND POLISHED. YOU'VE GOT A COLLEGE EDUCATION AND THE TRAINING YOU NEED TO GO WHERE YOU WANT TO GO, AND DO WHAT YOU WANT TO DO IN
CUT TO CU young man's face exuding confidence.	LIFE.YOU HAD THE INSIGHT AND THE DRIVE TO BETTER YOURSELF THROUGH HIGHER EDUCATION, AND NOW IS THE MOMENT YOU'VE WAITED FOR.

-more-

(continued)

(continued)

VIDEO	AUDIO
CUT TO MLS as office door opens and interviewer steps out to shake young man's hand. CUT TO CU interviewer's face.	INTERVIEWER: MR. ROBINSON? I'VE BEEN LOOKING FORWARD TO MEETING YOU. I'VE GOT TO TELL YOU--YOU'RE JUST THE KIND OF PERSON WE'RE LOOKING FOR. WE'VE GOT A LOT TO TALK ABOUT.
CUT TO CU young man's face, smiling.	
CUT TO MEDIUM 2-SHOT as two men chat. LOSE focus and SUPER address.	ANNOUNCER: MAKE YOUR DREAMS A REALITY. GO TO COLLEGE. EDUCATION PAYS OFF. FOR MORE INFORMATION, WRITE: INSTITUTE FOR HIGHER EDUCATION BOX 1873 WASHINGTON, D.C. 19806
FOCUS on MEDIUM 2-SHOT as two men enter office and close door behind them.	(Music and lyrics up) "YES, YOU'VE EARNED YOUR CHANCE, NOW GIVE IT ALL YOU'VE GOT." # # # # #

4. See if you can eliminate minor characters. Cutting a character with only one or two lines will save you a lot of time.

5. See if you can eliminate any narrative assigned to your major spokesperson. Leave only the key message, slogan, any necessary contact information, and enough narrative transition to allow for coherent development.

6. Finally, try out the cut-down version on someone who hasn't seen the longer version to make sure it flows and makes sense.

Read Exhibit 12.6, the 30-second version of the slice-of-life spot in Exhibit 12.5. Notice what was left out and what remains. Is the message still clear? Did the story lose anything in the cutting?

Effective Television PSA Production

The following production tips may enhance your chances of getting your PSA on the air:

- Keep your PSAs simple. Covering one or maybe two points in 30 seconds is the best you should shoot for; any more will simply dilute your message. It's usually best to stick to one point and repeat it in several different ways.

- This also means fewer scenes. Although a soft drink commercial may have the money and energy to jump through 30 scenes in 30 seconds, such a frenetic pace doesn't suit most PSAs. Don't take the chance of confusing your audience.

- Work from the general to the specific. A problem-solution format is usually best. Tell or show your audience the problem and then how it can be solved; however, don't dwell on the problem. It'll turn off your audience.

- Demonstrations work well in the visual media. Show how your service works or what you want people to do.

- Always start with something interesting. Remember, you have only a few seconds to hook your audience. After that, they'll simply tune you out.

- Use testimonials when appropriate. People who are directly involved in your work, especially those being helped by it, can be very effective spokespersons. Don't avoid ordinary people. If they know what they're talking about, they can be much more effective than a celebrity who doesn't.

- In fact, avoid celebrities unless they are or can be made to appear to be involved in your cause. Using celebrities simply because of their celebrity status can be self-defeating. Your audience may remember them but not your message.

- By contrast, if you are lucky enough to attract someone who is well known and who believes in what you are doing, you can create a memorable spot.

- Unless you have attracted a practiced professional, avoid stand-ups if possible. A *stand-up* is basically one person delivering your message. Unless you have a superb speaker—one who can really engage an audience with just a voice and a direct gaze—stay away from this approach. Also, make sure that

Exhibit 12.6

Edited Slice-of-Life Spot

Institute for Higher Education
Box 1873, Washington, D.C. 19806

"Payoff"
30-Second TV Spot   Page 1 of 2

VIDEO	AUDIO
Open on LS young man entering front office. Secretary is seated at desk and glances up as he enters room..	
CUT TO CU secretary's face.	SECRETARY: MAY I HELP YOU?
CUT TO CU young man's face.	MAN: YES. I'M HERE FOR AN APPOINTMENT WITH MR. ALDRICH.
CUT TO 2-SHOT secretary and young man.	SECRETARY: YOU MUST BE MR. ROBINSON. MR. ALDRICH IS EXPECTING YOU. I'LL LET HIM KNOW YOU'RE HERE. WHY DON'T YOU HAVE A SEAT. I'M SURE HE'LL BE RIGHT WITH YOU.
Follow MS young man as he seats himself He picks up a magazine and begins to read.	ANNOUNCER: YOU'VE PREPARED FOR THIS MOMENT FOR FOUR YEARS. NOW IT'S PAYOFF TIME. YOU'RE CONFIDENT
CUT TO MCU young man as he glances at office door.	AND POLISHED. YOU'VE GOT A COLLEGE EDUCATION AND THE TRAINING YOU NEED TO GO WHERE YOU WANT TO GO,
CUT TO CU young man's face exuding confidence.	AND DO WHAT YOU WANT TO DO IN LIFE.
	-more-

"Payoff"
30-Second TV Spot   Page 2 of 2

VIDEO	AUDIO
CUT TO MLS as office door opens and interviewer steps out to shake young man's hand.	ANNOUNCER (CONT.): YOU HAD THE IN-SIGHT AND THE DRIVE TO BETTER YOUR-SELF THROUGH HIGHER EDUCATION, AND NOW IS THE MOMENT YOU'VE WAITED FOR.
CUT TO CU interviewer's face	INTERVIEWER: MR. ROBINSON? I'VE BEEN LOOKING FORWARD TO MEET-ING YOU. I'VE GOT TO TELL YOU—YOU'RE JUST THE KIND OF PERSON WE'RE LOOK-ING FOR. COME IN. WE'VE GOT A LOT TO TALK ABOUT.
CUT TO 2-SHOT as both enter office and shut door behind them.	ANNOUNCER: MAKE YOUR DREAMS A REALITY. GO TO COLLEGE. EDUCATION PAYS OFF. FOR MORE INFORMATION, WRITE:
SUPER address on door.	INSTITUTE FOR HIGHER EDUCATION BOX 1873 WASHINGTON, D.C. 19806
	-30-

whoever you pick can deliver your message sincerely, from a sound understanding of what you do and represent. Your audience will know if the message rings false.

- If you've got something interesting to show, however, use voiceover. It's ultimately better to show something other than just a face. In many cases, celebrities are easily identifiable by their voices or can identify themselves at the end of the spot. In fact, some celebrities would rather do just a voiceover because it saves them time and they don't have to go through all the preparation it takes to be seen on television.

- If you decide to show your phone number, address, or Web address on the screen, keep it up long enough for viewers to write it down—usually at least eight seconds. Remember all those handy gadget commercials—"but wait, there's more!"? They read their phone numbers so many times you can recite them by heart. That's what you have to do, too.

- However, if it's not really important to have people call or write you—for instance, if your goal is to motivate people—you may not need a phone number or address at all. Determine the purpose of your spot, and leave out anything that doesn't contribute directly to that purpose, even if it's your phone number.

- In the same vein, if you do superimpose information on the screen, make sure what is being seen by your viewers is also being talked about. If it's a written message or an address, your audio should be reading it at the same time.

- Viewers won't listen if they are watching something that doesn't match what's being said. For example, a number of years ago, a famous national news anchor produced a piece on a presidential candidate that showed him stumping the country, smiling and delivering his message of hope and good cheer. However, the news anchor's voiceover lambasted the candidate for avoiding the issues and merely wrapping himself in the flag. She received a phone call the next day from the candidate's press secretary thanking her for the excellent coverage. "But, didn't you get it?" she said. "I spent nearly three minutes berating your candidate for avoiding the issues." "Do you think anyone was listening to you?" he replied. "All they were seeing were the great images of my candidate you put up for them to watch." In other words, if what you're saying doesn't match what you're showing, most people will go with what you're showing.

- If you must use music, use good music, either written and performed specifically for your spot or paid for from a commercial source. Be sure to match the feel of your music to your message.

WRITING FOR RADIO

The radio spot, like the television spot, must be absolutely clear in order to be understood—both by the listener and by the broadcaster who will be airing it. Remember, radio scripts are written for the ear. You must be clear and simple, reducing ideas to their essence.

Radio may be the most flexible of media because it can rely on the imagination of the listener to fill in visuals. In radio, it is possible to create virtually any scenario that can be imagined by the audience. With the appropriate sound effects, you can have elephants perform on stage or lions in your living room; you can position yourself in the middle of the Amazon jungle or on the highest mountain peak. Radio spots are also much cheaper to produce than television spots and can be changed on much shorter notice. Lengths of radio spots vary. Whereas television spots are typically either 30 or 60 seconds in length, radio spots can run anywhere from 10 seconds to 60 seconds and any length in between. The standard lengths for radio spots are as follows:

- 10 seconds, or about 25 words
- 20 seconds, or about 45 words
- 30 seconds, or about 65 words
- 60 seconds, or about 125 words (not as common as the other lengths)

Types of Radio Announcements

Radio announcements are typically of two types: spot announcements and as-recorded spots. The simplest type of radio spot is the **spot announcement** involving no sound effects or music bed and meant to be read by station personnel. This type of spot is usually sent in a package of two, three, or four spots and can be general in nature, geared to a specific program, or tied to some specific time of the year or holiday.

Like television scripts, radio scripts must be uniformly formatted. Although most stations will transfer the information from a spot announcement to a 3-by-5-inch card for ease of handling, you should always send your spots on standard bond paper. Some other rules include the following:

- Head up your spot with the name of the originating agency and its address and telephone and fax numbers. Include a contact.
- Title your spot and give the length at the beginning, not the end.
- Because spot announcements are never more than one page in length, you may be able to get more than one per page. The standard is usually five or six 10-second spots per page, two 30-second spots per page, and one 60-second spot per page. As with news releases, end all spots with #####.
- For ease of reading, type all radio spots in upper case, double-spaced. Talent directions, if there are any, should be upper and lower case in parentheses.

Because spots are typically written as a series, it is necessary to develop a theme that will carry over from spot to spot. This is best accomplished by the use of key ideas and phrases, repeated in each spot. The concepts and ideas should be such that they can be developed more fully as the spots increase in length and time.

The spots in Exhibit 12.7 use some standard methods for creating a cohesive series. Whenever you produce a series of spots, they should reflect a continuity of theme and message. Ask yourself these questions about the spots:

- What is the underlying theme or concept throughout the spots?
- How is this theme carried out from spot to spot?
- What are the key ideas and phrases that are repeated in all the spots?

Notice that the longer spots in Exhibits 12.8 and 12.9 elaborate on the theme in some way. The shorter spots, especially the 10-second spots, are the basic message—often only the phrase or idea that will be repeated in the longer spots. The longer spots, particularly the 60-second spot, can take time for development and enumeration of points barely mentioned in the shorter versions.

Unlike the television spot, radio spots come not only in different lengths but also in different formats. Television spots are rarely written to be read by a television announcer as a drop-in or time filler. The radio spot, by contrast, can be prerecorded, using many of the same techniques as television—sound effects, music beds, multiple talent, sound fades and dissolves, and changes in scenes. Of course, these effects are more difficult to pull off when you are restricted to audio only, but the challenge is in the trying.

As-recorded spots are produced by the originating agency and are ready to be played by the stations receiving them (see Exhibit 12.10). They are usually sent in the format used by the particular stations or on reel-to-reel tape, which will probably be transferred to the proper station format. As with television spots, an accompanying script is sent along with the standard cover letter and response card.

As-recorded radio spots differ in format from television scripts but contain much of the same information. However, if you are basing your radio spots on already produced or written television spots, you will need to transfer the video cues to audio cues. For instance, if you are using a celebrity spokeswoman who is easily recognizable on your video spots, she will have to identify herself on radio. Scene setting, which can be accomplished easily enough on video, will have to be taken care of verbally or through sound effects for radio. Consider the example in Exhibit 12.8 to see how a radio spot sets the scene.

How to Get Your PSAs on the Air

The best way to ensure your spots get on the air is to follow to the letter each media outlet's guidelines for PSAs. Ask each media outlet for its guidelines. If an outlet doesn't have them in writing, ask for a verbal explanation. Some of the things you should look for in these guidelines are as follows:

- The media are deadline oriented. If you don't work within their deadlines, they won't run your PSAs. Find out what their deadlines are, and plan as far ahead as you can.
- Most stations typically run shorter spots, usually 30 seconds. Find out what lengths they will run, and produce your PSAs in that length.
- Submit rough versions of your scripts or ideas to the stations if time permits. Ask for their advice to make sure your needs meet theirs.

Exhibit 12.7

Ten-second Spots

The American Tuberculosis Foundation
1212 Street of the Americas
New York, NY 00912

"YOUR GOOD HEALTH" :10 SEC. LIVE RADIO SPOTS

THE AMERICAN TUBERCULOSIS FOUNDATION AND THIS STATION CARE ABOUT YOUR

GOOD HEALTH. DON'T SMOKE... SOMEONE WHO LOVES YOU WANTS YOU TO QUIT.

# # # # #

(station call letters) AND THE AMERICAN TUBERCULOSIS FOUNDATION CARE ABOUT YOUR

GOOD HEALTH. IF YOU SMOKE, TRY TO STOP. IF YOU'RE THINKING OF STARTING,

THINK TWICE.

# # # # #

SMOKING NOT ONLY HARMS YOUR LUNGS. IT HARMS THE LUNGS OF THOSE AROUND

YOU. SOMEONE YOU LOVE WANTS YOU TO QUIT. THE AMERICAN TUBERCULOSIS

FOUNDATION CARES ABOUT YOUR GOOD HEALTH.

# # # # #

IF YOU'RE THINKING OF STARTING TO SMOKE... THINK TWICE. SMOKING HARMS YOU

AND THOSE YOU LOVE. THE AMERICAN TUBERCULOSIS FOUNDATION AND THIS STA-

TION CARE ABOUT YOUR GOOD HEALTH.

# # # # #

GOOD HEALTH MEANS TAKING CARE OF YOURSELF. DON'T START SMOKING. AND IF

YOU ALREADY SMOKE... TRY TO STOP. SOMEONE YOU LOVE CARES ABOUT YOUR

GOOD HEALTH. A MESSAGE FROM (station call letters) AND THE AMERICAN TUBERCULOSIS

FOUNDATION.

# # # # #

Exhibit 12.8

Thirty-second Spots

The American Tuberculosis Foundation
1212 Street of the Americas
New York, NY 00912

"YOUR GOOD HEALTH" :30 SEC. LIVE RADIO SPOTS

DO YOU SMOKE? IF YOU DO, DO YOU REMEMBER WHEN YOU STARTED? MAYBE YOU
WERE A TEENAGER AND YOUR FRIENDS THOUGHT IT MADE THEM LOOK "ADULT."
WHATEVER THE REASON, SMOKING ISN'T GROWN UP ANY MORE... IT'S JUST PLAIN
STUPID. THE AMERICAN TUBERCULOSIS FOUNDATION AND THIS STATION WANT YOU
TO KNOW THAT SOMEONE YOU LOVE CARES ABOUT YOUR GOOD HEALTH. WE WANT
YOU TO HAVE THE CHANCE TO ACT LIKE A GROWN UP. IF YOU'D LIKE TO STOP
SMOKING,WRITE US. OUR ADDRESS IS:

THE AMERICAN TUBERCULOSIS FOUNDATION
BOX 1892
NEW YORK, NEW YORK 00911

# # # # #

WHEN YOU SMOKE, YOU'RE NOT JUST HURTING YOURSELF, YOU'RE HURTING THOSE
AROUND YOU... AND MAYBE EVEN SOMEONE YOU LOVE. THE AMERICAN TUBERCULO-
SIS FOUNDATION WANTS YOU TO KNOW THAT YOU CAN QUIT. WE'VE DEVELOPED A
PROGRAM THAT WILL HELP YOU STOP SMOKING IN 30 DAYS, AND WE'LL SEND YOU
THAT PROGRAM FREE. ALL YOU HAVE TO DO IS WRITE US AT:

THE AMERICAN TUBERCULOSIS FOUNDATION
BOX 1892
NEW YORK, NEW YORK 00911

WE CARE ABOUT YOUR GOOD HEALTH.

# # # # #

Exhibit 12.9

Sixty-second Spots

The American Tuberculosis Foundation
1212 Street of the Americas
New York, NY 00912

"YOUR GOOD HEALTH" :60 SEC. LIVE RADIO SPOT

SMOKING CAUSES HEART DISEASE, EMPHYSEMA, AND CANCER. BUT DON'T STOP
SMOKING JUST BECAUSE YOU MIGHT DIE FROM IT. STOP SMOKING BECAUSE SOMEONE
YOU LOVE MIGHT DIE FROM IT. THAT'S RIGHT… SECOND-HAND SMOKE IS A PROVEN
CONTRIBUTOR TO HEALTH PROBLEMS IN NON-SMOKERS. WHEN YOU SMOKE AT
HOME, YOUR CHILDREN BREATHE THE SAME CANCER-CAUSING SMOKE YOU DO…
AND THEY DON'T HAVE ANY CHOICE. THEY CAN'T DECIDE TO QUIT SMOKING. BUT
YOU CAN. IF YOU WANT TO STOP SMOKING, WRITE US. WE'LL SEND YOU A FREE PRO-
GRAM THAT WILL HELP YOU STOP IN 30 DAYS. WRITE:

THE AMERICAN TUBERCULOSIS FOUNDATION
BOX 1892
NEW YORK, NEW YORK 00911

(repeat address)

REMEMBER, SOMEONE YOU LOVE CARES ABOUT YOUR GOOD HEALTH.

# # # # #

Exhibit 12.10

As-Recorded Radio Spots

Northwest Library Association
1342 Placer Ave.
Seattle, WA 98901

"Werewolf" 30 Sec. PSA—As Recorded

(sfx: sounds of wind, howling, and footsteps running)

WOMAN: DID YOU HEAR THAT? IT SOUNDED LIKE A WEREWOLF!

MAN: DON'T WORRY. WE'RE SAFE.

(sfx: loud sound of bushes rattling and sudden snarling)

WOMAN: (very frightened) IT IS A WEREWOLF! WHAT ARE WE   GOING TO   DO?

MAN: (reassuringly) I TOLD YOU NOT TO WORRY. I HAD PLENTY OF GARLIC ON MY

        PIZZA TONIGHT, REMEMBER?

WOMAN: (sarcastically) I CERTAINLY DO.

WEREWOLF:(in terror) GARLIC! (screams)

(sfx: sounds of rapidly retreating footsteps and howling fading into distance)

WOMAN: (relieved) HOW ON EARTH DID YOU KNOW THAT GARLIC WOULD FRIGHTEN A

        WEREWOLF AWAY?

MAN: I READ IT IN A BOOK AT THE PUBLIC LIBRARY.

WOMAN: (sarcastically again) AND DID THIS BOOK EXPLAIN THE EFFECTS OF GARLIC ON

        YOUR DATE?

MAN: WHOOPS...

ANNCR: YOU'D BE SURPRISED WHAT YOU CAN LEARN AT YOUR PUBLIC LIBRARY.

        GIVE READING A TRY... IT MAKES GOOD SENSE.

MAN: (voices fading as couple walks away) OH, COME ON CAROL, IT SAVED OUR LIVES

        DIDN'T IT... I'LL CHEW SOME GUM... I'LL BRUSH MY TEETH...

                                # # # # #

- Find out whether any of the stations will produce your spots for you. Some will, if you provide the script and it suits their needs. Look especially for cosponsorship opportunities through which the station can publicize its involvement with you.

- Be careful, though. Competing stations may not want to run spots produced by a rival station, especially if you use that station's "personalities." However, if a station merely produces your spots for you, find out if you can run them on other stations.

- Find out when each station is most likely to run PSAs. Although it might be best for you to get your message out during the Christmas season, the stations will probably be inundated with similar requests. You'll find that most stations have more available air time following major holidays.

Remember, broadcasting (and cable) still reach more people than any other media. The proliferation of cable channels has multiplied your opportunity for placement while further segmenting your audience for you. Don't automatically discount broadcast and cable because of costs. As this chapter has shown, there are ways to cut costs and still use the medium to its fullest advantage. Explore those avenues. It can only help your chances of being heard—and seen.

KEY TERMS

video news release (VNR)	spot	slice-of-life spot
actuality	script treatment	spot announcement
public service announcement (PSA)	shooting script	as-recorded spot
	accompanying script	
	talking heads spot	

EXERCISES

1. Monitor television programming for a two- or three-hour period. Ascertain the number of public relations–oriented commercials and PSAs. Be careful not to select pure product advertising. Answer the following questions:
   - If the spot or spots are PSAs, who is the sponsor?
   - Can you determine the producer (for example, Advertising Council)?
   - Is the producer different from the sponsor?
   - If the spot or spots are legitimate commercials, are they image oriented, public interest, or issue oriented?
2. Contact a radio or television station news or program director and ascertain the station's policy regarding the placement of PSAs. Present a report on the public service editorial policies of a station in town.

3. Write a 30-second script featuring a seated spokesperson asking for support for the United Way of Anytown, U.S.A. The appeal should be primarily to parents to support a new pediatric clinic to be built with United Way support.

4. Write a 30-second script featuring two celebrities (of your choice). They will be seen endorsing a "support cancer research" theme.

5. Tape a television commercial or PSA. Transcribe it in writing. Rewrite the television spot as a 30-second radio spot, taking care to convert the visuals into verbal cues in the transition.

CHAPTER

13

Speeches and Presentations

In this chapter you will learn:

- The types of speeches and their uses.
- The modes of delivery for speeches, and how they differ.
- How to prepare, write, and deliver a speech.
- How to handle a Q & A session.
- How to use presentation materials to accompany a speech and why.

Speech writing is putting words into someone else's mouth—and that's not an easy task. It requires that you know intimately the person for whom you are writing. You need to know his or her style of speaking, body language, tone of voice, speech patterns, and, most important, personality. When you write a speech you become the person you are writing for, and to an extent that person will become you at the moment he or she begins to speak your words.

Thus, speech writing is a truly collaborative effort. It requires the absolute co-operation of all parties involved. Think of famous speeches you have heard or read: Patrick Henry's "Give me liberty or give me death," Winston Churchill's "Blood, sweat and tears," John F. Kennedy's "Ask not what your country can do for you," and Martin Luther King's "I have a dream" are a few examples. Often, famous speeches such as these were written by the speakers themselves, but just as often, they were collaborative efforts by the speakers, professional speech writers, and others with valuable input into the process. As in all forms of public relations writing, everybody has something to say about what you write.

Whether you are preparing speeches for others or for yourself, this chapter serves as a good introduction. First I talk about how to prepare and write an effective speech or presentation and how to handle question-and-answer (Q & A) sessions. In the second half, I discuss using audiovisual materials as support.

TYPES OF SPEECHES

The public relations **speech** is as varied as the purposes to which the speech will be put. In fact, speeches are usually classified by purpose:

- A speech to *inform* seeks to clarify, instruct, or demonstrate.
- A speech to *persuade* is designed to convince or influence and often carries a call to action.
- A speech to *entertain* covers almost everything else including celebrations, eulogies, and dinner speeches.

The type of speech you use will be determined largely by the topic and the audience. The method of delivery and the degree to which the speech relies on audiovisual aids will also depend on these factors.

MODES OF DELIVERY

There are four basic modes of speech delivery: **extemporaneous, impromptu, scripted,** and **memorized.** For extemporaneous and impromptu speeches, the public relations writer is responsible primarily for the research and compilation of information, usually in outline form. The speaker then studies the notes carefully and is (theoretically) prepared to speak knowledgeably and fluently on the topic. Speeches delivered from script or from memory can be written entirely by the public relations writer.

For all modes of speaking, once the speech is prepared the primary responsibility of the public relations practitioner is to coach the speaker. This means, of course, that you must know how to give a good speech yourself. If you don't—and many public relations people don't—find someone who can and have that person coach the speaker. This often means hiring outside professionals to do the job, which may be costly, but in the long run may be well worth the effort and expense.

PREPARATION AND WRITING

Preparation is the most important element in any type of speech or presentation. Although some of us are able to speak off the cuff, it is a dangerous habit to get into. Think of the politicians who have lost elections because of candid off-the-record remarks or unwise ad libs. It is extremely important that you prepare in advance everything you will say and do during a presentation. Don't leave anything to chance.

The nuts and bolts of an effective presentation include the following:

- Specific purpose
- Clear understanding of your audience
- Well-organized ideas
- Adequate support
- Effective delivery

Specifying Your Purpose

Keep two important principles in mind here. First, the speech should be results oriented. Think of the effect you want it to have on the audience. Decide whether you want the audience to be persuaded, informed, or feel entertained by your presentation.

Second, the purpose of your presentation should be the basis for all the other decisions you make. This means that the way you organize your ideas, the kind of audiovisual support materials you use, even the way you deliver the presentation, will hinge on why you are giving it in the first place.

Analyzing Your Audience

Your presentation is given for your listeners. Even if you think it is the best presentation you have ever given, if it doesn't affect them, it will have failed.

Analyze the occasion: What is the reason this group is together at this time, and what do they expect to hear from you?

Analyze the people: What experience and knowledge about the subject do they bring to your presentation? What is their attitude toward the subject? Toward you?

Organizing Your Speech

Good organization lets your audience know that you know what you're talking about. A seemingly confused speaker loses credibility and wastes valuable time. Remember, no one will sit still for long—especially if you're not making sense. And the only way to make sense is to be organized.

It is worth repeating that the best way to organize a speech is to think of its purpose. Use that purpose as the basis for deciding what goes in your speech, how you structure it, what data you present, even for how you choose your style or wording.

Here is a typical speech format:

Introduction

- *Attention-getter.* Tell people why they should listen.

- *Establish rapport.* Create a bond with your audience. Show them what you have in common.

- *Preview.* Tell people what they are going to hear.

Body/Discussion

- *Main points, arranged logically* (usually in order of importance).

- *Data supporting each main point.*

Conclusion

- *Review.* Summarize the key points the audience has heard.

- *Memorable statement.* Create a desired frame of mind that will stay with the audience.

- *Call for action* (if applicable).

Building a speech is like building anything else: You've got to have a solid foundation. It helps if what you build has a look of continuity, coherence, and completion. No one likes a structure that looks haphazard or loosely constructed. For speechmakers, a solid structure implies a solid idea.

You can see from this outline that in speeches, it pays to be repetitious. Tell people what you are going to do, do it, and then tell them what you have done.

Most writers find it easier to work on the body of the presentation first, before thinking up a snappy introduction and conclusion.

The body of a speech may be developed in a number of ways:

- *Chronological.* Organized by time. For example, cover first this year's events, then next year's.

- *Spatial.* Organized by direction. For instance, talk about your company's development as it moved from the East Coast to the West Coast.

- *Topical.* Organized by topic. Cover one set of ideas that are related to each other, and then move on to the next set of related ideas.

- *Cause and effect.* Organized by need and fulfillment. Describe "what we need" and then "how to get it."

- *Problem and solution.* Organized by question and answer. Describe the problem and then the solution, or vice versa.

Pay attention to how you word the main points you want to make. Work for parallelism, balance, and good transitions between main points. (Notice how the five types of organization described here begin with parallel openings. Notice, too, that they are balanced in both length and sentence structure.)

With the body of the presentation in hand, attack the introduction. A good introduction is relevant to the audience and occasion, involves the audience personally, positively disposes them toward your presentation, and stimulates them.

A good introduction does not begin with the phrase "Today I want to talk to you about . . . ," nor does it necessarily include a joke. Good introductions can be questions, unusual facts, good examples, stories, illustrations, metaphors, analogies, or any one of a number of other devices.

Once you have an attention-getting introduction, you can work on the conclusion of your speech or presentation. The conclusion should summarize or reiterate the main points of your presentation (tell them what you have done). Finish with a memorable statement that makes the purpose of the speech clear and positions the audience firmly on your side. If your speech is intended to persuade, you will also call the audience to action—for example, to join the group you are pitching, or to call their local congressional representative about the issue you have just raised.

One of the best ways to organize a speech is to develop a summary sheet. Include at least the following information:

- *The audience.* What are the ages, educational backgrounds, and demographic characteristics of the audience members? How big is the audience?

- *The purpose.* Are you trying to inform, persuade, reinforce attitudes, or entertain? Complete the phrase "After listening to my speech, audience members will. . . ."

- *Organization of the speech.* Is it chronological, spatial, topical, cause and effect, or problem and solution?

- *Supporting materials.* What statistics, quotations, case histories, analogies, hypothetical illustrations, or anecdotes do you have to support your claim?

- *Purpose of introduction and conclusion.* How will you gain interest, create a need for listening, summarize, and call to action?

- *List of visual aids.* Which media will you use (slides, computer presentation, flip charts)? What content (words, charts and graphs, etc.)? How will visuals be integrated into the speech (during, following, support only, or stand-alone)?

For a complete sample summary sheet, see Exhibit 13.1.

Exhibit 13.1

Summary Worksheet

Preliminary Questions

I. What are the expectations of this audience?
Toward me?
Toward my topic?
Toward this specific situation? (Are there any extenuating circumstances that should be considered?)

II. How do I expect my audience to be affected by my presentation?
The general purpose of my presentation will be to inform, persuade, reinforce certain ideas, entertain?
The specific thesis: After listening to my speech, the audience will . . .

The Body of the Speech

III. What is the best structure to follow given I and II above?
Should my presentation be arranged chronologically? Spatially? Topically? By cause and effect? By problem and solution?
The structure I have chosen is the best in this particular situation because . . .

IV. What are the three or four main points suggested by the specific structure?
A.
B.
C.
D.

V. How will I support the main points?
Will I use statistics, examples, analogies, case studies, direct quotations?
A will be supported by:
B will be supported by:
C will be supported by:
D will be supported by:

VI. How should I adapt my language and word choice to suit audience expectations?
To what extent should I use jargon and buzz words?
To what extent should I be conscious of defining certain words?

VII. Should I use any visual aids?
What should be visualized?
How should it be visualized?
Why should it be visualized?

VIII. How should I introduce the speech?
　　　Why should my audience listen to this message?
　　　How will my audience benefit by listening to me?
　　　How can I make my audience want to listen?
　　　You should listen to me because . . .
　IX. How should I conclude the speech?
　　　How do I relate the conclusion to the main points I have covered?
　　　In conclusion . . .

Supporting Your Ideas

The detail or support you use to fill out your presentation must be sufficient to ensure that your listeners know precisely what you mean but should not be so overwhelming that you lose your audience in minutia.

Your support must be relevant to your listeners. If it makes no sense to them, you will fail to get their attention, gain their good will, or persuade them to your view. For example, if you are writing a speech that intends to persuade the audience to give money to your not-for-profit organization, you would want to include some concrete examples about how their money will be used (e.g., a pledge of $5 per month will deliver 100 hot lunches to shut-ins, but you don't need to detail the exact costs of each meal). Use any kind of support that is appropriate to your purpose and ideas. Facts and statistics are almost mandatory for many business presentations, and examples and illustrations can often make those hard numbers come alive. Quotations from a source your listeners respect can add proof that what you are saying is true. Analogies and metaphors can often be used to make concrete that which is abstract by putting the abstraction in human terms. Preachers use these two devices all the time. Remember, use enough support and detail to do the job but no more.

DELIVERY

Finally, you are standing in front of your listeners (assuming you are the speech or presentation giver). Now it is your job to make your ideas come alive. The secrets of effective delivery are thorough preparation and lots of practice. You cannot deliver a presentation effectively if you don't know what you want to say. That requires preparation. The only way you can become a fluent speaker is to practice. There is no shortcut!

Okay. You are thoroughly prepared and well practiced. Now you must stand up and do two things. First, stick to what you have practiced. Don't get distracted. Don't throw away your prepared presentation for an impromptu effort. Second, keep your eyes on your audience. Look at them. Watch their reactions to what you say. Don't get engrossed in your script. In fact, try not to use a script at all; use an outline or brief notes instead.

Also, don't get engrossed in your audiovisual material. Watch the audience, not the screen. Even if you are using 35-mm slides in a dark room, look out at your audience. You won't be able to see them well, but it is important that they get the feeling you can.

Another piece of advice: Look relaxed, even if you aren't. Smile, frown, move your arms, look around the room at everyone. Try to feel as though you are in the middle of a lively conversation with a group of friends. It will do wonders for your delivery.

THE Q & A SESSION

Anticipation is the key to successful Q & A sessions. If you're the type of speaker who has to have everything written out in advance, then Q & A is not for you. You need to know whether you can handle thinking, analyzing, and speaking off the cuff before you throw yourself to the lions. The best hedge against blowing a Q & A session is practice. It's advisable to have someone who is familiar with the topic of your presentation work with you on possible questions in advance. That way, you have at least some idea of what to expect when you face the real thing. The following advice will help you when you do:

- Repeat the question or paraphrase it in your own words.
- Make sure you understand the question before answering it. Seek clarification if necessary.
- Don't lie, fabricate, or distort information. If you don't know the answer, say so—but don't appear flustered. Offer to find the answer and get back to the questioner. Confidence breeds credibility.
- Refer to any visual aids that will help you answer the question.
- Be concise—don't give another speech.
- Don't allow a questioner to take you on a tangent. Stick to the main points of your speech.
- Don't allow an individual questioner to monopolize the Q & A session.

PRESENTATION MATERIALS

We live in a visual society today. Most of us watch television or go to the movies. Our magazines and newspapers are more and more visually oriented. And, increasingly, we spend a lot of time surfing the Internet. Although the Internet hasn't taken full advantage of melding visuals and words, it has come a long way, and it is fast becoming one of the most integrated media available to communicators. With all this focus on visual appeal, it's hard for a speech or presentation audience to maintain attention, even with the most persuasive of speakers, without something to look at. Used as integrated components of a speech, audiovisual materials can help keep the audience's attention and add valuable information.

Audiovisual support should be for impact—to develop audience interest and hold attention. Use it for effectiveness, to help your listeners remember more, longer. Don't use it simply because it is there. Use it only if it enhances your presentation. If you do use audiovisual support, consider the following points:

- Be sure it adds to your presentation.
- Do not let the support control the presentation. Your ideas must come first.
- Rehearse the presentation with the audiovisual materials. Learn how to use them.
- Do not talk to the visuals; talk to the audience.
- Talk louder. You are competing with the visuals for audience attention.
- Stand clear. Remember, visuals must be seen to be useful.

Preparing Audiovisual Materials

The most common support materials used with speeches are visual-only support materials such as graphs, diagrams, photographs, and handouts; and audiovisual support materials such as videotapes, slides, and multimedia programs. The advent of software programs such as Adobe Persuasion (now out of print) and Microsoft Powerpoint has ushered in a new age of audiovisual presentation. These programs, and others like them, combine the traditional support of slides with an entirely new element—motion. Now, instead of using charts and graphs on posterboard, a videotape, and a slide show, you can prepare all of these support materials in one place.

In the past, it took a lot of work and a pretty hefty investment in equipment just to add dissolves to your slide show (two projectors and a dissolve unit, at least). Today, you can add to your slide show not only dissolves but also fades, wipes, and myriad other effects just by pressing a few computer keys. You can also add music, moving images (captured video, for instance), and voices—all digitized and embedded in your slide show. And now, with the latest projection technology, these shows aren't even limited to your computer screen. They can be projected onto screens rivaling your local theater (they also cost about as much as your local theater's).

Even though the technology has changed drastically, the rules for developing a good slide presentation have not. A good slide show should add zip and clarity to information that may be otherwise dull. It requires that you be well organized, know your audience, and follow a few simple rules:

1. *Define your objective.* Be sure you know what you want to accomplish, what changes you want to take place in your listeners, and what behavior you want to affect.

2. *Analyze your audience.* Are they laypeople or experts? Do you aim for the lowest common denominator? The middle? The top? The more you know about your audience, the easier it is to make that decision.

3. *Work from an outline when creating your visual presentation.* Don't replicate everything you are going to say. Keep it to a concise summary of the major points and supporting materials needed to reach your objective with this audience.

4. *Decide what mood or treatment you want.* A light, humorous treatment may mean cartoons and a comic narration. Are you going to threaten? Cajole? Be low-key? Mood makes a difference in how you use color and pacing.

5. *Write a script, if you plan to use one.* This will include all of the details not reflected in your visual presentation.

6. *Plan your slides.*

   • Convert material originally designed for publication to slide format. *Hint:* You can scan this material and insert it into your slides as needed. In my experience, most of the presentation software accepts PICT format the best, and images saved in PICT format typically take up less memory. Also, if you're projecting directly from a computer, or showing your slide presentation on your computer, you don't need the highest resolution. Scan your images at no greater than 100 dots per inch (dpi).

   • Use a series of slides or charts, disclosed progressively, to build up complex ideas. *Hint:* If you have a long list of subpoints spread among several slides, be sure to use the same header on each slide so that your audience remembers your major point.

   • Keep all copy and symbols simple and legible. Projected letters should be at least two inches high and one-half inch wide. What this means to you is that your type size shouldn't go any lower than 18 points, or it won't be legible. *Hint:* Use a sans serif typeface, and keep it mostly bold. Serif type tends to be harder to read when projected.

   • Make all copy on slides short and to the point. Include no more than 15 or 20 words or 25 or 30 pieces of data per slide. Again, remember to keep the type size legible.

   • Keep slides simple and bold. Limit each slide or chart to one main idea.

   • Use charts and graphs rather than tables. Tables almost always look complicated and confusing.

   • Use variety in layout, color, charting, and graphics for change of pace. *Hint:* Don't use more than one slide background per slide show. The presentation software includes a dizzying selection of background templates. Pick one and stick to it for your entire presentation. *Second hint:* Pick uncluttered backgrounds and dark colors for use with light-colored lettering. Uncluttered backgrounds allow you more space to work, whereas light letters against dark backgrounds are easier to read.

   • Avoid mathematical formulas or equations on slides.

   • Keep photographs uncluttered.

   • Keep moving. Leave slides up only long enough for the audience to read. Remember, the slides are there to supplement and support your words and ideas, not to take your place. *Hint:* Most presentation software allows for manual or automatic mode. In most cases, you'll want to control the speed yourself by using the manual mode. Use the automatic mode only if your slide show is designed to run unaccompanied as a stand-alone display.

- Enlist the aid of a competent audiovisual specialist. Although the new programs aren't all that difficult to learn, your presentations can still benefit from someone trained in visual design.

7. *Edit your slide presentation.* Ask yourself the following questions:

- Are all major points covered?
- Does the content of each slide fit the narration?
- Are all slides legible?
- Are colors and visuals bold and effective?
- Does each slide depict one idea only?
- Is there good continuity from slide to slide?
- Does the program add up to form a visually coherent and pleasing presentation?

8. *Rehearse, rehearse, rehearse.*

9. *Visit the room where you will be making the presentation* prior to your presentation time to make sure the projector is there and in working order. Run through your program to make sure all is as you want it. *Hint:* Computer compatibility is still a problem, especially between electronic projectors and notebook computers. Ideally, you would have your own portable setup. If you don't, meet with the computer technician in charge of the facility where you will be presenting and make sure everything works before the curtain goes up.

10. Slide programs are almost always given in darkened rooms. The only other light may be the one on the lectern you use. Even the new computer projections units aren't any brighter than the old slide projectors. That means you must make a special effort to force yourself to look out into a darkened room at people you may be unable to see. Don't lose eye contact with them, because they can see you just fine. Remember, a slide show is an accompaniment. *You're* the real show.

Scripting for Audiovisuals

Scripts using visual accompaniment are formatted similarly to television scripts, with visuals on the left and narration on the right. No matter whether you are writing for a live presentation accompanied by visuals or a self-contained presentation that will run automatically with narration already added, the technique of scripting is the same. Remember, a script includes everything you are going to say, not just an outline of your visuals. Unless you, or your presenter, has done this particular presentation a number of times or is very good at *prompted extemporaneous speaking* (using visuals as reminders), you'll probably need a script.

Exhibit 13.2

Slide Script

Slide Script
"Building the Future" Page 1 of 5

1. Graphic—"BUILDING THE FUTURE ON THE PAST" over University coat-of-arms	1. BUILDING THE FUTURE ON THE PAST. THESE WORDS REFLECT BUTLER UNIVERSITY'S COMMITMENT TO INNOVATIVE RESEARCH AND EDUCATIONAL PROGRAMS.
2. Aerial shot of campus	2. A COMMITMENT TO DEVELOP THE PROMISE OF IDEAS INTO THE FOUNDATION OF HUMAN PROGRESS.
3. Same, with "RESEARCH" and "TEACHING" supered	3. THIS COMMITMENT TAKES MANY AND VARIOUS FORMS REFLECTING THE INTEL-LECTUAL DIVERSITY OF THE CAMPUS COMMUNITY.
4. Psychology researcher with experimental subject	4. IMPORTANTLY, THE BOLD AND UNCOMPROMISING INQUIRY SO TYPICAL OF RESEARCH AT THE UNIVERSITY MORE OFTEN THAN NOT PROVIDES THE BASIS FOR THE BEST IN TEACHING AND PUBLIC SERVICE.
5. IEC researcher testing solar cell	5. IT HAS BEEN SAID THAT THE FUTURE IS PURCHASED BY THE PRESENT.

-more-

The audiovisual script should be easy to follow. Visuals appear exactly opposite their audio counterparts, often with numbers corresponding to the slide placed within the script narration to indicate the exact point at which the slide will be changed.

The major difference between audiovisual scripts and television spots is length. Slide presentations are usually longer with fewer visual changes. To keep them lively, count on changing slides every 5 to 10 seconds. Much depends on the type of presentation. For instance, if you are presenting the annual budget report, you might be severely limited as to the type and number of slides shown. If the slide contains written information, gauge the amount of time it will take to read it by reading it aloud. If you are dealing strictly with visual images, then the 5- to 10-second time allotment should be just about right The new technology allows for a number of special effects that can alleviate some of the boredom of static slides (e.g., points popping on the screen one at a time, graphics moving in and out). Just don't overdo the movement.

Exhibit 13.2 is a simple slide presentation script, but you'll notice it follows the same format as a television script (see Chapter 12).

KEY TERMS

speech	impromptu speech	memorized speech
extemporaneous speech	scripted speech	

EXERCISE

Prepare a brief presentation about your school or college, selling it as a great place to get an education. Hit heavily on its strengths (location, educational reputation, etc.). Use the format presented in this chapter for combining words and visual aids. If you have access to presentation software, develop your full audiovisual support that way. Try developing a support slide show and a full, stand-alone presentation.

CHAPTER

14

Design, Printing, and Desktop Publishing

In this chapter you will learn:

- What design is and why it is important in communication.
- The principles of design.
- How to choose the appropriate typeface, ink, paper, and printing process for a publication.

- What desktop publishing is and how it has changed the design and printing process.
- How to work well with a printer.

Design is central to the success of any communication. In fact, most designers would go so far as to suggest that design is just as important an element of a publication as writing. Don't get me wrong: If your writing stinks, graphic cartwheels and high design acrobatics won't cover up the smell. But the point must be made that good design attracts and holds readership, whereas bad design repels and discourages it. If you don't get them in the tent, they won't see the show.

Like it or not, we read externally first and internally second. That is to say, we judge publications not only by their covers but also by their overall visual appearance. Design provides an outward structure upon which we further communicate our messages, sell our soap, project our images, inform our publics, and otherwise hang our corporate hats. Although most companies pay plenty of attention to the design of their ads, packaging, logos, and other images, they often lose sight of the importance of design when it comes to their publications.

But make no mistake. Whether the publication is internal (a newsletter, benefits folder, or employee recruitment kit) or external (a brochure, annual report, or company magazine), its design requires careful planning. Without structure, visual thought, and order, a publication will not get the attention it deserves. No matter how well written and carefully edited your message may be, readers will pass over poorly designed print materials. It's as simple as that.

For these reasons, then, I want to spend some time talking about design. First, as a public relations writer, you must understand and be able to use basic design principles. Second, you need to develop a design vocabulary, so that you can communicate clearly with designers, printers, and other publication professionals. Third, you must know how the eye moves through a page (so that you can direct and redirect visual traffic) as well as understand how to attract and hold readers. Finally, you need to comprehend the "parts of sight" as clearly as you know the parts of speech.

DESIGN: WHAT IT IS AND WHY IT MIGHT BE GREEK TO YOU

Before venturing further, I need to define what I mean by design. Essentially, design is the act of bringing order to whatever surrounds us. It is planning and organizing physical materials and shaping and reshaping our environment to accommodate specific needs. There's nothing particularly mysterious about design, but many of us are intimidated by it.

For one thing, few of us have had much visual education. That fact is especially ironic when you consider how much our learning and survival depend on sight. Think about it: With few exceptions, our verbal literacy is learned, broadened, and specialized through vision—that is, through reading and writing skills. We study letters, words, spelling, vocabulary, grammar, syntax, style, writing, and literature. Grammar is apt to be central to our language studies from third grade through our first year of college. Writing begins before we start our formal educations and runs fully through all the years of our educations. Visual studies, however, tend to end somewhere between the second and third grades when crayons are either thrown or taken away.

Another reason why we underestimate the impact of design is the effortless nature of sight itself. Our eyes are designed to receive and process lines, shapes, textures, colors, intricate spatial relationships, and other complex visual information almost instantly. So long as we keep our eyes open, we don't run red lights, fall down stairs, open the wrong end of a soda can, or trample people. That sight works so easily is both good and bad. Good in that our visual sense operates automatically, is well greased, and complete beyond our wildest dreams. Bad in that we take it for granted and often assume that to have sight is to have visual literacy. Of course, this is no more the case than to assume that to be able to speak a language is the same as to read and write that language.

It should come as no surprise, then, that design seems foreign to most of us. It enjoys its own vocabulary, grammar, syntax, composition, and meaning. Additionally, it possesses a unique literature, history, and heritage—one that, in fact, precedes written language. But, happily, acquiring this new visual language is considerably less painful than the average root canal procedure. Let's get started.

DESIGNING PUBLIC RELATIONS MATERIALS

Do different print formats require different design approaches, principles, and strategies? Or, more simply stated, do you design differently for different formats? Well, yes and no. Or, as Winnie the Pooh might say, it all depends.

A set of design principles applies to whatever we create, regardless of format, medium, intent, or audience. In each instance, we plot a visual course that becomes the blueprint for our publication's architecture. And although publication formats vary, just as buildings differ, they possess similar structural principles—just as skyscrapers, shopping malls, museums, and homes have some characteristics in common. Publications, like buildings, use a structural plan that mixes serious pragmatic and aesthetic concerns while providing a sound framework and foundation.

But every publication deserves a good design that takes into account its format, medium, intent, and audience (see Exhibit 14.1).

- *Format.* The exaggerated vertical format of a brochure presents a set of spatial concerns much different from those of a poster. The brochure's long, relatively small, and narrow area is arranged in a series of panels—of equal or unequal size—that can be folded two, three, or more times, vertically or horizontally. These properties make the brochure's continuity and sequence especially important. A poster, by contrast, presents a single face to its reader and is, therefore, designed much more like a print ad with a point of emphasis for entry and a series of guides leading the reader through the integrated communication.

- *Medium.* The medium also brings its own eccentricities and needs to the design. Although an annual report may bear a strong resemblance to a magazine—and the best ones seem to—special care is required to design a report that communicates with its many audiences while conforming to exacting Securities and Exchange Commission requirements that prescribe everything

Exhibit 14.1

Connection Newsletter

Inside: *New fiber line, a look at Wilton Connor, our retail strategy, ethics training and more…*

Weyerhaeuser Company
Containerboard Packaging and Recycling
EC2-2D7
P.O. Box 9777
Federal Way WA 98063-9777

PRESORTED
Standard Rate
U.S. Postage
PAID
Seattle WA
Permit No. 3597

The newsletter of **Weyerhaeuser Containerboard Packaging and Recycling**   **May/June 2003**

Not a moment to spare

At a glance: Getting in there JIT

As companies react to the strict requirements of mega-retailers, many are going to a just in time (JIT) con cept — reducing their inventories and asking for product only when they need it. For box plants, that means coming up with quick and creative packaging solutions.

Quick service
"Customers are being more and more driven by their customers — like Wal-Mart. If Wal-Mart's needs change, so do our customers', and they come to somebody like us to meet their needs," says Andy Fescoe, general manager at the Rochester,

N.Y., box plant. "We try to think of ourselves as a service company with a product. We provide a product, but we have to be able to react very quickly to an ever-shortening time frame."

Speedy solutions
Two of Rochester's customers, Kodak and Sentry, continually put the team to the test.

For Kodak, Rochester services multiple divisions and runs hundreds of SKUs. "Over time, the delivery requirements have become shorter and shorter," says Andy. "They have reduced inventory but still need the product available quickly and at a reasonable cost."

Three methods are used to meet Kodak's needs:

■ Delivering made-to-ship orders, which are called in five days in advance.

■ Maintaining inventory at the plant of 15 popular items. Orders are faxed in at night, and the boxes are delivered each morning — meeting a four-hour turnaround requirement.

■ Delivering orders as small as 25 boxes to Kodak's internal warehouse, called the Kodak Hub. Those orders require a four-hour turnaround.

Changing the system
Although the Kodak Hub solves Kodak's JIT needs, the requirements are hard for the Rochester team to meet, and it's costly.

"Presently, we're working at a way to exit the Kodak Hub situation and begin 'self-hubbing.' We're working with Kodak now on establishing the logistics necessary here to be able to accommodate the four-hour turn-around requirement," says Andy. "We have our IT people as well as Kodak's IT people working diligently to come up with a method of

Continued on page 2

▲ Weyerhaeuser

The Weyerhaeuser newsletter *Connection* is a 12-page tabloid, printed in two colors (a different second color each issue) and full of large graphic photos and images.

(continued)

(continued)

Not a moment... Continued from page 1.

communication that will still allow the four-hour turnaround."

Different looks, one box

Another way Rochester helps speed up its response time is through label application. Its customer Sentry, a metal-safe manufacturer, needs similar-sized boxes but requires quick deliveries of many different models going to different retailers. Boxes are generic until the product-specific labels are applied.

> "But whether you are bringing in a day's worth or an hour's worth of material, inventory is required someplace. And at some point, the lines of economy and space cross."

"In this case, we can inventory for them but not in the finished-goods form," says John McCormick, sales manager at Rochester. "We can bring the boxes off the corrugator, and even diecut them in some cases, prior to having the labels applied. And we can react rapidly when Sentry calls — even if it's within a 48-hour time frame."

Who's holding the box?

Although inventory creates flexibility and often allows a plant to meet the time-sensitive specs, it is expensive.

"In my opinion, there's a paradox with the JIT delivery concept," says John. "Everyone is trying to eliminate inventory. But whether you are bringing in a day's worth or an hour's worth of material, inventory is required someplace. And at some point, the lines of economy and space cross."

Maximizing the machine

There are other hidden costs associated with JIT delivery besides just inventory.

"In our business, you have to set up your finishing equipment for each specific order," says Andy. "It doesn't make sense to run a machine five minutes if it has a setup time of 45. We want to spread that setup over a much larger quantity of boxes so it is more effective — and that is part of the JIT trade-off."

Open lines of communication

But despite the costs, the trend is set. Customers continue to want less quantity, larger varieties and quicker turnarounds. To achieve that requires fine-tuned logistics.

"Communication is the cornerstone of it all," says Mike Rougeux, plant superintendent at the Elmira Heights, N.Y., box plant, which serves customers such as Corning Glass and Leprino Foods.

"We've really had to hone the "can-do" attitude," says Mike. "Our customers' needs are complicated, and we have to understand them. And it's the open communication between ourselves and our customers that gives us the flexibility to work through obstacles."

Some steps the team takes to ensure JIT deliveries include:

■ A design review process for all new items. A cross-functional team studies expectations and obstacles.

■ Limiting work behind each machine to remain as flexible as possible.

■ Scheduling by customer service of the lineup behind converting machines for maximum efficiency.

■ Strong partnering with quality vendors for tooling and quality raw materials.

"We have a 98 percent on-time delivery since we started tracking," says Mike. "We have strong processes in place, but we also have strong relationships, whether it's between our customers and ourselves or internally between sales and manufacturing. You have to all work together to meet the customers' needs. When you start acting independently, you lose."

Andy agrees, "You have to continually work together to come up with a workable solution, because it's an ever-changing climate."

MAKING THE RIGHT DECISION

Steve Rogel leads SMT in discussion on ethical business practices

At a glance: Ethics training coming this spring

A new employee who has not been fully trained dumps solvent down a storm drain. What should you do? As it turns out, this very situation may be one of the topics you will be discussing in the upcoming 2003 ethics training.

The code

Every three years, Weyerhaeuser revises its code of ethics. This year's 6th edition, entitled *Our Reputation: A Shared Responsibility,* includes:

■ A new section on privacy.

■ Reformatting to make it more reader-friendly.

■ A rewritten section on electronic resources for easier understanding.

■ Revised language to reinforce compliance with new laws and regulations.

Every employee will be receiving a copy of the updated document.

Training

Following distribution, training will be conducted companywide. The objective is to ensure that all employees are aware of the company's current guidelines for conducting business in an ethical manner. It also provides information on how to raise any concerns or report potential unethical or illegal activity.

Weyerhaeuser has a well-earned reputation for conducting business ethically. Nurturing this ethical culture is important because it:

■ Provides a competitive advantage in the marketplace.

■ Enables us to attract and retain good people who share our values.

■ Provides us with credibility in the marketplace.

■ Gains support from the communities where we do business.

Adding excitement

Neil Moir, manager, ethics and business conduct, admits that some may find the code a little dry. "That's why we've tried to put a little life into the training," he says. "The first segment will be familiarizing people with the program. The second part is much

more interactive. There is a video where different scenarios are presented to open up dialogue on a range of issues. It's set up to get people thinking and talking about the code in daily practice.

"In the video, employees can see how ethical dilemmas affect them, which gets the ethical juices flowing," says Neil. This year, the SMT will be featured throughout the video, giving guidance in certain situations.

Top to bottom

On March 17, Steve Rogel led a training session for his direct reports. The training will start "cascading" through the businesses June 1, 2003. The SMT will give the course to the leaders under them, who will take it the supervisors under them, and so on, until everyone has received the training.

"Our business will continue the cascading approach until every employee has received the training from their manager. We expect that bulk of that training will be completed by the end of 2003. This training is refreshed every two years," said Jim Keller, senior vice president, CBPR.

Sonja Narcisse, CBPR HR director, will be communicating the deployment and tracking process to managers in mid May.

"We want to remind folks that this training is not a change in the company's ethics," says Jim Keller, senior vice president of CBPR and the CBPR BMT. "Our employees are ethical and know this information. Integrity is a part of everything we do. This is a refresher course — one with the support of Mr. Rogel, the Board of Directors and the SMT."

Contact:

Weyerhaeuser Business Conduct office: Neil Moir, 253-924-4955 CBPR & process questions: Sonja Narcisse, 253-924-2821

from logistics to point size. Designing a poster that will be read from across a room by a moving audience—or that may itself be moving—presents a different challenge.

- *Intent.* Intent also figures squarely into the design formula. Let's assume that a company has had a financially disastrous year. Although it can easily afford a full-blown, four-color report with portraits of smiling CEOs in three-piece suits, perceptive company planners might decide that a more austere approach is warranted. Or, perhaps due to a corporate takeover or a major image overhaul, a company decides to completely reposition itself and court a changed or new audience. To do so, it redesigns everything from its newsletter to its logotype. Simply put, your purposes affect the look and structure of what you publish.

- *Audience.* All publications should be designed with their audience in mind. Too often we forget the audience by neglecting to notice that it has changed dramatically or is in the process of a major change. Or, we're so insulated that we don't measure what we publish by the most important touchstone— our consumers. There's nothing like a sudden decline in readership for the company newsletter to alert an editor to potential problems.

PRINCIPLES OF DESIGN

Most of us don't pay much attention to a design when everything is correctly ordered. In fact, the average person seldom sees design in anything at all. We read newspapers daily without noticing the skeletal framework that orders the headlines, photography, graphics, text, and other style elements of a page. Similarly, we raise our wineglasses to toast without realizing that stems are designed to keep our hands from warming the wine. The best design is like that: It exists but doesn't call attention to itself. As a friend once remarked, "A good designer doesn't design for design's sake. The best design serves its purpose, period—without calling attention to itself."

Although a number of basic **design principles** exist, most public relations writers can get by well enough if they understand only an indispensable few. These principles are balance, proportion, sequence, emphasis, and unity. Other design choices facing the public relations writer involve grids, alignment, and typefaces. I'll discuss these issues, too.

Balance

Most of us intuitively understand balance—at least to the extent that we notice immediately if something is out of balance. As children, we seemed to just know that if the person on the other end of the teeter-totter was bigger than us, we had to sit closer to the end to counterbalance his or her weight. In a way, we might say that balance is natural to human beings. We seek it in our lives, our budgets, and in the way we view the world. The very fact that we walk upright (at least most of the time) suggests that we understand balance somewhere deep in our genetic programming.

In its simplest form, balance as it relates to design means that what is put on one side of a page should "weigh" as much as what is on the other side. All the elements you place on the page have weight, even the white space you leave by not placing elements. Size, color, and degree of darkness all play a part in balance.

There are two ways to achieve balance (see Exhibit 14.2). The easiest is the *symmetrical approach*. To balance symmetrically means to place exactly the same amount of weight in exactly the same positions on either side of the page (or spread). Symmetrically balanced pages tend to appear more formal and can be used to impart a nonverbal conservatism to your layout. The *asymmetrical approach* is generally more interesting. The technique involves shifting weight on one side of a page or spread to balance the opposite side (much like in the teeter-totter example). For example, if a two-page spread has a big photo near the gutter (center line of a two-page spread) on one side of the layout, you can achieve balance by placing a smaller picture closer to the outside edge of the opposite page. Remember, this arrangement works with all elements of varying weight, including white space. An asymmetrical layout appears less formal than its symmetrical counterpart.

When you increase the number of elements on a page or spread, you increase the difficulty of working with symmetrical balance. It is difficult, for instance, to ensure that all your photos will be the same size, all your illustrations roughly the same shape, or all your headlines the same length (especially if you want to emphasize a story over others on the page). In fact, you are almost forced into asymmetry on most layouts unless you plan carefully for the opposite effect.

For the beginner, you can check whether your layout is balanced in a number of ways, all based on looking at it from an altered perspective: For example, you can squint at your layout. The blurring attained through narrowing your eyes tends to block out the light areas and bring the darker areas of your layout to the forefront. Or you can turn your layout upside down or look at it in a mirror. Both of these methods provide you with an opposite view and, thus, a new look at your layout. Balance, or lack of it, will jump out at you almost immediately.

Proportion

We tend to think of proportion in terms of comparison. For instance, a picture on a page is bigger or smaller than another picture on the page, or it is the largest element on the page in comparison to the other elements. Thus, proportion is a measure of relationship in size. It helps to show one object's relationship to other objects in your layout. For example, articles and their accompanying pictures, cutlines, and pull quotes typically will form a proportional whole in relationship to the rest of the page. Or the space that separates articles from one another may be greater than that which separates the elements within an article. We use proportion to tell us what belongs with what on a page.

Exhibit 14.2

Balance

The easiest way to achieve balance is through pure symmetry (top). Place identically weighted elements on either side of the center axis of the page. Symmetry can also be affected by centering objects. Asymmetry, by contrast, requires more practice to achieve (bottom). The fundamental rule in asymmetrical balance requires visualizing your layout as a teeter-totter. Balance the objects on either side of your vertical axis according to weight and distance from the fulcrum. In this case, the large image is counterbalanced by the white space and headline on the left.

Our sense of proportion has, or should have, a parallel in nature. Pythagorus, the Greek mathematician and philosopher, noticed this over 2,000 years ago when he suggested that the most pleasing proportion is based on a roughly 2:3 ratio. In Pythagorian terms, the lesser dimension in a plane figure is to the greater as the greater is to the sum of both. Using the 2:3 ratio, 2 is to 3 what 3 is to 5. Get it?

Fortunately, there is a simpler method of explaining the concept. Think of a page of typing paper. It is 8½-by-11 inches—roughly, a 2:3 ratio. In other words, it has an asymmetrical proportion rather than a 1:1, symmetrical proportion. For designers, this means avoiding dividing a page into halves, or any increment of a 1:1 ratio, such as 4:2 or 6:3. Not that this rule has to be followed religiously, but it does add visual interest to your layout. A layout based on halving the page is more formal, more constrained.

A more practical—and easier—method of working with a page layout is the **rule of ground thirds.** This method requires that you divide a page into thirds, and that you balance the page using a two-thirds to one-third ratio (see Exhibit 14.3). You've probably already noticed that two-thirds is roughly equivalent to three-fifths, the Greek's favorite aspect ratio. This two-thirds to one-third ratio is commonly used in newsletter layout, but it is most often apparent in print advertisements in which a large graphic image takes up two-thirds of the page while the copy takes up the other third.

Don't get the idea that you have to group two-thirds of your elements into two-thirds of every page. This ratio can be achieved in a number of ways. For instance, you can have a page two-thirds full and one-third empty. Or you can have a page that is two-thirds empty and one-third full (although your boss might think this a little wasteful).

Sequence and Emphasis

When we look at a page, we tend to move from big elements to smaller elements, dark areas to lighter areas, colored elements to black-and-white elements, bright colors to muted colors, and unusual shapes to usual shapes. A proper sequence, or order, of the elements on your layout will literally lead your readers through your page (see Exhibit 14.4).

Emphasis has to do with focusing your readers' attention on a single element on a page (see Exhibit 14.5). This is what you want them to see first and is usually where you want them to start interpreting your page. We emphasize elements by assigning them more optical weight than other items on the page. These emphasized elements are larger, darker, more colorful, oddly shaped. They draw the readers' attention first among all the other items on the page.

A number of simple techniques exist that, if used properly, will show your readers exactly where to look first and where to go from there. Although these guidelines are meant specifically for newsletter layout, they can be adapted to many other types of layout as well:

- *All elements.* Elements placed high on the page will gain emphasis; elements placed at or near the bottom will have less emphasis. Placement near or at

continued p. 290

Exhibit 14.3

Proportion

VIRTUE ETHICS & THE GREEKS

THE GREEKS DIDN'T CARE SO MUCH WHAT A PERSON DID AS WHAT A PERSON WAS. CHARACTER WAS THE MORAL BULDING BLOCK ON WHICH EVERTHING ELSE THAT WAS GREEK DEPENDED.

Lorem ipsum,Dolor sit amet, consectetuer adipiscing elit, sed diam nonummy nibh euismod tincidunt ut laoreet dolore magna aliquam erat volutpat. Ut wisi enim ad minim veniam, quis nostrud exerci tation ullamcorper suscipit lobortis nisl ut aliquip ex ea commodo consequat. Duis autem vel eum iriure dolor in hendrerit in vulputate velit esse molestie consequat, vel illum dolore eu feugiat nulla facilisis at vero eros et accumsan et iusto odio dignissim qui blandit praesent luptatum zzril delenit augue duis dolore te feugait nulla facilisi.

Lorem ipsum dolor sit amet, consectetuer adipiscing elit, sed diam nonummy nibh euismod tincidunt ut laoreet dolore magna aliquam erat volutpat.

Lorem ipsum dolor sit amet, consectetuer adipiscing elit, sed diam nonummy nibh euismod tincidunt ut laoreet dolore magna aliquam erat volutpat. Duis autem vel eum iriure dolor in hendrerit in vulputate velit esse molestie consequat, vel illum dolore eu feugiat nulla facilisis at vero eros et accumsan et iusto odio dignissim qui blandit praesent luptatum zzril delenit augue duis dolore te feugait nulla facilisi.

Lorem ipsum dolor sit amet, consectetuer adipiscing elit, sed diam nonummy nibh euismod tincidunt ut laoreet dolore magna aliquam erat volutpat. Ut wisi enim ad minim veniam, quis nostrud

A VIRTUE IS ACQUIRED BY HABITUAL PRACTICE. IT ISN'T SOMETHING A PERSON IS BORN WITH.

exerci tation ullamcorper suscipit lobortis nisl ut aliquip ex ea commodo consequat.

Lorem ipsum dolor sit amet, consectetuer adipiscing elit, sed diam nonummy nibh euismod tincidunt ut laoreet dolore magna aliquam erat volutpat. Duis autem

vel eum iriure dolor in hendrerit in vulputate velit esse molestie consequat, vel illum dolore eu feugiat nulla facilisis at vero eros et accumsan et iusto odio dignissim qui blandit praesent luptatum zzril delenit augue duis dolore te feugait nulla facilisi. Lorem ipsum dolor sit amet, consectetuer adipiscing elit, sed diam nonummy nibh euismod tincidunt ut laoreet dolore magna aliquam erat volutpat.

Ut wisi enim ad minim veniam, quis nostrud exerci tation ullamcorper suscipit lobortis nisl ut aliquip ex ea commodo consequat. Duis autem vel eum iriure dolor in hendrerit in vulputate velit esse molestie consequat, vel illum dolore eu feugiat nulla facilisis at vero eros et accumsan et iusto odio dignissim qui blandit praesent luptatum zzril delenit augue duis dolore te feugait nulla facilisi.

Lorem ipsum dolor sit amet, consectetuer adipiscing elit, sed diam nonummy nibh euismod tincidunt ut laoreet dolore magna

Proportion is achieved by using the Greek principle of ground thirds. In this example, the headline and copy take up approximately two-thirds of the page and the picture occupies the other third.

Exhibit 14.4

Sequence

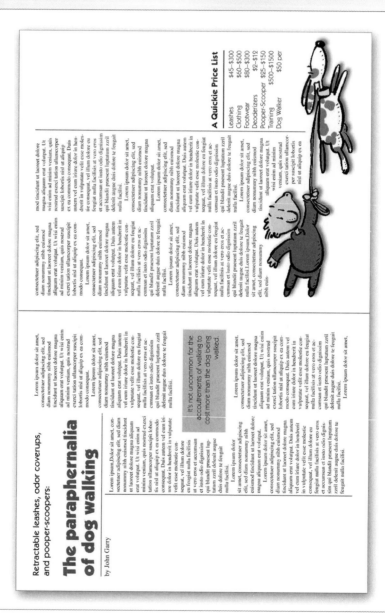

In this example, the headline bleeding into the white space in the upper left corner draws your eye naturally to the starting point (helped by our natural inclination to look there anyway). The natural column flow, the pull quote, and the final graphic (moving off the page to the right) all lead you to the exit point at the lower right of the layout.

Exhibit 14.5

Emphasis

Use of strong graphics, color, unusual shapes, or large type will indicate to your readers where you want them to look first; however, this may not mean you want them to start reading there. Although emphasis can be used to establish sequence, it can also be used simply to draw attention to something, with the understanding that the reader should then know where to look to begin reading. In this example, that entry point is established by the headline.

the center of the page will also gain emphasis, especially if used in conjunction with another form of emphasis such as color or size. The left side of a page or the left page of a two-page spread has priority over the right. The outside margins of a two-page spread (the left margin of the left page and the right margin of the right page) are focal points as well.

- *Headlines.* For heavier emphasis, place headlines at the top or near the center of the page. The eye naturally falls in these areas. Additional emphasis can be gained by using a larger point size or stretching the headline over more than one column width. Typical options, then, are one–column heads in a smaller point size, more than one–column heads in a smaller point size, one–column heads in a larger point size, and more than one–column heads in a larger point size.

    Depending on the number of columns you are working with and the range of point sizes you choose, the degrees of emphasis are many. Keep in mind, however, that you should vary headline size by no more than a few basic increments. For example, if minor heads are set at 18 points, major heads should not be larger than 24 or 30 points. This closeness in point size adds to the unity of your design. The rare exception might be the major headline on the front page of your newsletter. You might go all the way to 36 points, but be sure that your headline doesn't then conflict with and lessen the impact of your banner or nameplate.

- *Articles.* Place lead articles at or near the top of the page. Also place continued articles at or near the top. Because continuation lines (e.g., "continued from page 1") are usually small, you can still emphasize another article on the same page as a jumped article by working with the headline. By using boxes and tint blocks (see Exhibit 14.6), you can emphasize an article by setting it off from other elements on the page. Also, dividing your page into ground thirds and placing an emphasized article in either portion by itself will get it attention.

- *Graphics.* Larger photographs and other graphic devices impart greater emphasis, no matter where they are placed. Smaller elements placed at the top or bottom of the page can also gain emphasis. A small photo, for example, placed at or near the bottom of a page might help balance a large headline placed at the top of the page.

    Again, graphic elements should follow the general restrictions of your grid (the number of columns you are using; see discussion below). Thus, a three–column grid will allow photos of one, two, or three columns in width. Remember, too, that the darker the graphic element, the more emphasis it will have. This applies to boxed articles and tint blocks as well.

- *White space.* White space is not usually thought of as an element of emphasis. Rather, it is usually an element of contrast—that is, it is used to emphasize something else, not to draw attention to itself. The one rule to remember when using white space is, don't surround it with other elements. White space should be pushed to the outside of your pages, not the inside. On a two-page spread, the only white space between the two pages should be the

Exhibit 14.6

Tint Boxes

Boxes and tint blocks can be used as effective design elements, if they are used correctly. For example, never allow your text to "bump up against" the lines of you boxes or the edges of your tint blocks. This makes the text and the layout look crowded. Also be very careful not to indicate too dark a screen or your copy will be unreadable. The best way to check on screen darkness is to print it out on the ultimate output printer you are planning to use, or seek the advice of your printer.

20%

Boxes and tint blocks can be used as effective design elements, if they are used correctly. For example, never allow your text to "bump up against" the lines of you boxes or the edges of your tint blocks. This makes the text and the layout look crowded. Also be very careful not to indicate too dark a screen or your copy will be unreadable. The best way to check on screen darkness is to print it out on the ultimate output printer you are planning to use, or seek the advice of your printer.

30%

Boxes and tint blocks can be used as effective design elements, if they are used correctly. For example, never allow your text to "bump up against" the lines of you boxes or the edges of your tint blocks. This makes the text and the layout look crowded. Also be very careful not to indicate too dark a screen or your copy will be unreadable. The best way to check on screen darkness is to print it out on the ultimate output printer you are planning to use, or seek the advice of your printer.

50%

Boxes and tint blocks can be used as effective design elements, if they are used correctly. For example, never allow your text to "bump up against" the lines of you boxes or the edges of your tint blocks. This makes the text and the layout look crowded. Also be very careful not to indicate too dark a

60%

When using tint blocks, take care that your type will read well over the percentage screen you've chosen. Top to bottom are 20, 30, 50, and 60 percent screens.

gutter. Wide side margins, heavy **drops** (the amount of white space at the top of a page), or uneven bottoms all add contrast. The creative use of white space will add an air of affluence to your publication, making it look more sophisticated. Too much white space, by contrast, will make a newsletter look like its editor ran out of stories. Remember, white space is weighted just like any other design element. Using it effectively requires a lot of practice.

Unity

Unity is one way of providing readers with a whole by drawing relationships among its various parts. This means that body type and headline type should be compatible. Photos should be either all black and white or all color. The layout should be all formal or all informal. In other words, unity is the creation of a recognizable pattern (see Exhibit 14.7)

Perhaps the best way to gain unity of design has more to do with an overall look, a unifying design. Following are some basic guidelines for gaining unity in your publication:

- Stick with one or two typefaces (described in detail below). You can gain a lot of variety by simply changing size and weight and working with the various forms that any one particular typeface offers. For example, some faces come in light, text, regular, bold, black, and ultra, not to mention the italic versions of these variations. Two typefaces should be plenty.

- Use justified type for a formal look, unjustified type for an informal air (see discussion of alignment below). To increase the formality of unjustified type, just increase the hyphenation. This will make your lines less ragged on the right and, thus, more formal.

- Use rules (lines), tint blocks, and boxes for more formality; eliminate them for informality.

- Use top and bottom **anchors** (lines or strips of color) for more formal layouts.

- Make sure all illustrations are of the same type. If you are using cartoons, stick with cartoons throughout. If you're using pen-and-ink illustrations, stick with those. Too much variation in artwork will lend an air of confusion to your publication.

- Increase white space for a more informal look. The same goes for the use of larger graphics, especially those that are unboxed.

Grids

As already noted, a **grid** is another term for the columns used in a layout (see Exhibit 14.8). Although the use of grids is most common to newsletter, annual report, and magazine layout, they also can be valuable for complex brochures and flyers as well as ad layouts.

For publications such as newsletters, the most common formats are three– and four–column layouts. Both formats are quite flexible. Three–column layouts are

Exhibit 14.7

Unity

Unity means using compatible elements in your layout (type, artwork, photos, design, etc.). The best way to lose unity is to combine too many disparate elements in a single layout. In this simple brochure layout, only three typefaces (headline, subhead, and body copy) and a single illustration style are used.

Exhibit 14.8

Grids

(Clockwise from upper-right) A three–column grid laid out "newspaper style" with two-thirds of the layout at the top; a four–column grid with an illustrated table of contents in the bottom third; a two–column grid, also in newspaper style, with two stories on the front page; and a two–column grid with a large feature story column to the left and a boxed sidebar as the second column.

more appropriate for smaller formats and 4–column layouts for larger. Remember, the more columns you have, the narrower they will have to be and the smaller your type needs to be to accommodate the column width.

If you're just beginning, try a basic three–column grid for all your pages. The column width is enough to give you a readable type and to use graphics in legible sizes. The basic rule of laying out a newsletter is to use the columns as your grid and lay out all your elements (in our three–column grid) in one–, two–, and three–column widths.

Alignment

Alignment refers to the way your copy is arranged in relation to column margins (see Exhibit 14.9). The two most typical alignments are *flush left* (sometimes called *ragged right*) and *justified.* Flush left copy is getting to be quite common for newsletters, some in-house magazines, and other types of publications. It imparts a less formal look, involves less hyphenation, and takes up more space.

Justified copy looks more formal, is more hyphenated, and takes up less space. However, when using justified copy, keep in mind that the width of your columns severely affects word spread. The narrower your columns, the more your words will separate from one another in order to maintain justification. Computers allow for minute adjustments to word and letter spacing to help correct this spread, but the best way to avoid it is to keep your columns at the average or maximum width for your type size.

Other alignment possibilities exist, such as *flush right* and *centered.* Flush right copy should be avoided because it is difficult to read. However, it is sometimes useful for very brief text blocks such as pull quotes that appear in outside left margins. Centered body text should always be avoided. Centered headlines are not in fashion these days, although centered pull quotes are still found quite a bit.

The best idea is to pick either flush left or justified for your body copy and not to deviate. Stick with flush left for headlines. Use either flush left or justified for pull quotes and captions.

Type and Typefaces

Type is the generic term for the lettering used in printing, whereas **typeface** refers to the nearly limitless alphabets and ornaments available as type. **Font** is the classification within a given typeface, such as bold or italics. The array of type and typefaces you can choose from is truly bewildering. But if you learn a few basics now, that array can be narrowed down to just a few choices for you and your public relations material.

The first thing to know is how to classify type. Let's start with the most general, and useful, classification for publication purposes. First of all, type is measured in *points* (in type, this is a vertical measurement). There are 72 points in an inch. Imagine trying to designate 11-point type in inches and you know why printers have traditionally used a different scale. Small type, up to 14 points, is called **body type.** Type that is 14 points and above is called **display type**

Exhibit 14.9

Text Alignment

What's the difference between a therapist, psychologist, psycho-therapist, psychiatrist, and counselor? If you don't know, you're among the millions of people who are confused about the multi-tiered mental health counseling field.

In an effort to clear up some of the confusion, the American Mental Health Counselors Association (AMHCA) has "hired" a university student group to produce a public information campaign for them.

The Public Relations Student Society of America (PRSSA) at the University of Oregon has been retained by the Association to develop a program of information that will better define the various roles contained under the umbrella term "mental health counselor." Jane Weiskoff, regional director of AMHCA says that the confusion seems to stem from a mis-

What's the difference between a therapist, psychologist, psycho-therapist, psychiatrist, and counselor? If you don't know, you're among the millions of people who are confused about the multi-tiered mental health counseling field.

In an effort to clear up some of the confusion, the American Mental Health Counselors Association (AMHCA) has "hired" a university student group to produce a public information campaign for them.

The Public Relations Student Society of America (PRSSA) at the University of Oregon has been retained by the Association to develop a program of information that will better define the various roles contained under the umbrella term "mental health counselor." Jane Weiskoff, regional director of AMHCA says that the

What's the difference between a therapist, psychologist, psycho-therapist, psychiatrist, and counselor? If you don't know, you're among the millions of people who are confused about the multi-tiered mental health counseling field.

In an effort to clear up some of the confusion, the American Mental Health Counselors Association (AMHCA) has "hired" a university student group to produce a public information campaign for them.

The Public Relations Student Society of America (PRSSA) at the University of Oregon has been retained by the Association to develop a program of information that will better define the various roles contained under the umbrella term "mental health counselor." Jane Weiskoff, regional director of AMHCA says that the

Notice that the justified text (left) takes up less space than the flush left text (center). The flush right text (right) is nearly impossible to track (move from end of one line to the beginning of the next).

(normally headlines). Most typefaces come in both body and display sizes; however, there are subtle differences between the sizes. The best way to choose type is to look at a complete alphabet in all the sizes and weights you are going to be using and check out the differences for yourself. Look for straight or curved serifs, for example, or whether the loops close or are left open on certain letters. Most of these distinctions boil down to a matter of taste. Only you know which is best for your job.

Next, type can be broken down into five other, fairly broad categories: black-letter, script, serif, sans serif, and italics. For our purposes, we'll look at just the last three (see Exhibit 14.10):

- *Serif.* Most **serif typefaces** are distinguished by a variation in thick and thin strokes, and by *serifs*—the lines that cross the end strokes of the letters. Serif type can be further broken down into Romans and slab or square serif faces. Romans have the traditional thick and thin strokes whereas slab serif faces

Exhibit 14.10

Type Samples

Serif Type

Times

Serifs are the small lines that cross the end strokes of the letters in serif type. Roman serifs have the traditional thick and thin strokes.

Lubalin

Square or slab serifs have fairly uniform thicknesses of both the letter strokes and their serifs.

San Serif Type

Helvetica

In this example of sans serif type (Helvetica), notice the uniformity of stroke width. This is characteristic of most, but not all, sans serif type.

Optima

Optima is one of several sans serif typefaces with some interesting variation in strike width. This variation (along with a hint of serifs) tends to make the face more readable.

Italic/Oblique Type

Type *Type*

There is quite a bit of difference between a true italic face (Palatino italic) left, and a slanted version of the upright face, right. Type designers would just as soon you didn't distort their original typeface designs.

Type *Type*

Sans serif typefaces don't have italic versions per se. Instead, they have obliques. Like italics, obliques are specifically designed to be set at a slant. They are not simply slanted versions of the upright face.

---

have relatively uniform strokes and serifs. Serif faces are usually considered easier to read, especially in body type sizes.

- *Sans serif.* **Sans serif typefaces** are without serifs (*sans,* from the French, meaning *without*). They are usually, but not always, distinguished by uniformity of strokes. They usually impart a more modern look to a publication, especially if used as display type. Setting body type in sans serif is unwise because the uniformity of the strokes tends to darken your page and makes for difficult reading. There are some exceptions. Optima, for example, has some variation in stroke and reads fairly well in smaller sizes. Additionally, Stone Sans, a new face designed by Sumner Stone of Adobe Systems, makes excellent use of thin and thick strokes.

- *Italics.* Some typographers don't consider italics a separate category of type because most typefaces today come with an italic version. However, true Roman italic versions of many typefaces are completely different from their upright versions. Since the advent of desktop publishing, editors have had the option of italicizing a typeface with a simple keystroke. This method typically only slants the existing face; it does not always create a true italic version of that typeface. Only by selecting a typeface that has been designed specifically as an italic do we get true italics. Because they are slanted, italics tend to impart an informality and speed to your message. However, because of the slant, they are more difficult to read and should be used for accent only.

  Just as a point of interest, italics refers only to a version of a serif face. A slanted version of a sans serif typeface is called *oblique.* Like italics, true obliques are designed as separate fonts (a complete alphabet, number series, and set of punctuation points and miscellaneous marks) and are not simply the original face at a slant.

If you are typesetting or desktop publishing your publication, then you will have to select typefaces. Following are some of the most common questions regarding that selection:

- *Can I use just one typeface?* Yes. The safest route to take is to stick with one typeface. Using a single face lends your written material unity and consistency. Pick one that comes in as many variations as possible—style, weight, size, and width.

  Most typefaces come in regular and/or light versions. These are sometimes called *book* or *text.* They also come in *upright* (Roman) and italics (or oblique, if the typeface is sans serif). In addition, they may have *demibold* and *bold* versions in both upright and italics or oblique (these versions may be called *heavy* or *black;* or heavy and black versions may be in addition to bold). And the demibold and bold versions may come as *extended* or *condensed* (referring to the width of the letters).

  The greater the variety available, the more flexibility you have in a single typeface. For example, you could use the regular version for body type, the bold version for headlines, and the regular italic version for captions, pull quotes, and subheads (in different point sizes).

- *Can I use more than one typeface?* Although you may have access to a type library of 400 or more faces, try to limit yourself to no more than two different typefaces in a publication, and make sure they don't conflict with each other. This is the most difficult part of using more than one face. Here are a few guidelines to remember:

  - If your body type is serif, try a sans serif for headlines. Two different serif faces will probably conflict with one another.

  - If you are using a light body type (as opposed to its regular version), use a regular or demibold headline type. You don't want your headline weight to overpower your text weight.

- Above all, don't pick your type just by looking at a type chart. Have a page set, complete with body copy and headlines, to see for yourself whether your two faces are going to harmonize.

- *Where do I go to select type?* If you are working on a computer, you probably have 20 or so typefaces that come with either your system software or your layout software or both. In addition, you can easily add anywhere up to 500 choices, depending on the sophistication of your desktop publishing system. Stick with a small array of type. It's easier and saves a lot of frustration in the long run. If all you have is Times Roman, use it. If you have Times Roman and Helvetica, use Times for the body copy and Helvetica for the headlines. If you have access to a larger type library on your computer, explore your options by experimenting with several combinations, printing out a page with each one.

  Don't forget to try several different point sizes for body copy also. Readability can vary a great deal between 12-point Times and 12-point Palatino, as well as between 12-point Palatino and 10-point Palatino, for example.

  Be aware that your type will also look different when printed on different printers. Decide which printer you're going to use to print your final camera-ready copy and check its print quality against your type choice. Typefaces with thin serifs may not print as well on a dot-matrix printer as on a laser printer, or as well on a laser printer as on an imagesetter. Bold or heavy faces (especially if condensed) will tend to clog and fill on dot-matrix and laser printers but will print cleanly on an imagesetter. If you don't have access to different typefaces on your computer, ask your printer for samples of type set in copy blocks and as display type. Most printers can provide you with more than just a type chart.

WORKING WITH PRINTERS

The relationship between the writer-designer and printer should be a symbiotic one; however, both of you will probably have to work at it for a while until you get comfortable with the relationship. The trick to working successfully with printers is to know what you are talking about—there's no substitute for knowledge. You have to know a bit about the printing process in order to get along with your printer. Every writer can tell you horror stories about printers who, after seemingly understanding exactly what you want, proceed to print exactly what they want. This is not to say that it is hard to get along with printers. It simply means that you have to know what you want and be able to explain it in printer's terms. I recommend that you try out several printers and work with those who not only give you the best deal but also are willing to give you guidance. This is not an easy process, but it does pay off in a lower frustration factor in the long run.

  It used to be that printers took over as soon as you handed them your copy. These days, however, it's just as likely that you've not only written the copy but also designed the piece and laid it out before you ever talk with a printer. You no longer have to go through a typesetter, for instance. However, most printers can still desktop publish your piece for you if you don't know how. And although you can often even download your work directly to a printer's file server, it is still wise to speak with them in person first in order to avoid the almost inevitable hardware and software incompatibilities.

For example, does the printer carry the typefaces you use in your publication? If not, can you legally supply them or do you have to "print" your publication to a Postscript file, thus embedding all the fonts in the publication itself? Do you even know how to print to a Postscript file? Do you know what a Postscript file is? You're probably beginning to get the picture. No matter how sophisticated we may get, for the foreseeable future we will still be relying on printers for much of what we need in the way of finished product.

In addition, printers can be an invaluable aid in selecting printing methods, papers, inks, bindings, and so on. Even the seemingly simple process of picking a paper can be mind-numbing. Literally thousands of papers are available for printing, and you can size, fold, and otherwise decorate your printed product in an unlimited number of ways. Just remember, you can get what you want if you know how to ask for it.

Printing Processes

Many writers simply entrust the choice of printing method to the printer. Although a number of printing processes are available to you, the two you will likely have the most contact with are offset lithography and quick printing or quick copying. Most collateral pieces and many newsletters are simply offset printed, which is one of the fastest and cheapest methods to get good quality printing today. Quick-print and quick-copy methods will usually result in a loss of quality. Other, more detailed printing jobs, such as embossing or special paper shapes, may require specialty printing. Be advised that specialty printing is costly. Make sure that you are willing to bear the extra cost before you decide on that gold-foil stamp on the cover of your new brochure.

Offset Lithography

The most common printing process used today is offset lithography. The process is based on the principle that oil and water don't mix. During the printing process, both water and ink are applied to the printing plate as it revolves. The nonprinting area of the plate accepts water but not ink, while the image, or printing, area accepts ink but not water. It is named offset printing because the plate isn't a reverse image as in most printing processes (see Exhibit 14.11). Instead, the plate transfers its right-reading image to an offset cylinder made of rubber (which reverses the image), and from there to the paper. Because the plate never comes in contact with the paper, it can be saved and used again and again, saving cost on projects that have to be reprinted periodically—unless, of course, you make changes.

Most public relations documents are printed using offset lithography. It is relatively inexpensive, compared to other processes, and it results in a high-quality

Exhibit
Exhibit 14.11

Offset Printing

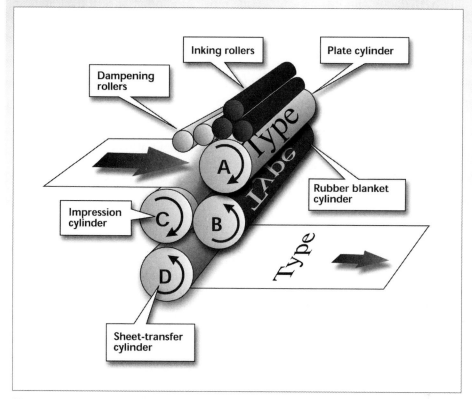

Offset gets its name from the indirect printing process in which the printing plate's image is offset to a rubber blanket that puts the ink on the paper. Notice how the type and image go from right-reading to reversed to right-reading again.

image. Although small press runs of 1,000 or less can be made using offset lithography, it is especially cost-effective for larger runs, because presses are capable of cranking out hundreds of copies a minute.

Quick Print and Quick Copy

The quick-print and quick-copy processes involve two methods of reproduction.

Quick print involves a small cylinder press using paper-printing plates. The plates are created using a photo-electrostatic process that results in a raised image created with toner (much like the toner used in photocopy machines). This raised image takes the ink and is imprinted directly onto the paper.

Quick copy used to mean exclusively xerography; however, many of the newer quick-copy setups, such as Xerox's Docu-Tech, don't use this now familiar process at all. Instead, these machines (literally computers) use laser technology to print. The result is a rapid-print method that is not limited to black and white, like xerography, but can present a wide range of grays. This is a great boon to newsletter editors who use a lot of photographs, for example. Anyone who has ever photocopied a photograph knows how bad the quality can be. The larger-model photocopiers used in this process can rapidly produce multiple copies in sizes up to 11-by-17-inches.

Neither of these processes is useful for two-color work, but both are inexpensive and fast. If you are going to use quick copy, reserve it for rush projects or those that won't suffer from single-color xerography. Also, there can be major differences between photocopiers, and even between copies run on the same machine. A copier that ran your last job beautifully may not repeat the same quality the next time if the toner hasn't been changed recently. Don't be afraid to ask for a test print of your most difficult page to make sure the blacks are really black and there is no fade out on any part of the page.

Paper Choice

Paper choice is one of the most important aspects of producing effective public relations documents, particularly a collateral piece such as a brochure. Your choice of paper may determine whether your brochure is picked up and read; whether it lasts more than one or two days before it falls apart; or whether it even works well with your chosen type style, graphics, and ink color.

When choosing a paper, you will need to consider three major criteria. First, does the paper suit the use to which it will be put? In other words, does it have the right look, feel, color, durability, and so on? Second, how much does it cost? Third, are you using a laser printer?

Suitability

In judging the suitability of your paper choice to your job, you must first determine the nature of your information. Some pieces, such as flyers or announcements, are printed on relatively cheap and lightweight stock and are meant to be thrown away soon after reading. Others need to be more permanent. A brochure outlining company benefits to employees, for example, probably will be kept and used over and over again. It will need to be on a heavier and more durable stock. A company magazine printed in four colors will need a durable paper that will take constant opening, closing, and general handling without tearing because the publication will probably be passed on to other readers.

Aside from durability, three other factors need to be considered in judging the suitability of your paper: weight, texture, and color.

- *Weight.* Papers come in various weights. Weight is determined by taking 500 sheets of the paper and weighing it. Although a heavier weight usually indicates a thicker stock, it doesn't have to. One 25-pound bond paper may be thicker than another. Likewise, one 60-pound book paper may be lighter and less durable than another. The best way to judge weight versus thickness is to handle the paper for each type of stock personally. Most printers have hundreds of samples of paper stock and can help you select the weight and thickness you want for your job. As a general rule, stick with text weights for newsletters and magazines and heavier, or cover, stocks for magazine covers and brochures.

- *Texture.* Texture is also an important consideration when choosing a paper. Heavily textured paper may impart a feeling of quality or a feeling of roughness, depending on the paper stock and the method of manufacture. Basically, papers break down into two broad categories for texture: matte finish and coated stock. *Matte finish paper* ranges from a paper with a rather smooth but nonglossy surface to heavily textured paper. *Coated stock paper* refers to any paper that is slick or glossy. Again, the range is considerable. Photographs often reproduce better on coated stock, which is what most magazines use. Using a matte stock will soften the color and give a photograph an entirely different feeling. Some heavily textured stocks may not take ink well but may be perfect for foil stamping or embossing. The best way to tell if your idea will work on a certain texture stock is to ask the printer, look at some samples, and come to an informed decision.

- *Color.* Paper color has to complement all the other graphic elements of your collateral piece: typeface, ink color, photographs, and artwork. It will also set the mood of your piece. Color preference is a very personal matter. Remember, however, that you are producing pieces to be read by certain target publics who may or may not like your color choice. Thus, to an extent, color choice is a matter of gauging your intended audience's reaction to a particular color. Research has shown, for instance, that businesspeople will not respond to questionnaires printed on hot-pink paper (not much of a surprise). They will respond well to beige and various shades of white, but respond very little to pale blue and green. All colors carry connotations for most people. You need to stay away from outrageous combinations and any color you think might not get the desired response to your information piece.

Cost

The determining factor in your paper choice may well be cost. Don't despair, though, just because your budget may be limited. Paper comes in thousands of weights, colors, and textures, and one of them will fit your cost restrictions. Remember that a few extra dollars on a good grade paper may well pay off in the long run by impressing your readership.

Paper for Laser Printing

Some papers are made specifically for laser printers, and some papers definitely should be avoided. Ask yourself three questions when you pick laser printer paper:

I. Will the laser copy be used as a finished piece or for reproduction?

2. Does the paper say what you want it to say? In other words, what is its look and feel?

3. Does the paper run well in your printer?

Keeping in mind the paper specifications presented earlier, consider the following guidelines when you select the paper for your needs and your printer:

- Brighter paper reproduces well on laser printers. (This doesn't mean whiter paper; there are varying degrees of brightness even among white papers.) Brighter papers are also good for reproduction masters. In fact, several manufacturers make papers specifically for laser printer output that will be used for reproduction. Also, because it's hard to predict the degree of darkness of your printer, the brighter the paper, the more contrast you are likely to have between the print and the paper. In general, avoid colored paper; however, some interesting effects can be obtained with lighter colors such as gray and beige.

- Stay away from heavily textured paper. The heavier the texture, the more broken your type will look, because it will be harder for the toner to adhere to the paper's surface. Texture also affects any large, dark areas such as screens and display type. Some texture, like that found in bond paper and linen stock, is fine. The trick here is to experiment.

- Avoid heavy papers weighing 90 pounds or more (like cover stock), unless you enjoy removing jammed paper from your printer. Similarly, extremely light papers, such as onion skin, may stick to the rollers or jam as they feed into the printer. Don't experiment much here. Just settle for a text-weight paper (generally around 60 pounds), and consign the choice of cover paper to your commercial printer.

- Use a fairly opaque paper, especially if the laser-printed copy is to be your final version. If you use a paper with high opacity, be sure it isn't also heavily textured.

- Don't expect heavily textured papers to retain their texture. Unlike offset presses, laser printers flatten the paper as it moves through the printer. In most cases, any texture will be lost.

- By the same token, don't use embossed or engraved papers in your laser printer because they might jam the mechanism and will flatten out anyway.

- Make sure your paper is heat resistant. Because laser printers work at temperatures of around 4,000 degrees Fahrenheit, certain letterhead inks may melt or stick and any metal or plastic will certainly ruin your printer. Above all, don't use acetate in your laser printer unless it has been specifically designed for your particular printer.

Ink Choice

Choosing an ink can be a nightmare for the novice. Even the most experienced designers often have a short list of their favorite inks. Inks come in virtually limitless color combinations. And each color will be affected by the paper on which it is printed. For example, coated paper will result in brighter colors whereas matte finish paper will soften the color. The texture of the paper also affects ink color, as does the use of colored paper.

There are no easy ways to learn what inks to use. The best way for a beginner to choose an ink is to look at other work done using the same ink-and-paper combination. Also, obtain a copy of the Pantone Color Matching System. It's really just a color sample book, like the ones you see when you pick out a house paint, but it is the most commonly used system among printers and designers. You'll be amazed at the variety of colors available to you. Don't be embarrassed, however, to stick to the basic colors to begin with. They are usually the safest to work with. Your printer will usually have a Pantone book you can use while there. Pantone's address is on the sample book. Just write them and ask about obtaining your own copy.

If you don't want any surprises, ask to see samples of work your printer has done using different papers and inks. Most printers take great pride in their work and will be more than happy to share it with you.

Color brings an added dimension to any publication, whether it's as simple as a second color to help accent, unify, or dress up a publication, or as complete as full color. To use color effectively, you should have a rudimentary understanding of how the different color processes operate.

Spot Color Printing

Spot color printing (also known as *two-color printing*) is the placement of a second color (black—or whatever the primary inking color—being the first) in a publication. (Note that in printing, black is counted as a color.) Unless you're using a multicolor press, applying the second color means an additional press run. That translates into more ink, materials, handling, press time, and money.

In two-color printing, two sets of printing plates are made, one for each color run. Often, a designer will use the black (or other first color) for the type and use the second color for the art and graphic highlights—such as dropped-initial letters. This also means that you have to create two originals, one for the black plate and one for the second color. This is not an easy process for most people and is usually left to a designer or printer. Check with your printer first to determine their requirements for two-color printing.

Process Color Printing

Process color printing (also known as *four-color printing*) is used for reproducing full-color artwork or photography. This illusion of full color is accomplished by optically mixing the three primary colors—yellow, red (actually magenta), and blue (called cyan)—along with black. Four-color plates are shot through a screen to reduce solid areas to printable, graduated dot patterns. Because each color is shot through a slightly different angle screen, the screened halftone of each blends through the overlaid dot patterns.

During printing, each color is applied separately, one plate at a time and one color atop the others. The quality of this four-color overprinting method largely depends on the quality of the original work; the quality of the cameras, plates, and printing press used; and the skills and professionalism of those who operate the equipment. Process color is best left to your printer to handle for you. As always, ask the printer in advance about their requirements.

Binding

With binding, as with everything else, if you want to know what to expect, ask your printer, and seek out samples on your own. Basically, there are two types of binding: that used for relatively thin publications such as magazines and pamphlets, and that used for thicker publications such as books. I discuss only those most applicable to public relations output here.

Regardless of what you are binding, it will probably be organized either into signatures or single pages. **Signatures** are groupings of pages printed on both sides, usually 16 to a signature, but sometimes less, as long as they're in multiples of 4 (pages printed for binding are usually printed 4 to a two-sided sheet of paper).

After signatures or single pages have been collated, they may be bound. Among the most common bindings that public relations people are likely to use are *saddle stitching* (stapled signatures), *perfect binding* (glued, single sheets), or *spiral binding* (hole-punched single sheets bound in plastic or wire). Most quick printers can do saddle stitching and spiral binding; however, only larger printers will be able to do perfect binding. More traditional forms of binding, such as *case binding* (for hardcover books) are reserved for publications you want to last longer than you will.

Swipe Files

One of the best ways to tell your printer what you want is to show them an example. A **swipe file** is a collection of your favorite pieces done by other people or companies. They will help you a great deal with design, layout ideas, and writing style, as well as with communicating your ideas to printers. You may find a particular brochure, for instance, that is exactly the right size and design for the information piece you want to produce. You may decide to use similar paper, ink color, or even design. Most graphic artists, designers, and printers use ideas generated from a variety of sources. Don't plagiarize your source, however, and don't steal the artwork right off the source brochure. Be careful to differentiate between emulation and plagiarism. If you do decide that you must borrow directly from another piece, obtain permission from its originator in advance of the publication of your piece.

Keep a swipe file of samples to show your printer. If you find a piece that you would like to emulate, show it to the printer to get an idea how much it will cost to produce. The printer can tell you what the type is and whether your copy will fit in that size, as well as the paper stock and weight, ink color, and mechanical specifications—all of which will affect the price. For the beginner, a sample is worth a ten-thousand word explanation.

Computer Layout Preparation for Printing

The final stage of layout is the *mechanical,* the finished camera-ready layout that goes to the printer. The computer has revolutionized this process. If you are diligent, exact, and working with a limited range of graphics, you can present your printer with a mechanical in one piece—with no pasted-up parts. Computer imagesetters, such as the Linotronic, print out your layouts onto paper exactly as you have designed them, ready to be shot into printer's negatives. You can even go directly to negative film from an imagesetter, saving the cost of shooting negatives from a positive mechanical—but only if you are completely satisfied with your layout.

Assuming you are working in black and white, there are several ways to construct your mechanical:

- You can have it run entirely off an imagesetter, either from your computer disks or through a network or telephone line hookup. This requires that all of the elements on your mechanical be computer generated: word-processed text and display type; borders, boxes, and rules produced in your page-layout program; photos scanned, cropped, and sized either in a photo manipulation program (such as Adobe Photoshop) or right in your layout program; illustrations created in a paint, draw, or illustration program and imported or placed in your layout program; and any color separations already performed by your software.

- You can run the basic mechanical (text, display type, rules, and boxes) on an imagesetter and have photos and art shot separately and stripped into the negative before the printing plate is made. If you don't have a scanner or access to electronic clip art, this is probably the closest you'll get to having the whole thing done in one step. Even at this level, the savings in typesetting and paste-up alone are worth it.

- You can run your mechanical on a laser printer at either of the above two levels. This assumes you either don't have access to an imagesetter or don't feel that the extra quality is needed for your particular publication. Some very nice newsletters and brochures can be offset printed directly from laser-printed mechanicals. Most office-quality laser printers are capable of printing to plain paper at anywhere from 300- to 1200-dpi resolution.

  An imagesetter can print either to resin-coated paper positives or directly to right-reading film. Printing to film greatly enhances resolution, especially of scanned photographs, because it eliminates one step in the printing process—the shooting of negatives from camera-ready copy. When image-setting directly to film, always ask for a proof prior to final printing.

Print Order Preparation

The most important interface between the desktop publisher and the printer is when the print order is submitted. Following are several sets of suggestions for getting your publication out of your computer and onto paper:

In General

Always call your chosen printer in advance to see how they can meet your publishing needs. Find out the following:

- If they support your computer platform (Macintosh or Windows).
- If they can use your fonts, have their own versions of the fonts you used, or accept only PostScript files.
- If you can download directly to the printer or if you have to bring your work in on disk.

When you submit your material, include the following:

- The name and version (3.0, 5.4, etc.) of the software application you used to create your publication.
- File names under which your publication is stored.
- Hardcopy of the publication (if you've laid it out already).
- Type of output desired (imagesetter, laser printer, offset lithography).

Regarding Photos and Artwork

If you do not include your artwork and photos directly in your file and require that the printer either mechanically or digitally work with your graphics, observe the following guidelines:

- Photos and artwork should be cropped and marked with the finished size, either a percentage of the original or the final image dimensions.
- Place crop marks in margins of photos and artwork. If there are no margins, then tape the piece to a larger sheet and indicate crop marks.
- Use a felt tip pen to put instructions on the backs of photos. Marks made by graphite pencil or ball point pen can leave impressions on the face of the photo that reproduce. Avoid putting paper clips or staples on photos.
- Keep photos and artwork free of dirt, glue, wax, and other foreign material.
- If you mark instructions near artwork or copy, it is best to use light blue pencil or pen.
- Avoid rolling maps, charts, or artwork into tubes. Keep these items flat if possible.
- Find out in advance the maximum sizes that can be handled by your printer's reproduction equipment.
- Find out the maximum sizes that their digital scanners can accommodate.

Proofs

- Read proofs carefully and mark corrections plainly so that they can be seen easily; a red pencil or pen is best. Use standard proofreader's marks.

- Avoid changes on **bluelines** (the final printer's proof) unless they are essential. Changes at this stage are costly because the plate (if it is to be offset printed) has already been made.

A WORD ON DESKTOP PUBLISHING

Anyone who assumes the responsibilities of writing and laying out a publication for an organization has a lot to learn. The availability of desktop publishing software and hardware designed specifically to augment those tasks has made the job, if not easy, at least manageable by a single person. What once had to go through the traditional writing, editing, typesetting, paste-up, and printing processes can now be done in fewer steps and with the involvement of fewer intermediaries. Although a desktop publishing system won't make you an instant designer, it does provide the writer, editor, and designer with more tools to better accomplish their respective jobs. Without the knowledge and experience gained through a study of the basics of writing, editing, and design, however, even the best hardware and software won't help you.

The greatest benefit of desktop publishing to the public relations writer is that it allows you to control your own output, right down to the printing. Its greatest drawback is that it allows you to control your own output, right down to the printing. In other words, its greatest asset is its greatest deficit, and you are the deciding factor. Unless you become skilled at not only writing and editing but also layout and design, the complete benefits of desktop publishing may never be realized for you. But that's okay. What you really need to do is to realize exactly what you can do, what you are willing to learn to do, and how much you can afford to spend to get it all done. Remember, everybody has to begin somewhere, and, fortunately for us, there is a wealth of programming to fit every need.

Ultimately, your final, printed publication is going to determine how successful your desktop publishing system is—and a lot of that success depends not on your hardware and software, but on you. You are the final ingredient in this system. Your energy, talent, interest, and organizational abilities will be the final determinant in the success or failure of your publications. Truthfully, you can get by on a lot less than you think you can if you possess the right attitude and the requisite abilities. Fancy hardware and expensive software only enhance and streamline a process you should already have down to a fine art. Computers have made and are continuing to make a tremendous difference in publishing. But always remember that the multi-thousand-dollar system you sit down in front of every day is only a tool. The system doesn't make you an artist, just as sitting in front of a typewriter doesn't make you a writer. Dedication, hard work, and talent do.

Keep in mind the following points:

- Don't expect desktop publishing to give you something you don't already possess.

- If you're looking for an answer to your design problems, check out your own abilities first. However, if you're expecting the technology to streamline the process and save you some money, it probably will.

- Are you willing to take the time needed to make yourself an expert on your system? If you aren't willing to become an expert, you're wasting your money. Anyone can learn the basics (or just enough to cause trouble), but if you're serious about desktop publishing, you'd best dedicate yourself for the long haul. Be prepared to immerse yourself in the process, the programs, and the machinery. The more you know, the more streamlined the process becomes.

Above all, don't set yourself up for frustration. Realize the limitations of your system and of desktop publishing in general. Understand how it works and why it does what it does. You don't have to become a computer expert to gain a fairly complete understanding of your hardware and software. The more you know, the less frustrated you'll be when something does go wrong. Most of the frustration of working with computers comes from not knowing what's happening in software or hardware problem situations. Keep those technical support hotline numbers close at hand and use them. Don't be afraid to ask questions, but read the manuals first so that you'll know what to ask.

Finally, take it all with a grain of salt. A computer is just a tool of the trade. Misuse it, and your shortcomings will become apparent to everyone who looks at your work. Use it wisely, and it will show off for you.

KEY TERMS

design principles	type	sans serif typeface
rule of ground thirds	typeface	signature
drop	font	swipe file
unity	body type	bluelines
anchor	display type	
grid	serif typeface	

EXERCISES

I. Find one example each of the following design principles shown in action:

balance (symmetric and asymmetric)
proportion
emphasis
sequence
unity

Your example can be any printed piece including brochures, newsletters, print ads, posters, flyers, etc. Be prepared to discuss your choices and how they reflect these design principles.

2. Pick a brochure or newsletter that you like particularly well. Take it to two different printers and get printing estimates from each. Assume that you will be reprinting the piece exactly as it is now printed—same paper, ink, color, etc. You will be running 1,000 copies. Ask the printer to include the cost of folding in the estimate. Tell the printer that you will bring the piece to them on computer disk fully laid out. Take notes on what each printer asks and what they say they can and can't do for you. Be especially mindful of anything you didn't know you needed until you talked to the printer, and make a list of those items you'd need to confirm prior to actual printing.

15

Computer Writing and the Internet

In this chapter you will learn:

- How to compose on a computer, both on your own and in collaboration with others.

- What intranets are and how they are used for internal corporate communication.

- What the Internet is and how corporations use it to communicate with external publics.

- The basics of designing a Web site.

- How to write for Web sites.

Although scientists may disagree, I believe that the two greatest boons the computer has granted us are word processing and desktop publishing. Of course, that's from a public relations writer's perspective.

Back in the dark ages, public relations writers used typewriters (this was right after carving in stone became unsatisfactory because of too many last-minute changes). Typewriters, as you may recall, evolved from click-clicking mechanical monsters to electronic marvels over the course of about 100 years. Following the advent of the personal computer, it took only about 10 more years for typewriters to become completely obsolete. Today, if they have typewriters at all, most people just use them to type addresses on envelopes—another job rapidly being taken over by more advanced computer printers.

Typewriters, of course, were a vast improvement over having to write by hand; and they did mimic typesetting, which made reading a good deal easier. But editing? That's another story entirely. At first, you had to erase with a very rough little instrument designed, apparently, to tear typewriter paper to shreds. Then there was something called erasable bond paper, but its surface was so slick that the paper seemed to erase on its own much of the time. Next came correction fluid (e.g., Wite-Out). The mother of one of the Monkees (yes, the 1960s "rock" group) invented that one—and made a fortune. But the stuff looked awful, and you could never get it off your hands. Finally, there was correcting ribbon for electric typewriters, which appeared to lift the letters right off the page.

If all of this seems like an odd and long-winded preamble to a chapter on writing with and for the digital media, it's not—because the greatest benefit of computers in our end of the business is that we no longer have to erase, paint over, or lift off anything. This may seem obvious to many of you, but those of us who actually remember typewriters in all their manifestations breathe a prayer of thanks to the wizards of science every time we sit down to compose a press release. Those of you who don't remember will just have to take my word for it.

This chapter is about how to write both on and for the computer—how to use this marvelous tool to your best benefit and how to write public relations material intended to be published on a digital site.

WRITING ON THE COMPUTER

Personal computers and word-processing software allow us to manipulate words in all sorts of ways—ways that would have been unimaginable on a typewriter. To name a few, words can be put down faster, corrected almost as fast, rearranged, reorganized, counted, parsed, and printed. I'm not going to waste your time here recommending word-processing software. There are far too many good software packages on the market for you to go very wrong. Just remember to match your software to your needs. Most of the popular word-processing packages include rudimentary layout and graphic insertion capabilities, which is fine if you don't know how to use a basic desktop publishing program. However, at this point, even the most sophisticated word-processing program doesn't come close to being as flexible as a basic layout program. So pick one that is good at writing, not layout.

You'll need a program that is easy to understand yet can automate complex jobs such as outlining, page numbering, bulleting, indenting at various levels, moving text rapidly, font exchange and stylizing, spell checking, and word counting. For me, these are the basic requirements. Some writers have special needs, such as an online thesaurus, the ability to insert or design tables and charts, mail merge, macro design, and so on. Just remember: Unless you really want to become a designer (and add to your workload), stick with writing—which means stick with a program that handles writing well. If you don't need all the bells and whistles, don't pay for them.

For those of us who learned to write in other ways—on a typewriter or by hand—computer writing is very different. For all the reasons stated above, writing on a computer is easier. That doesn't make it necessarily better, however. Remember what I said at the very beginning of this book: Good writing is good writing. No piece of software will make you a good writer, just like relying on a spell checker won't make you a good speller—or make up for you being a bad won. (See what I mean?) With that caveat in mind, let's look at some ways to get the most out of computer writing.

On Your Own

Most writers are a solitary lot by nature and generally prefer to work alone. And computers have made working alone more congenial than ever before. A computer seems to do some of the work for you. As I am typing this now, my software is noting misspellings as I go along. In fact, it just added an *s* to *misspellings* because I apparently spelled it with only one. Even a solitary writer sometimes has the feeling that he or she is collaborating with someone else. Under most circumstances, I would suggest therapy; however, all writers need a little help occasionally, and the interactive nature of software today provides much of that help automatically. This often imparts the illusion of near companionship. The trick is not to let it literally go to your head. You're still in charge here, no matter how smart your computer seems to be. You're still the writer—it's the tool. Take advantage of this marvelous tool as you work through three key steps as a lone writer: brainstorming, writing, and editing and proofreading.

Brainstorming

Computers have made brainstorming incredibly easier than it used to be. Of course, nothing substitutes for your creativity, but computers can help stimulate that creativity. Try these tricks:

- *Free write.* In other words, write without a thought to grammar, spelling, or logic. Take an idea and simply write about it, stream of consciousness. This was possible prior to the computer, obviously, but a computer makes working with your free writing much easier in the organizing and editing stages (see below). Free writing tends to stimulate creativity, but don't get in the habit of thinking that it's a substitute for good writing. It's just an exercise.

- *Blind write.* Another easy trick to try is to write blindly. Turn down your monitor's brightness, and write without looking at what you are saying. This reduces the tendency all writers have to edit as they go along. It may take several attempts before you become comfortable with this technique, but it can produce some interesting results.

- *Use your swipe files.* All good writers and designers keep swipe files. For designers, these are pieces that spark your imagination and present you with a design idea that you can mimic (see Chapter 14). For writers, a swipe file contains all of the pieces you have written in the past. Ideally, they are on computer disks and are properly labeled so that you can find them. You'd be amazed how much boilerplate you can borrow from other pieces you have written and adapt to current needs. That company intro you wrote for the open house brochure two years ago can now be used in your backgrounder or your annual report. All you need to do is create the transitions between the old material and the new. A word of caution here: Be sure not to borrow from someone else's writing, unless it is company property. This is not called borrowing by the courts; it's called plagiarism. If something has been written for your organization by someone else and you want to use it, just make sure it is yours, free and clear. Typically, if it was done for your organization, even by a freelancer, it is company property.

- *Start a "phrase" file.* For want of a better word, I've used *phrase.* This used to be an old poet's trick. Every poet comes up with lines that can't be fit into the current poem he or she is working on. Sometimes the line even stimulates the idea for the poem itself, but when the poem is finished, the line no longer seems to fit. In any event, poets catalogue these lines or phrases for future use in other poems. Similarly, your file could contain a number of headings, and the contents could be composed of either unused phrases or phrases that bear repeating. For example:

  - *Headlines or titles.* These could be anything from book titles to headlines from newsletters or magazines. If possible, try to further subcategorize them by topic.

  - *Leads or intros.* Include good leads from news releases, feature stories, and the like. Even if the subject is different, the construction or turn of phrase can still be used again. The same type of file could be created for good endings as well.

  - *Quotes.* There's nothing like a good quote. I've got hundreds of quotes catalogued by author and by subject. Thousands of quotes are now on the Internet and available in an instant. Either way, these are handy for speech writing or feature stories. Just remember to attribute them to the right source. For instance, I was recently notified via e-mail from someone I'd never met that a biblical quote I'd used on a Web site was not from Ezekiel but from Daniel. Nothing like publicly embarrassing yourself, especially if you're a writer.

- *Catalogue your ideas.* Catalogue your best ideas, used and unused. Look at this list regularly to help stimulate your creativity. That idea you discarded last month may be just the right thing this week.

- *Browse the Internet.* It's amazing how many good ideas you can get simply from browsing. Some of my best ideas have come from the hours I used to spend wandering the library aisles. Today, much the same thing can be accomplished without ever having to leave your desk chair. (Of course, you don't burn nearly as many calories.) Just sign on to the Internet, pick a search topic, and browse. Download anything that interests you, remembering that this, too, is copyrighted material. Also remember that you do have a job to do and surfing the Internet can be addictive. I've found that setting aside an hour a day for surfing, and sticking to it, keeps my productivity steadier.

Writing

At some point, you have to stop brainstorming and begin to write. Here again, the computer can prove invaluable. You should become familiar with some of the following techniques:

- *Use layout and publishing tools to organize.* Most programs enable you to move words, sentences, and paragraphs with ease by simply highlighting and moving the text with the mouse, or by cutting and pasting. The more sophisticated programs allow for the rearrangement of entire pages, sections, or chapters. This is perhaps the greatest benefit of using a computer to compose. Organization is the key to all good writing, and a computer makes reorganization a snap. *Tip:* As you move things around, don't leave copies of the original words or paragraphs in their original places. In other words, cut them and re-place them. Don't copy them. If you copy them, before long you'll have redundancy everywhere you look. If you're not sure where to put material you've cut out, put it into a separate file by splitting your screen. Be sure to save this file in case your computer crashes. You can also use the "strike through" function included in most word-processing programs. This function visually indicates text that may be edited out at a later time.
- *Take advantage of windows.* Most computer platforms utilize windows, which allow you to work with multiple documents simultaneously. Most programs also indicate how many windows you have open at any one time and allow you to switch from one to another with some ease. This makes copying and pasting among documents extremely easy. Just remember not to *cut* from other documents to your master, just *copy*, leaving the other documents intact. *Tip*: Don't open more than three documents at a time, or use the "window shade" function some platforms support to "roll up" documents you are not currently working on. Having more than three documents open requires a mental juggling act that usually ends in confusion.

Proofreading and Editing

Whether you're doing your own editing or someone else is working with you, you're going to want to proofread your work. You don't want to look *too* bad to your editor or fellow writers. Here are some tips for using your computer to help you:

- *Use proofreading tools.* Most software programs, and even some design programs, come with spell checkers. Word-processing software also comes with grammar checkers, thesauruses, word counters, and, sometimes, even readability checkers (see Chapter 16). I always use a spell checker and often a word counter, especially for magazine articles that have to be a certain length. I rarely use a grammar checker because I don't believe they can substitute for a good grasp of grammar and are wasted on good writers who don't usually make egregious errors in that department anyway. *Tip*: Don't rely on your spell checker to catch everything. As already mentioned, they don't catch all errors and often flag things that aren't problems. Be even more cautious with grammar checkers. If you feel you have to use one, your job as a writer may be in jeopardy.

- *Check your organization.* Take a last-minute stroll through your piece to check for organizational problems. If you find any, correct them by using the methods discussed above. Also make sure your paragraphs reflect a single idea or subject. Read with your cursor as a pointer. If you come to a point within a paragraph at which ideas have changed, just position the cursor and hit "return."

- *Use "search and replace."* If you do locate an error that you suspect might have been repeated elsewhere, or if you decide to substitute one word or phrase for another you've used throughout, use the "search and replace" function to make the changes. *Tip*: You can also use this function as an editing tool. For example, if you are compiling a lengthy document with a number of references to illustrations or charts, you might have to wait until your graphics are assembled to insert text references (e.g., "see Exhibit 9.1"). You can enter these references into your text in advance by inserting a character that you can search for later when your exhibits are in order. For example, using [brackets] as a search character usually works because most of us use them only for editorial comment anyway. Or you could enter a string of characters that wouldn't normally appear in writing, such as *?????*.

- *Change typeface or size.* By simply enlarging your font size or changing typefaces, your written piece takes on a new look. This new look may help you spot mistakes more easily. In most cases, this sort of temporary change doesn't disturb your formatting. Bullets in one typeface will usually be bullets in another. These formatting options are part of the program itself and not generally typeface dependent.

In Collaboration

T. S. Eliot's famous poem *The Wasteland* was twice the length in draft form than in final published form. In fact, by some accounts, it was unfathomable. Eliot's friend and editor, Ezra Pound, cut the work nearly in half, thereby ensuring that Eliot would become recognized as one of the finest poets in the English language. We'd all like to have editors like that, of course; however, we more often benefit as much from simple collaboration. Here again, the computer can be extremely useful. Let's look at some of the ways you can use your computer to collaborate with other writers and with editors:

- *Real-time collaboration.* This can be accomplished in a number of ways. If you share a local area network (LAN) with your collaborators, you can literally work online with them, in real time. It's possible, and not all that annoying, to write together by "trading" phrases, rewriting each other's work, and re-ordering points, all without laying eyes on each other (unless you have video capabilities on your computer and like to see who you're talking to). This sort of collaboration requires absolute teamwork and a willingness to let others contribute to your work as it is being created. There is an old poetry game in which each person makes up a stanza of a poem, the final poem being a linked chain of all the contributed stanzas. Collaborative writing in real time is something like this game.

- *Online collaboration.* This is roughly the same as real-time collaboration except that you don't work in real time. Instead, you submit your drafts either to a fellow writer or to an editor sharing the same network as you, and your collaborator returns your work along with suggestions or edits keyed right into the text.

- *E-mail.* This is perhaps the slowest of the online methods, especially if you are communicating with someone outside your LAN. However, it beats waiting days or weeks for your work to be edited and turned around in the regular mail (or snail-mail, as it is becoming known). It also requires that you have compatible software in order to download attached files. Otherwise, your text has to be included as the mail message itself—a bit clumsy, to say the least. The book you are reading now was rewritten and edited in this way, saving weeks of time. The editor and I sent our revisions back and forth to each other, and then the editor sent each completed chapter to the publisher, all via e-mail—the only part of the book that had to be sent by regular mail was the artwork.

    If you do use this method, make sure you understand who is responsible for the final draft. That person must see to it that all edits and corrections are made and the piece is ready to go to its final destination. *Tip*: Date all drafts, file them according to some logical scheme (don't put multiple drafts in the same folder), and purge those that are out of date. Nothing is more confusing than to try to remember which draft included the latest information. Don't rely on the computer dating that is automatic with your system. You may have put that new piece of information into yesterday's draft and mistakenly opened an older one today. This will redate your old one, making it seem newer than the other. And don't store your work on more than one computer. Instead, use disks to move files around.

WRITING FOR THE COMPUTER

Recent changes in technology have allowed organizations to reach out to their constituencies in ways never before imaginable. The computer has not only spawned word processing and desktop publishing, it has also allowed us to reconfigure our communications and our modes of delivery. Additionally, technology has expanded the scope of both internal and external communications beyond that of traditional media. The role of everything from the news release to the corporate magazine has been broadened by the ability to make what was once a static delivery system now interactive. Nowhere has this change been more apparent than in employee communications.

Employee Communications: Intranets

As mentioned in Chapter 9, employee publications such as newsletters and magazines have gone through an evolutionary process that has resulted in publications less focused on entertainment and more focused on information. However, recent research has shown that employee publications alone aren't perceived as sufficient in providing information that employees need and want, especially during times of change. In addition, the employee publication has traditionally been considered a one-way form of communication in that it does not allow employees to ask questions of or provide feedback to their employers. New technology not only has changed the speed at which information can be delivered to employees but also has allowed for a range of interactivity not available to print media. For our purposes, the most relevant of these technologies is the company Intranet.[1]

The development of the Internet and the Web has in many ways revolutionized the way people communicate with each other, as well as how they access information. Through the Internet (which I discuss in more detail shortly), information can be shared electronically from all over the globe. An **intranet** is essentially an internal version of the Internet. Organizations have discovered the potential for developing intranets that enable their employees to access information within the confines of the organizational walls that can be used to help them with their jobs.

From a technical standpoint, an intranet is similar in design to the Web. Documents are organized into home pages that contain information on a particular subject, often punctuated with graphics or audio. The type of information available on an intranet can be determined by management or, in some cases, by employees themselves who might design their own home pages. At the most sophisticated level, an intranet can provide employees with access to information about an organization's financial data, daily news updates, customer profiles, sales figures, and meeting minutes.

---

[1] For an excellent Internet site dealing with intranet design and strategies, visit *CIO* magazine's Web site at http://www.cio.com/research/intranet/intranet_sites.html. The site contains numerous case studies, links to how-to articles, and an annual Web site award.

One of the added benefits from an employee communication perspective is that an intranet allows for greater interaction between employees as well as between employees and management. This enables employees to provide feedback to each other and to their supervisors. Cisco Systems saves more than $75 million annually as a direct result of its Web-based employee services applications. The Employee Connection keeps Cisco's 26,000 employees in the know with features such as an employee and resource directory, an automated expense reimbursement tool, technical documentation, and patent tracking.[2] According to Cisco,

> Most Cisco employees begin their workday with . . . Cisco Employee Connection. It's here that employees compare meeting schedules, procure office equipment, request workplace repairs or technical assistance, review employee benefits, make business travel arrangements, attend distance-learning classes, and even order catered items for upcoming meetings.
>
> And while the financial savings have been impressive, workforce optimization has other significant advantages, including employee empowerment, streamlined administration, and improved recruiting and benefits management.[3]

Cisco reports that the Web provides a number of benefits for building a workforce optimization program:

- Web applications are quicker and easier to deploy than client-server applications.
- Open standards enable the company to reach all constituents all around the world with the same application platform.
- Because employees can find information and complete tasks without the help of third parties, they have greater control and can complete tasks faster.[4]

Other examples demonstrate how readily organizations adopt these new, and seemingly successful, approaches to communication:

- Ketchum Public Relations developed myKGN as a way to reach both employees and clients with an online service suited specifically to their needs. myKGN is the first personalized enterprise portal for the public relations industry. Via myKGN, Ketchum professionals and their clients can customize access to hundreds of useful Web sites, subscription media services, line-of-business applications, and the industry's most extensive knowledge management system. By putting this information at everyone's fingertips and letting them manage it in their own way, myKGN helps Ketchum associates and their clients think smarter, execute faster, and collaborate more effectively. Usage of myKGN has grown every month since it was launched in November 2000. Today, approximately 1,200 internal Ketchum associates

---

[2] *CIO* online magazine's Web Business Awards, 2003, http://www.cio.com/archive/120101/winners.html.

[3] "Empowering Employees," *IQ Magazine*, 2002, Cisco Systems online, http://www.cisco.com/warp/public/3/middle_east/solutions/iq/wo/wo4/wo15.htm.

[4] "Empowering Employees," *IQ Magazine*, 2002, Cisco Systems online, http://www.cisco.com/warp/public/3/middle_east/solutions/iq/wo/wo4/wo15.htm.

and 100 clients use the portal. A recent employee survey showed that 92 percent of Ketchum professionals believe myKGN has had a positive influence on the way they work.[5]

- The U.S. Army even has a Web presence designed just for active-duty military. The Army's vast corporate portal, known officially as Army Knowledge Online, or AKO, was built to accommodate the electronic information needs of the Army's 1.2 million individuals and is the culmination of some four years of work. From a single interface users can get to their e-mail accounts, personnel information, and additional applications based on their access rights.[6]

Communicating with Other Publics: The Internet

In addition to the changes in delivering news releases (covered in Chapter 7), the most obvious example of using new technology to communicate with external publics is the **Internet.**

The Internet, which stands for "interlocking networks," is a large computer network that links several already established computer networks together with a common language. The Internet is a computer network made up of thousands of networks worldwide. No one knows exactly how many computers are connected to the Internet. It is certain, however, that these number in the millions. The result is a sharing of information over vast distances with the ease of dialing a phone. What once took days, weeks, or even months to accomplish now takes only minutes. As with the use of an intranet to enhance employee communications, the use of the Internet can be used to better meet the demands of external publics.

No one is in charge of the Internet. Certain organizations develop technical aspects of this network and set standards for creating applications on it, but no governing body is in control. The Internet backbone, through which Internet traffic flows, is owned by private companies.

An Internet user has access to a wide variety of services: electronic mail, file transfer, vast information resources, interest group membership, interactive collaboration, multimedia displays, real-time broadcasting, shopping opportunities, breaking news, and much more.

A quick tour of corporate **Web sites** will "net" you a rather complete picture of an organization's mission, products and services (and how to purchase them if the site is retail), economic situation, investment opportunities, frequently asked questions (FAQs), and myriad other topics. Primarily, such sites serve two, sometimes mutually exclusive, purposes: retail sales and image building. Of course, most public relations writers would be more concerned with image-building sites.

[5] Ketchum Public Relations online site, http://www.ketchum.com. Specific information on myKGN taken from Ketchum's press release, http://www.ketchum.com/DisplayWebPage/0,1003,310,00.html.
[6] *Portal Magazine*, 2003, http://www.portalsmag.com/articles/default.asp?ArticleID=4379.

Writing for Web Sites

Here is where you probably think you're going to find the secret to digital success. Wrong. My advice? Use the formats and styles outlined elsewhere in this book (including this chapter) when you write for the Internet. A news release is still a news release. A feature is still a feature. Ad copy is still ad copy. A FAQ section is just a question-and-answer section. You get the idea.

The most glaring difference seems to be the huge amount of chatter on the Internet. Fortunately, this is mostly confined to chat rooms and e-mail; however, a casual perusal of Web sites will quickly alert you to the inability of many site owners to write or, seemingly, express themselves in any coherent manner. The lesson is this: Don't succumb to the temptation to be chatty. Public relations writing is professional writing, even on the Internet. Follow the dictates of good writing, no matter what vehicle you are using, and you can't go wrong.

In an online editorial for *E&P Interactive* (part of the *Editor & Publishers* Web site at http://www.mediainfo.com), Steve Outing reviewed Crawford Kilian's book, *Writing on the Web* (International Self-Counsel Press, 1999). Kilian offers some sage advice for those who are already engaged in that dubious activity. First, he cites well-known Internet guru Jakob Nielsen as saying that Web readers read 25 percent slower than print readers. Kilian concludes that "if we read 25% slower on screen, then perhaps we owe our readers 25% less text."

Although Kilian cautions that Web site writing rules should be taken with a grain of salt because they are constantly evolving, here are his six general principles about writing for the online medium:

1. Web writing requires orientation, information, and action. That is, provide background information and navigation aids; provide the information itself; and provide a way for a reader to respond.

2. Web writing should be understandable at first glance.

3. Web writing should be the least you can possibly present to effectively deal with the subject. Excess information is a disservice to the Web reader.

4. Web writing displays a positive attitude to problems. Even if dealing with a negative topic like some injustice, offer the reader something constructive to do to deal with the injustice (taking advantage of the interactive nature of the online medium).

5. Web writing presents facts and ideas in terms of the reader's advantage. A smart Web writer uses "I" and "we" seldom, and "you" and "your" very much.

6. Web writing displays correctness, clarity, and consideration—correct organization, format, names, addresses, spelling, and grammar; appropriate language, proper tone, concision, coherence, and consideration of the reader's needs.

Do these rules sound familiar? They should. They are basically what this book is all about, and they pretty much bolster my long-held argument that good writing is good writing, no matter where you read it.

Kilian also reminds us not to forget to know our target audiences. Are they sophisticated about the topic? If so, we can use jargon common to the subject; if not, we must avoid using potentially confusing terms. Similarly, some audiences will need a more straightforward design with easy-to-interpret signposts leading them from one place to the next, whereas other, more sophisticated audiences may respond readily to a more complex design. As with any other publication, suit your design to your audience.

The single, glaring message Outing brings home in his review is that we shouldn't let technology overbear the message. Much the same as design done just for the sake of design will probably deter the serious seeker of information, a technologically stunning Web site may hinder your task of communicating successfully. The warning is well timed. I increasingly counsel students who are whizzes at Web site design, but who still can't write a coherent paragraph, on their job prospects. Sadly, they continue to believe that knowing the technology is all they need.

Remember: The difference between writing *for* a Web site and writing *on* the computer is that the computer is a writing tool, just like a typewriter or a pen, whereas a Web site is a communication vehicle, just like a newsletter. A well-written piece of communication is what you get paid to produce as a public relations writer. Ultimately, you will be judged by how well you write.

DESIGNING A WEB SITE

Just as public relations writers often are both designers and writers for other information pieces—newsletters, brochures, and the like—so too are you likely to be called upon to design your company's Web site. Thus, it is important to understand the basic premises behind Web sites and be able to contribute to them. It is not my intention to discuss the details of Web site construction here but rather to simply point out some generalities that will help you get started.

Although the computer screen doesn't replicate the printed page exactly, many of the techniques common to print layout are valid for Web site design. Some critics counter that this is exactly the problem: Computers shouldn't attempt to replicate print. (Many people believe that television made the same mistake in replicating radio programming and not exploring its full potential as a visual medium.) For the foreseeable future, however, people will continue to react to computer screen layout the same way they react to the printed page. As such, a Web site should be designed to attract, hold, and guide the inquiring reader (or viewer)—just like any other vehicle used for the dissemination of information. Keep in mind, however, that as the technology develops and as more and more users gain sophistication, "reading" Web sites will continue to evolve. We already see the first generation of users who are familiar with the language and the structure of the Web as a whole, and are quite capable of navigating its congested waters with ease. This expertise should not deter you, though, from constructing a site that is readable by all who use it, not just the Web sophisticates.

The single biggest detractor from a readable Web site is clutter. A great temptation exists with Web sites, as with any other publication, to overstate your design. Surf several corporate sites and you will immediately notice differences.

Retail locations often sell advertising to allied companies in the form of animated banners and other links. Although these features may help to offset the cost of maintaining a Web site, they add decidedly to the clutter. Web sites devoted to company image and information usually keep to the simpler formats, understanding that you must guide in order to inform.

Here are some very basic tips for getting the most out of your Web site:

- *Begin with a goal.* What is your Web site's mission? Is it to inform, persuade, sell, or open two-way communication?

- *Develop an outline.* Write down, in order, what you would like to include in your Web site. Remember: The term *Web site* refers not only to your home page but also to any local links (links within your site). You might want to make each major heading a separate linked site (see Exhibit 15.1).

- *Decide what you want to include on your home page.* This is your introduction. Keep it simple and to the point. Many home pages are just opening remarks with links to more complex information. Don't clutter this most important first contact point.

- *Rough out a basic design for your home page.*

- *Keep it simple.* In my opinion, the best designs are still the simple ones, the ones that incorporate the basic principles of design. Despite all the talk about nonlinear thinking, we still view layout in a linear fashion: left to right, top to bottom. And we still need the same visual cues to lead us. You really can't go wrong if you stick with the basic design rules laid out in Chapter 14.

- *Avoid going with the latest "cute" device.* For example, how many Web sites have you seen with annoying little animation pieces on them moving through a set range of motion and then repeating it endlessly? Waving flags, jumping frogs, runners, you name it; they all detract rather than attract. I liken this to the use of novelty type in print publications—avoid it at all costs.

- *Include an index or table of contents on your home page.* These are located typically across the top or down the left margin of the page. Each entry should be a link to one of your other outline's points. It is also advisable to repeat this index at each site connected to your home page as a way of providing a common reference point.

- *Use graphics wisely.* Visuals are undoubtedly one of the strengths of the computer in all its forms. Once thought of as merely a word processor (originally a number cruncher), the computer's ability to integrate sight, sound, and motion now make it a leading vehicle for communication. As with any other element, however, graphics can be overused. Again, avoid clutter. Use only the best graphics, and make them central to your layout. Follow the advice found in Chapter 14 on the uses of emphasis and sequence as you lay out your page. *Tip*: Use movies only if you feel they are absolutely indispensable to your communication effort. Although movies on the computer screen are certainly novel to most of us, they are also difficult to play (software requirements vary) and they use an incredible amount of memory. Remember, the slower your page runs, the less patient your reader-viewer becomes.

Exhibit 15.1

Web Site Outline

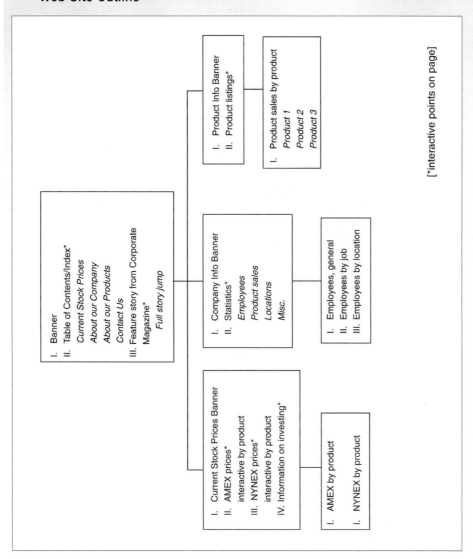

It is best to schematize your outline in the form of a chart, much like an organizational chart, with connections shown from site to site. Your outline can become fairly large and complex very quickly, proving the old advertising acronym, KISS: "Keep It Simple, Stupid."

Exhibit 15.2

Sample Web Site

Here are two Web pages designed for two entirely different audiences and for two entirely different reasons. The not-for-profit home page (top) is simple, straightforward, and relatively easy to maintain. It's designed to be used primarily by potential donors and volunteers. The Intel Press Room site (bottom) is more complex yet still simple to navigate with a lot of pertinent information and no excesses. It's designed to be used primarily by journalists.

- *Integrate graphics and copy carefully.* As with print publications, use visuals to break up heavy copy. The Internet accommodates a lot of copy effectively, but reading it from a screen can be tedious. That's why so many people still download text from Web sites rather than read it online. Try not to go for too long without graphic interruption.

- *Keep introductory material brief.* Although you may include lengthy written pieces in your site, introductions to that material should be brief. They should stand out the same way headlines stand out in print publications (of course, you may use headlines as well to draw attention to material).

- *If possible, make your successive pages consistent with your home page design.* For example, repeat your index on each page in the same location. Use the same background, or wallpaper, for each page. And be sure to include links back to your home page and to the top of the current page at regular intervals— especially if the page is long.

- *Keep it simple.* I know, I've already said this. This time, however, it means keep the level of complexity in your overall site down. Too much information is just as deadly as not enough. Limit the number of links you use, and make them as clear and as logical as possible. One of the greatest dangers of Web site design is that your readers-viewers will be distracted from their purpose (and from yours). Set an agenda and make sure everything on your Web site has some bearing on it. If it doesn't, don't include it. This also goes for those courtesy links to similar sites. Do you really want your readers to jump to another location? Knowing the siren song of the Internet as well as I do, I wouldn't bet on them returning any time soon.

Exhibit 15.2 shows a sample Web site.

KEY TERMS

intranet
Internet
Web site

EXERCISES

1. With a classmate or coworker, write a one- to two-page collaborative piece on the public relations–related topic of your choice. Be prepared to discuss the process—how you communicated, how it worked (or didn't), how it differed from writing alone, etc.

2. Locate two Web sites, one retail oriented and one image oriented. Using Kilian's rules for writing on the Web as your guide, critique the sites and make suggestions for their improvement.

CHAPTER 16

Writing for Diverse Audiences

In this chapter you will learn:

- How to write for diverse audiences, including global audiences, ethnically diverse audiences, and low-literacy audiences.

- How to use symbols properly for diverse audiences.

- How to effectuate "bias-free" writing.

- How to use readability formulas.

Recognizing that audiences are diverse is the first step toward realizing that your writing style may have to be adjusted to suit the needs of your readers. Of course, you already knew that, but this recognition is more than just realizing that target publics are demographically or psychographically diverse. It is a realization that your audiences may be ethnically or culturally diverse. They may be internationally diverse or simply domestically diverse. For example, is there a southern culture? A western culture? A northeastern culture? They may even be diverse in their level of literacy. What follows then is a discussion of some of the issues you will have to consider to ensure that your readers are (a) getting the message you intended them to get, (b) understanding it in the way you wanted them to, (c) are not offended by anything you've said, and (d) can respond to your message in a way you'll understand.

WRITING FOR THE GLOBAL AUDIENCE

Increasingly, public relations writers find themselves engaging in conversations with constituents who are not from the United States, may never have been to the United States, and don't speak English as a first language. It is extremely important that your writing be clear and that your information be understood by all types of audiences. These audiences will generally fall into four categories:

- Those who read information in English, and English is their primary language.

- Those who read information in English, but English is not their primary language.

- Those who read information that has been translated from English into their primary language.

- Professional translators who will translate documents into their native language.

In a recent article appearing in the University of Southern California Annenberg Center for Communication online magazine, *Online Journalism Review*, Andrew Stroehlein, a pioneer of Internet journalism, notes that we can no longer assume that visitors to our Web publications will have English as a first language.[1]

> True, the United States still has the largest number of users, and English is still the leading language, but other countries and languages now make up more than 50% of the Web, according to The Face of the Web, the annual study of Internet trends by international research firm Ipsos-Reid (15 May 2001).
>   Not only are less than half of all Web sites in English (48%), there are countries where Internet penetration and use are greater than in the USA (Canada and Sweden, for example).[2]

---

[1] Andrew Stroehlein, "Writing for a Global Audience," *Online Journalism Review*, http://www.ojr .org/ojr/world_reports/1017960259.php.
[2] Andrew Stroehlein, "Writing for a Global Audience," *Online Journalism Review*, http://www.ojr .org/ojr/world_reports/1017960259.php.

Stroehlein also stresses awareness of cultural differences, especially regarding the kind of things most of us take for granted. Once you move beyond your own state, in many cases, there will be cultural differences. Crossing national borders with your writing increases that likelihood greatly. Stroehlein suggests that serious organizations dealing with multinational audiences hire an international staff. Another suggestion is to include as much background on likely cultural trip-ups as possible. For example, a story about a regulated industry in the United States would need to include information on regulatory policy specific to that industry. Although many industries are regulated internationally, restrictions vary.

The next few sections include a number of style tips for writing for diverse audiences. Not all of these tips will be applicable all the time. You need to decide which are most usable for a given communication.[3]

Style Tips

The following style suggestions can help ensure your information is clear for all types of audiences:

- Use short and simple sentences. Remember, the average length of a sentence in public relations writing is about 16 words. Certainly, less than 25 words would be best.

- Use relative pronouns.

- Define abbreviations and acronyms and avoid jargon. Certain industries are heavy with jargon and acronyms. Explain any necessary jargon (most can simply be avoided), and spell out acronyms and abbreviations.

- Use correct English punctuation.

- If you use lists, make sure they are introduced by a complete sentence.
  - Make each item in the list a complete sentence or complete phrase.
  - Make list items parallel in structure.

- Avoid slang, humor, sarcasm, colloquialisms, and metaphors. Humor is one of the hardest emotions to portray across cultures. What one culture finds funny might be considered offensive by another culture. Also remember that most non-native-English speakers understand formal English, not colloquial English.

- Do not use Latin abbreviations (i.e., e.g., etc.).

- Avoid negative constructions. For example, use "It is like the previous request" rather than "It is not unlike the previous request." Or, use "Log on again to reconnect" instead of "You cannot reconnect without logging on again."

---

[3] Much of what follows was gleaned from IBM's excellent Web presentation on communicating globally through their software and hardware, http://www-3.ibm.com/software/globalization/index.jsp. The site provides changing topics targeted to those presenting information to a global and diverse audience.

- Avoid ambiguity.
- Choose examples that are appropriate for the intended audience.

Grammar Tips

Appropriate grammar enables easier, more accurate translations and enhances audience understanding:

- Always use correct, English grammar.
- Write in active voice whenever possible, and use the present tense.
- Avoid the infinitive *(to create)*, present participle *(creating)*, and past participle *(created)* forms of verbs in the beginning of sentences. These verbs are less direct, and the subject of the clause is not always obvious. The phrase "completing steps" could mean "When you complete the steps" or "Because you complete the steps."
- Avoid complex sentences that use several adverbs or other modifiers. If you use complex sentences, include whatever words are necessary to make the subject clear.
- Avoid using words in multiple grammatical categories (verb, noun, adjective). In English, many words can change their grammatical category. In most other languages, the same word cannot be a verb, a noun, and an adjective. (For example, use "during the restore operation" instead of "during the restore.")
- Avoid ambiguous pronoun references in which the pronoun can possibly refer to more than one antecedent. For example, in the statement "If there is prompt text for the completed field, it does not change," it is not clear whether the "prompt text" or the "completed field" does not change.
- Use simple and clear coordination so that the reader can identify the relationships between the elements of a sentence. For example, "the file or result field definition" could mean any of the following: "the result-field definition or the file," "the file definition or the result-field definition," "the file-field definition or the result-field definition," "the definition of the file or of the result field," or "the field definition of the file or of the result."
- Ensure the elements of a sentence are parallel. Words, phrases, and clauses should be grammatically equal. For example, use "network management, databases, and application programs" rather than "network management, databases, and writing application programs."
- Avoid using too many prepositions in a sentence, but do not omit prepositions or articles that are necessary. The sentence "This is a list of the current status of all event monitors for this process" could be rewritten as "This lists the current status of all event monitors for this process."
- Do not use the dash parenthetically (as in "It is at this point—the start point—that designers and writers meet"). Use either commas or actual parentheses instead. Translators will accept the dash being used to show an

extension of a sentence (as in "The most important people in IBM are the customers—they pay us").

Terminology Tips

The following terminology guidelines will help make your text easier for international audiences to understand:

- Use correct and consistent terminology. Define new or unfamiliar terms in a product glossary. Minimize the creation of new terms.
- Avoid referring to culture-specific standards.
- Avoid the overuse of abbreviations and special symbols. If you must use abbreviations, define them the first time they are used in the body of the text. Use only standard abbreviations and symbols.
- If your product uses the # symbol, don't refer to it as "the pound sign." Use "the number symbol (#)," and explain clearly how it is used.
- Include explanatory context for all product-specific and specialized terms.
- Ensure information is free of typographical errors.
- Avoid terms such as *domestic* and *foreign*.

Punctuation Tips

Pay close attention to how you punctuate text:

- Always use the punctuation style consistent with the language in which you are writing—in most cases, American English. Remember that British English uses punctuation differently (especially regarding the use of quotation marks).
- Do not use a slash to mean *and/or*. Rewrite the sentence to indicate the exact meaning, for example: "You can choose the green one, the blue one, or both."
- Do not use an ampersand (&) to mean *and*.

ICONS AND IMAGES

Cultural sensitivity is important. When you write information or create graphics for culturally diverse audiences, remember that the words and images you develop might be read differently by people from cultures other than your own. Some information and graphics might cause minor offense, and others could have major consequences.

Keep in mind a fundamental rule while designing international icons: Icons are not universal. Pictures and symbols create powerful and different associations in each culture and context. Following are some tips for developing international icons for clear communication that avoids culture and translation issues:

- *Text-based icon.* Text often fits awkwardly into icons. Even though the text in the base language may be short, the translation can be very long. For example, the English *on* translates to *aktiveret* in Danish.

- *Puns.* Puns may work well in one language but be absolutely meaningless or hard to translate into other languages or cultures.

- *Hand and arm gestures.* Almost every hand gesture that is acceptable in one country is obscene in another. For instance, the American "okay" sign formed by a circle between the thumb and first finger is considered obscene in other cultures. Also, hand symbols can be confused with the various sign languages used by speech- and hearing-impaired groups in different countries.

- *Animal icons.* Animals can represent different things from culture to culture:
  - An owl might be seen as intelligent in Western countries but is considered a dumb bird in some Asian countries.
  - Dogs are beloved pets for some people but a food source for others.
  - Snakes are viewed as sneaky by some but represent rebirth or cycles to other people.
  - Similar differences exist for a wide range of animals, including the pig, cow, and rabbit.

- *Colors.* Certain colors evoke distinct images in various cultures and countries, from political parties and countries to companies and sports teams. For example, black is a color of mourning in the West whereas white is the color of mourning in Japan. As a guide, use colors to reinforce messages that work in black and white.

- *Body parts as metaphors.* Parts of the anatomy can be used effectively to symbolize functions in many countries, but you must still be careful in their use:
  - Ear: hearing, audio control, audio input.
  - Nose: smell.
  - Mouth: food, eating, taste, breathing; however, an open mouth may be considered rude in parts of Asia.
  - Teeth: various uses, including associations with anger.
  - Tongue: often associated with rude gestures in many lands.
  - Eye: vision, video, video input; however, an eye symbol can indicate the "evil eye" in limited areas of Italy and Latin America.

- *Facial expressions.* The human face is incredibly expressive, but many expressions can be interpreted differently by various cultures. The smile is fairly universal, but showing teeth might be considered rude to some. Cartoon happy faces and sad faces are not far from the limit of reliable facial expressions.

- *Body language.* Body language might seem universal, but even something as common as nodding and shaking the head for yes and no can be reversed in some countries.

- *Sexual images.* These can be effective or deadly: Liberal societies appreciate them whereas conservative societies deplore them. In general, countries with secular governments are more liberal than those under religious rule.

- *Local symbols.* Any number of visual clichés are suitable only for local usage because they are often meaningless or unfamiliar in other countries (e.g., mailboxes, bride and groom, the nuclear family, the Lincoln penny).

- *Reading direction.* Iconic representation in calendars, books, graphs, flow-charts, and other materials can be complicated by the reading direction of various languages. For example, Hebrew and Arabic are written right to left, and Asian languages may be written from top to bottom with columns going right to left.

- *Political symbols.* Political symbols such as the donkey and elephant for the United States's Democratic and Republican parties can be very powerful but also very local. Use icons selectively for effect within specific countries.

- *Flags.* Some nations do not permit their flags to be used in commercial applications, whereas the United States and Britain do allow it. If you use national flags on icons, be prepared to have alternative icons for countries in which they are not allowed.

- *Monetary symbols.* Although the dollar sign is an appropriate symbol of money or wealth in some countries, the pound sterling, yen sign, and others are appropriate to other countries. A sack of coins, nonspecific bills, or other neutral money metaphors should be used as an alternative.

- *Symbols of authority.* Symbols of law and order vary according to locale, from a British judge's wig and an American judge's gavel to the headdress of an aboriginal tribe's chief.

- *Symbols of violence.* Avoid using metaphors of violence such as guns, knives, and bombs.

- *Tools and instruments.* Many tools and instruments are roughly similar in many lands, from construction tools such as saws, screws, and hammers to tools of science and medicine such as stethoscopes and scalpels. If details on the images are reduced, the generic image is more widely acceptable.

- *Indication of handicaps.* The wheelchair icon is a widely recognized international symbol for all types of physical handicap, intended as a metaphor not just for an inability to walk but also for limited strength, dexterity, and mobility. Black glasses on an outline of a face can be a good indicator of visual handicaps.

- *Nature icons.* Like animals, plants and other natural images can have strong local connotations yet provide powerful and flexible metaphors for icons. Climatic phenomena such as clouds, sun, snow, rain, and lightning offer distinctive and learnable metaphors regardless of the local climate.

- *Math and music.* Mathematical symbols and musical notation are widespread and uniform. However, some common math symbols require sensitive treatment:

- Asterisk for multiplication: This symbol is not universal, because it can also be a raised dot or stylized ×, and at times could be interpreted as the Jewish Star of David if the asterisk has six points.

- Plus sign for addition: Because this symbol can be interpreted as a cross, Israel and some Muslim countries may use substitutes for the plus sign.

- Decimal indication: Both the period and comma are used in a variety of countries to indicate a decimal function.

BIAS-FREE WRITING

We are increasingly reminded that our language must be **bias** free. That is, it should not "offend, demean, or exclude people on the basis of gender, ethnic group, religion, age, ability/disability, or sexual orientation."[4] Developing a writing style free of bias is not an easy task, because much of writing is an unconscious act. For example, we might be in the habit of using *he* as the common pronoun designation in our writing. To alternate with *she* or to use *she/he* may seem a forced, conscious act—and it probably is. However, we all need to be attuned to potentially offensive language.

The trick is to recognize when a phrase, term, or word may be troublesome and learn to deal with it automatically. What follows are some tips developed by the University of Wisconsin and used widely by other institutions as writer's guidelines for avoiding bias.[5] Keep in mind that a particular usage that a group prefers today may change tomorrow. The trick is to write in a way that is respectful of all people.

- Avoid identifying people by race or ethnic group unless it is relevant. We don't usually point out that an individual is white or of Anglo-Saxon heritage. The same rule should apply to other groups.

Inappropriate
Maria Duran, a Hispanic professor of physics, has been promoted to associate professor.

Recommended
Maria Duran, a professor of physics, has been promoted to associate professor.

Inappropriate
Alpha Beta Gamma, the black fraternity, wants to reroof its building.

Recommended
The Alpha Beta Gamma fraternity wants to reroof its building.

---

[4] Oregon State University Extension Family & Community Development, http://osu.orst.edu/dept/ehe/nutrition.htm.
[5] "Guide to Bias-Free Communications," Office of University Publications, University of Wisconsin, Madison, 1991. Second printing, August 1992.

- Avoid the term *non-white,* which sets up white culture as the standard by which all other cultures should be judged. Also avoid *culturally disadvantaged* and *culturally deprived.* These terms imply that the dominant culture is superior to other cultures or that other groups lack a culture.

- Refer to individuals as "member of a minority group" or specify the minority group (e.g., Latino) when minority group identity is pertinent. (*Minority* refers to a group and serves as a modifier in the term *minority group*.)

Example
Women and minorities are encouraged to apply.

Recommended
Women and members of minority groups are encouraged to apply.

Example
Minorities attended the meeting.

Recommended
Members of the Hmong and Korean communities attended the meeting.

- Avoid words, images, or situations that reinforce stereotypes and that imply all people of a particular race or ethnic group are the same.

Example
Not surprisingly, the Asian-American students did best in the math contest.

The Problem
Assuming it is relevant to point out that this group excelled, the phrase "not surprisingly" may reinforce the stereotype that all Asian Americans have superior aptitude in math.

- Be sure your communication does not patronize or give token mention to members of racial or ethnic groups. Exaggerated focus on people's accomplishments or insincere and gratuitous references to their concerns imply that they are not usually successful or accomplished, or are not considered to be in the mainstream of society.

- Stay attuned to the current terminology by which racial and ethnic groups refer to themselves. Usage changes (e.g., from *Negro* to *African American,* from *Oriental* to *Asian American*). National newspapers and television news are good indicators of current usage. Also, ask people what term they prefer.

  People who trace their ancestry through the Caribbean or Central and South America may identify themselves as coming from any one of a number of different cultures and ethnic groups. For instance, the terms *Hispanic, Latino/a, Chicano/a,* and *Puertorriqueno/a* all have different meanings. Many people whom the U.S. Census would describe as *Hispanic* prefer the term *Latino or Latina.* Some people with Spanish-sounding surnames may have indigenous Indian, German, or Asian ancestry or prefer to be referred to by their nationality (e.g., Colombian, Nicaraguan, Guatemalan). Others may prefer that no reference be made to their nationality or ancestry.

People whose ancestors originally populated North America may want to be identified with specific communities, such as Winnebago or Chippewa, or they may prefer to be referred to as *American Indian* or *Native American* rather than *Indian*. If in doubt, ask.

Also, attention must be paid to the punctuation used in referring to racial and ethnic groups. The terms *African American, Asian American,* and the like are nouns and should not be hyphenated. However, when these terms are used as modifiers (e.g., "the Asian-American students," they should be hyphenated.

- Be sensitive to religion when referring to various ethnic groups. Don't make assumptions. For instance, just as not all Arabs are Muslims, most nationalities and ethnicities will embody different religious practices. Avoid stereotyping a race, nationality, or ethnic group with a specific religion.

- Review written communications and visual materials to ensure that, where appropriate, all groups—women, men, minority and ethnic group members, older people, and disabled people—are represented.

This does not mean that every publication, video, or similar material must include all groups at all times or that participation of particular groups should be exaggerated or overstated. But generic campus publications, such as college bulletins or communications that are part of a continuing series (such as newspapers or annual reports), should aim for reasonable representation of all groups involved.

WRITING FOR LOW-LITERACY AUDIENCES[6]

Half of all Americans read below the 10th-grade level. Poor reading skills limit many people in their ability to lead productive lives, affecting their families and communities as well as themselves. For those of us in the writing business, we need to know our audience in depth. If that audience is composed in whole or in part of those whose literacy level is considered to be low, we must adjust accordingly. If materials are written at too high a level, people receiving them cannot read or understand them. Others may not make the effort. Consider the following statistics:[7]

- Twenty-three percent of adult Americans (44 million adults) are functionally illiterate (they read somewhere below eighth-grade level).
- More than 700,000 illiterate youths graduate from U.S. high schools each year.
- Almost 40% of all 17 year olds in minority groups are functionally illiterate.

[6] "Writing for a Changing World: Reaching Low Literacy Audiences with Print Material," Minnesota Extension Service, 1993.
[7] The Condition of Education, International Adult Literacy Survey, National Center for Education Statistics, U.S. Department of Education, 1998.

These statistics show that you might, at some time, be writing to an audience that cannot fully understand what you are saying.

Where Do You Start?

Once you are aware of the need for more readable educational materials, it's easy to feel uncertain about your writing. You begin to look critically at everything you read. Whether or not you need to develop lower literacy materials as part of your normal work, consider using some of the following techniques in your everyday writing for greater clarity:

Organization

- Use headings and subheadings (these tell the reader what is coming next and break up long columns).
- Present only the most important information.

Language and style

- Use short sentences: not more than 25 words.
- Use short paragraphs: not more than 60 words.
- Write in the active voice, not passive voice: "Read the instructions before beginning" is easier to understand than "Instructions should be read before beginning."
- Use concrete examples to illustrate a point: "You get Vitamin A in dark green leafy vegetables and deep orange vegetables: spinach, carrots, orange vegetables" or "Spinach, carrots, or squash are vegetables that have Vitamin A."
- Repeat new or unfamiliar information to reinforce learning.
- Avoid clichés and jargon: "Labels let you in on the inside" may be too abstract. "Container labels can tell you a lot about what's inside the package" is better.
- If you must use a technical, unfamiliar word, explain the word with a simple definition or example.
- Repeat new or unfamiliar words several times to make them more familiar to the reader.
- Use positive statements: "Follow safe practices" is better than "Do not follow unsafe practices."

Design

- Use an unjustified right margin.
- Use larger, easy-to-read type for text (10–12 point).
- Use upper and lower case letters, which are easier to read than all capitals.

Readability Formulas and Computer Programs

More than 40 **readability formulas** exist that assess the degree of difficulty of written material. Two of the more common ones are the *Gunning Fog Index* and the *Flesch Formula* (see Exhibit 16.1). Most of these formulas look at word difficulty and sentence length. Applying these formulas by hand requires some calculation and time.

A number of software programs can automate running readability formulas, such as SpellCatcherPlus (http://www.rainmakerinc.com) and GrammarExpert-Plus (http://wintertreesoftware.com). In addition, the most widely used word processing programs, such as WordPerfect and Microsoft Word, can also analyze documents using the Flesch method. Remember that computer programs can assess only the readability of written pieces. Other factors, such as page setup, type size, and use of illustrations, affect how easy the material is to read and understand.

Exhibit 16.1

Readability Formulas

The Gunning Fog Index

1. Select a sample of 100 words from the middle of your piece.
2. Count the number of sentences and divide that number into 100 to find the average sentence length.
3. Count the number of words consisting of three syllables or more in the 100 words. Do not include proper nouns, compound words like *typesetting*, or words that end in *ed* or *es*.
4. Add the totals from steps 2 and 3 and multiply by 0.4.

The resulting score approximates the number of years of schooling required to read the piece. College graduates usually can read at about a score of 16 whereas most bestsellers are written at a 7–8 level. Obviously, if your piece is intended for vertical distribution, such as a company magazine, you will need to reach an average audience. Newspapers, for instance, are written at about the sixth-grade level.

The Flesch Formula

1. Select a sample of 100 words from the middle of your piece.
2. Count the number of sentences and divide that number into 100 to find the average sentence length (ASL).

(continued)

(continued)

3. Count the number of syllables in the sample and divide this figure by 100 for the average word length (AWL).

4. Plug the resulting figures from steps 2 and 3 into the following formula: Readability = $206.835 - (84.6 \times AWL) - (1.015 \times ASL)$

5. Interpret the scores based on the following scale:

70–80 = very easy (romance novels)

60–65 = standard (newspapers, *Readers Digest*)

50–55 = "intellectual" magazines (*Harpers, Atlantic Monthly*)

30 and below = scholarly journals, technical papers

This formula is based on ease of reading determined, to a large extent, by the length of words. This assumes that polysyllabic words slow down and often confuse the reader. Other formulas gauge the degree of familiarity by noting personal pronouns, for instance.

KEY TERMS

bias
readability formula

EXERCISES

1. Select a paragraph from each of three of your school or organizational publications—something written in narrative form, not a bulleted list or an outline of any kind. Answer the following questions:

   - Who do you think the target audience is for this publication? Try to describe the audience's general demographic characteristics.

   - Why do you think your school or organization wants to reach this audience?

   - Do you think they are successful? (An educated guess will be fine.)

2. Now, run both the Gunning Fog Index and the Flesch Formula on the paragraphs. Given what you described in the first exercise, do you think the writing level and style match the target audience's abilities?

3. Locate printed materials designed to reach diverse audiences, both culturally and for level of literacy. These materials can usually be found at state employment offices, social service agencies, certain college campus programs, agencies serving primarily minority audiences, or organizations dealing with international or crosscultural audiences. Analyze these materials for some of the points covered in this chapter. Do you think they are successful at reaching their target audiences?

Glossary

The chapters in which a term is highlighted are indicated in parentheses at the end of the definition.

A

Accompanying script. The version of a television script sent with the taped spot to the stations that will run it. The accompanying script is stripped of all but its most essential directions. It is intended to provide the reader with a general idea of what the taped spot is about, and is to be used only as a reference for broadcasters who accept the spot for use. (12)

Actuality. An audio- or videotape that features newspeople describing an event, interviews with those involved in the event, or ambiance or background of the event itself for a voice-over. (12)

Advocacy advertising. Presents a point of view. This may range from political to social and, by inference, positions the company as an involved citizen of the community or the nation. (11)

Anchor. A line or strip of color used at the top or bottom of the page to gain unity in a publication. (14)

Angle. The hook in a news release that attracts media attention. (7)

Annual report. One of the most-produced organizational publications, annual reports not only provide information on the organization's financial situation, they also act as a vehicle for enhancing a corporation's image among its various internal publics. (8)

Appeal strategies. A type of **compliance strategy** that persuades the audience by calling upon it to help or come to the aid of the communicator or some third party represented by the communicator. (3)

Argument strategies. Persuasive strategies designed to oppose another point of view and to persuade. There are two types: reasoned argument and emotional appeal. Both attempt to persuade by arguing one point of view against another. (3)

As-recorded spot. A radio spot produced by the originating agency and ready to be played by the stations receiving it. They are usually sent in the format used by the particular station or on reel-to-reel tape, which will probably be transferred to the proper station format. (12)

Attribution. A stylistic device whereby quotes are credited to their sources. *Said* is the most common form for journalistic style; however, *says* is commonly used by public relations writers to add immediacy. (7)

B

Backgrounder. Basic information pieces providing background as an aid to reporters, editors, executives, employees, and spokespersons. This is the information used by other writers and reporters to "flesh out" their stories. (7)

Bias. Writing that offends, demeans, or excludes people on the basis of gender, ethnic group, religion, age, ability/disability, or sexual orientation. (16)

Blind headline. A headline that imparts no information useful to the reader's understanding of the story it accompanies. (10)

Blueline. A printer's proof that should be checked for accuracy before a print job is started. (14)

Body type. Type set smaller than 14 points and used for body copy. Distinguished from display type, which is 14 points and larger. (14)

Bridge. The part of a brochure that explains the purpose of the piece and refers to the title or headline. (10)

C

Caption. The informational description that appears below or next to a photograph or other illustration. Also known as a **cutline.** (9)

Command headline. A type of headline that orders the reader to do something. (11)

Command strategies. A type of **compliance strategy** that persuades through three forms: (3)

- Direct requests with no rationale or motivation for the requests
- An explanation accompanied with reasons for complying
- Hints in which circumstances are suggested from which the audience draws the desired conclusions and acts in the desired way

Commercial speech. As defined by the Supreme Court, the concept of commercial speech allows a corporation to state publicly its position on controversial issues. The Court's interpretation of this concept also allows for political activity through lobbying and political action committees. (4)

Compliance strategies. Persuasive strategies designed to gain agreement through coercion. (3)

Consequence. One of the characteristics of newsworthiness of information. Relates to whether the information has any importance to the prospective reading, listening, or viewing public. Is it something that the audience would pay to know? (5)

Contact log. A record of all telephone calls from the media or other parties inquiring about a crisis. This will help to ensure that the many callbacks required are not overlooked. It will also assist in the postcrisis analysis. (6)

Controlled information. Information over which you have total control as to editorial content, style, placement, and timing. Examples of controlled information are institutional (image) and advocacy advertising, house publications, brochures, and paid broadcast material (if it is paid placement). Public service announcements (PSAs) are controlled as far as message content is concerned but uncontrolled as to placement and timing. (1)

Copyright. Legal protection of intellectual property (e.g., writing, artwork) from use by others without permission. (4)

Corporate advertising. Advertising paid for by corporations but not related directly to products or services. Corporate or institutional advertising takes three basic forms depending on the purpose of the message: **public interest advertising, public image advertising,** and **advocacy advertising.** (11)

Crisis team. A group of people specifically designated to handle and respond to crises. This group is generally composed of managers in key areas including those areas most likely to be hit by a crisis. (6)

Crossheads. Small, transitional heads within an article. (9)

Curiosity headline. A type of headline that invites the reader to read further in order to answer a posed question. (11)

Cutline. The informational description that appears below or next to a photograph or other illustration. Also known as a **caption.** (9)

Dateline. A brief notation at the beginning of a press release used to indicate the point of origin. (7)

Defamation. Any communication that holds a person up to contempt, hatred, ridicule, or scorn. (4)

Delayed lead. A type of news release lead used to add drama to a story. This type of lead is usually reserved for feature stories and is not appropriate for straight news. (7)

Descriptive data. Information gathered from research that paints a picture of the public being studied by its distinctive demographic characteristics—descriptors such as age, income, sex, education, nationality, and so on. This is information needed for a reader profile. (2)

Design principles. The five basic principles that comprise good design: (14)

- *Balance.* The concept that what is put on one side of the page should "weigh" as much as what is on the other side. All the elements placed on the page have weight, even the white space left by not placing elements. Size, color, and degree of darkness all play a part in balance.

- *Emphasis.* Focusing readers' attention on single elements on a page. Elements are emphasized by assigning them more optical weight than other items on the page. These elements are larger, darker, more colorful, or oddly shaped. They draw the readers' attention first among all other items on the page.

- *Proportion.* A measure of relationship in size. It helps to show one object's relationship to other objects in a layout.

- *Sequence.* The order of the elements on a layout. It will literally lead readers through a page.

Display type. Type larger than 14 points, used for headlines and other emphasized elements. (14)

Dissonance theory. A theory formulated in the 1950s which says that people tend to seek only messages that are "consonant" with their attitudes; they do not seek out "dissonant" messages. In other words, people don't go looking for messages they don't agree with already. This theory also says that about the only way you are going to get anybody to listen to something they don't agree with is to juxtapose their attitude with a "dissonant" attitude—an attitude that is logically inconsistent with the first. (3)

Downward communication. Communication within an organization that imparts management's message to employees. Ideally, even downward communication channels such as newsletters permit upward communication through letters to the editor, articles written by employees, surveys, and so forth. (9)

Drop. The amount of white space at the top of a page layout. (14)

E

Emotional appeal. Using emotional techniques to persuade an audience. The most common techniques are use of symbols, emotive language, and entertainment. (3)

Entertainment. A communication strategy that encapsulates information within a format that makes it easier to accept or understand. (3)

Exclusive. A press release or other information intended for only one media outlet. The same information may not be released to other outlets in any form. (7)

Exposition. An information strategy that involves the dissemination of pure information. Two of the most-used forms of exposition are narration and description. (3)

Extemporaneous speech. A speech given on the spur of the moment, usually with little or no preparation. Basically synonymous with **impromptu speech.** (13)

F

Fact sheet. An information piece that contains just that—facts—and nothing more. It should elaborate on already presented information, such as a news release, and not merely repeat what has already been said. (7)

Feature style. A less objective style of writing that provides less hard information than straight news style. Features generally take a point of view or discuss issues, people, or places. The style is more relaxed, more descriptive, and often more creative than straight news style. (9)

Financial release. This type of **news release** is used primarily in shareholder relations but is also of interest to financial media. (7)

Font. The classification within a given typeface, such as bold, or italic. (14)

Format (1). The type of music a radio station plays or the information it provides. For example, some stations play only Top-40 hits. These stations usually cater to a teenage audience. Other stations play only Classic Rock or jazz, or provide news. Their listeners vary according to their format. (5)

Format (2). The way you arrange your brochure—its organizational characteristics. (10)

G

Ghostwriting. Writing something for someone else. Writing that will appear under someone else's name. Examples are corporate letters to the editor and speech writing. (4)

Grid. Another term for the columns used in a layout. (14)

H

Hard news. Information that has immediate impact on the people receiving it. By journalists' definition, it is very often news people need rather than news they want. (5)

I

Impromptu speech. A speech given on the spur of the moment, usually with little or no preparation. Basically synonymous with **extemporaneous speech.** (13)

Inferential data. Information gathered from research that allows for generalizing about a larger group or population. This means that the people chosen for the survey must be entirely representative of the larger population comprising the target audience. This allows sampling of a small segment of the target public in order to infer from their reactions the reactions of the larger audience. Inferential research can work only if the sample is chosen completely at random from the larger population. (2)

Interest. One of the characteristics of newsworthiness of information. Relates to whether the information is unusual or entertaining. Does it have any human interest? (5)

Internet (interlocking networks). A large computer network that links several - already established computer networks together with a common language. The Internet is a computer network made up of thousands of networks world-wide. (15)

Intranet. An internal network devoted usually to employee or organizational issues and accessed via an internal network or the Internet through a password-protected gateway. (15)

Inverted pyramid style. A straight news story: It begins with a lead, expands on the lead, and proceeds to present information in decreasing order of importance. Also known as straight news style. (7)

Issue statement. A precise definition of the situation, including answers to the following four questions: (2)

1. What is the problem or opportunity to be addressed?
2. Who are the affected parties?
3. What is the timing of this issue?
4. What are your (or your organization's) strengths and weaknesses as regards this issue?

K

Kicker. Usually a slogan or a headline-type phrase coming at the end of the body copy. Used to reiterate the message of the headline. (11)

L

Language fallacies. Typically unethical persuasive strategies that involve the actual use of language, including: equivocation, amphibole, and emotive language. (4)

Lead. The opening sentences of a straight news story or feature article. In a straight news story, the lead should include the *who, what, when, where, why,* and *how* of the story. Feature leads generally begin by setting the scene of the story to follow. (7)

Logic fallacies. Persuasive techniques codified by the Roman orators over a thousand years ago. Commonly referred to as logic fallacies because they are both illogical and deceptive by nature, they include, among others: cause and effect, personal attack, bandwagon, and inference by association strategies. (4)

M

Media directory. A good directory is an indispensable tool for the media relations specialist. Publishers of directories offer formats ranging from global checkers that include a variety of sources in every medium to specialized directories dealing with a single medium. (5)

Media list. A personalized list that contains details about local contacts and all the information you need to conduct business in your community. Media lists may include regional and even nationwide contacts, depending on the scope of your operation. A media list, once compiled, should be updated by hand at least once a month. (5)

Memorized speech. A fully scripted speech that the speaker has completely memorized for delivery. (13)

Message and media center. A location during a crisis from which information can be disseminated to the media and other interested parties. It should be some distance from offices of the crisis communication team, spokesperson, and emergency operations center to ensure that media don't end up in the middle of the action and can't "accidentally" bump into people to whom they shouldn't be talking. (6)

Message strategy. Developing a message, or messages, that will reach and have the desired effect on your target audiences. Message strategies should logically follow your objectives and contribute either directly or indirectly to them. (3)

N

Newsletter. A brief (usually four pages) printed publication distributed either vertically or horizontally. A newsletter usually contains information of interest to a narrowly defined target audience. The various types of newsletters include the following: (9)

- *Association newsletters* help a scattered membership with a common interest keep in touch.

- *Community group newsletters* are often used by civic organizations to keep in touch with members, announce meetings, and stimulate attendance at events.

- *Institutional newsletters,* perhaps the most common type of newsletter, are usually distributed among employees.

- *Publicity newsletters* often create their own readers. They can be developed for fan clubs, resorts, and politicians.

- *Special-interest newsletters,* developed by special-interest groups, tend to grow with their following.

- *Self-interest or "digest" newsletters* are designed to make a profit. The individuals or groups who develop them typically offer advice or present solutions to problems held in common by their target readers. These often come in the form of a sort of "digest" of topics of interest to a certain profession.

News release. The most widely used of all public relations formats. News releases are used most often to disseminate information for publicity purposes and generally are of three types: **publicity releases, product releases,** or **financial releases.** (7)

Objectives. The concrete steps you need to take to reach your goal. A project's objectives must relate to the purpose of your message and should be realistic and measurable. For public relations writing, there are three types of objectives: informational, attitudinal, and behavioral. (2)

P

Persuasion. An information strategy that involves moving someone to believe something or act in a certain way. (3)

Placement agency. An organization that will take information, such as a press release, and send it out to media outlets using its own regularly updated media lists and computerized mailing services. (5)

Positioning. Placing your piece in context as either part of some larger whole or as a standout from other pieces. (10)

Press kit. One of the most common methods of distributing brochures and other collateral information pieces. Press kits are produced and used for a wide variety of public relations purposes, including product promotion presentations, press conferences, and as promotional packages by regional or local distributors or agencies. (5)

Primary research. Data collected for the first time and specifically for the project at hand. (2)

Privacy. One of the legal terms used to describe infringement. Often referred to as *invasion of privacy.* Its most common forms are as follows: (4)

- *Appropriation.* The commercial use of a person's name or picture without permission

- *Intrusion.* The literal invasion of a person's private space by such means as using telephoto lenses, audiotaping, or trespass

Product release. This type of **news release** deals with specific products or product lines and is usually targeted to trade publications within individual industries. (7)

Profile. A feature story written specifically about a person, product or service, or an organization or some part of it. It profiles the subject by listing facts, highlighting points of interest, and tying the subject to the organization being promoted. (9)

Prominence. One of the characteristics of newsworthiness of information. Relates to whether the information concerns or involves events and people of prominence. (5)

Proximity. One of the characteristics of newsworthiness of information. Relates to whether the information is local. (5)

Public image advertising. Tries to sell the organization as caring about its employees, the environment, the community, and its customers. Unlike the public interest ad, the public image ad always focuses on the company and how it relates to the subject. (11)

Public interest advertising. Provides information in the public interest such as health care, safety, and environmental interests. In order to have these ads placed free, they must meet stringent guidelines. (11)

Publicity. Information dissemination that is not generally paid for but is picked up and passed on by another entity, such as the media. The most common forms of publicity are press conferences and **news releases.** (7)

Publicity release. This type of **news release** covers any information occurring within an organization that might have some news value to local, regional, or even national media. (7)

Public service announcement (PSA). A radio or television spot aimed at providing an important message to its target audience. The PSA is reserved strictly for organizations that qualify as nonprofit under federal tax laws. (12)

Pull quote. A magazine or newsletter device of "pulling" out quotations from the text, enlarging the point size, and setting them off from the text to draw a reader's attention to a point within an article. (9)

Q

Quarterly report. Similar to **annual reports** except they are issued every three months and are less comprehensive. (8)

R

Readability formula. A calculation used to determine the degree of reading difficulty of written material—often determining either the grade level or the type of publication for which the material is suited. (16)

Reasoned argument. Also known as logical argument, this persuasive strategy uses the techniques of rhetoric as handed down from the ancient Greeks. For persuasive messages it is important to build the message around a thorough understanding of the psychological state of the audience. (3)

Referral ending. A type of ending for a feature story in which the beginning of the story is referred to in some way in order to bring closure to the story. (9)

Response ending. A type of ending for a feature story in which a call to action is included. (9)

Rule of ground thirds. A method of working with a page layout that requires that the page be divided into thirds and balanced using a two-thirds to one-third ratio. (14)

S

Sanction strategies. A type of **compliance strategy** that persuades by using rewards and punishments controlled by either the audience themselves or as a result of the situation. (3)

Sans serif typefaces. A category of typeface without *serifs*—the lines that cross the end strokes of the letters (*sans,* from the French, meaning "without"). They are usually, but not always, distinguished by uniformity of strokes. They usually impart a more modern look to a publication, especially if used as display type. (14)

Script treatment. An informal narrative account of a television spot. It is not written in a script format but may include ideas for shots and transitions. (12)

Scripted speech. A speech that has been fully scripted and from which the speaker reads, often from a teleprompter. (13)

Secondary research. Data previously collected, often by third parties, for other purposes and adapted to the current needs. This can include demographic information already gathered by another department in your organization, or information gained from research done by other parties entirely outside your company. (2)

Serif typefaces. A category of typeface distinguished by a variation in thick and thin strokes, and by *serifs*—the lines that cross the end strokes of the letters. Serif type can be further broken down into *Romans* and *slab* or *square serif* faces. Serif faces usually are considered easier to read, especially in body type sizes. (14)

Shooting script. Includes all of the information necessary for a complete understanding of a TV spot idea. It fleshes out camera shots, transitions, audio (including music and sound effects), narrative, acting directions, and approximate times. (12)

Signature. Groupings of pages printed on both sides, usually sixteen to a signature, but sometimes fewer, and always in multiples of four. (14)

Slice-of-life spot. A television commercial that sets up a dramatic situation complete with a beginning, middle, and end. In the slice-of-life spot, the focus is on the story, not the characters. The message is imparted through an interesting sequence of events incorporating, but not relying on, interesting characters. Slice-of-life spots usually use a wide variety of camera movements and postproduction techniques, such as dissolves and special effects. (12)

Social audit. An investigation, sometimes conducted by outside firms, to determine areas in which an organization has acted responsibly or could use improvement. (8)

Social responsibility report. A year-end report of business activities that can be construed as social responsibility. The basis of the social responsibility report is good citizenship—especially in the areas of economic, environmental, and social responsibility. (8)

Soft news. News people want rather than news they necessarily need. (5)

Special. A press release or other information written in a style intended for a specific publication, but being released elsewhere as well. (7)

Speech. A form of communication, usually interpersonal and somewhat formal, in which a group of people are addressed simultaneously. Types of speeches are typically classified by purpose: (13)

- A speech to *inform* seeks to clarify, instruct, or demonstrate.
- A speech to *persuade* is designed to convince or influence and often carries a call to action.
- A speech to *entertain* covers almost everything else including celebrations, eulogies, and dinner speeches.

Spot. A broadcast message, either paid-for advertising or a public service announcement. (5, 12)

Spot announcement. The simplest type of radio spot, a spot announcement involves no sound effects or music bed and is meant to be read by radio station personnel. (12)

Statistical supplement. Report of larger corporations that provides financial information, such as statement data and key ratios, which can be dated back 10–20 years. (8)

Style sheet. A listing of all of the type specifications you use in a newsletter or other publication. (9)

Subhead. May be (a) a display line enlarging on the main headline, usually in smaller size, or (b) a short heading within the copy used to break up a long block of text. (9)

Summary ending. A type of ending for a feature story in which the main points are summarized. (9)

Summary lead. The most common type of news release lead. A good summary lead will answer the key questions—who, what, when, where, why, and how. (7)

Swipe file. A collection of publications and designs done by other people or companies used to help with design, layout ideas, and writing style, as well as to communicate ideas to typesetters and printers. (14)

T

Talking heads spot. A television spot in which the primary image appearing on the television screen is the human head—talking. (12)

Target audience. The end users of your information—the people you most want to be affected by your writing. (2)

Testimonial approach. A type of headline that features a firsthand quotation. (11)

Thumbnail. A rough sketch, usually small, of a graphic layout. (11)

Timeliness. One of the characteristics of newsworthiness of information. Relates to whether the material is current. If it isn't, is it a whole new angle on an old story? Remember, the word news means "new." (5)

Trademark. Legal protection of product names, images, phrases, or slogans from use by others without permission and in a prescribed manner dictated by the trademark holder. (4)

Two-fold. The most common type of brochure fold resulting in a six-panel brochure. (10)

Type. The generic term for the lettering used in printing. (14)

Typeface. The nearly limitless alphabets and ornaments available as type. (14)

Uncontrolled information. Information that, once it leaves your hands, is at the mercy of the media. The outlet in which you want it placed has total editorial control over the content, style, placement, and timing. Such items as press releases are totally uncontrolled. Others, such as magazine articles, may receive limited editing but are still controlled as to placement and timing. (1)

Unity. One way of providing readers with a whole by drawing relationships among its various parts. Perhaps the best way to gain unity of design has more to do with an overall look, a unifying design. (14)

Upward communication. Communication within an organization that provides employees a means of communicating their opinions to management. (9)

Video news release (VNR). Originally prepackaged publicity features meant to be aired on local, regional, or national television, VNRs now are news releases designed as feature stories, usually for local television news programs. (12)

Web site. An internet "publication" composed of any number of Web pages, each hyperlinked to each other and to various other Web sites. (15)

Index